稲垣理一郎

Riichiro Inagaki

To research the Mount Fuji parts in volumes 10 and 11, I actually tried to climb the mountain.

I trained my tired old body beforehand so that I'd be prepared for anything... or so I thought. Due to days of work pressure, I ended up pulling an all-nighter before leaving for the climb.

I was so tired I thought I was going to die... All you good little kids out there, don't ever try that!

Next up, Mount Everest without sleep... not! I would definitely die.

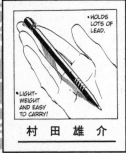

• HOLDS LOTS OF LEAD.

• LIGHT-WEIGHT AND EASY TO CARRY!

村田雄介

Yusuke Murata

My Most Treasured Possession

It's a mechanical pencil that I received from Morita-sensei when I visited his home.

I heard that he drew Mr. Kawato and Taison with this pencil, so it ought to be placed on the household altar. But it would be such a shame not to use it for its original purpose, so now I use it to draft Sena and the others. It goes without saying how great it is for drawing.

Note: Morita-sensei is manga creator Masanori Morita. Mr. Kawato is a character from his series *Rookies* and Taison is from *Rokudenashi Blues*. Ed.

Eyeshield 21 is the hottest gridiron manga to hit the scene. A collaborative effort between writer Riichiro Inagaki and artist Yusuke Murata, *Eyeshield 21* was originally serialized in Japan's *Weekly Shonen Jump*. An OAV created for Shueisha's Anime Tour is available in Japan, and the *Eyeshield 21* hit animated TV series debuted in spring 2005!

EYESHIELD 21

Vol 11: Open Season

The SHONEN JUMP ADVANCED Manga Edition

STORY BY RIICHIRO INAGAKI
ART BY YUSUKE MURATA

Translation & English Adaptation/Allison Markin Powell
Touch-up Art & Lettering/James Gaubatz
Cover and Graphic Design/Sean Lee
Editor/Yuki Takagaki

Managing Editor/Frances E. Wall
Editorial Director/Elizabeth Kawasaki
VP & Editor in Chief/Yumi Hoashi
Sr. Director of Acquisitions/Rika Inouye
Sr. VP of Marketing/Liza Coppola
Exec. VP of Sales & Marketing/John Easum
Publisher/Hyoe Narita

Printed in the U.S.A.

Published by VIZ Media, LLC
P.O. Box 77010
San Francisco, CA 94107

SHONEN JUMP ADVANCED Manga Edition
10 9 8 7 6 5 4 3 2 1
First printing, December 2006

PARENTAL ADVISORY
EYESHIELD 21 is rated T+ for Older Teen and is
recommended for ages 16 and up. It contains
graphic fantasy violence and crude humor.

THE WORLD'S MOST
CUTTING-EDGE MANGA

SHONEN JUMP ADVANCED

www.shonenjump.com

www.viz.com

Vol. 11
Open Season

Story by **Riichiro Inagaki**   Art by **Yusuke Murata**

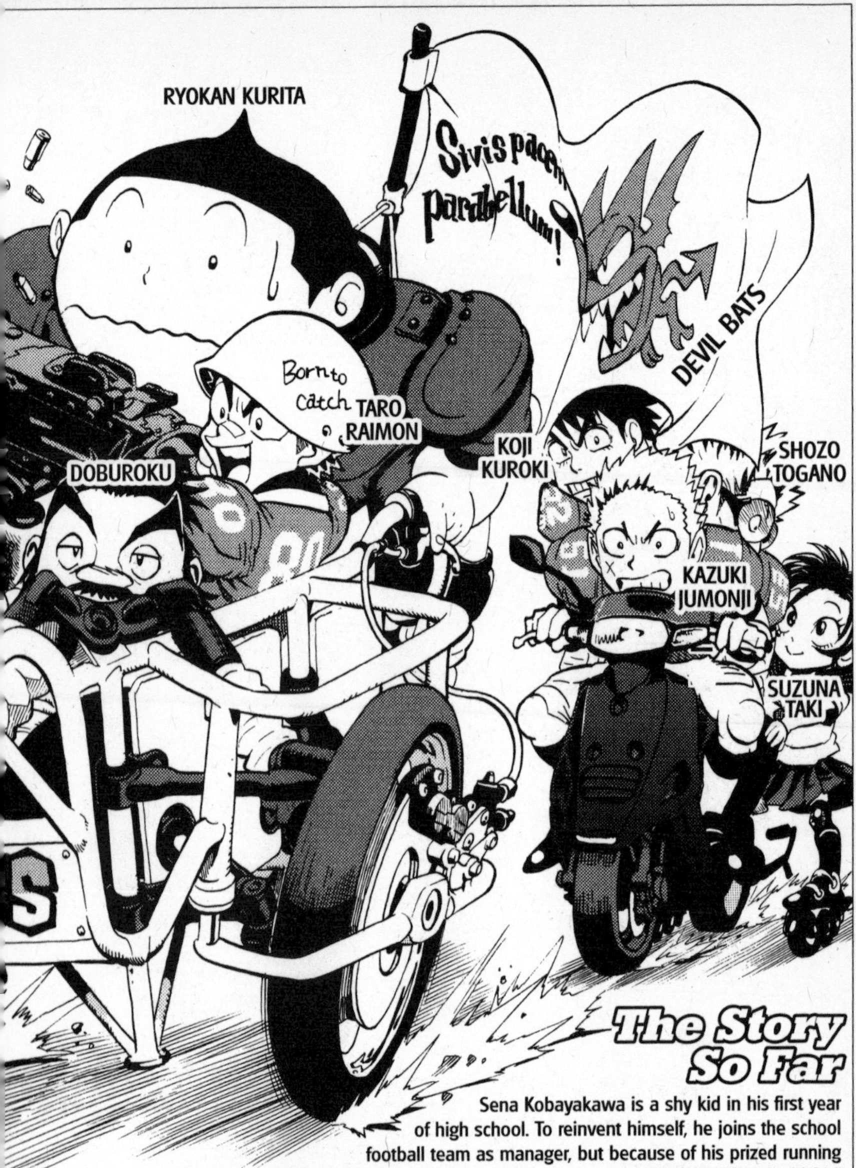
RYOKAN KURITA
Si vis pacem parabellum!
DEVIL BATS
Born to catch
TARO RAIMON
KOJI KUROKI
SHOZO TOGANO
DOBUROKU
KAZUKI JUMONJI
SUZUNA TAKI

The Story So Far

Sena Kobayakawa is a shy kid in his first year of high school. To reinvent himself, he joins the school football team as manager, but because of his prized running ability he is forced to play on the team under an assumed identity, "Eyeshield 21." Sena's desire to win continues to grow, now that he has played against Ojo, Taiyo, and the Aliens, and been matched with top athletes like Shin and Panther. Next stop: the Christmas Bowl! Determined to win, the Devil Bats complete their training from hell in America. No one is eliminated during the brutal "death march," and the team is now on their way home with their trainer, Doburoku, a potential new player, Taki, and his sister. When the fall season finally begins, will all their training pay off?!

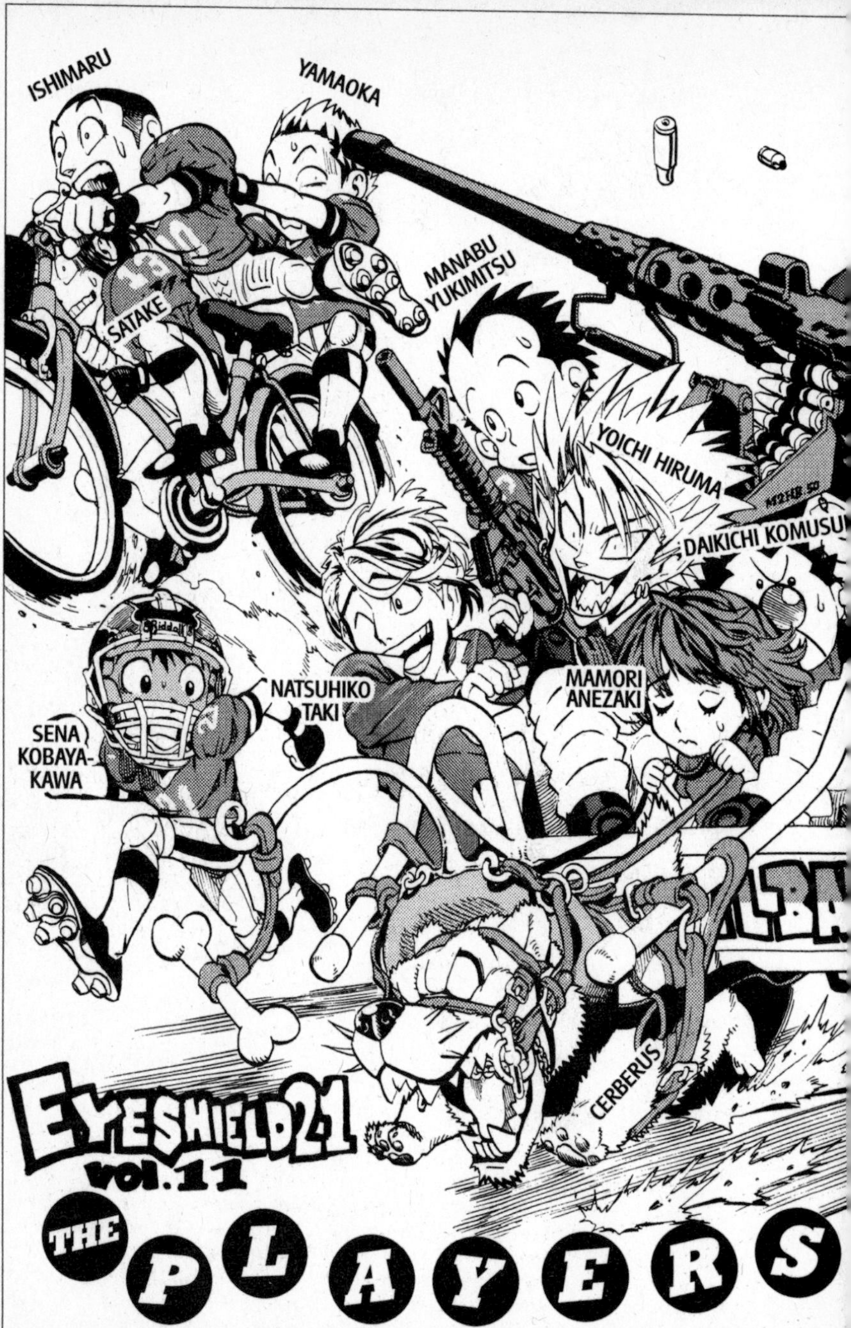
ISHIMARU
YAMAOKA
SATAKE
MANABU YUKIMITSU
YOICHI HIRUMA
DAIKICHI KOMUSUBI
NATSUHIKO TAKI
SENA KOBAYAKAWA
MAMORI ANEZAKI
CERBERUS
EYESHIELD 21
vol. 11
THE PLAYERS

Vol. 11
Open Season

CONTENTS

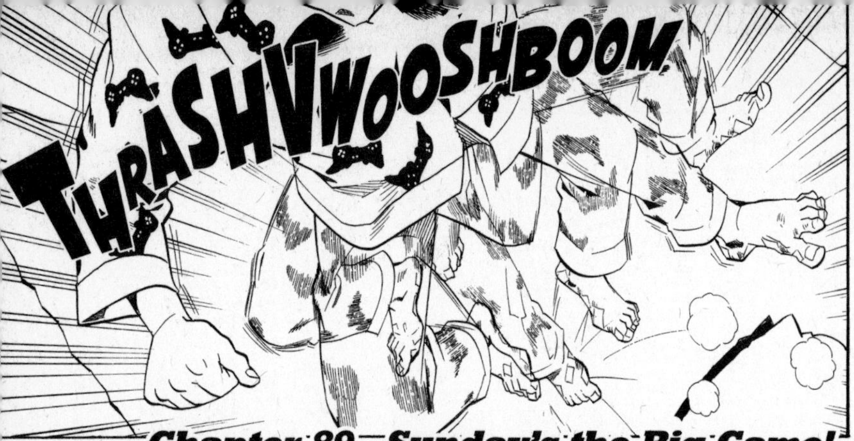
THRASHVWOOSHBOOM

Chapter 89 Sunday's the Big Game!

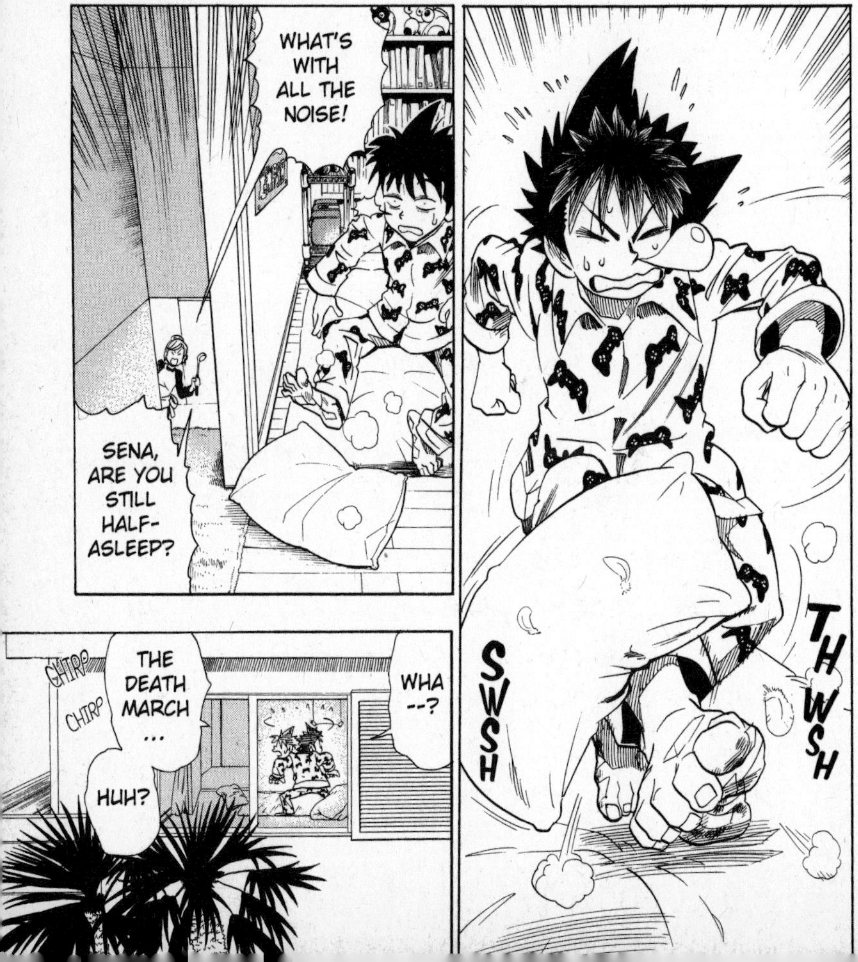
THWSH
SWSH
WHAT'S WITH ALL THE NOISE!
SENA, ARE YOU STILL HALF-ASLEEP?
WHA--?
THE DEATH MARCH ...
CHIRP
CHIRP
HUH?

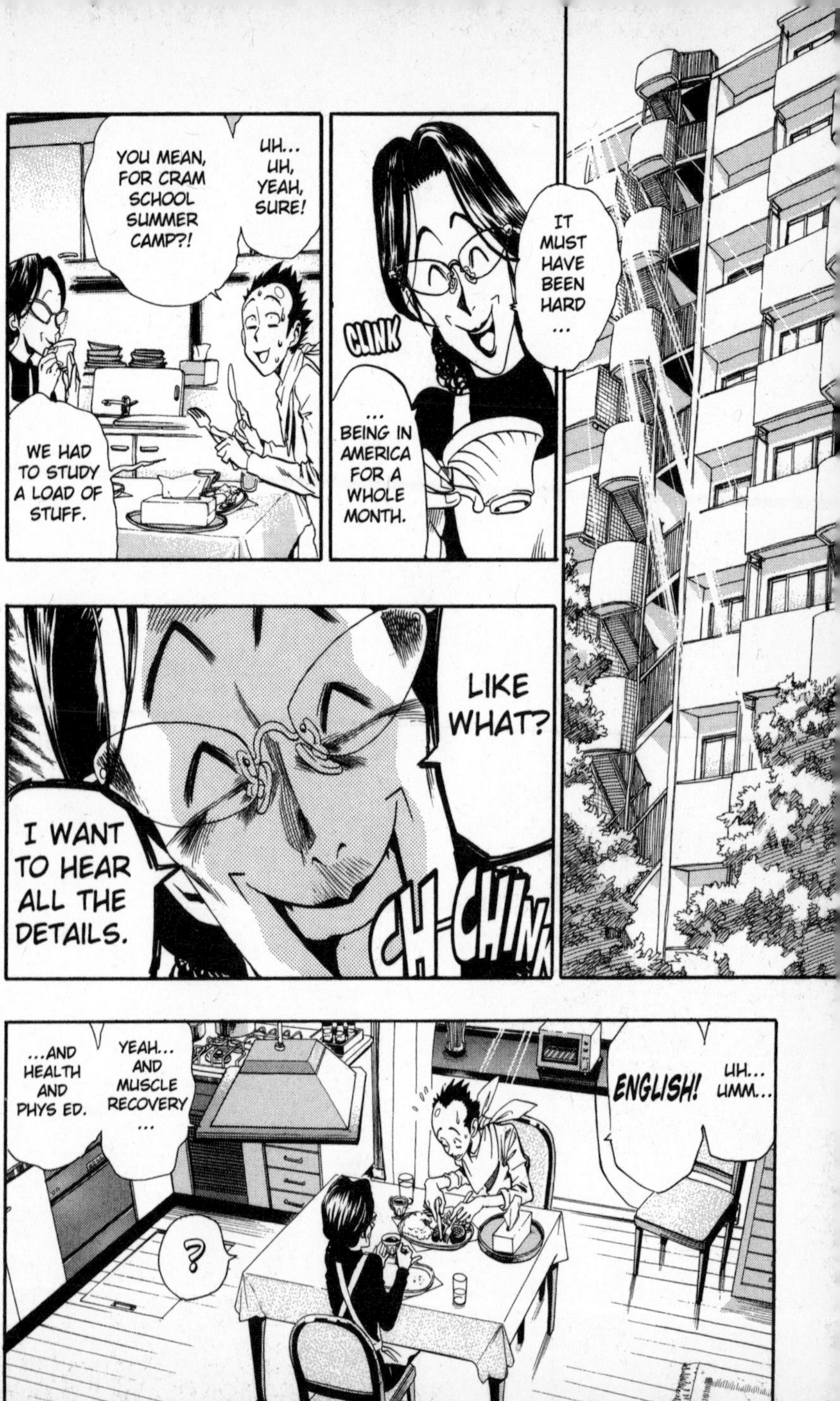
IT MUST HAVE BEEN HARD...
CLINK
...BEING IN AMERICA FOR A WHOLE MONTH.
UH... UH, YEAH, SURE!
YOU MEAN, FOR CRAM SCHOOL SUMMER CAMP?!
WE HAD TO STUDY A LOAD OF STUFF.
LIKE WHAT?
I WANT TO HEAR ALL THE DETAILS.
CH-CHINK
UH... UMM...
ENGLISH!
YEAH... AND MUSCLE RECOVERY...
...AND HEALTH AND PHYS ED.
?

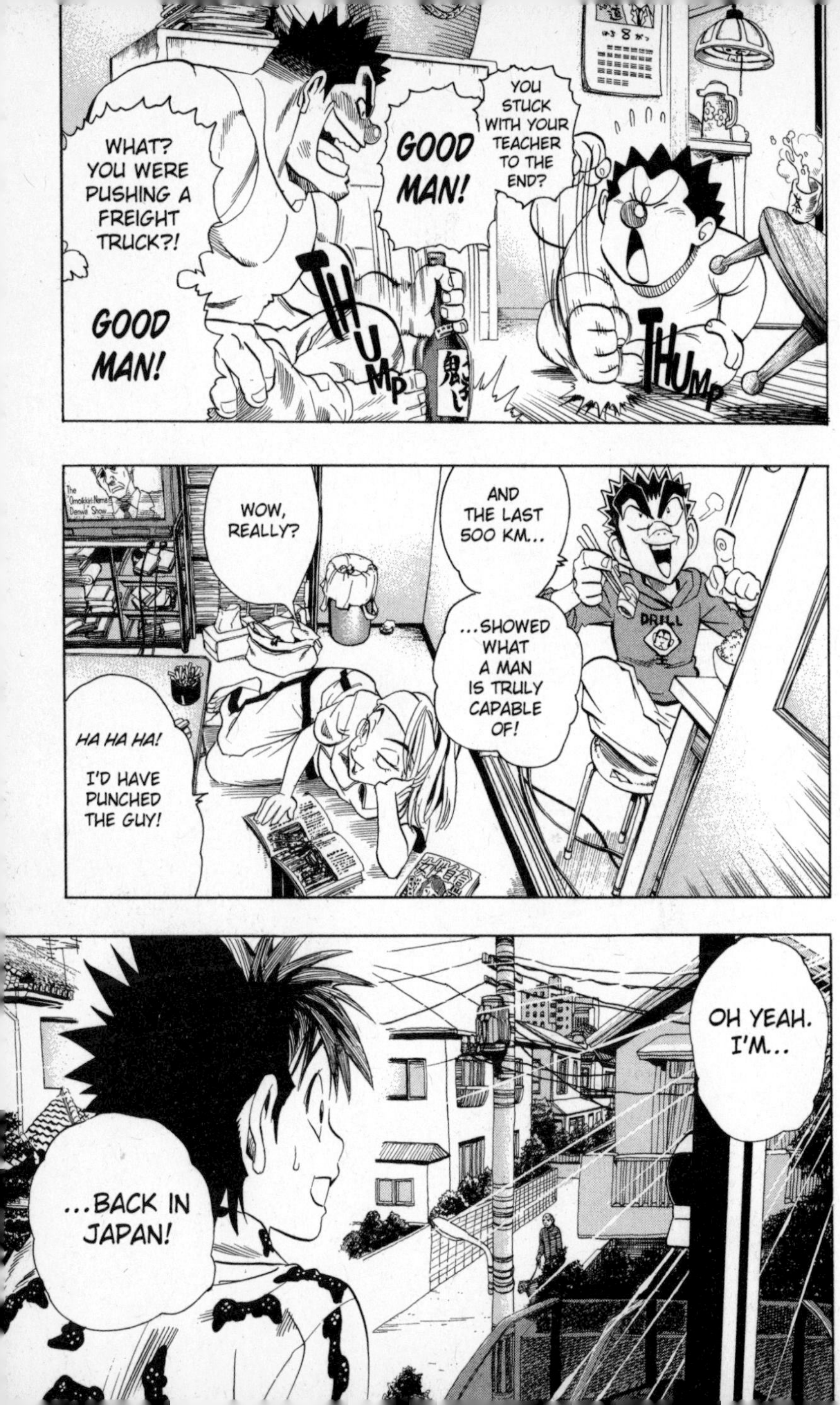
YOU STUCK WITH YOUR TEACHER TO THE END?
THUMP
GOOD MAN!
WHAT? YOU WERE PUSHING A FREIGHT TRUCK?!
THUMP
GOOD MAN!
AND THE LAST 500 KM...
...SHOWED WHAT A MAN IS TRULY CAPABLE OF!
DRILL
WOW, REALLY?
HA HA HA!
I'D HAVE PUNCHED THE GUY!
OH YEAH. I'M...
...BACK IN JAPAN!

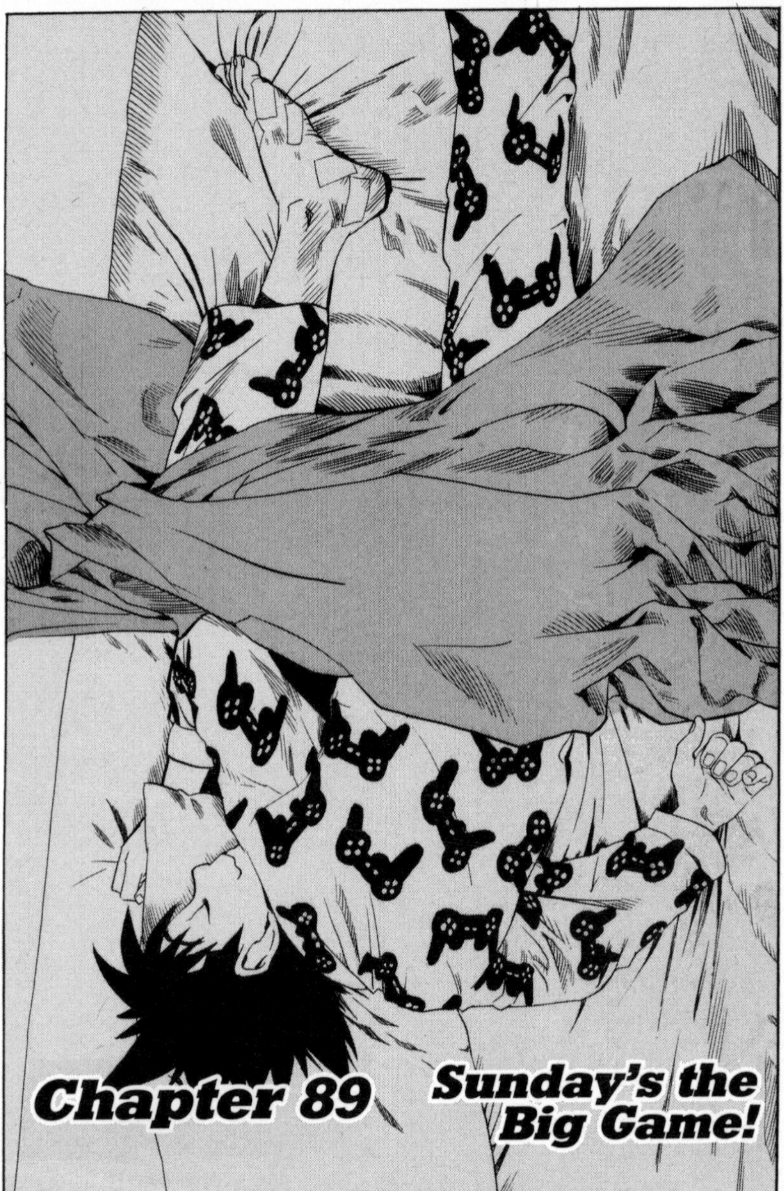
Chapter 89
Sunday's the Big Game!

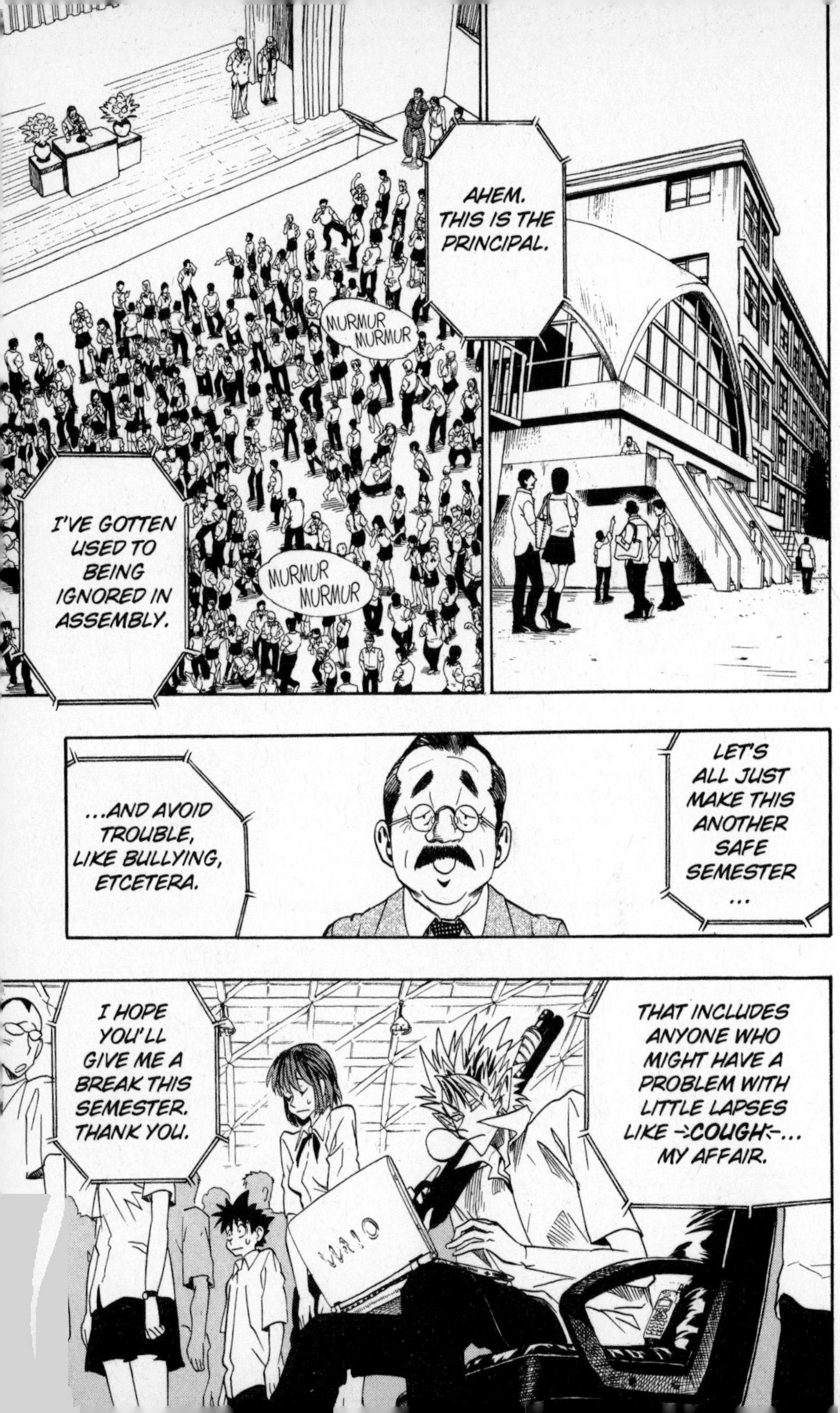
AHEM. THIS IS THE PRINCIPAL.
MURMUR MURMUR
MURMUR MURMUR
I'VE GOTTEN USED TO BEING IGNORED IN ASSEMBLY.
LET'S ALL JUST MAKE THIS ANOTHER SAFE SEMESTER ...
...AND AVOID TROUBLE, LIKE BULLYING, ETCETERA.
THAT INCLUDES ANYONE WHO MIGHT HAVE A PROBLEM WITH LITTLE LAPSES LIKE -:COUGH:-... MY AFFAIR.
I HOPE YOU'LL GIVE ME A BREAK THIS SEMESTER. THANK YOU.
VAIO

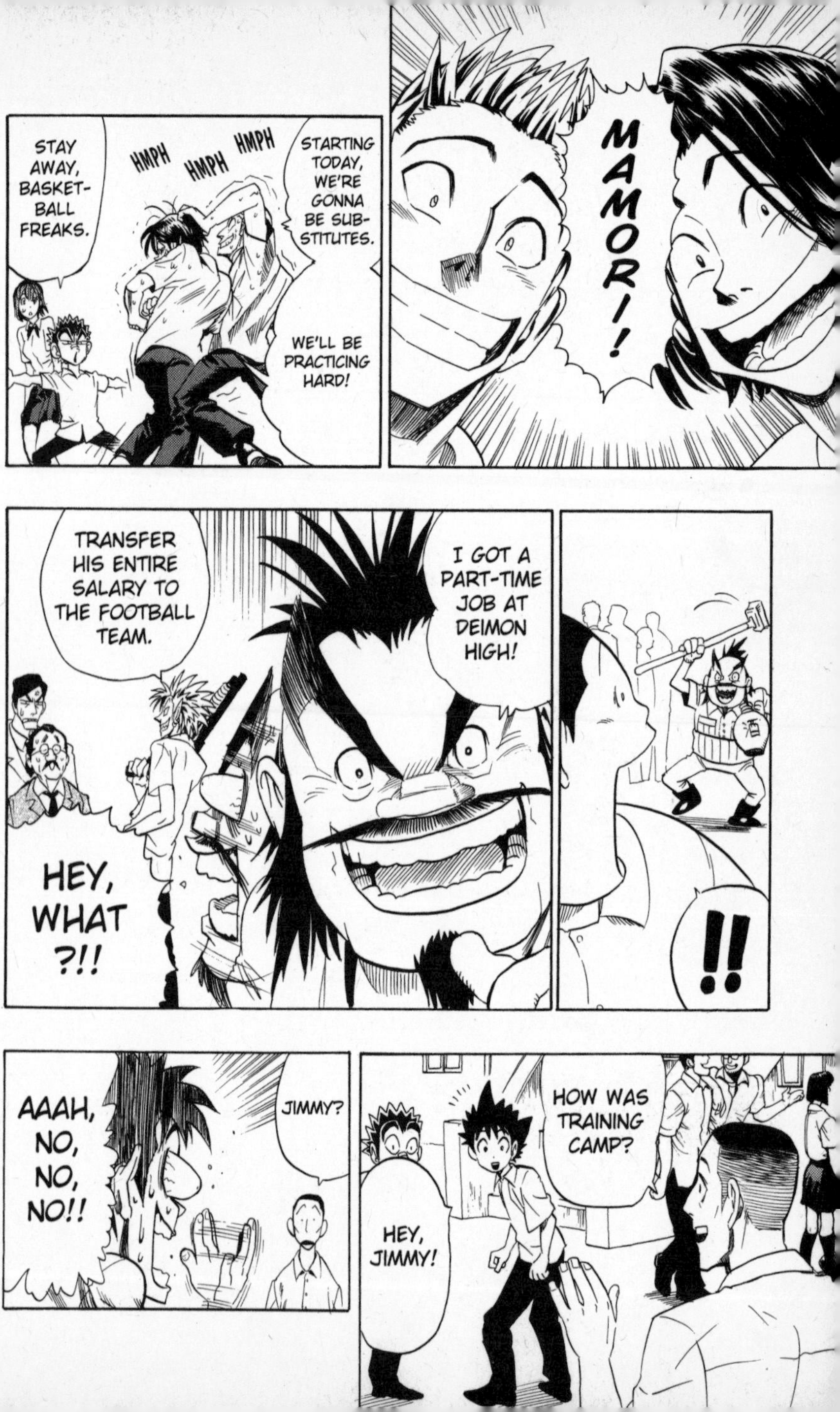
MAMORI!!
STARTING TODAY, WE'RE GONNA BE SUB-STITUTES.
WE'LL BE PRACTICING HARD!
HMPH
HMPH
HMPH
STAY AWAY, BASKET-BALL FREAKS.
!!
I GOT A PART-TIME JOB AT DEIMON HIGH!
TRANSFER HIS ENTIRE SALARY TO THE FOOTBALL TEAM.
HEY, WHAT ?!!
HOW WAS TRAINING CAMP?
HEY, JIMMY!
JIMMY?
AAAH, NO, NO, NO!!

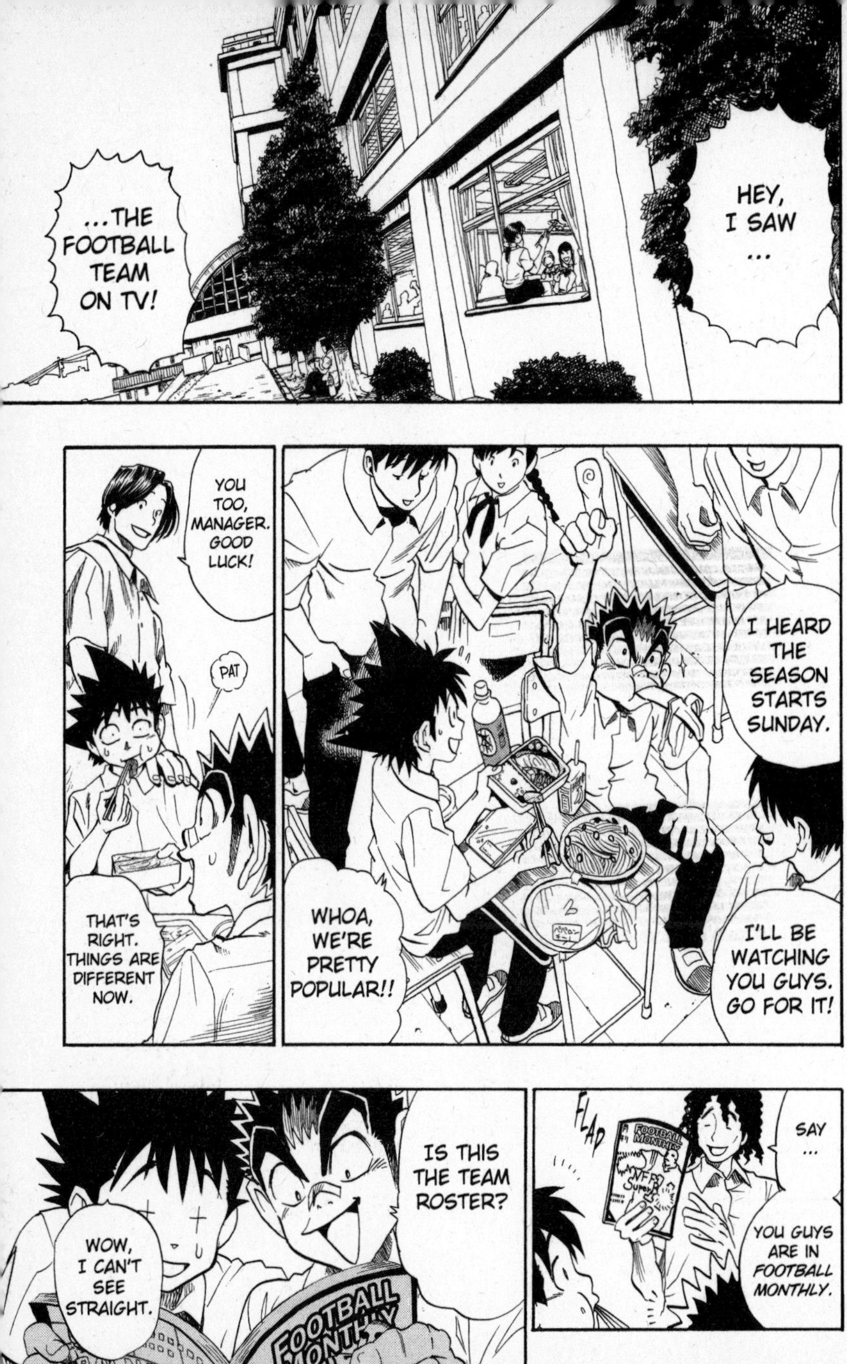
HEY, I SAW ...
...THE FOOTBALL TEAM ON TV!
I HEARD THE SEASON STARTS SUNDAY.
I'LL BE WATCHING YOU GUYS. GO FOR IT!
WHOA, WE'RE PRETTY POPULAR!!
YOU TOO, MANAGER. GOOD LUCK!
PAT
THAT'S RIGHT. THINGS ARE DIFFERENT NOW.
FLAP
SAY ...
FOOTBALL MONTHLY
YOU GUYS ARE IN *FOOTBALL MONTHLY.*
IS THIS THE TEAM ROSTER?
WOW, I CAN'T SEE STRAIGHT.
FOOTBALL MONTHLY
NFF

"A" BLOCK

HASHIRATANI DEERS

RUNNING	PASSING
B	C
LINE	**DEFENSE**
A	B

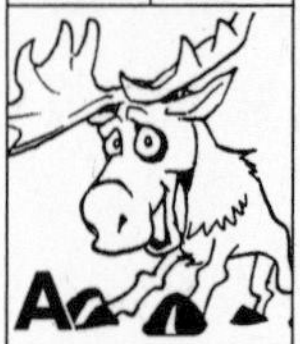
A

A strong veteran team. They make the most of their small size, using their speed to disarm opponents. Playing opponents of the same size, they are still superior.

KYOSHIN POSEIDONS

RUNNING	PASSING
C	D
LINE	**DEFENSE**
D	D

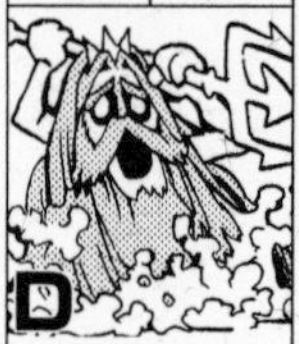
D

The players all have slight builds, despite the team's name. They're hurting because every one of their bigger players is on the bench.

ZOKUGAKU CHAMELEONS

RUNNING	PASSING
D	C
LINE	**DEFENSE**
D	B

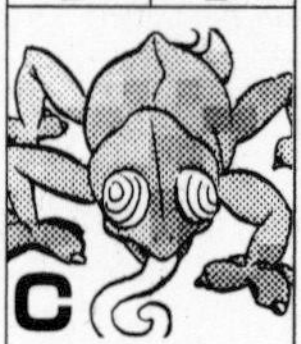
C

Being able to adapt their strategy to their opponents' will be a plus in the tournament, but right now it's not working. We're counting on Rui Habashira's special training.

TSUKUFU SUPER EAGLES

RUNNING	PASSING
C	D
LINE	**DEFENSE**
D	D

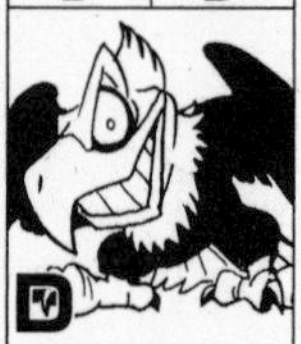
D

They base their strategy on fast plays (running and passing) that develop in center field. This means they're weak on the sides.

KOIGAHAMA CUPIDS

RUNNING	PASSING
D	D
LINE	**DEFENSE**
D	D

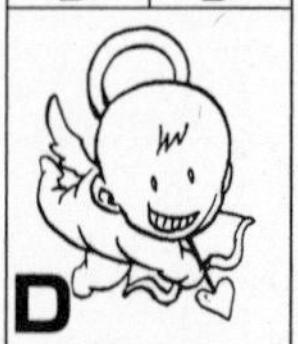
D

Is quarterback Hatsujo the one to watch, since he can do everything, including kick? Their first opponent seems a bit much for them…

SEIBU WILD GUNMEN

RUNNING	PASSING
C	S
LINE	**DEFENSE**
A	D

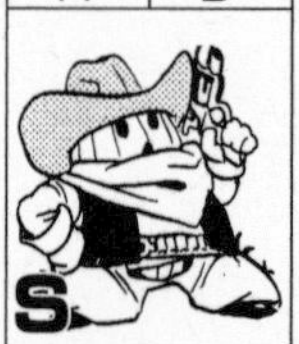
S

Their high-spee shotgun pass, a cause for fear in the spring, has been further refined. They are the season's most destructive force!

S = "special"--Ed.

TAMAGAWA BLUE SHARKS

RUNNING	PASSING
C	C
LINE	**DEFENSE**
D	D

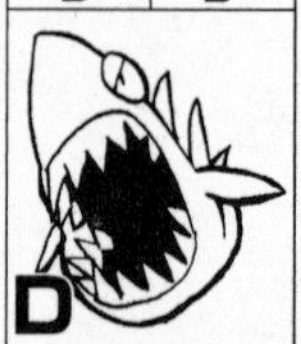
D

The team is made up of average players and could therefore use one really strong player.

URA-HARAJUKU BOARDERS

RUNNING	PASSING
C	D
LINE	**DEFENSE**
D	B

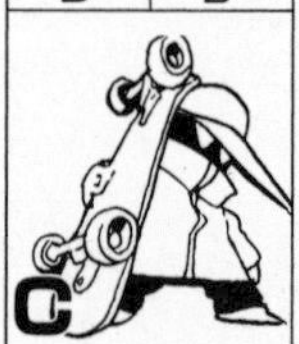
C

ach player has solid skills, but they might need more practice. How far will they go, relying on noseguard Gairo?

YUHI GUTS	
RUNNING	PASSING
D	D
LINE	DEFENSE
C	D

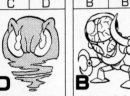

D

All of Yuhi's sports teams are highly regarded, except for their terrible football team. But the athletes' enthusiasm is refreshing.

AMINO CYBORGS	
RUNNING	PASSING
C	C
LINE	DEFENSE
B	B

B

Each year Amino takes the season by storm in a different sport. Will they dominate the football world with their medical knowledge?

DEIMON DEVIL BATS	
RUNNING	PASSING
A	C
LINE	DEFENSE
D	D

C

When they're on a roll, they have offensive power approaching NASA High School's, but they are erratic. The tournament dark horse.

JUJIKA PRIESTS	
RUNNING	PASSING
C	C
LINE	DEFENSE
D	D

D

They won the Fair Play Award in the spring season. Despite their modest abilities, they are a gentleman's team worth rooting for.

DOKUBARI SCORPIONS	
RUNNING	PASSING
C	C
LINE	DEFENSE
C	C

C

Their speed and power leave something to be desired, but for some reason they have a very good record. Could it be from researching the other teams?

TO THE FINALS

GINGA ROCKETS	
RUNNING	PASSING
D	C
LINE	DEFENSE
D	D

D

They were inspired this season to change their name after seeing NASA High School on TV. How far will they get with their brand-new "shuttle" pass?

CHUODAI PANTHERS	
RUNNING	PASSING
D	D
LINE	DEFENSE
C	D

D

They idolize Panther after seeing him on TV... not! Actually, the team has been around for 20 years, and their first game will likely be a break-through one!

HORI FANTASY MONSTERS	
RUNNING	PASSING
C	C
LINE	DEFENSE
D	C

C

They're strong overall but will they be able to handle the peculiar strengths of the opposing teams?

EDOMAE FISHERS	
RUNNING	PASSING
C	B
LINE	DEFENSE
C	A

A

They've improved a lot since spring and are already going after Seibu. They'll have to make sure to neutralize Tetsuma. Can they demolish the golden duo?

WASEDA KILLERS	
RUNNING	PASSING
B	D
LINE	DEFENSE
D	D

D

Their offensive strength comes from their running. They'd be a better team, though, if they were better at passing.

"B" BLOCK

KARIBU PIRATES

RUNNING	PASSING
C	D
LINE	**DEFENSE**
B	D

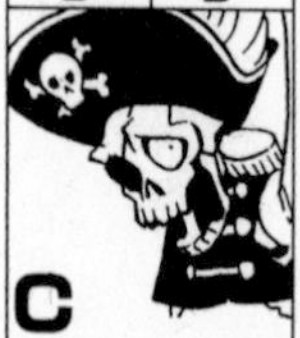

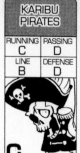

C

Besides their rough-and-tumble nature and Spartan-like training, watch out for their incredible stamina!

OIYAMA LIONS

RUNNING	PASSING
C	D
LINE	**DEFENSE**
D	C

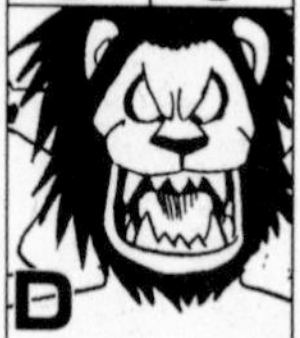

D

They've developed with the first-years who joined two years ago. Now in their third year, they're betting everything on this tournament.

NOROI OCCULTS

RUNNING	PASSING
C	D
LINE	**DEFENSE**
D	D

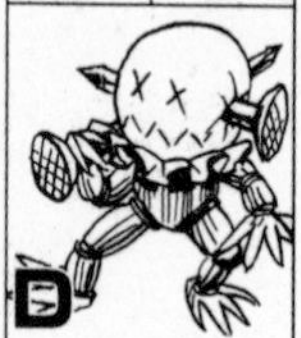

D

Can they force a win by thwarting their opponents with black magic? Every day they're focused on practicing their spells. Go play football!

JONANDAI GIANTS

RUNNING	PASSING
D	C
LINE	**DEFENSE**
C	C

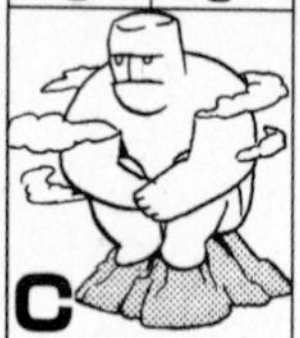

C

Tall and powerful, with overwhelming destructive power! They have giant… cheerleaders, but their players are of average size.

ARITO GRASS-HOPPERS

RUNNING	PASSING
C	C
LINE	**DEFENSE**
D	D

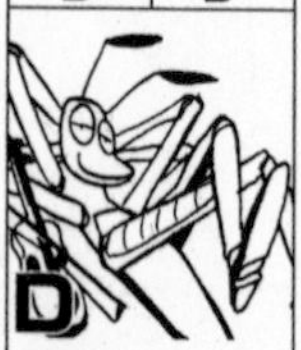

D

They've perfected their basic offensive practice, but they are clearly in need of defensive practice. Their average score is a 50-point loss.

NAKABA 99ERS

RUNNING	PASSING
D	B
LINE	**DEFENSE**
C	D

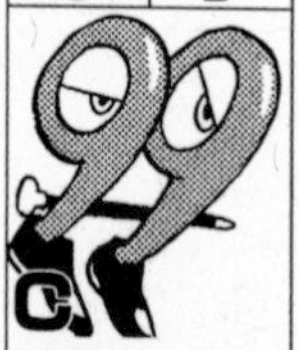

C

Having the most players (99), they're at their best when they line up on the field. Could they overwhelm their opponents by attacking as a human wave?

NIHON MACHINE GUNS

RUNNING	PASSING
C	D
LINE	**DEFENSE**
D	D

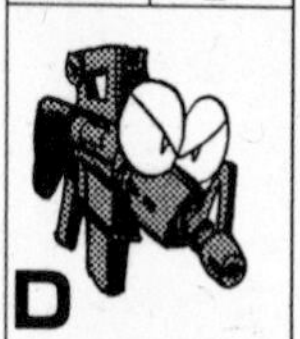

D

With virtually no huddle, they reel off plays like a machine gun would—which would be fine, except they never hit their target.

GENSHIJIN FIGHTERS

RUNNING	PASSING
B	B
LINE	**DEFENSE**
B	B

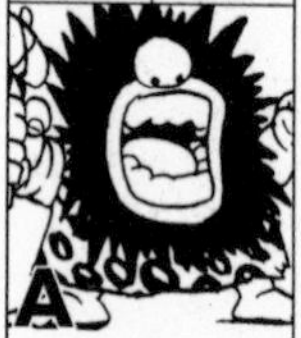

A

They have a strong defense and offense, but their strategy needs improving.

SENGOKU SAMURAI

RUNNING	PASSING
A	B
LINE	DEFENSE
B	C

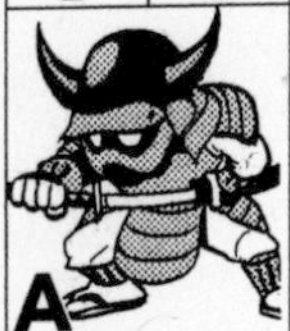

A

They have a solid coaching system because of their ties to influential Sengoku University. With their powerful offense, they're likely to go to the finals.

KYOKODAI MUSCLE BOMBERS

RUNNING	PASSING
D	D
LINE	DEFENSE
C	D

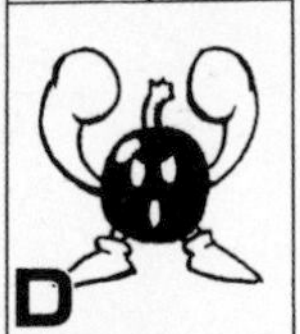

D

Their penetration down center field ought to be unstoppable but, well, they don't have that kind of power.

RATEN MATADORS

RUNNING	PASSING
C	C
LINE	DEFENSE
D	D

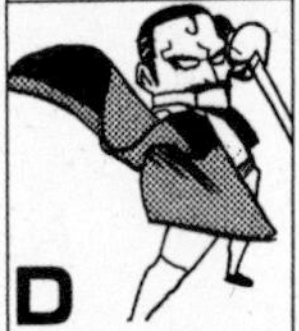

D

This is a good-looking team that wears bullfighter-style uniforms. They tackle with a light touch that still packs a surprising punch.

OJO WHITE KNIGHTS

RUNNING	PASSING
C	C
LINE	DEFENSE
B	A

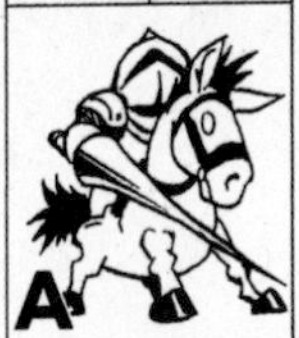

A

Has the team become just Shin and their defense? And without their so-called "golden generation," could Ojo be eliminated early on?

SANKAKU PUNKS

RUNNING	PASSING
B	C
LINE	DEFENSE
B	C

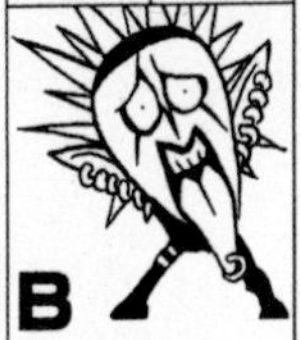

B

Sister school to powerful Taiyo High School. They gave Ojo a run for their money in a deadly showdown in the spring.

TO THE FINALS

HANAZONO BUTTERFLIES

RUNNING	PASSING
D	A
LINE	DEFENSE
D	D

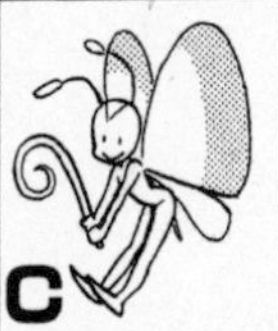

C

Their aerial game is their strength, thanks to light footwork. Their weak spot is their feeble line.

NANSEI HAWKS

RUNNING	PASSING
D	D
LINE	DEFENSE
D	D

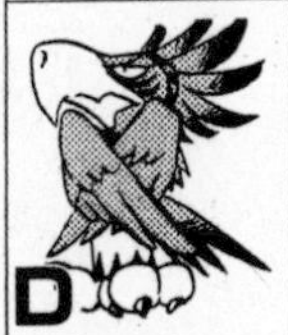

D

This year's rookie team. They've finally grasped the rules and will enjoy competing against the other teams.

BANDO SPIDERS

RUNNING	PASSING
D	D
LINE	DEFENSE
D	C

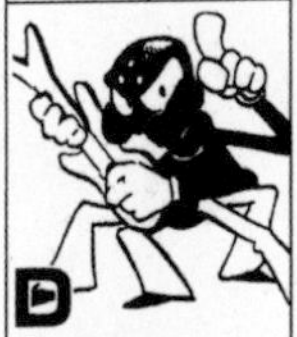

D

They have a capable kicker in Kotaro Sasaki, so at least they have excellent kicking, but other than that...

MITAMA MARINERS

RUNNING	PASSING
C	C
LINE	DEFENSE
C	B

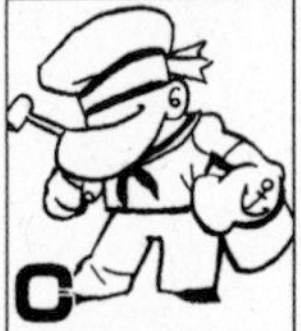

C

They are a crack team, having only 22 players on offense and defense. Will it take a team with special skills to beat them?

KITA ESKIMOS

RUNNING	PASSING
D	D
LINE	DEFENSE
D	D

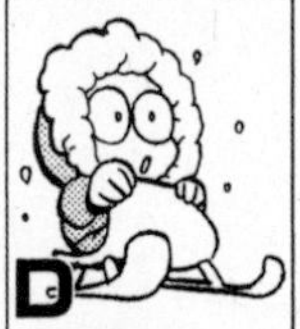

D

Being from the coldest climate, they can't attract players. They don't even have ten players to form a team, so how will they compete?

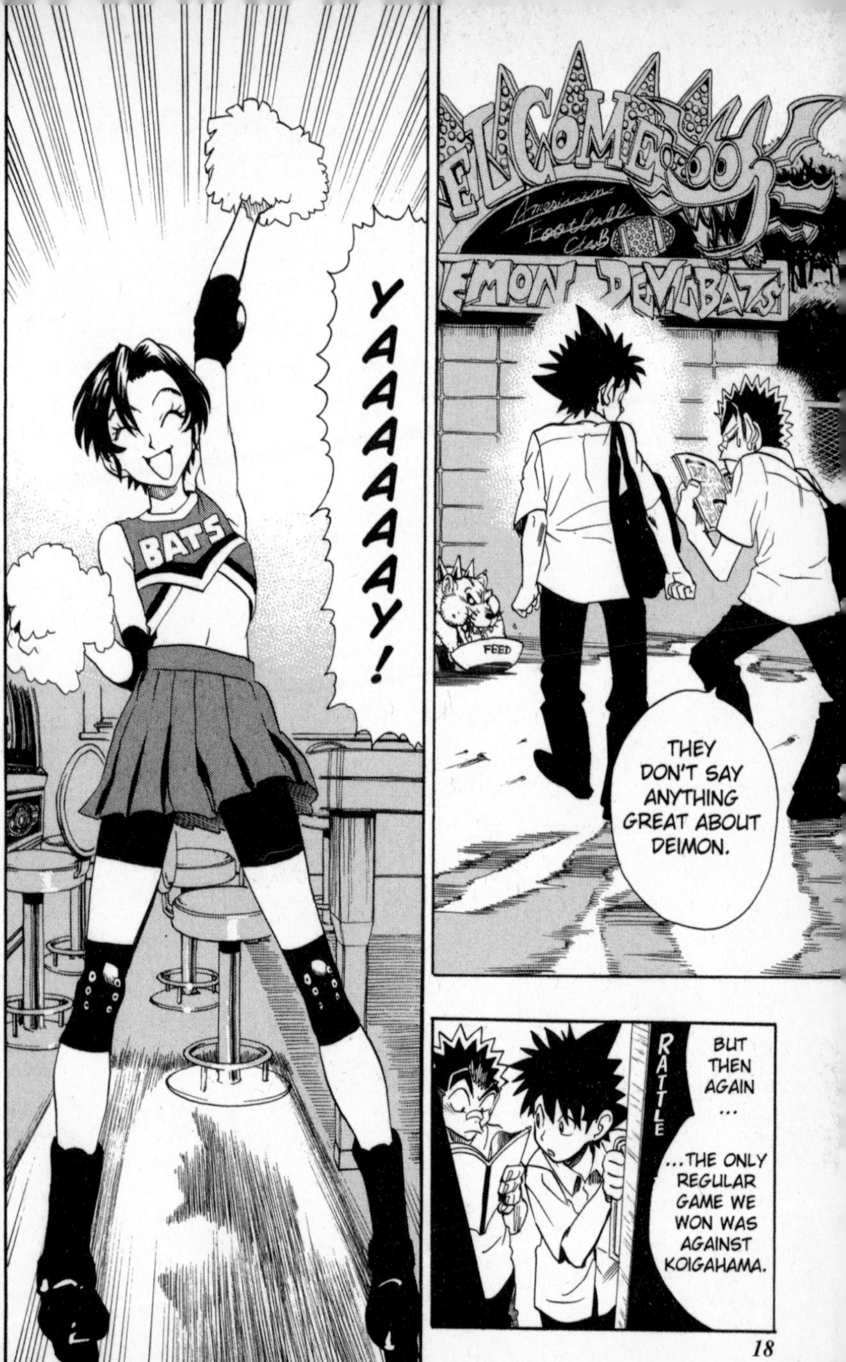
American Football Club
THEY DON'T SAY ANYTHING GREAT ABOUT DEIMON.
FEED
RATTLE
BUT THEN AGAIN ...
...THE ONLY REGULAR GAME WE WON WAS AGAINST KOIGAHAMA.
BATS
YAAAAAAAY!

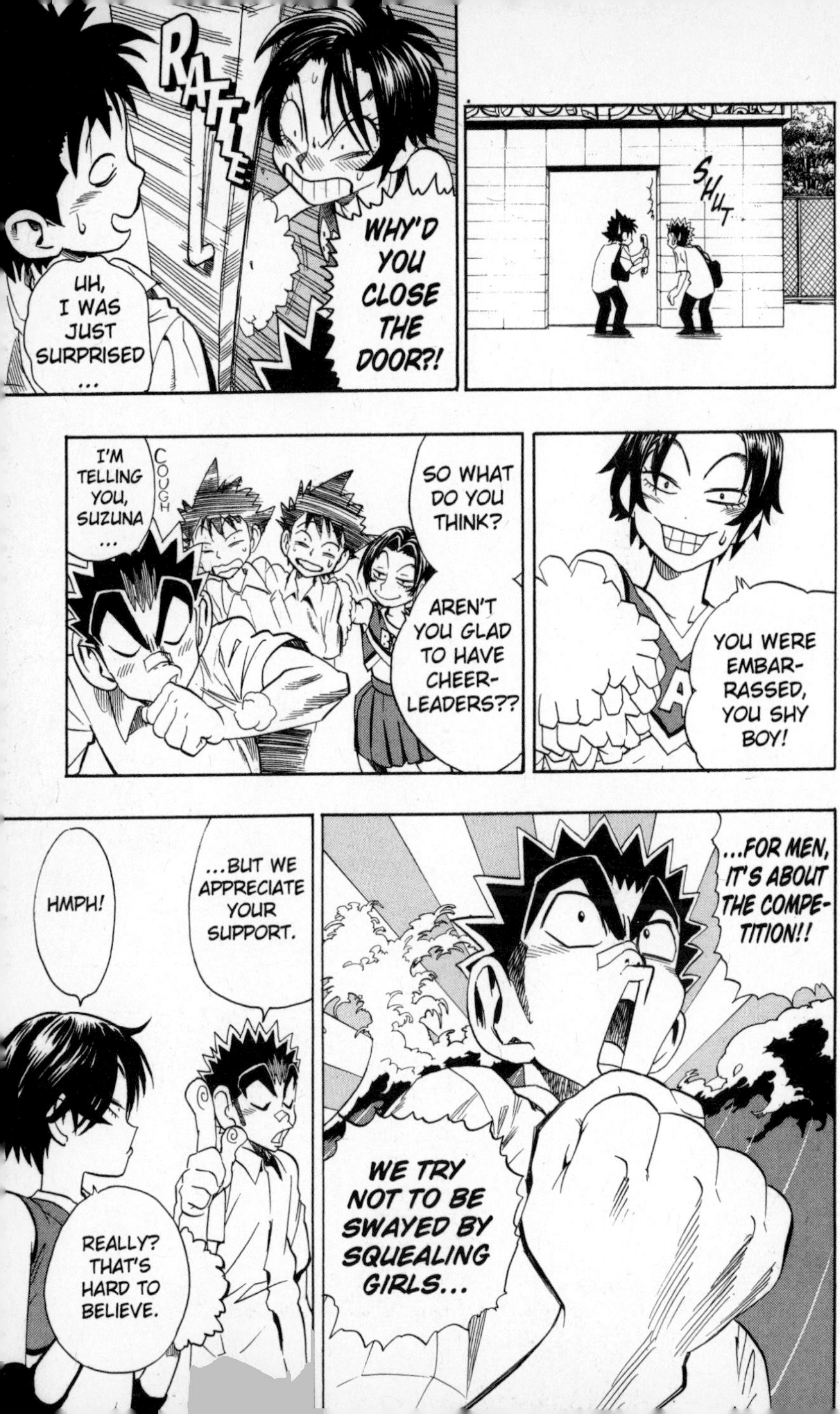
SHUT
RATTLE
WHY'D YOU CLOSE THE DOOR?!
UH, I WAS JUST SURPRISED...
YOU WERE EMBARRASSED, YOU SHY BOY!
SO WHAT DO YOU THINK?
AREN'T YOU GLAD TO HAVE CHEERLEADERS??
COUGH
I'M TELLING YOU, SUZUNA...
...FOR MEN, IT'S ABOUT THE COMPETITION!!
WE TRY NOT TO BE SWAYED BY SQUEALING GIRLS...
...BUT WE APPRECIATE YOUR SUPPORT.
HMPH!
REALLY? THAT'S HARD TO BELIEVE.

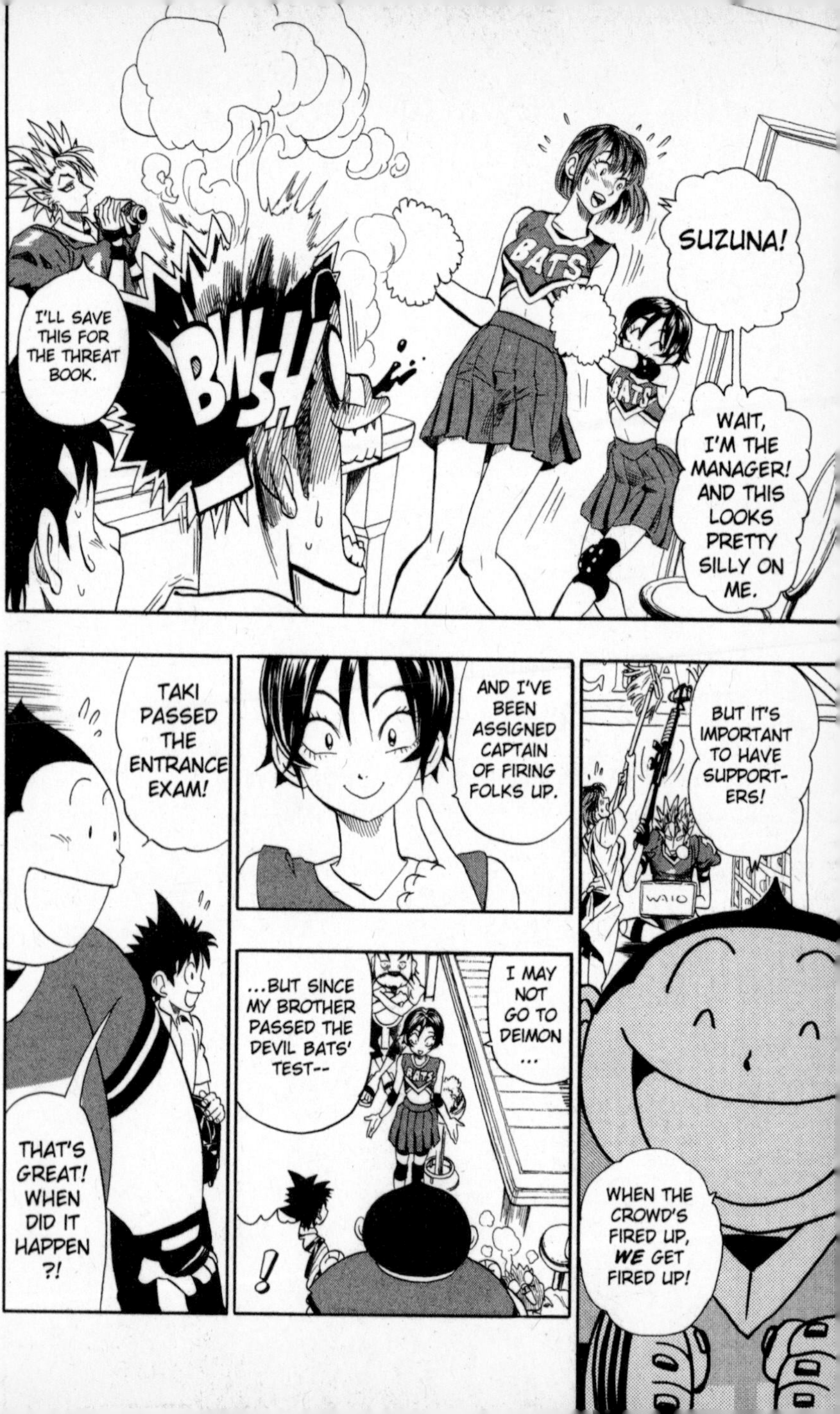
SUZUNA!
WAIT, I'M THE MANAGER! AND THIS LOOKS PRETTY SILLY ON ME.
BWSH
I'LL SAVE THIS FOR THE THREAT BOOK.
BUT IT'S IMPORTANT TO HAVE SUPPORT-ERS!
WAIO
WHEN THE CROWD'S FIRED UP, **WE** GET FIRED UP!
AND I'VE BEEN ASSIGNED CAPTAIN OF FIRING FOLKS UP.
I MAY NOT GO TO DEIMON...
...BUT SINCE MY BROTHER PASSED THE DEVIL BATS' TEST--
!
TAKI PASSED THE ENTRANCE EXAM!
THAT'S GREAT! WHEN DID IT HAPPEN?!

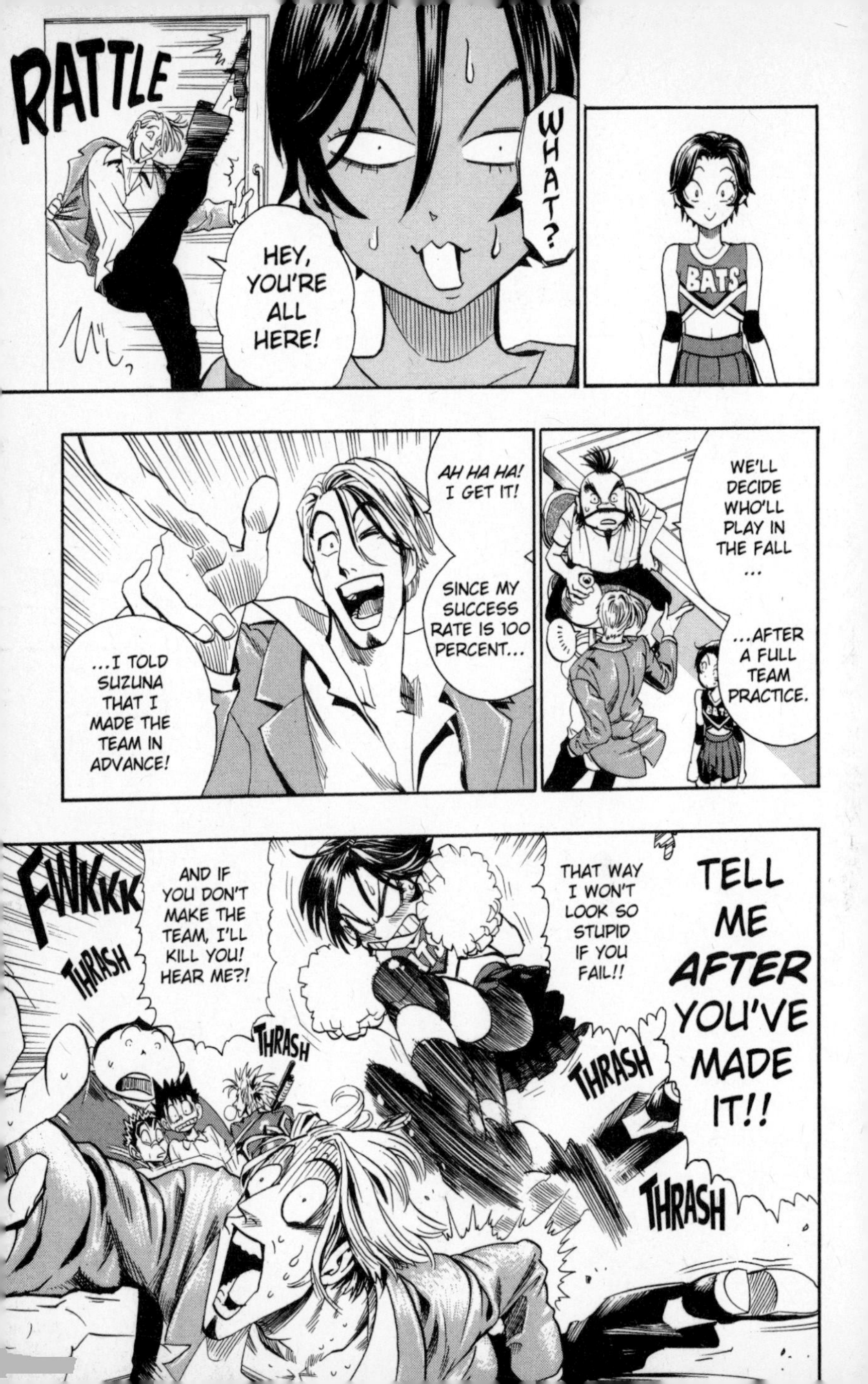
WHAT?
HEY, YOU'RE ALL HERE!
RATTLE
WE'LL DECIDE WHO'LL PLAY IN THE FALL...
...AFTER A FULL TEAM PRACTICE.
AH HA HA! I GET IT!
SINCE MY SUCCESS RATE IS 100 PERCENT...
...I TOLD SUZUNA THAT I MADE THE TEAM IN ADVANCE!
TELL ME AFTER YOU'VE MADE IT!!
THAT WAY I WON'T LOOK SO STUPID IF YOU FAIL!!
AND IF YOU DON'T MAKE THE TEAM, I'LL KILL YOU! HEAR ME?!
FWKKK
THRASH
THRASH
THRASH
THRASH

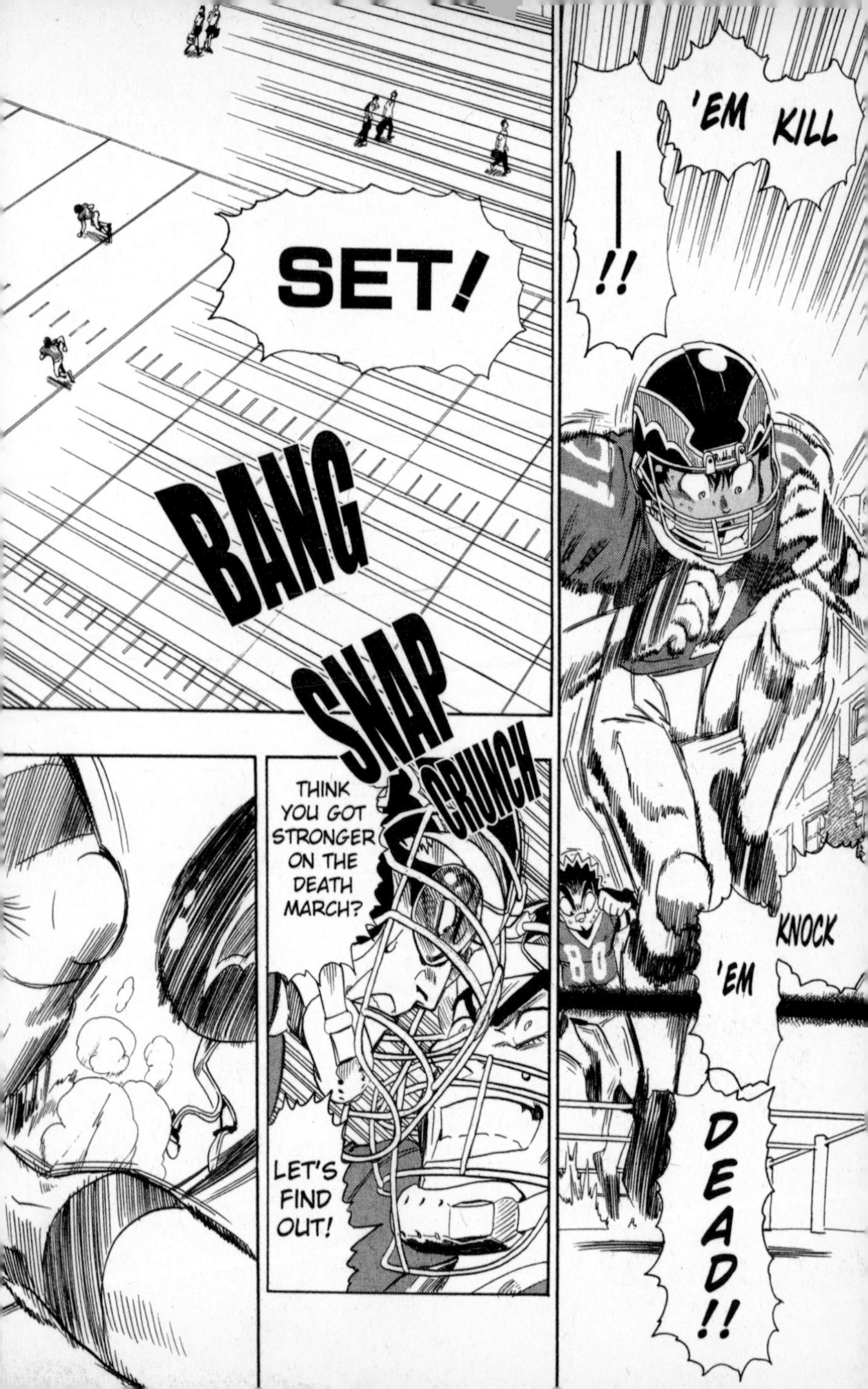
KILL 'EM
——!!
KNOCK 'EM DEAD!!
SET!
BANG
SNAP
CRUNCH
THINK YOU GOT STRONGER ON THE DEATH MARCH?
LET'S FIND OUT!

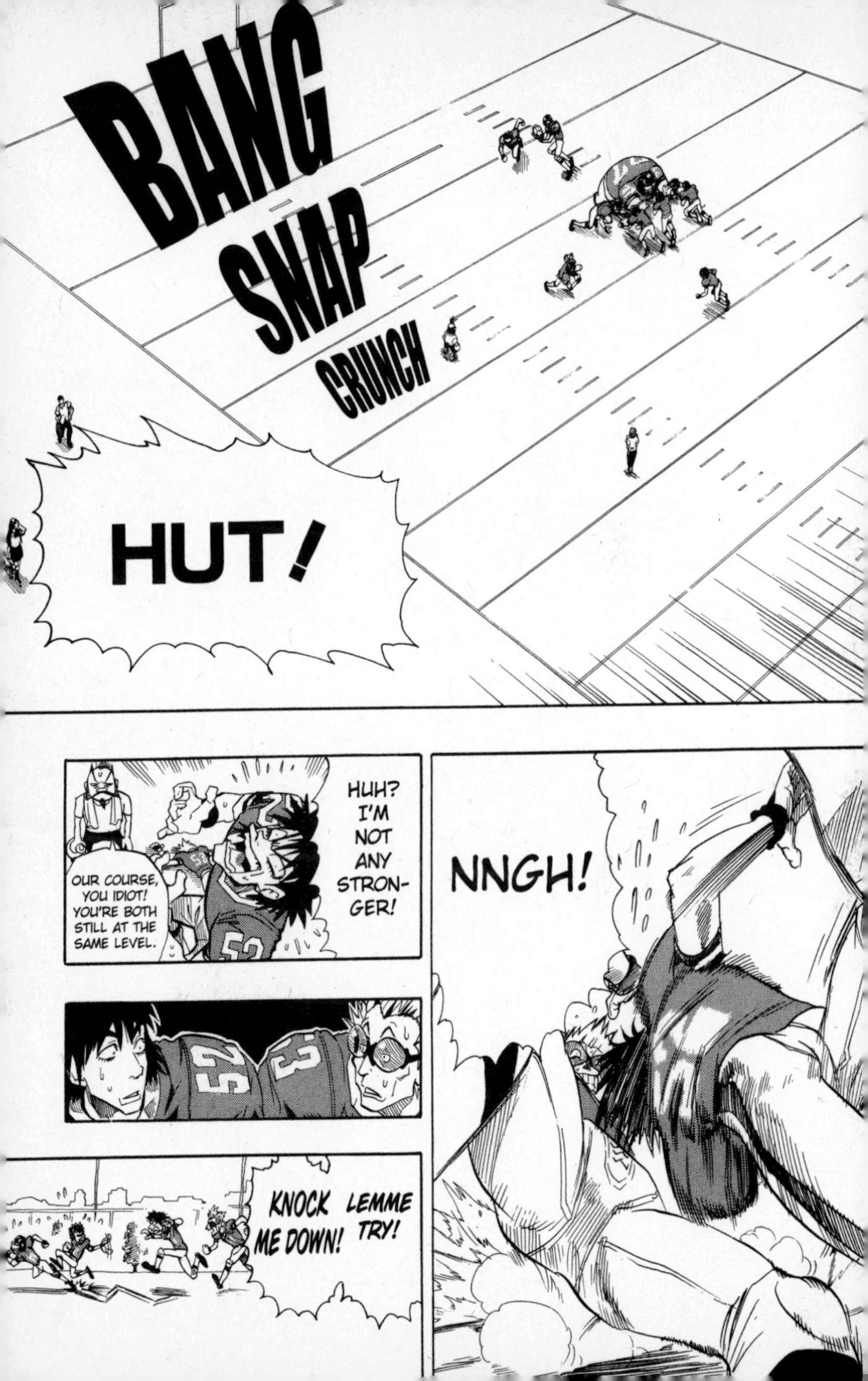
BANG
SNAP
CRUNCH
HUT!
NNGH!
HUH? I'M NOT ANY STRONGER!
OUR COURSE, YOU IDIOT! YOU'RE BOTH STILL AT THE SAME LEVEL.
LEMME TRY!
KNOCK ME DOWN!

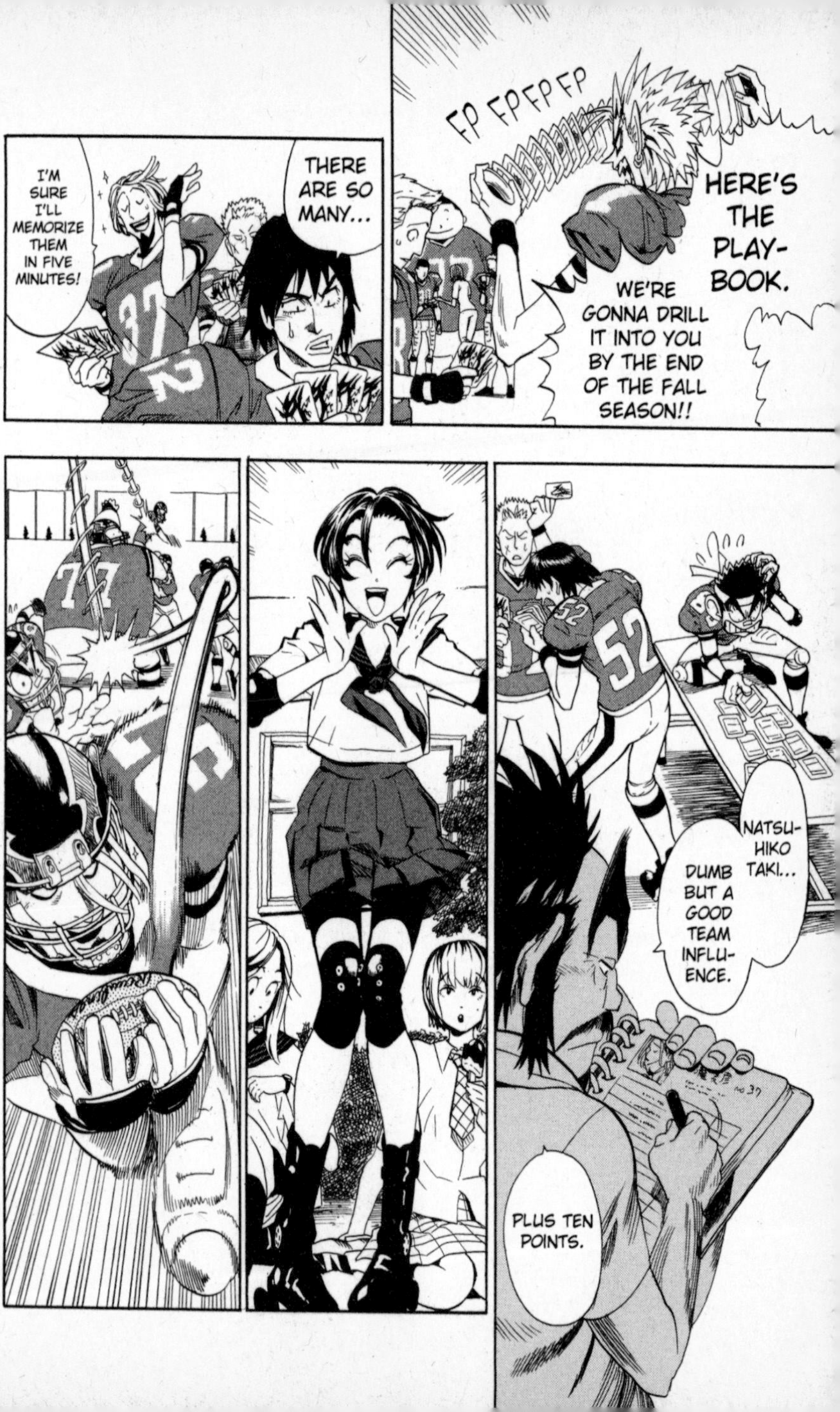
FP FP FP FP
HERE'S THE PLAY-BOOK.
WE'RE GONNA DRILL IT INTO YOU BY THE END OF THE FALL SEASON!!
THERE ARE SO MANY...
I'M SURE I'LL MEMORIZE THEM IN FIVE MINUTES!
NATSU-HIKO TAKI...
DUMB BUT A GOOD TEAM INFLU-ENCE.
PLUS TEN POINTS.

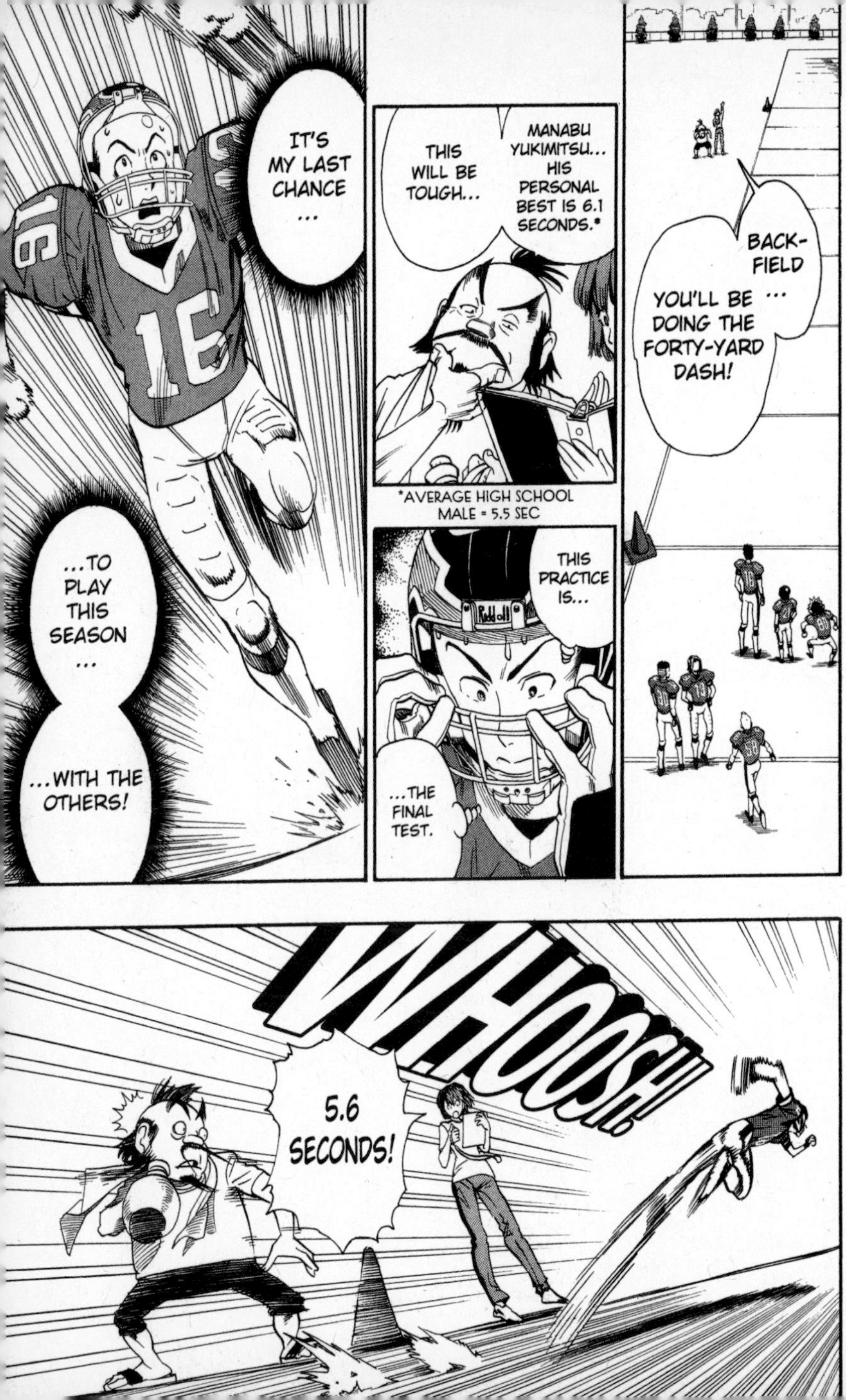
BACK-FIELD ...
YOU'LL BE DOING THE FORTY-YARD DASH!
MANABU YUKIMITSU... HIS PERSONAL BEST IS 6.1 SECONDS.*
THIS WILL BE TOUGH...
*AVERAGE HIGH SCHOOL MALE = 5.5 SEC
THIS PRACTICE IS...
...THE FINAL TEST.
IT'S MY LAST CHANCE ...
...TO PLAY THIS SEASON ...
...WITH THE OTHERS!
WHOOSH!!
5.6 SECONDS!

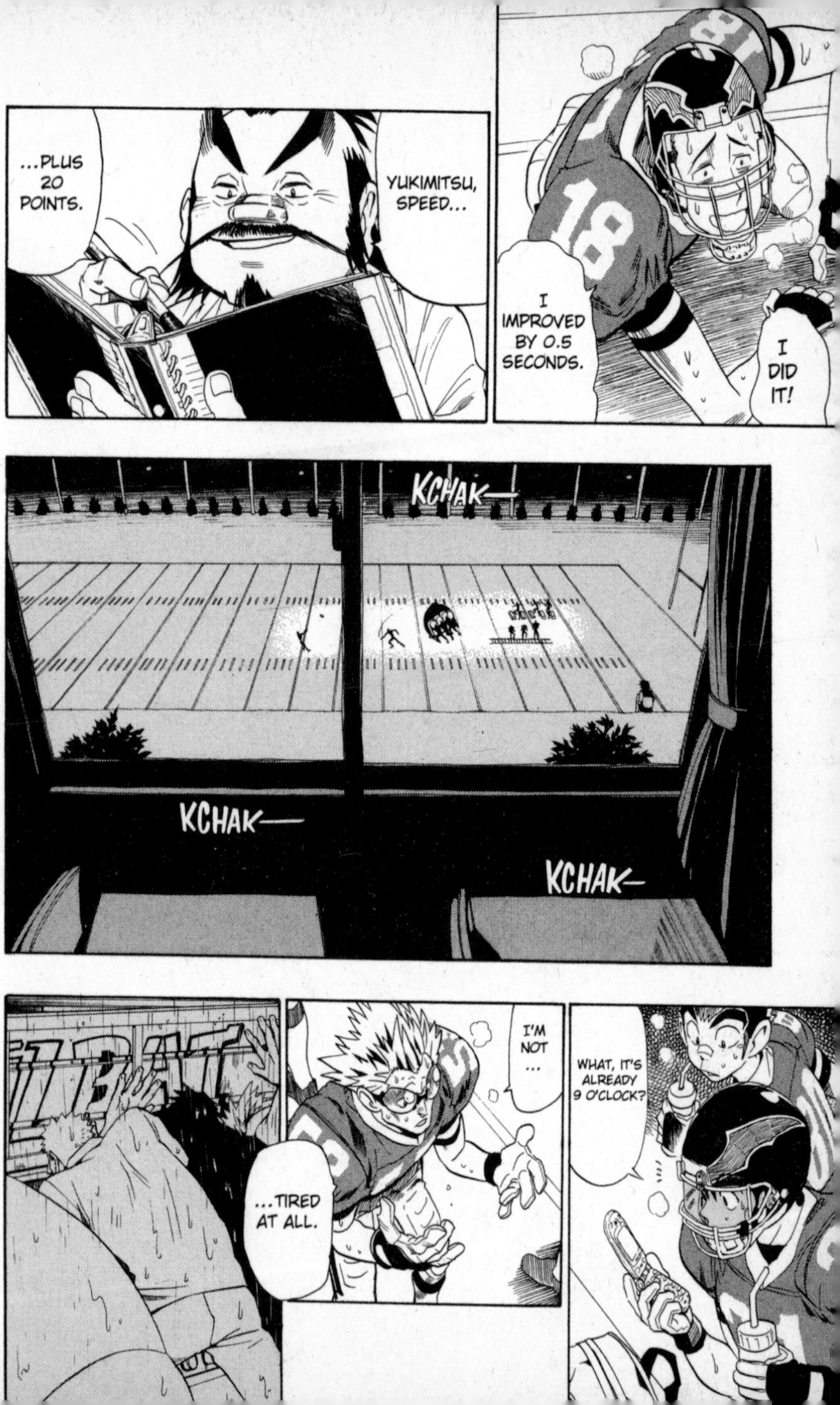
I DID IT!
I IMPROVED BY 0.5 SECONDS.
YUKIMITSU, SPEED...
...PLUS 20 POINTS.
KCHAK—
KCHAK—
KCHAK—
WHAT, IT'S ALREADY 9 O'CLOCK?
I'M NOT...
...TIRED AT ALL.

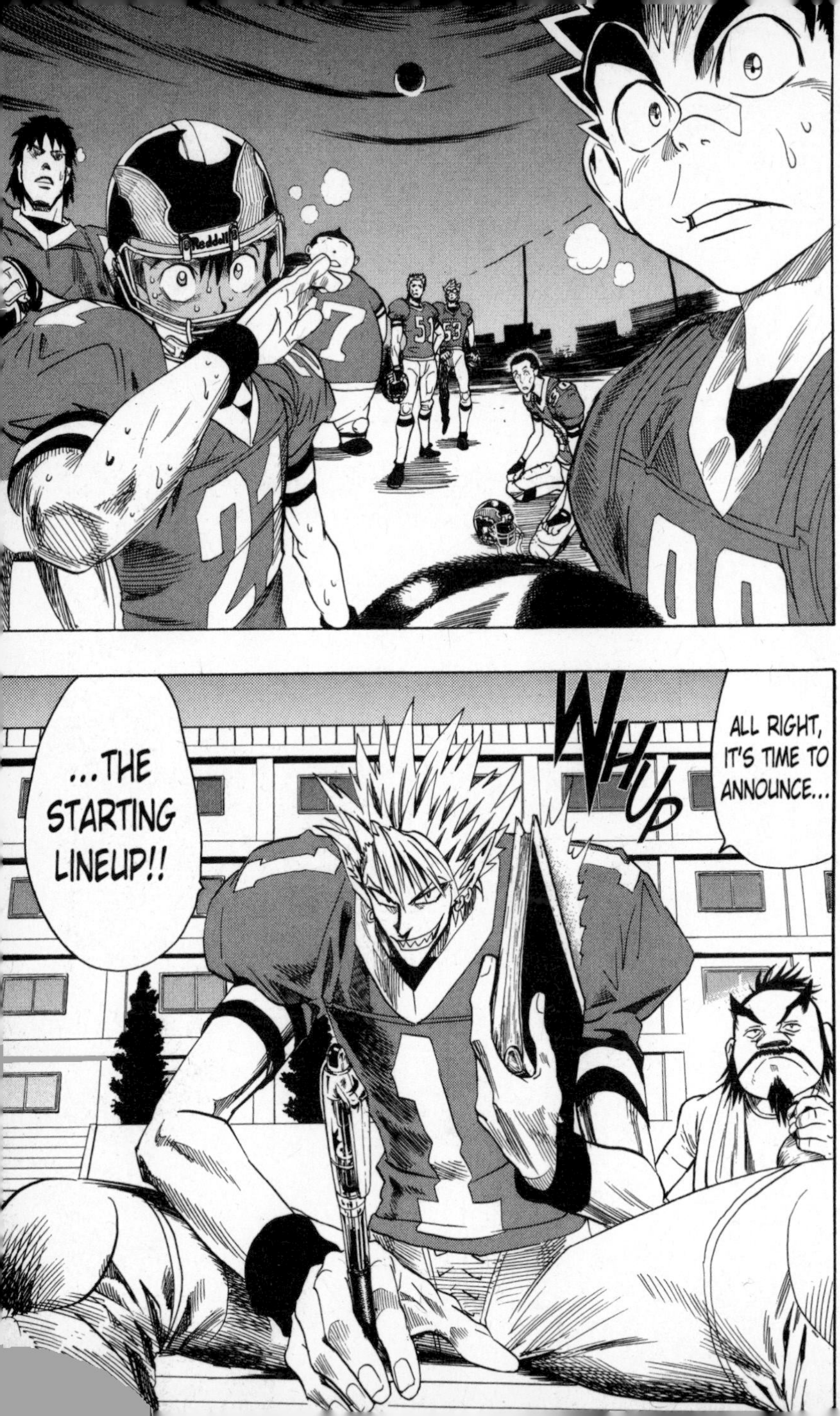
ALL RIGHT, IT'S TIME TO ANNOUNCE...
WHUP
...THE STARTING LINEUP!!

Eyeshield 21 Survey Corner **Devil Bat 021**

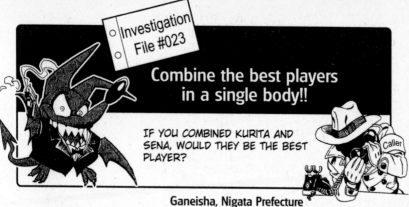

Investigation File #023

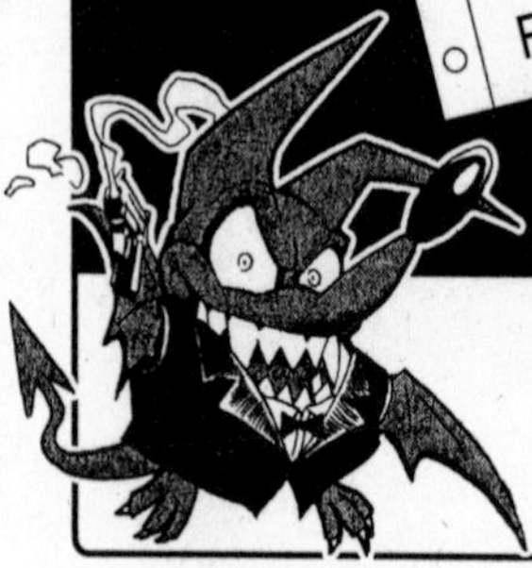

Combine the best players in a single body!!

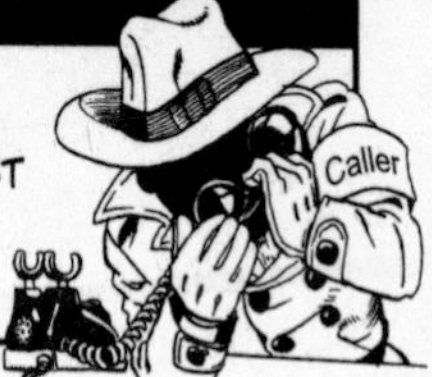

Caller

IF YOU COMBINED KURITA AND SENA, WOULD THEY BE THE BEST PLAYER?

Ganeisha, Nigata Prefecture

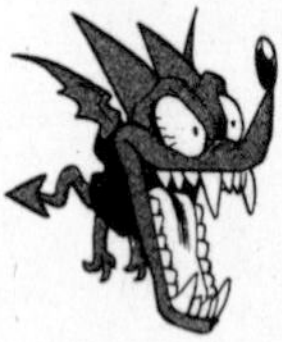

YOU MEAN, COMBINE KURITA'S AWESOME STRENGTH WITH SENA'S AMAZING SPEED?!

HEE HEE HEE! LEAVE IT TO ME!

KURISENA, THE BEST FOOTBALL ATHLETE, IS BORN!!

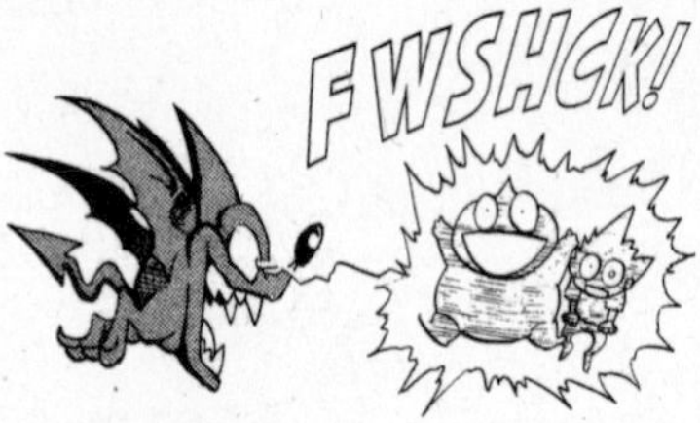

FWSHCK!

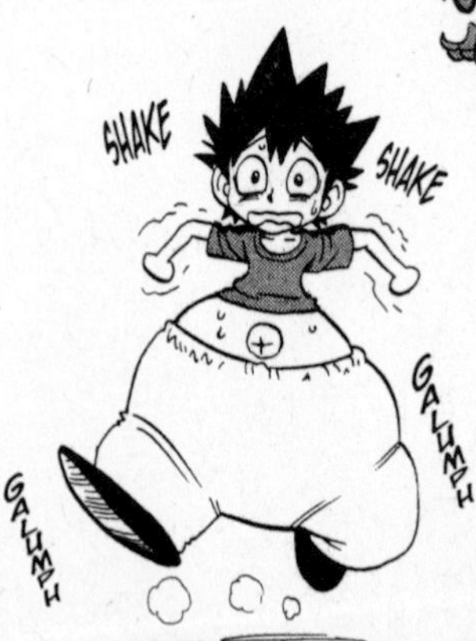

SHAKE
SHAKE
GALUMPH
GALUMPH

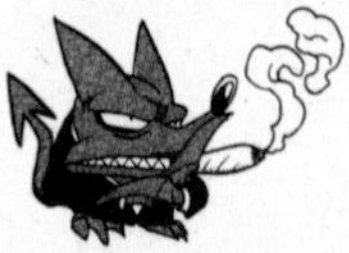

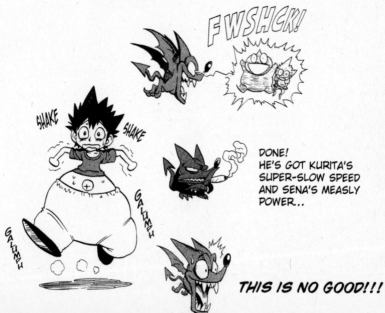

DONE!
HE'S GOT KURITA'S SUPER-SLOW SPEED AND SENA'S MEASLY POWER...

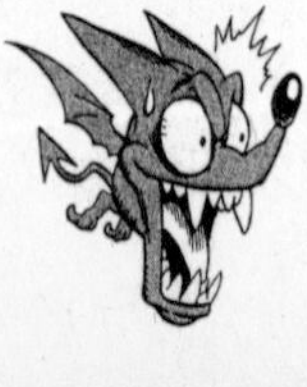

THIS IS NO GOOD!!!

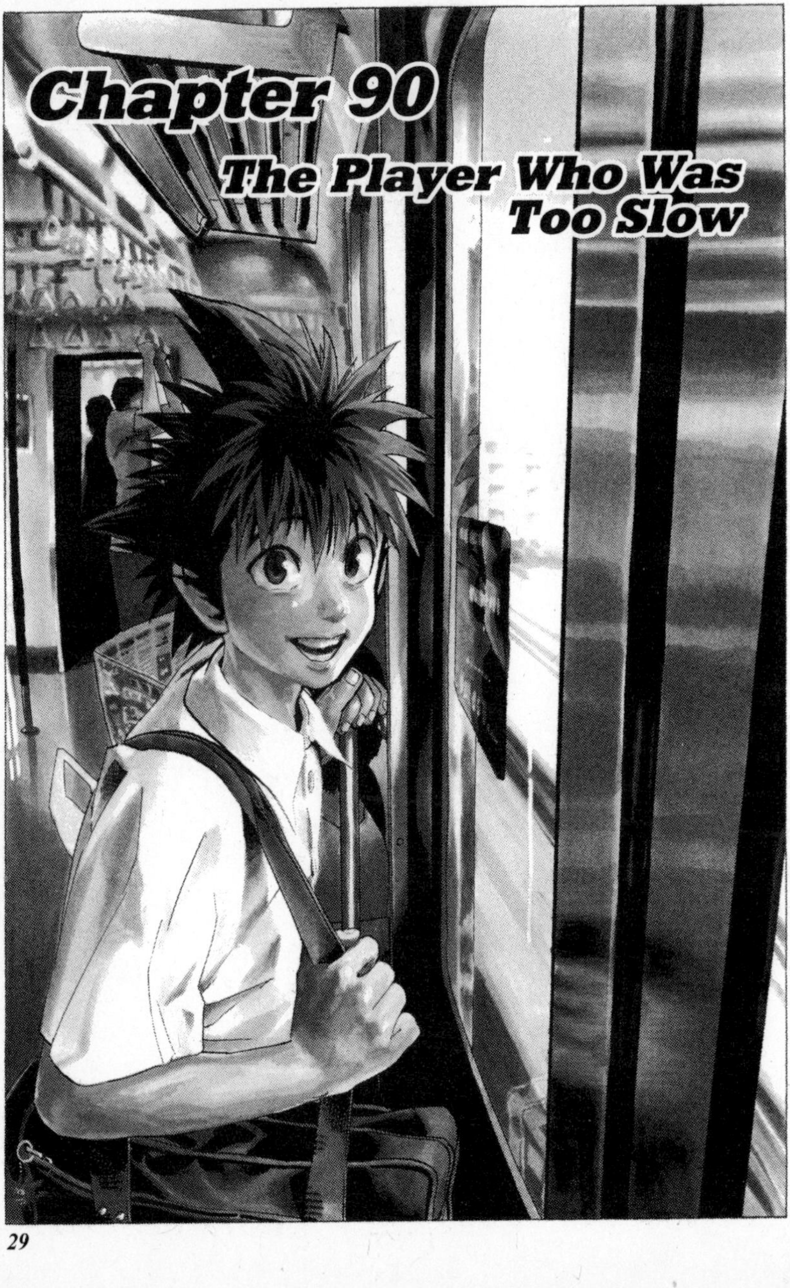
Chapter 90
The Player Who Was Too Slow

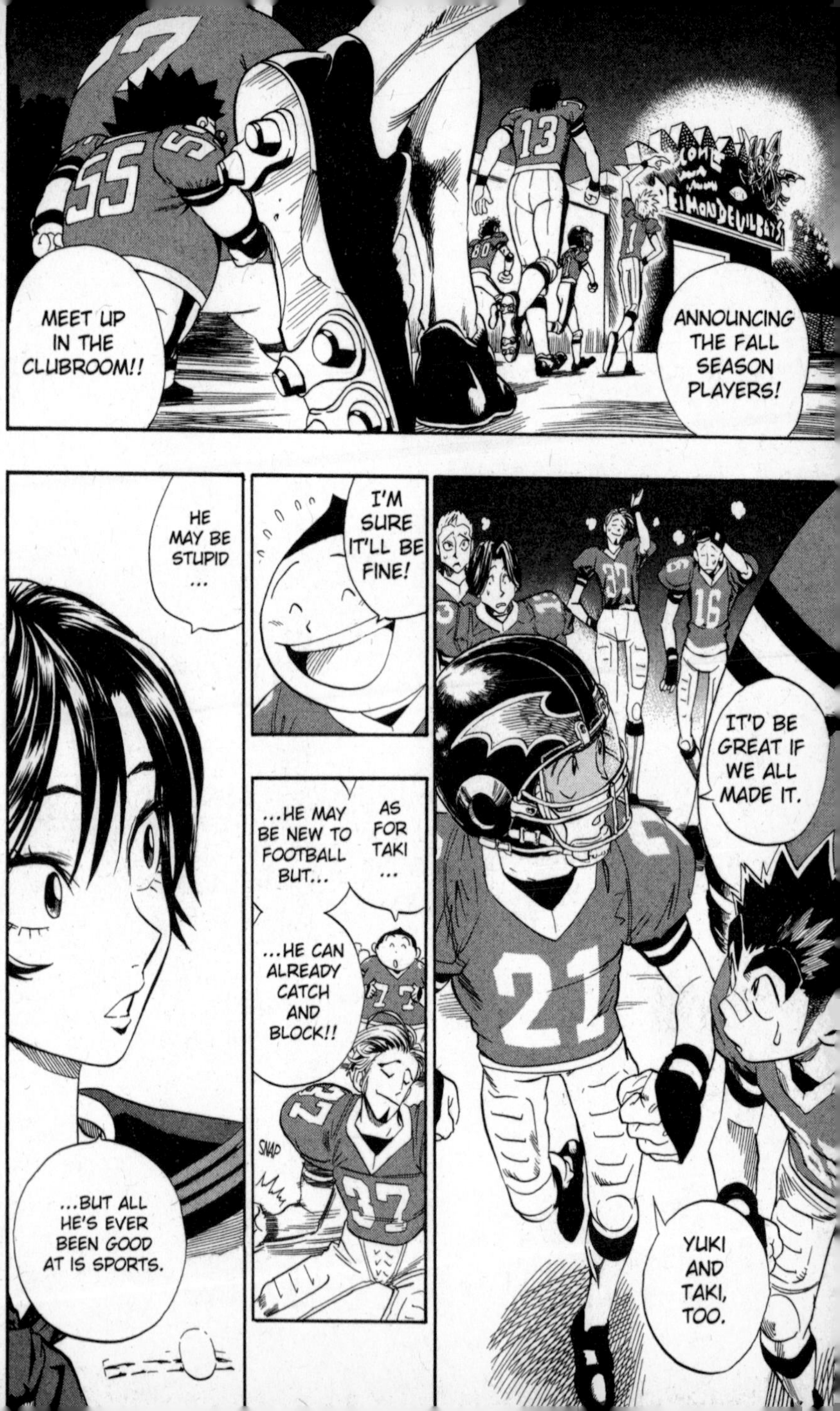
ANNOUNCING THE FALL SEASON PLAYERS!
MEET UP IN THE CLUBROOM!!
IT'D BE GREAT IF WE ALL MADE IT.
YUKI AND TAKI, TOO.
I'M SURE IT'LL BE FINE!
AS FOR TAKI...
...HE MAY BE NEW TO FOOTBALL BUT...
...HE CAN ALREADY CATCH AND BLOCK!!
SNAP
HE MAY BE STUPID...
...BUT ALL HE'S EVER BEEN GOOD AT IS SPORTS.

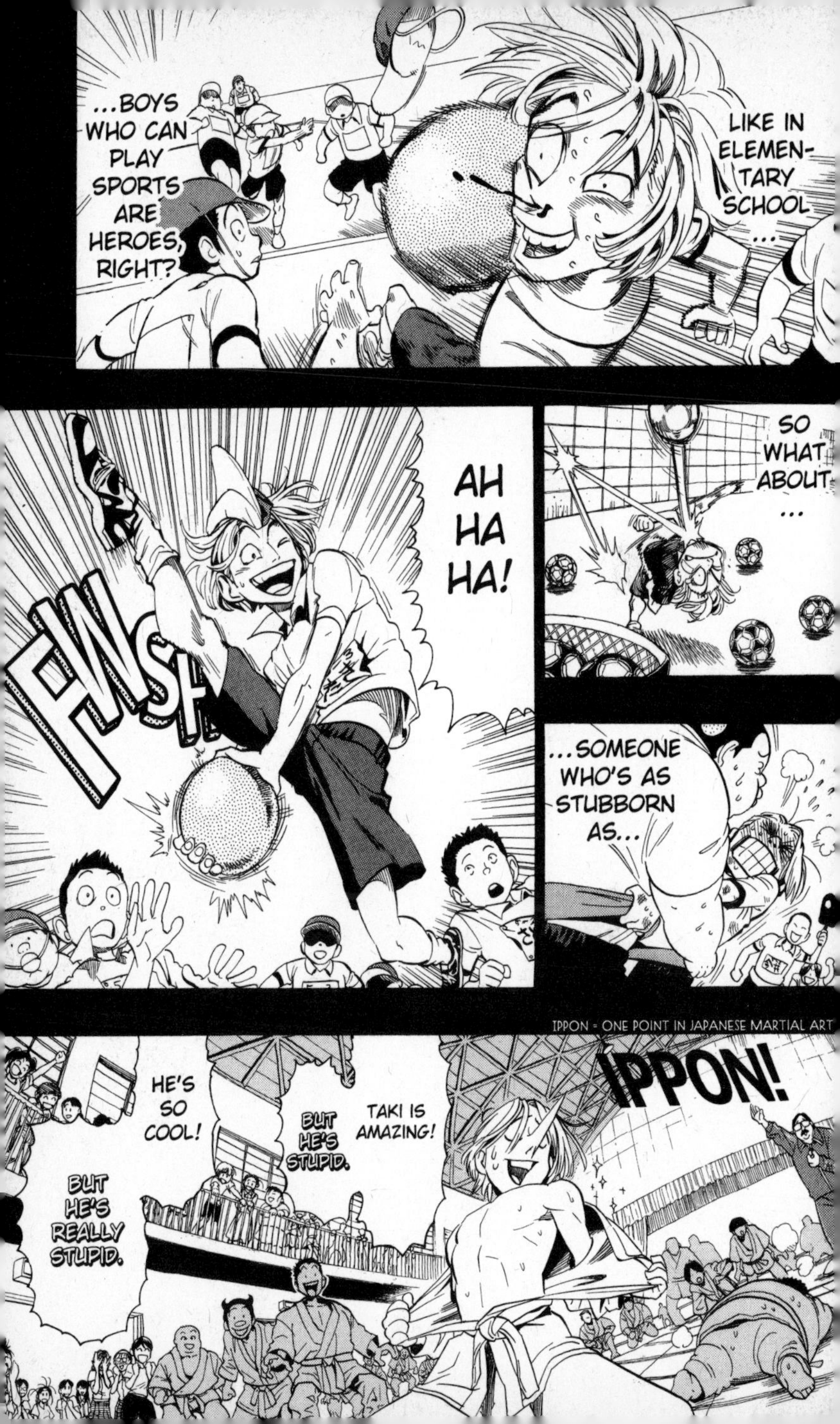

LIKE IN ELEMENTARY SCHOOL...
...BOYS WHO CAN PLAY SPORTS ARE HEROES, RIGHT?
SO WHAT ABOUT...
...SOMEONE WHO'S AS STUBBORN AS...
AH HA HA!
FWSH
IPPON = ONE POINT IN JAPANESE MARTIAL ART
IPPON!
TAKI IS AMAZING!
BUT HE'S STUPID.
HE'S SO COOL!
BUT HE'S REALLY STUPID.

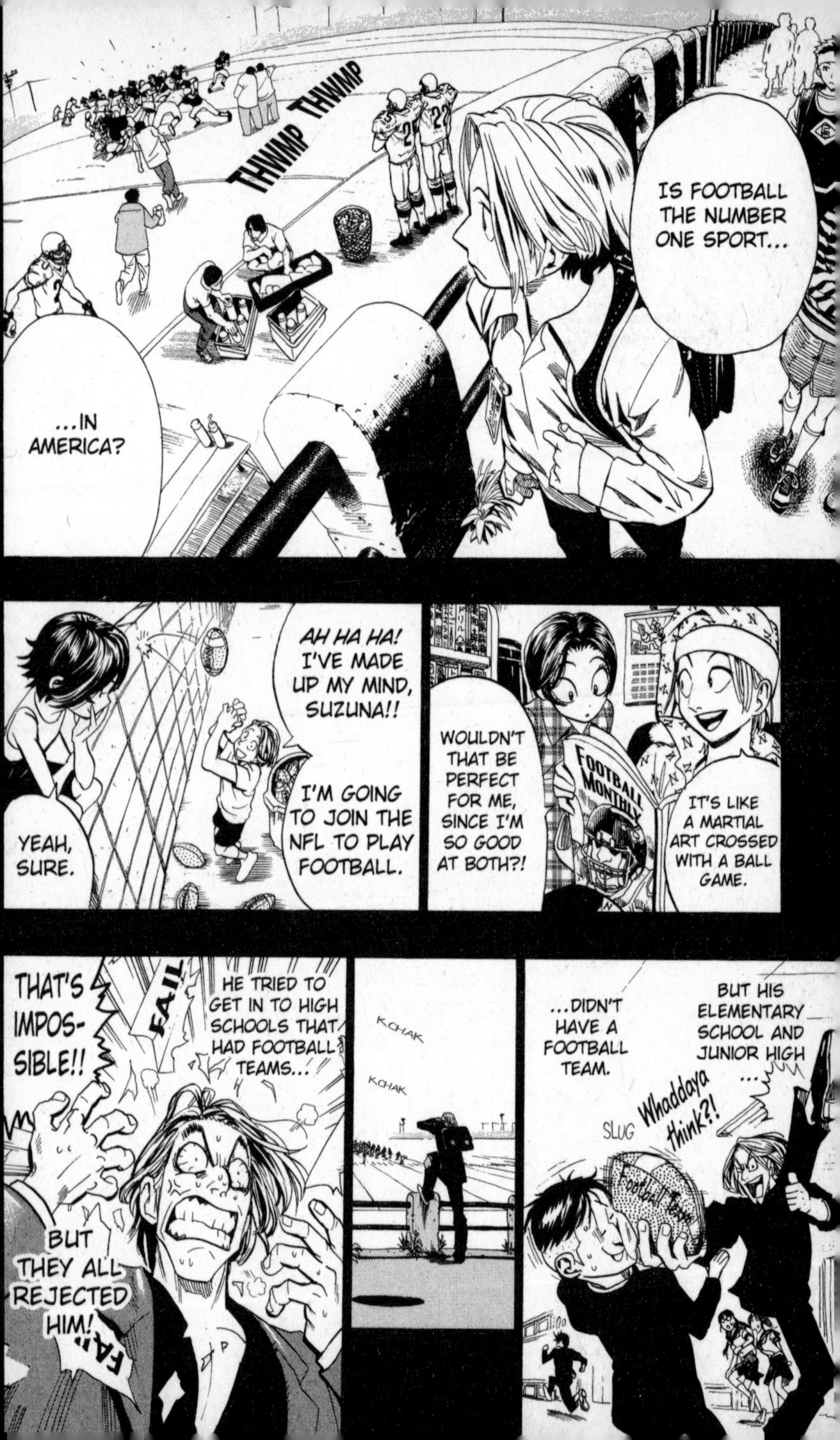
IS FOOTBALL THE NUMBER ONE SPORT...
THWMP THWMP
...IN AMERICA?
IT'S LIKE A MARTIAL ART CROSSED WITH A BALL GAME.
FOOTBALL MONTHLY
WOULDN'T THAT BE PERFECT FOR ME, SINCE I'M SO GOOD AT BOTH?!
AH HA HA! I'VE MADE UP MY MIND, SUZUNA!!
I'M GOING TO JOIN THE NFL TO PLAY FOOTBALL.
YEAH, SURE.
BUT HIS ELEMENTARY SCHOOL AND JUNIOR HIGH...
Whaddaya think?!
SLUG
Football Team
...DIDN'T HAVE A FOOTBALL TEAM.
K-CHAK
K-CHAK
HE TRIED TO GET IN TO HIGH SCHOOLS THAT HAD FOOTBALL TEAMS...
THAT'S IMPOSSIBLE!!
FAIL
BUT THEY ALL REJECTED HIM!
FAIL

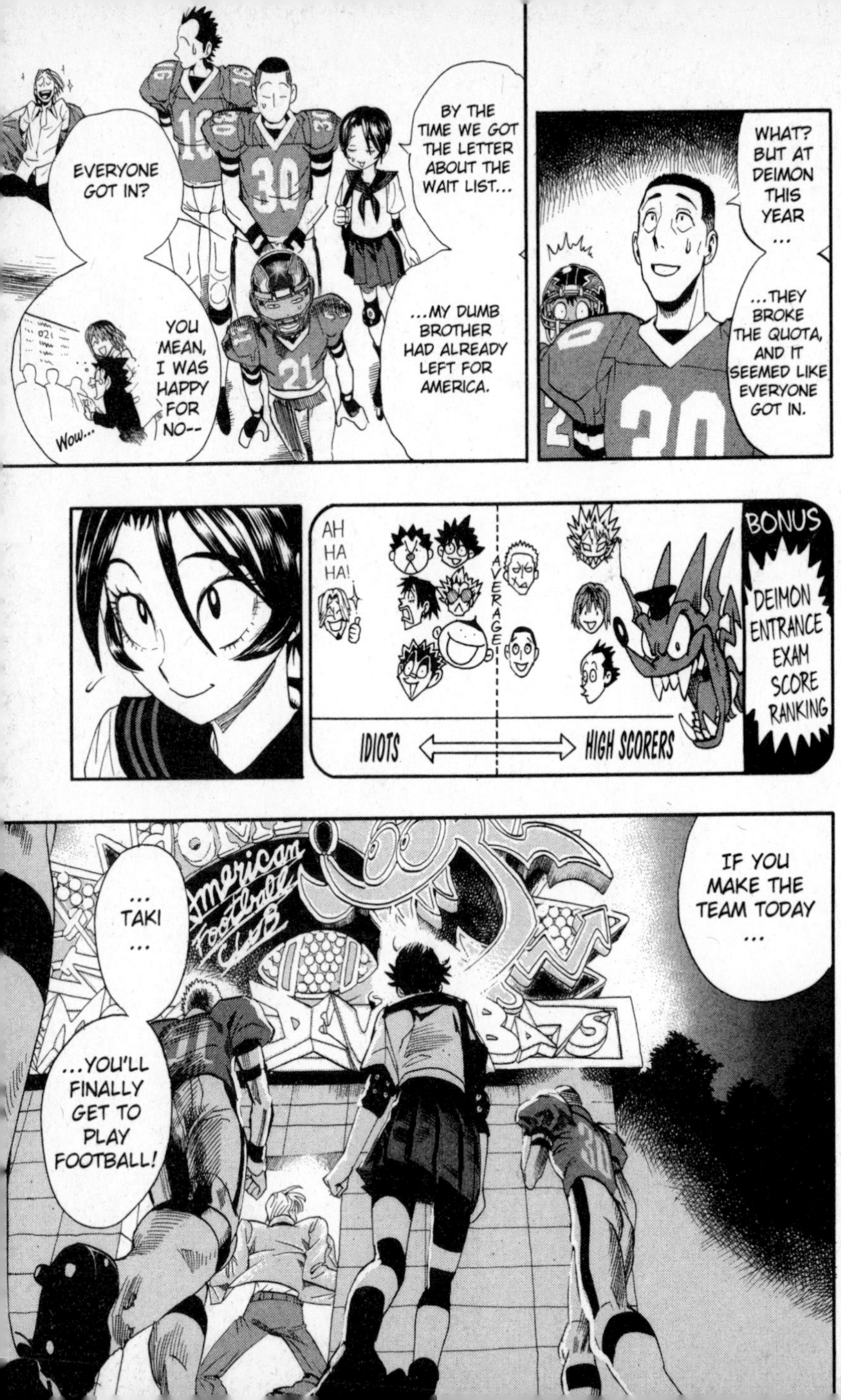
WHAT? BUT AT DEIMON THIS YEAR ...
...THEY BROKE THE QUOTA, AND IT SEEMED LIKE EVERYONE GOT IN.
BY THE TIME WE GOT THE LETTER ABOUT THE WAIT LIST...
...MY DUMB BROTHER HAD ALREADY LEFT FOR AMERICA.
EVERYONE GOT IN?
YOU MEAN, I WAS HAPPY FOR NO--
Wow...
BONUS
DEIMON ENTRANCE EXAM SCORE RANKING
AH HA HA!
AVERAGE
IDIOTS
HIGH SCORERS
IF YOU MAKE THE TEAM TODAY ...
... TAKI ...
...YOU'LL FINALLY GET TO PLAY FOOTBALL!
American Football Club
DEVIL BATS

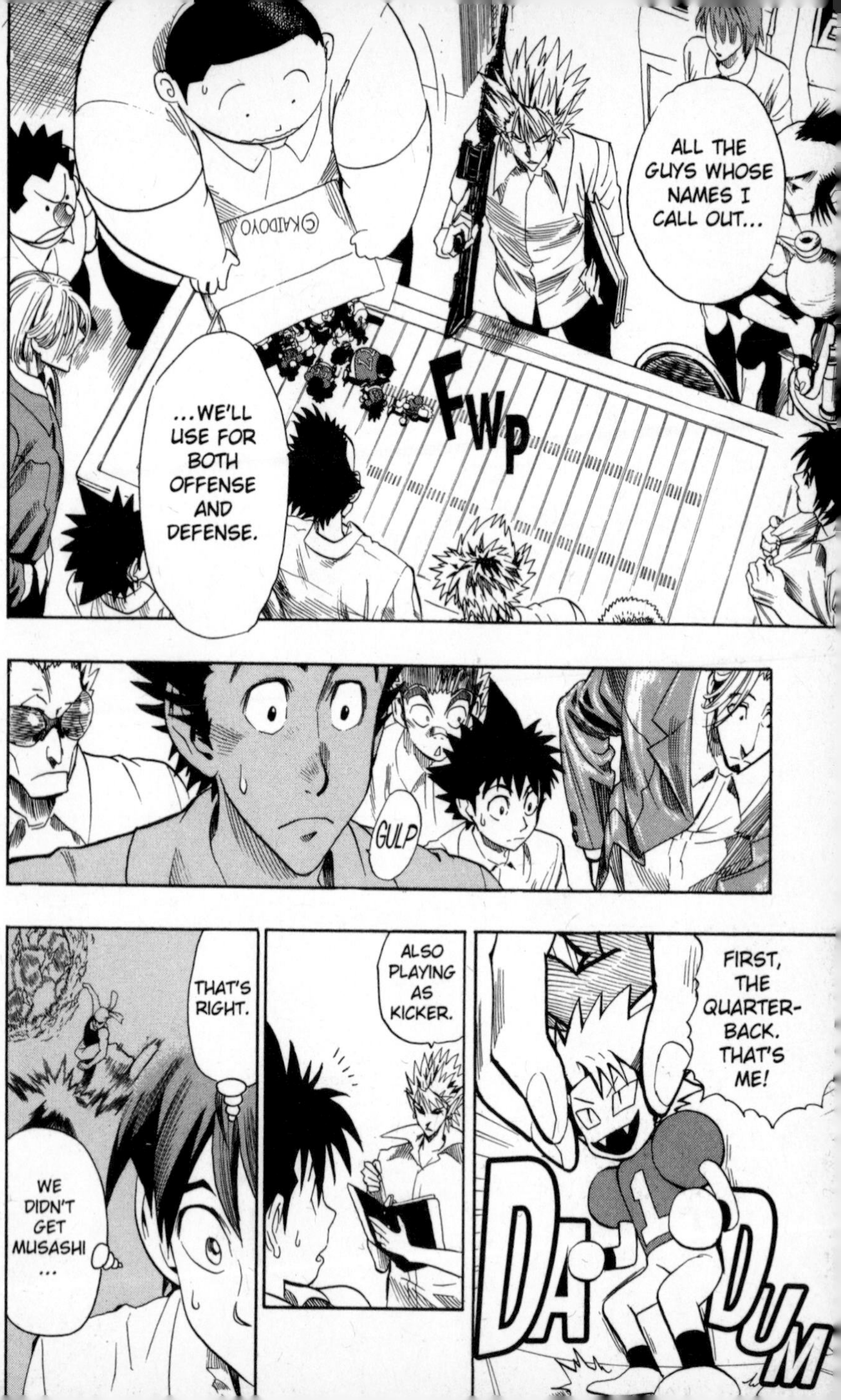
ALL THE GUYS WHOSE NAMES I CALL OUT...
...WE'LL USE FOR BOTH OFFENSE AND DEFENSE.
FWP
GULP
FIRST, THE QUARTER-BACK. THAT'S ME!
DA-DUM
ALSO PLAYING AS KICKER.
THAT'S RIGHT.
WE DIDN'T GET MUSASHI ...

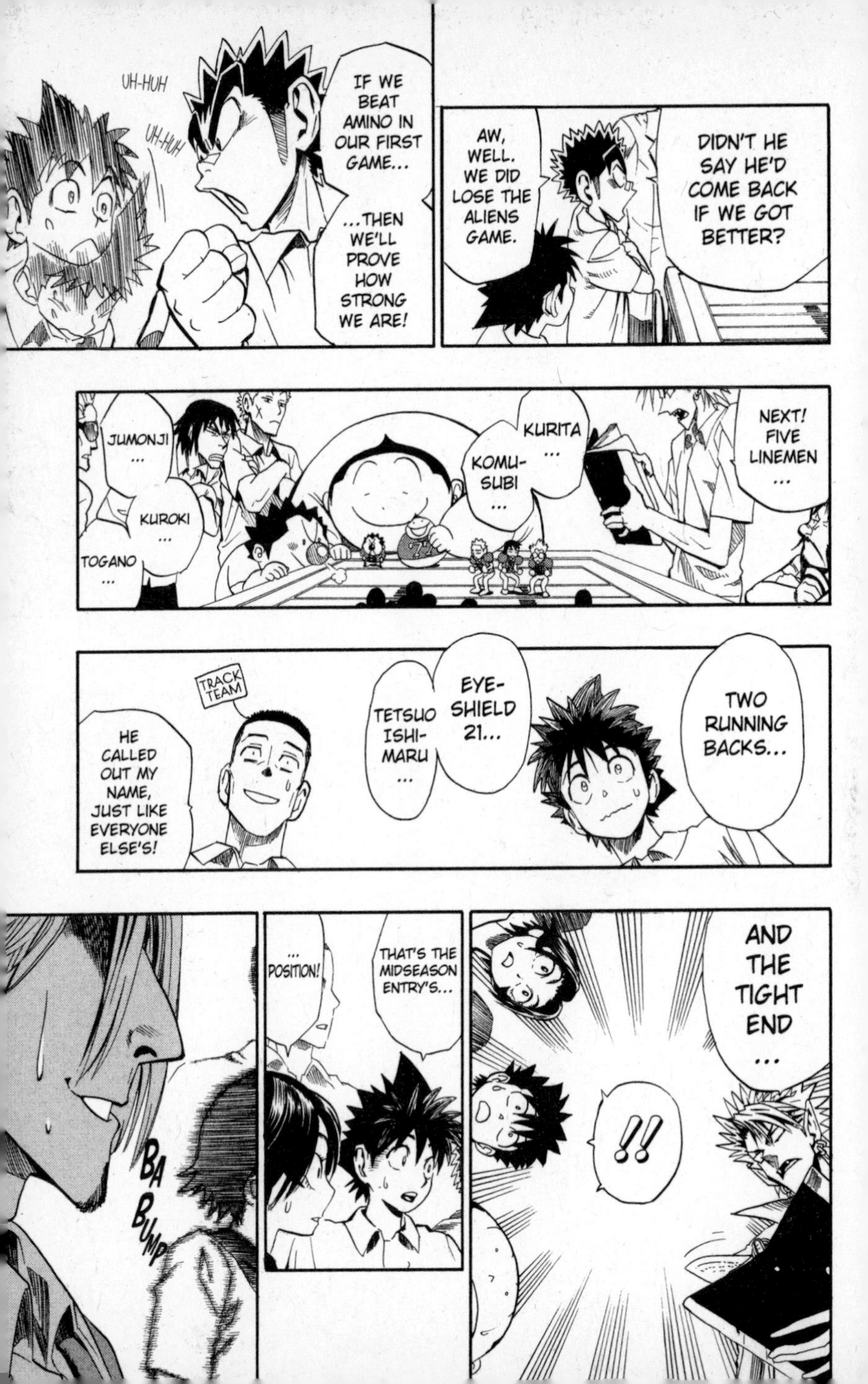
DIDN'T HE SAY HE'D COME BACK IF WE GOT BETTER?
AW, WELL. WE DID LOSE THE ALIENS GAME.
IF WE BEAT AMINO IN OUR FIRST GAME...
...THEN WE'LL PROVE HOW STRONG WE ARE!
UH-HUH
UH-HUH
NEXT! FIVE LINEMEN...
KURITA...
KOMU-SUBI...
JUMONJI...
KUROKI...
TOGANO...
TWO RUNNING BACKS...
EYE-SHIELD 21...
TETSUO ISHI-MARU...
TRACK TEAM
HE CALLED OUT MY NAME, JUST LIKE EVERYONE ELSE'S!
AND THE TIGHT END...
!!
THAT'S THE MIDSEASON ENTRY'S...
...POSITION!
BA BUMP

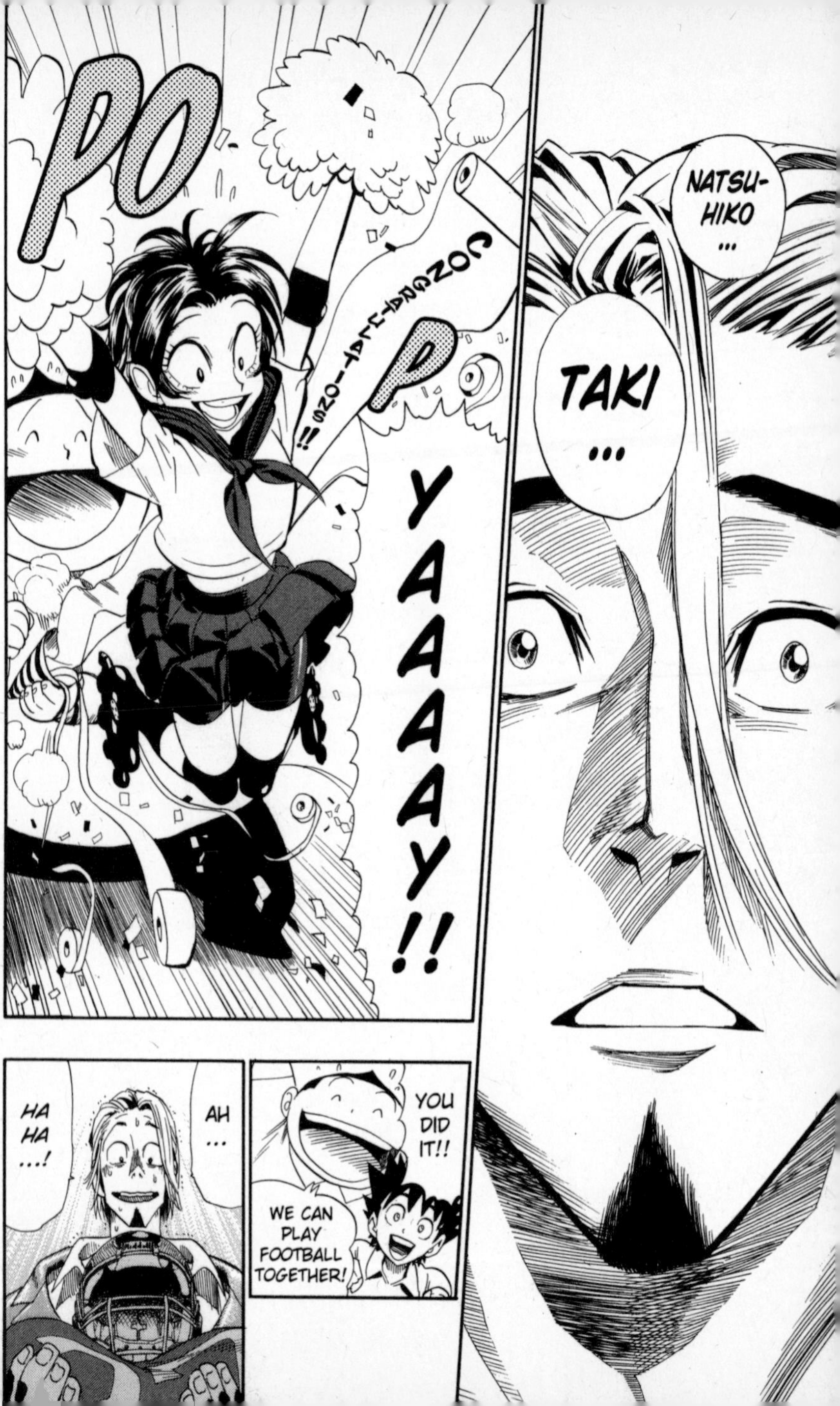
NATSU-HIKO ...
TAKI ...
PO
CONGRATULATIONS!!
P
YAAAAY!!
YOU DID IT!!
WE CAN PLAY FOOTBALL TOGETHER!
AH ...
HA HA ...!

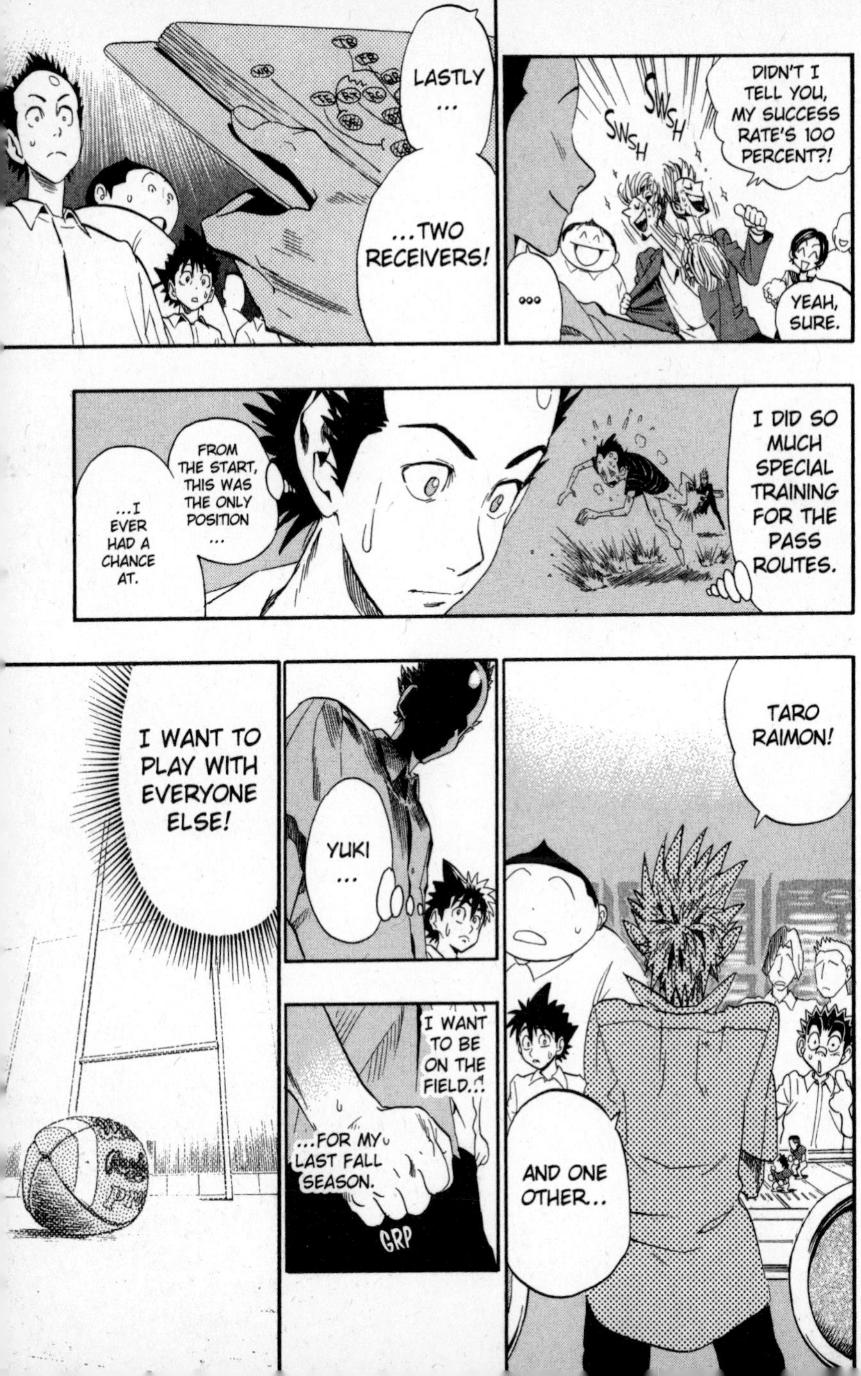
DIDN'T I TELL YOU, MY SUCCESS RATE'S 100 PERCENT?!
SWSH
SWSH
YEAH, SURE.
...
LASTLY ...
...TWO RECEIVERS!
I DID SO MUCH SPECIAL TRAINING FOR THE PASS ROUTES.
FROM THE START, THIS WAS THE ONLY POSITION ...
...I EVER HAD A CHANCE AT.
TARO RAIMON!
AND ONE OTHER...
YUKI ...
I WANT TO BE ON THE FIELD...
...FOR MY LAST FALL SEASON.
GRP
I WANT TO PLAY WITH EVERYONE ELSE!

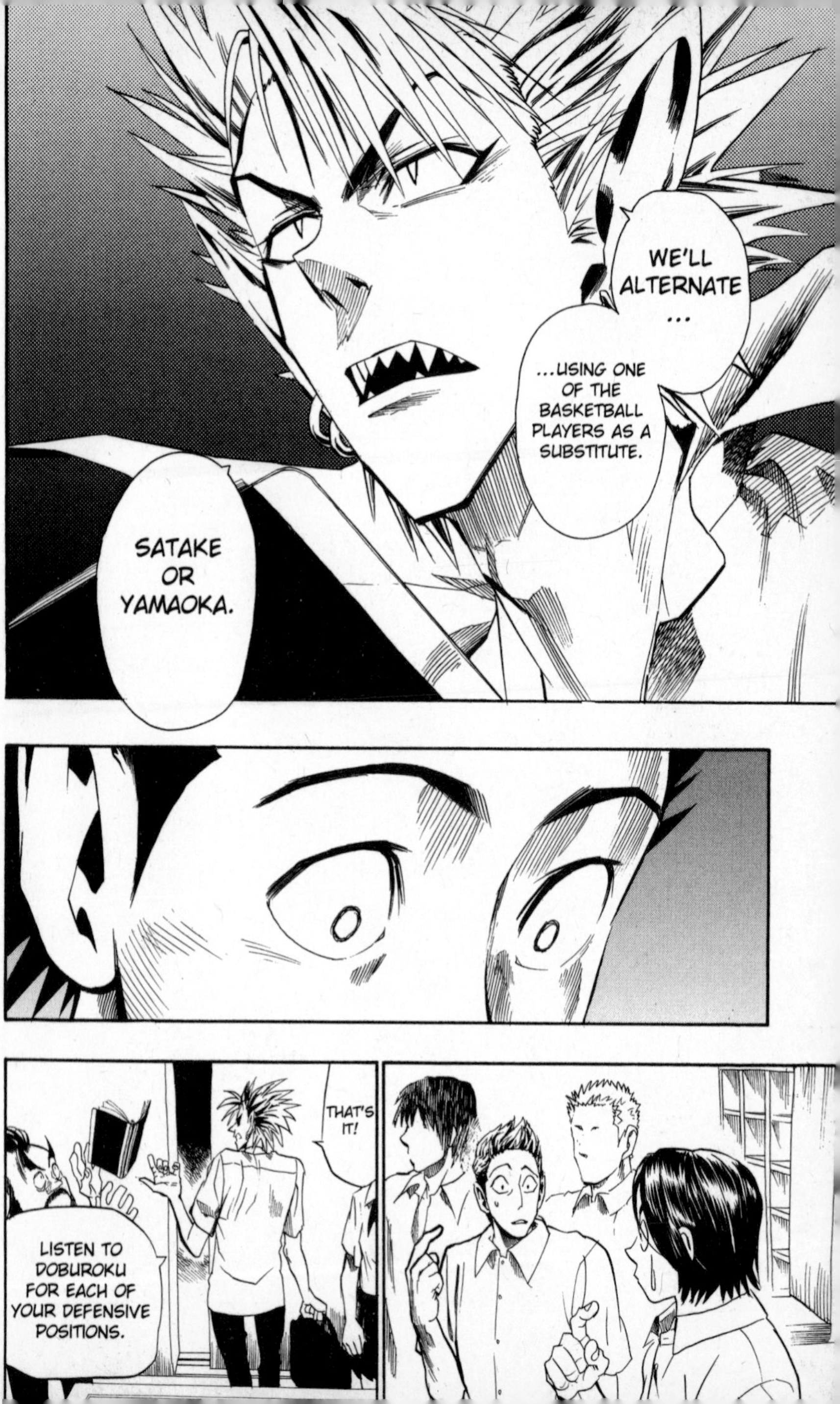
WE'LL ALTERNATE ...
...USING ONE OF THE BASKETBALL PLAYERS AS A SUBSTITUTE.
SATAKE OR YAMAOKA.
THAT'S IT!
LISTEN TO DOBUROKU FOR EACH OF YOUR DEFENSIVE POSITIONS.

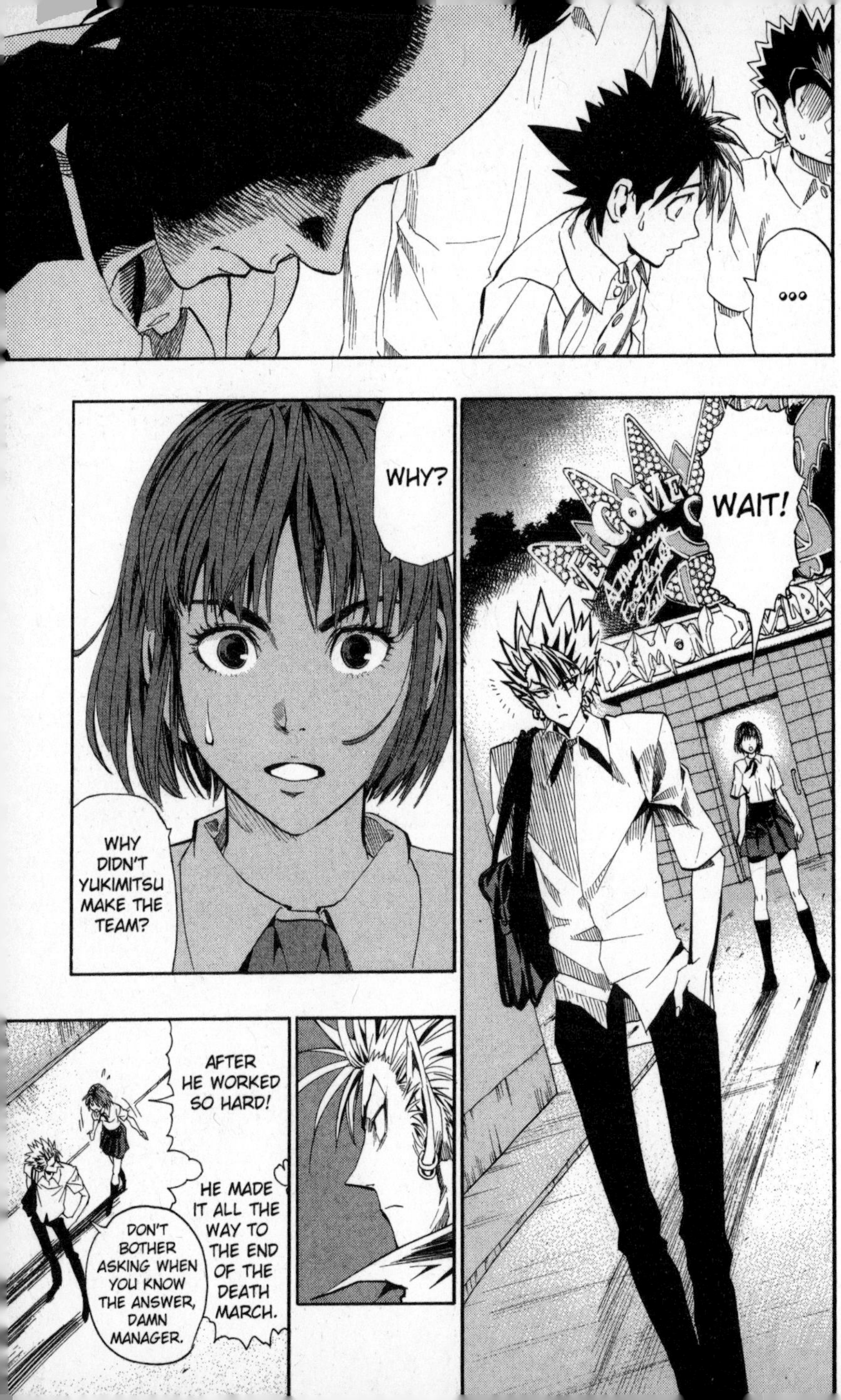
...
WAIT!
WHY?
WHY DIDN'T YUKIMITSU MAKE THE TEAM?
AFTER HE WORKED SO HARD!
HE MADE IT ALL THE WAY TO THE END OF THE DEATH MARCH.
DON'T BOTHER ASKING WHEN YOU KNOW THE ANSWER, DAMN MANAGER.

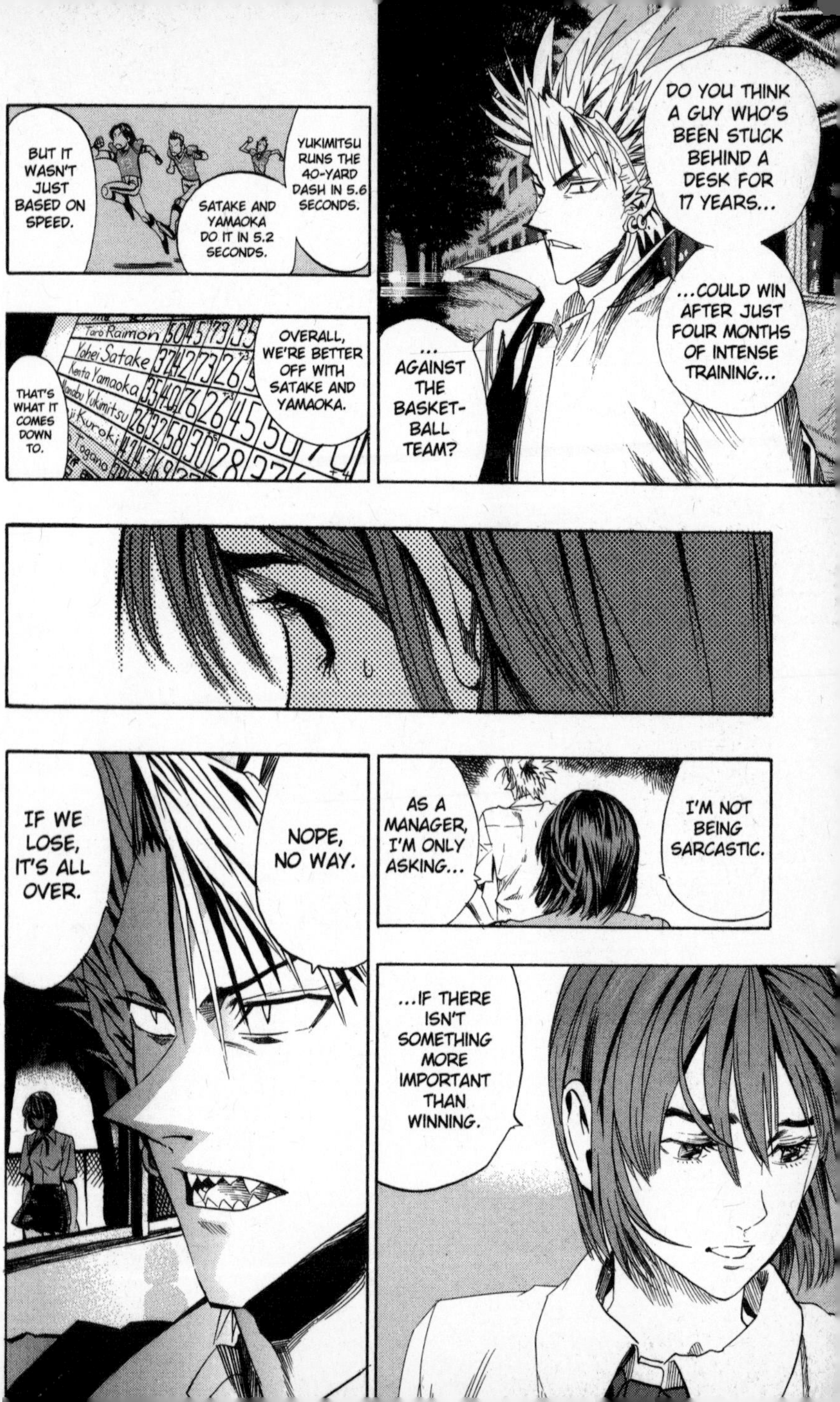
DO YOU THINK A GUY WHO'S BEEN STUCK BEHIND A DESK FOR 17 YEARS...
...COULD WIN AFTER JUST FOUR MONTHS OF INTENSE TRAINING...
...AGAINST THE BASKETBALL TEAM?
YUKIMITSU RUNS THE 40-YARD DASH IN 5.6 SECONDS.
SATAKE AND YAMAOKA DO IT IN 5.2 SECONDS.
BUT IT WASN'T JUST BASED ON SPEED.
Taro Raimon
Yohei Satake
Kenta Yamaoka
Manabu Yukimitsu
Kuroki
Togano
OVERALL, WE'RE BETTER OFF WITH SATAKE AND YAMAOKA.
THAT'S WHAT IT COMES DOWN TO.
I'M NOT BEING SARCASTIC.
AS A MANAGER, I'M ONLY ASKING...
...IF THERE ISN'T SOMETHING MORE IMPORTANT THAN WINNING.
NOPE, NO WAY.
IF WE LOSE, IT'S ALL OVER.

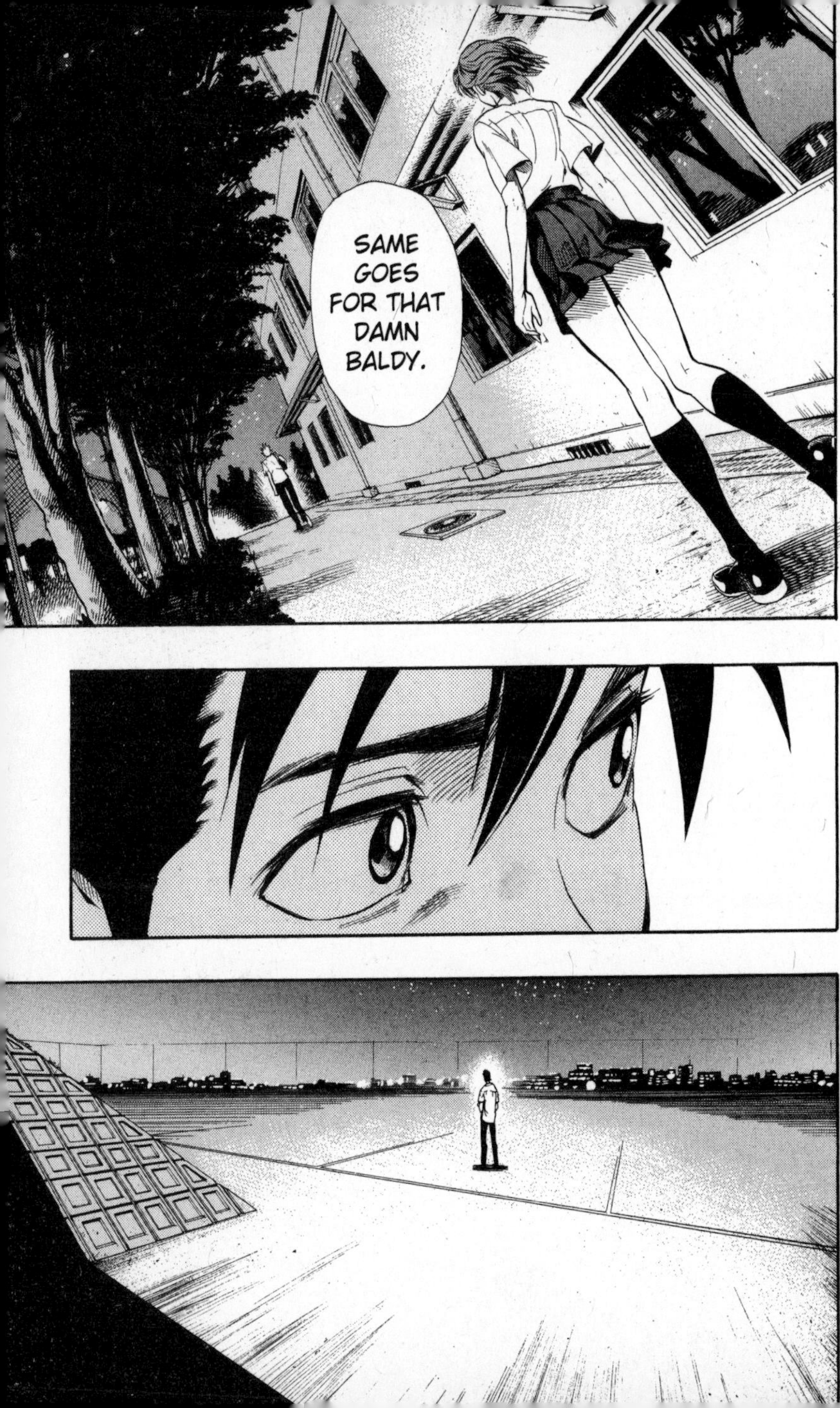
SAME GOES FOR THAT DAMN BALDY.

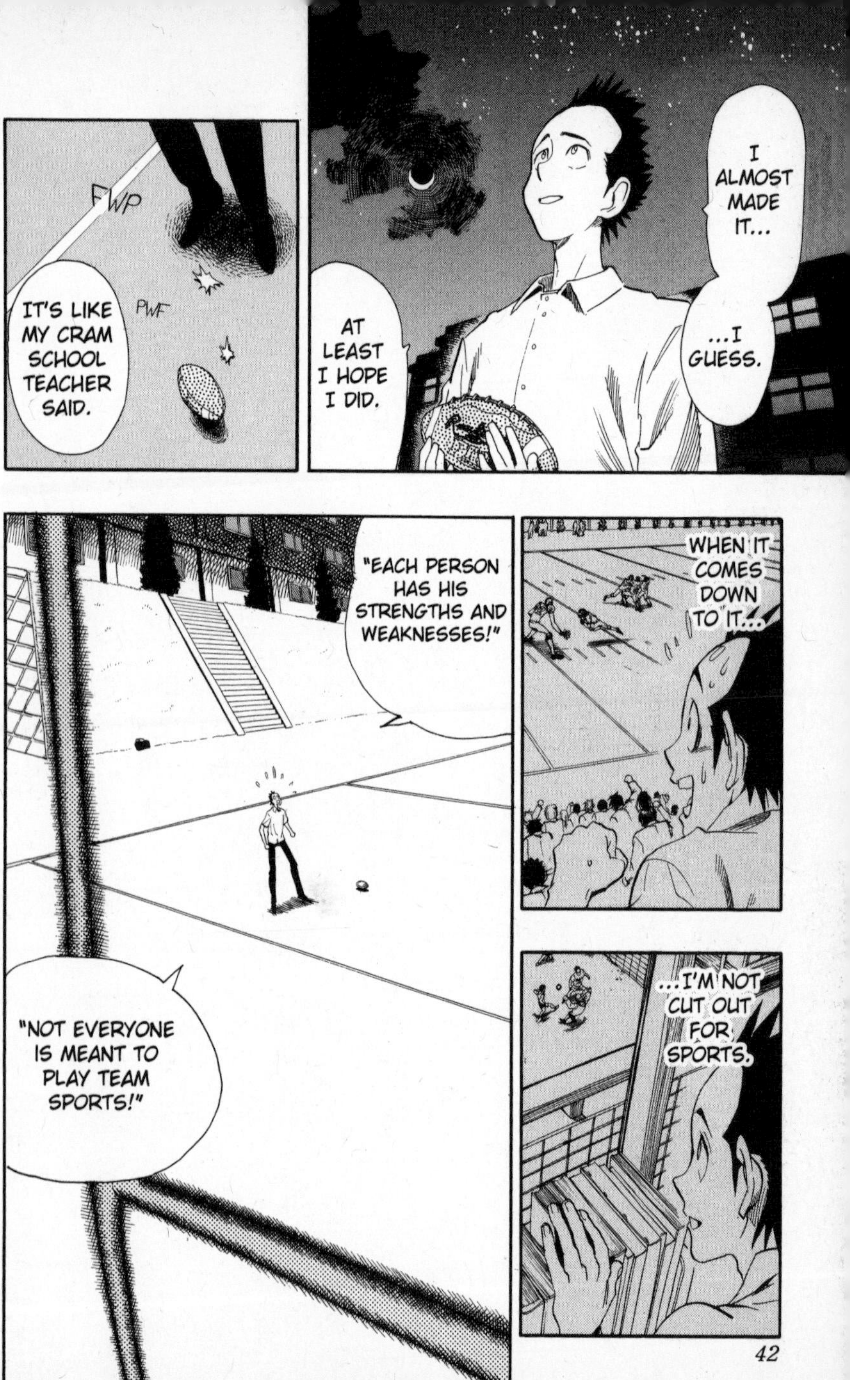
I ALMOST MADE IT...
...I GUESS.
AT LEAST I HOPE I DID.
FWP
PWF
IT'S LIKE MY CRAM SCHOOL TEACHER SAID.
WHEN IT COMES DOWN TO IT...
...I'M NOT CUT OUT FOR SPORTS.
"EACH PERSON HAS HIS STRENGTHS AND WEAKNESSES!"
"NOT EVERYONE IS MEANT TO PLAY TEAM SPORTS!"

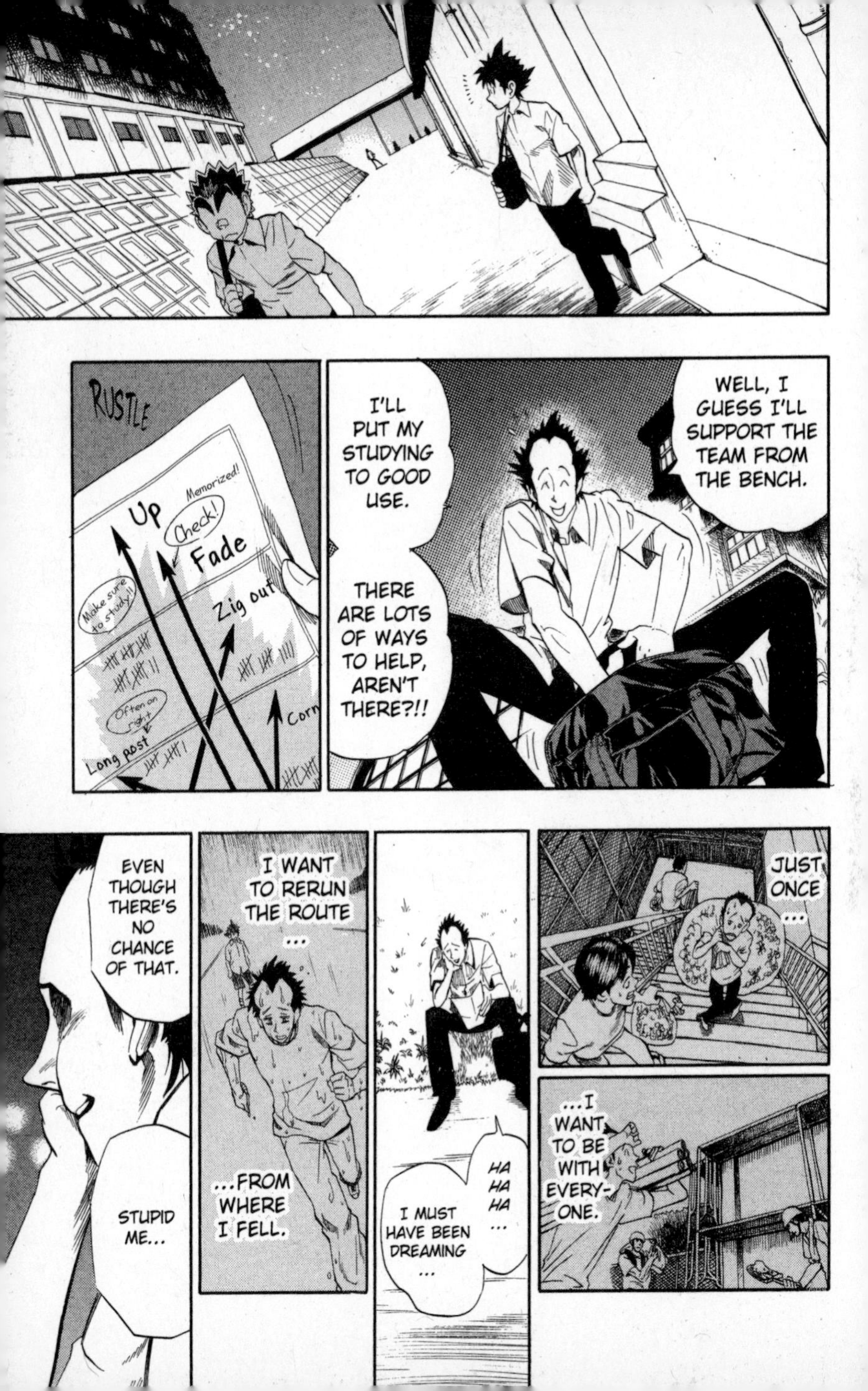
WELL, I GUESS I'LL SUPPORT THE TEAM FROM THE BENCH.
I'LL PUT MY STUDYING TO GOOD USE.
THERE ARE LOTS OF WAYS TO HELP, AREN'T THERE?!!
RUSTLE
Memorized!
Up
Check!
Fade
Make sure to study!!
Zig out
Often on right
Long post
JUST ONCE...
...I WANT TO BE WITH EVERY-ONE.
HA HA HA...
I MUST HAVE BEEN DREAMING...
I WANT TO RERUN THE ROUTE...
...FROM WHERE I FELL.
EVEN THOUGH THERE'S NO CHANCE OF THAT.
STUPID ME...

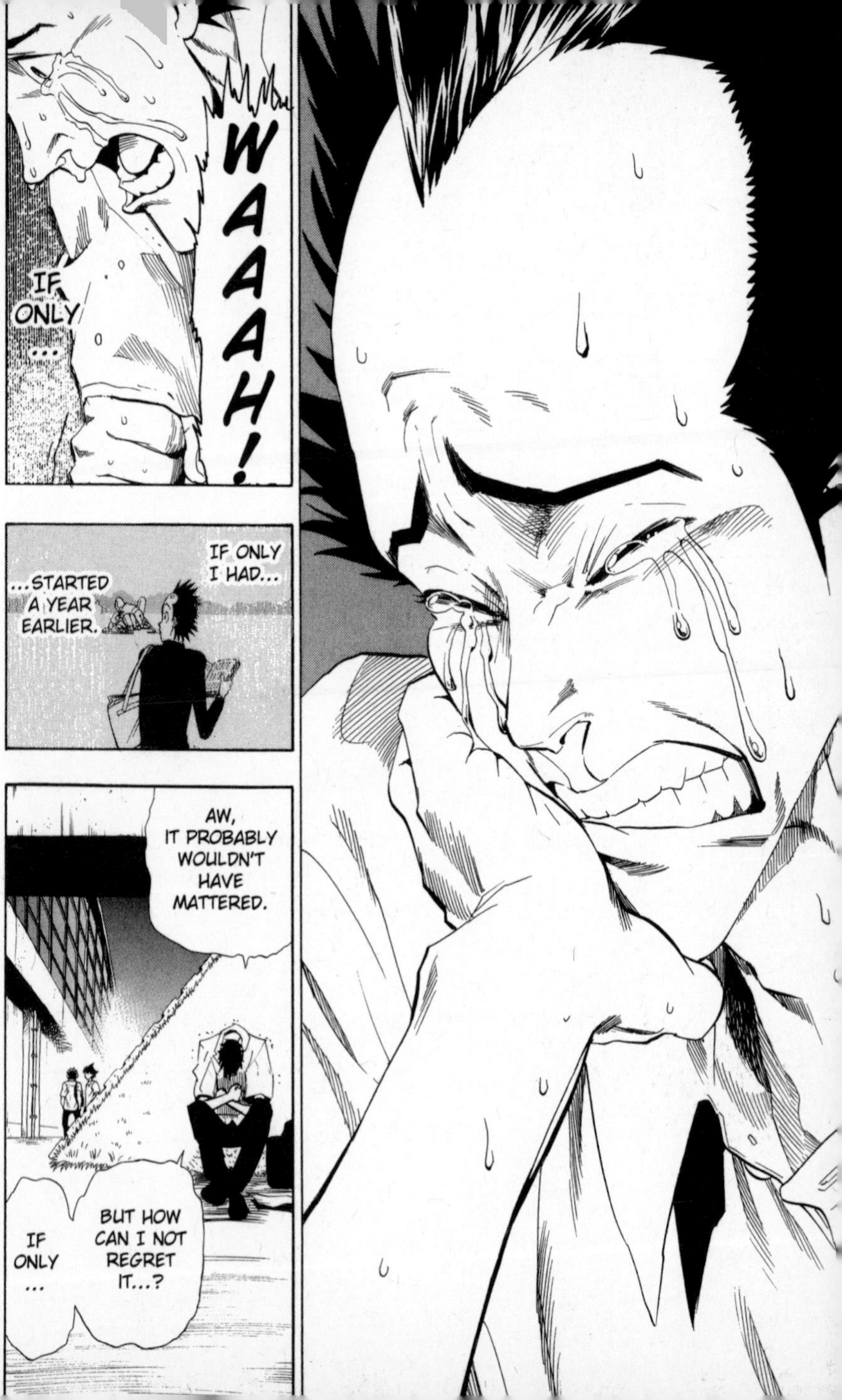
WAAAAH!
IF ONLY ...
IF ONLY I HAD...
...STARTED A YEAR EARLIER.
AW, IT PROBABLY WOULDN'T HAVE MATTERED.
BUT HOW CAN I NOT REGRET IT...?
IF ONLY ...

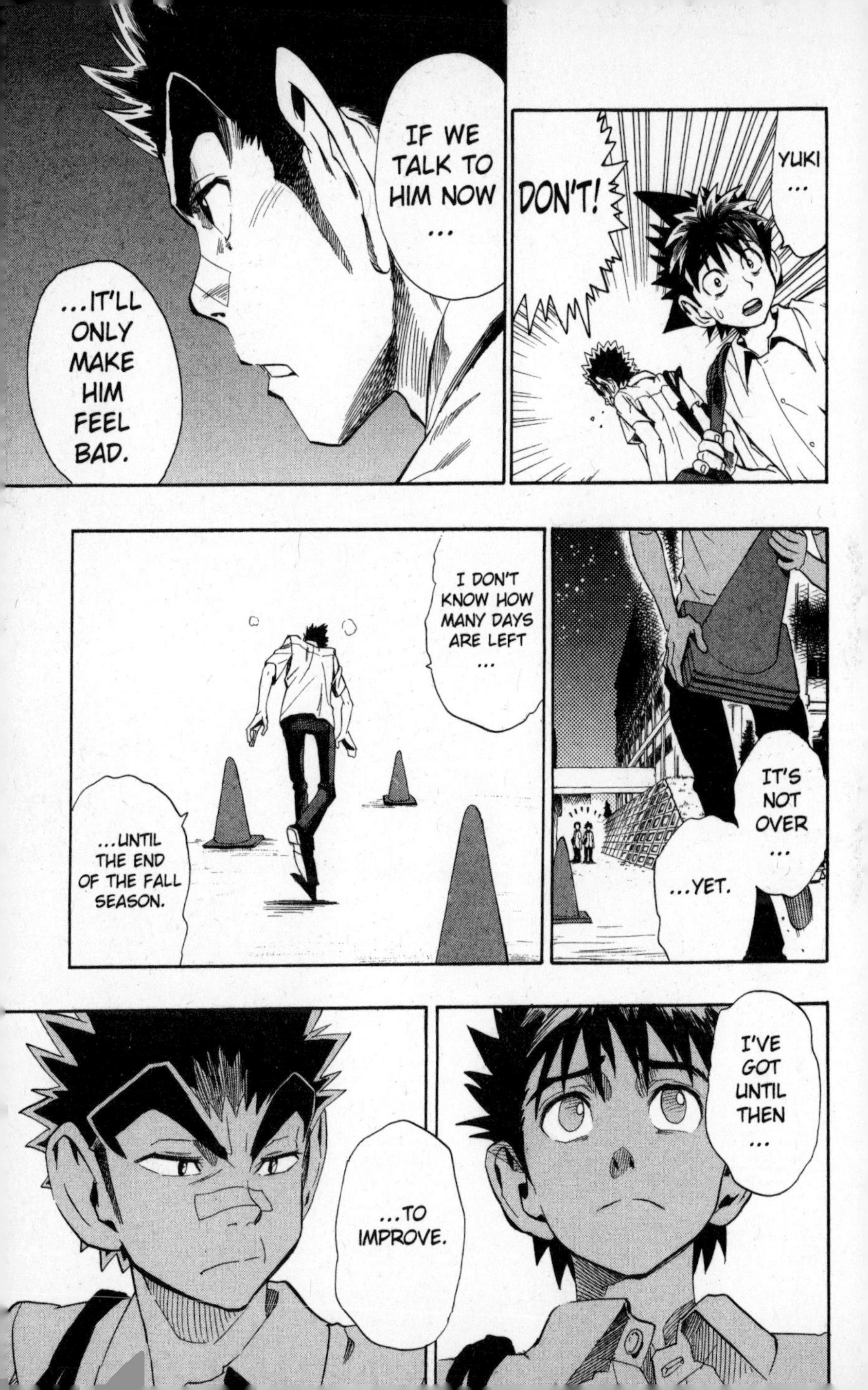
YUKI ...
DON'T!
IF WE TALK TO HIM NOW ...
...IT'LL ONLY MAKE HIM FEEL BAD.
IT'S NOT OVER ...
...YET.
I DON'T KNOW HOW MANY DAYS ARE LEFT ...
...UNTIL THE END OF THE FALL SEASON.
I'VE GOT UNTIL THEN ...
...TO IMPROVE.

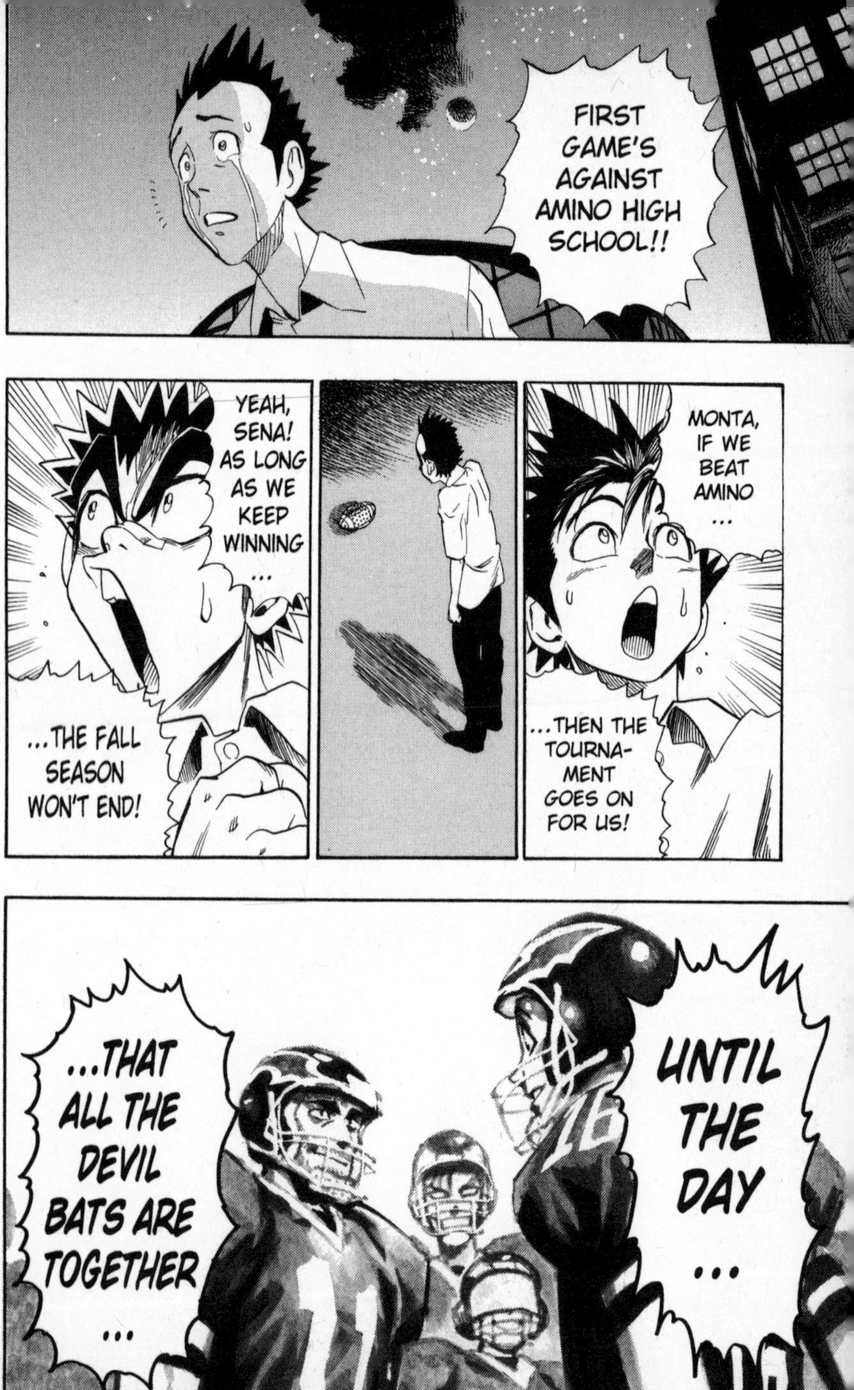
FIRST GAME'S AGAINST AMINO HIGH SCHOOL!!
MONTA, IF WE BEAT AMINO...
...THEN THE TOURNA-MENT GOES ON FOR US!
YEAH, SENA! AS LONG AS WE KEEP WINNING...
...THE FALL SEASON WON'T END!
UNTIL THE DAY...
...THAT ALL THE DEVIL BATS ARE TOGETHER...

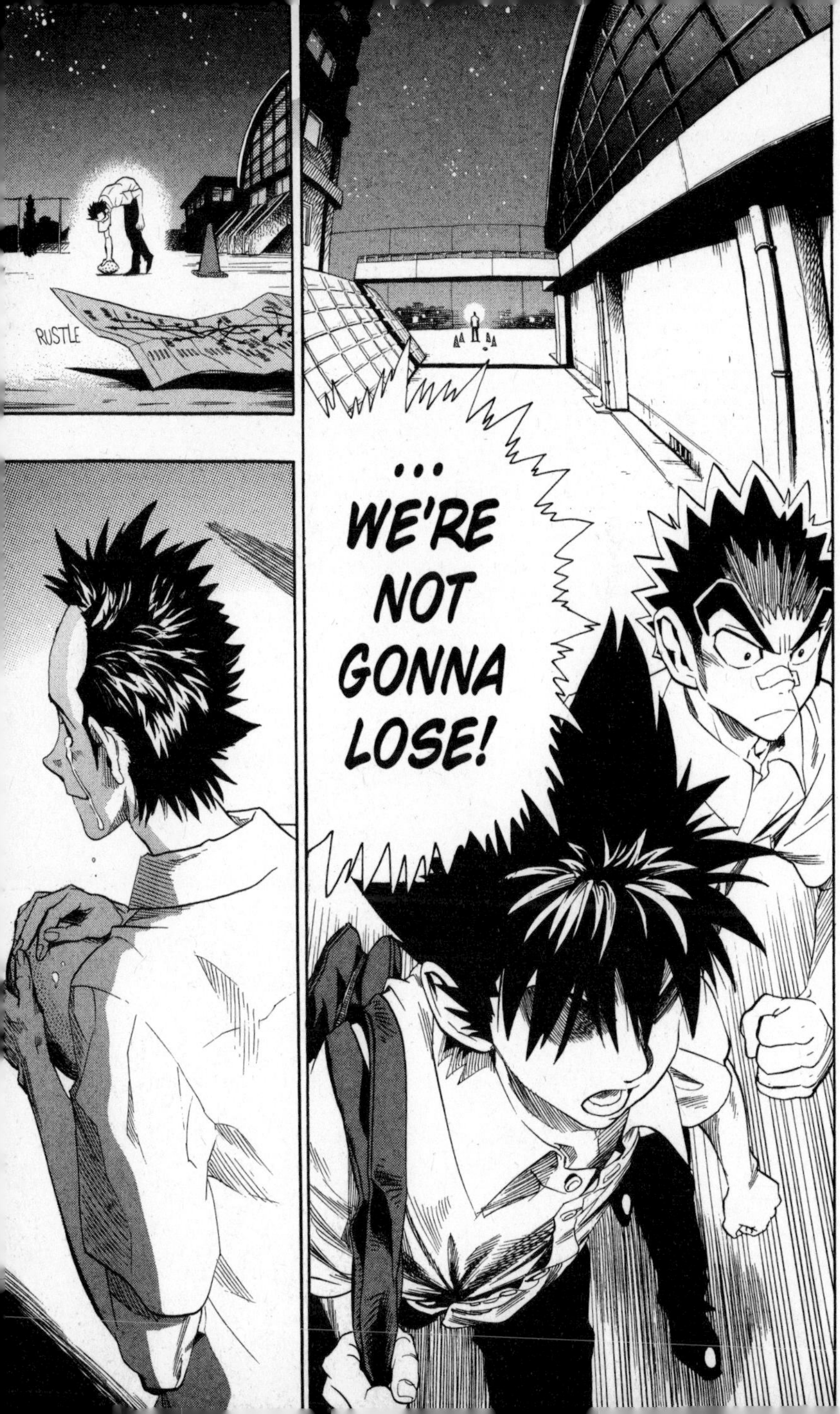
...WE'RE NOT GONNA LOSE!
RUSTLE

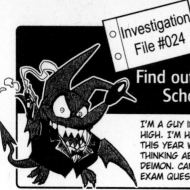

Investigation File #024

Find out what's on Deimon High School's entrance exam!!

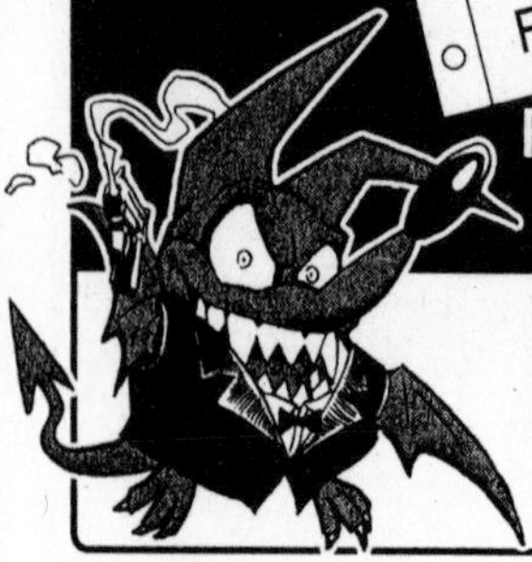

I'M A GUY IN MY THIRD YEAR OF JUNIOR HIGH. I'M HAVING A REALLY HARD TIME THIS YEAR WITH MY EXAMS, SO I WAS THINKING ABOUT APPLYING TO DEIMON. CAN YOU TELL ME WHAT THE EXAM QUESTIONS ARE LIKE?

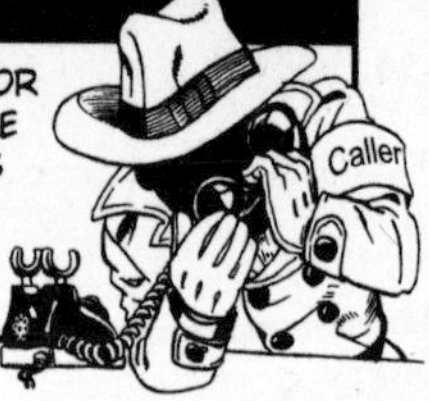
Caller

T.T., Shizuoka Prefecture

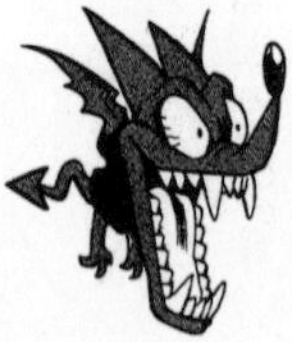

WE FOUND MATH QUESTIONS THAT THE PRINCIPAL MADE UP FOR THIS YEAR'S EXAM!

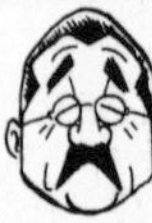

Deimon High School Math Exam Questions

QUESTION 1: $3 + 1 = ?$

QUESTION 2: IF $\zeta(S) = 0$ IS A FUNCTION OF $\zeta(S) = \sum_{n=1}^{\infty} \frac{1}{n^s}$ AND IS WITHIN THE RANGE $0 < Re(S) 0 < 1$ THEN PARTIALLY PROVE THAT $\zeta(S) = \sum_{n=1}^{\infty} \frac{1}{n^s}$ ALWAYS EQUALS $Re(S) = \frac{1}{2}$

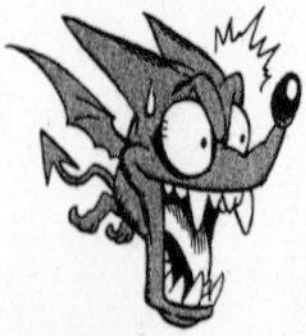

THE PRINCIPAL HAS REALLY HIGH EXPECTATIONS!

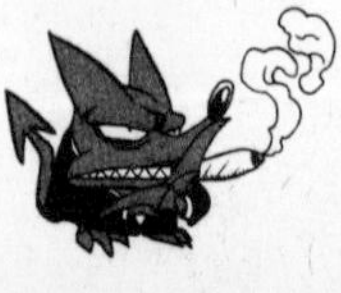

OH YEAH, RIGHT.
SINCE EVERYONE WHO TAKES THE TEST GETS IN, IT DOESN'T MATTER WHAT THE QUESTIONS ARE!

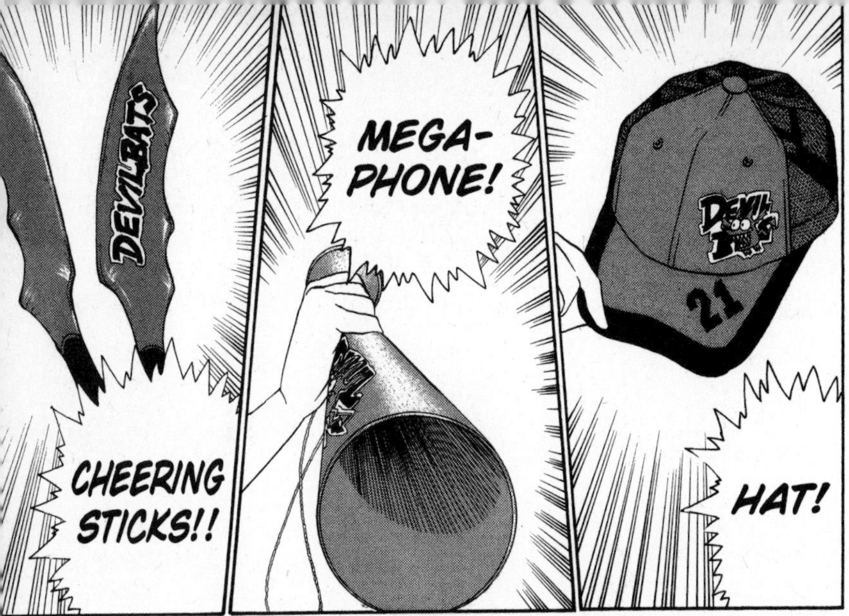
HAT!
MEGA-PHONE!
DEVILBATS
CHEERING STICKS!!

Chapter 91 Reach for the Stars

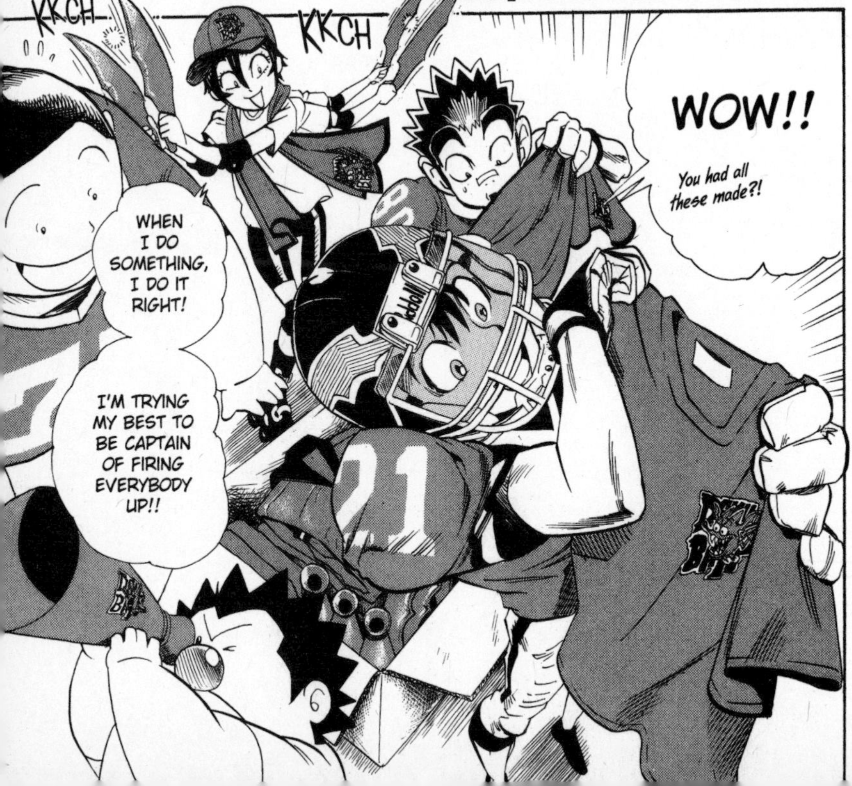
WOW!!
You had all these made?!
KKCH
KKCH
WHEN I DO SOMETHING, I DO IT RIGHT!
I'M TRYING MY BEST TO BE CAPTAIN OF FIRING EVERYBODY UP!!

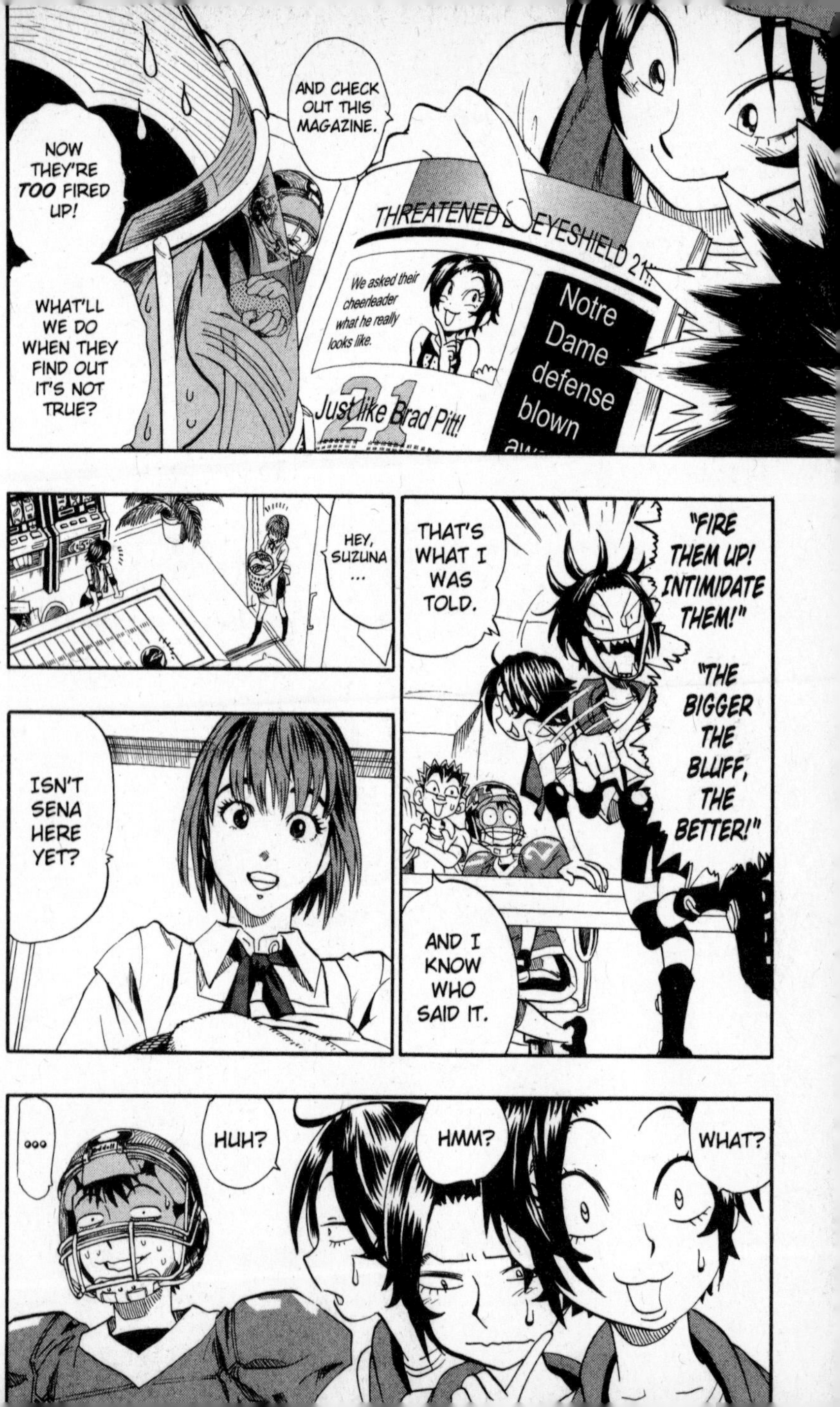
AND CHECK OUT THIS MAGAZINE.
THREATENED B EYESHIELD 21!!
Notre Dame defense blown
We asked their cheerleader what he really looks like.
21
Just like Brad Pitt!
NOW THEY'RE *TOO* FIRED UP!
WHAT'LL WE DO WHEN THEY FIND OUT IT'S NOT TRUE?
"FIRE THEM UP! INTIMIDATE THEM!"
"THE BIGGER THE BLUFF, THE BETTER!"
THAT'S WHAT I WAS TOLD.
AND I KNOW WHO SAID IT.
HEY, SUZUNA ...
ISN'T SENA HERE YET?
WHAT?
HMM?
HUH?
...

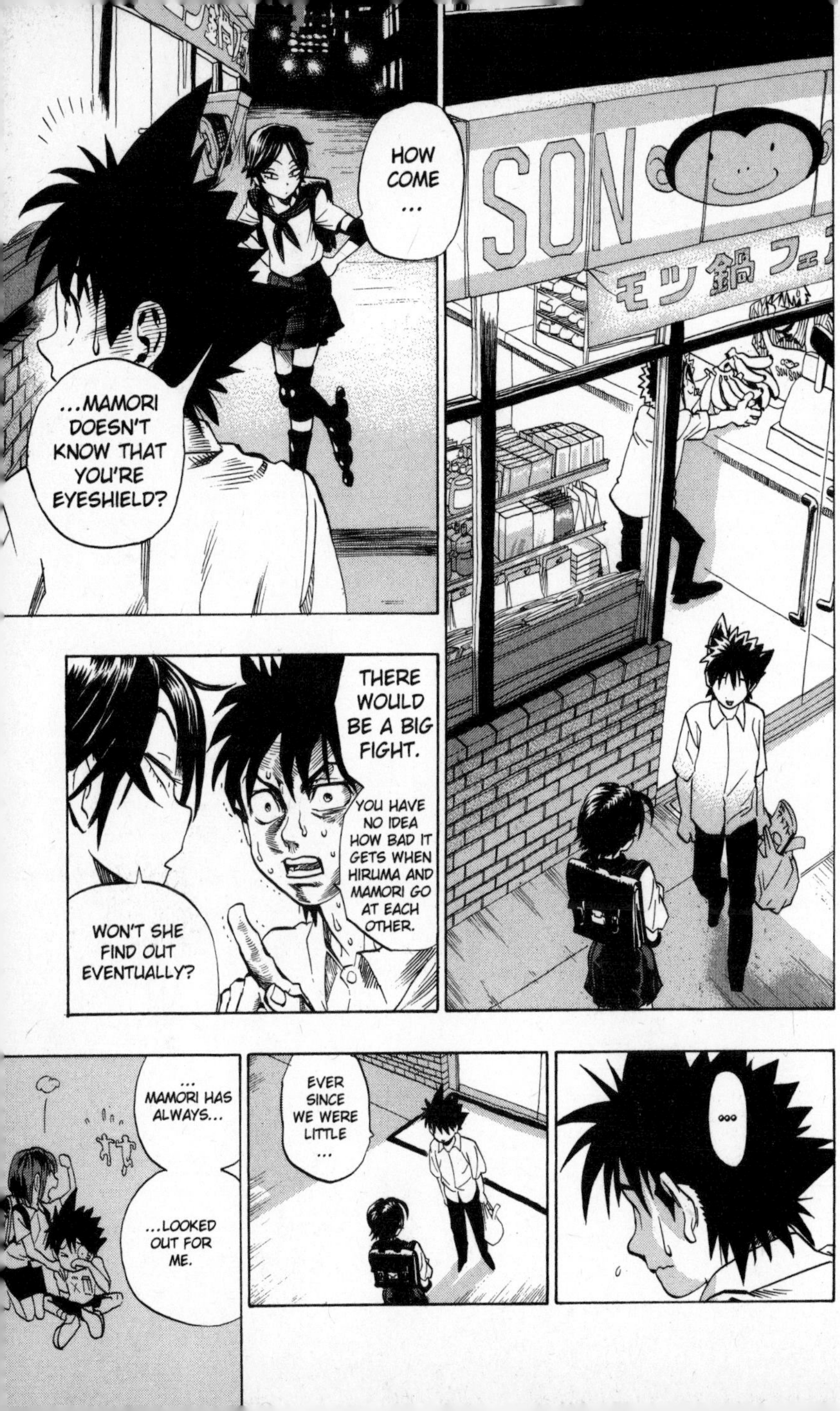
SON
モツ鍋フェ
HOW COME ...
...MAMORI DOESN'T KNOW THAT YOU'RE EYESHIELD?
THERE WOULD BE A BIG FIGHT.
YOU HAVE NO IDEA HOW BAD IT GETS WHEN HIRUMA AND MAMORI GO AT EACH OTHER.
WON'T SHE FIND OUT EVENTUALLY?
...
EVER SINCE WE WERE LITTLE ...
... MAMORI HAS ALWAYS...
...LOOKED OUT FOR ME.

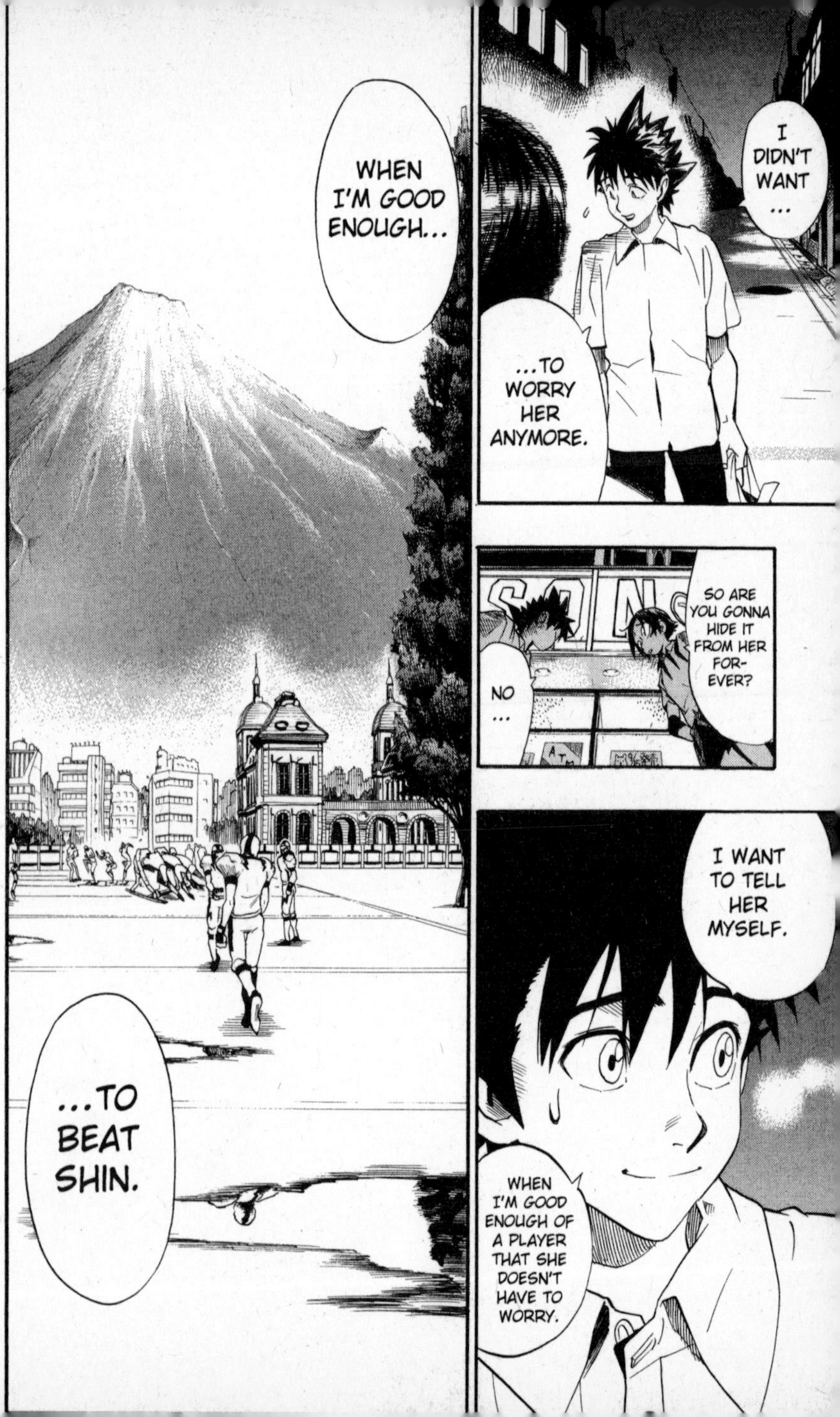
I DIDN'T WANT ...
...TO WORRY HER ANYMORE.
SO ARE YOU GONNA HIDE IT FROM HER FOR-EVER?
NO ...
I WANT TO TELL HER MYSELF.
WHEN I'M GOOD ENOUGH OF A PLAYER THAT SHE DOESN'T HAVE TO WORRY.
WHEN I'M GOOD ENOUGH...
...TO BEAT SHIN.

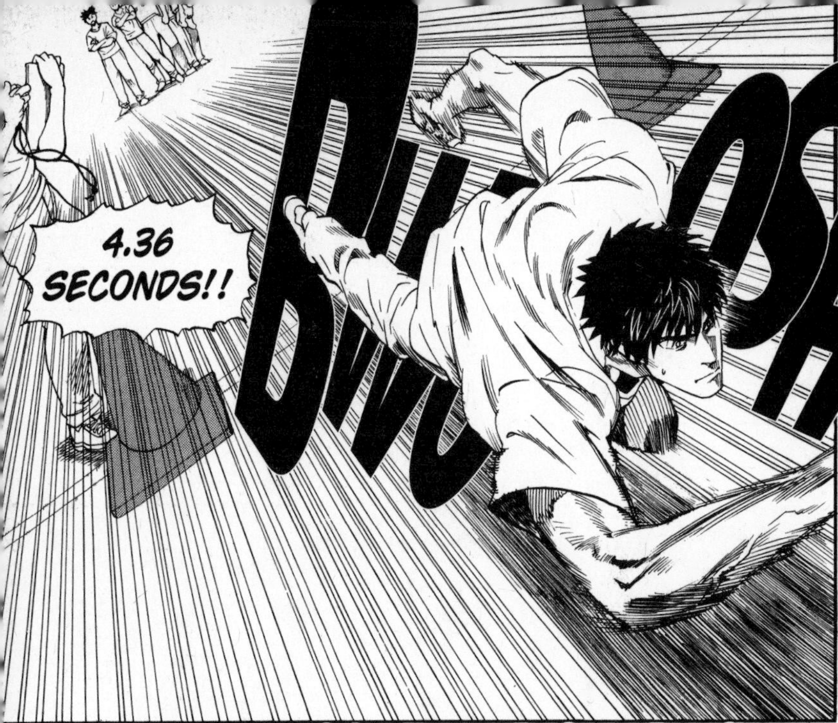
4.36 SECONDS!!

Chapter 91 Reach for the Stars

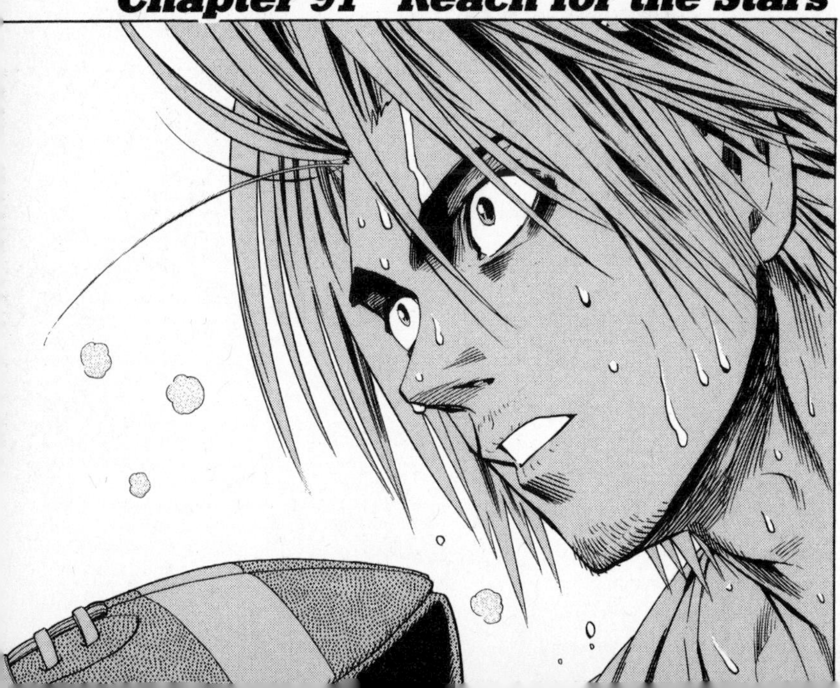

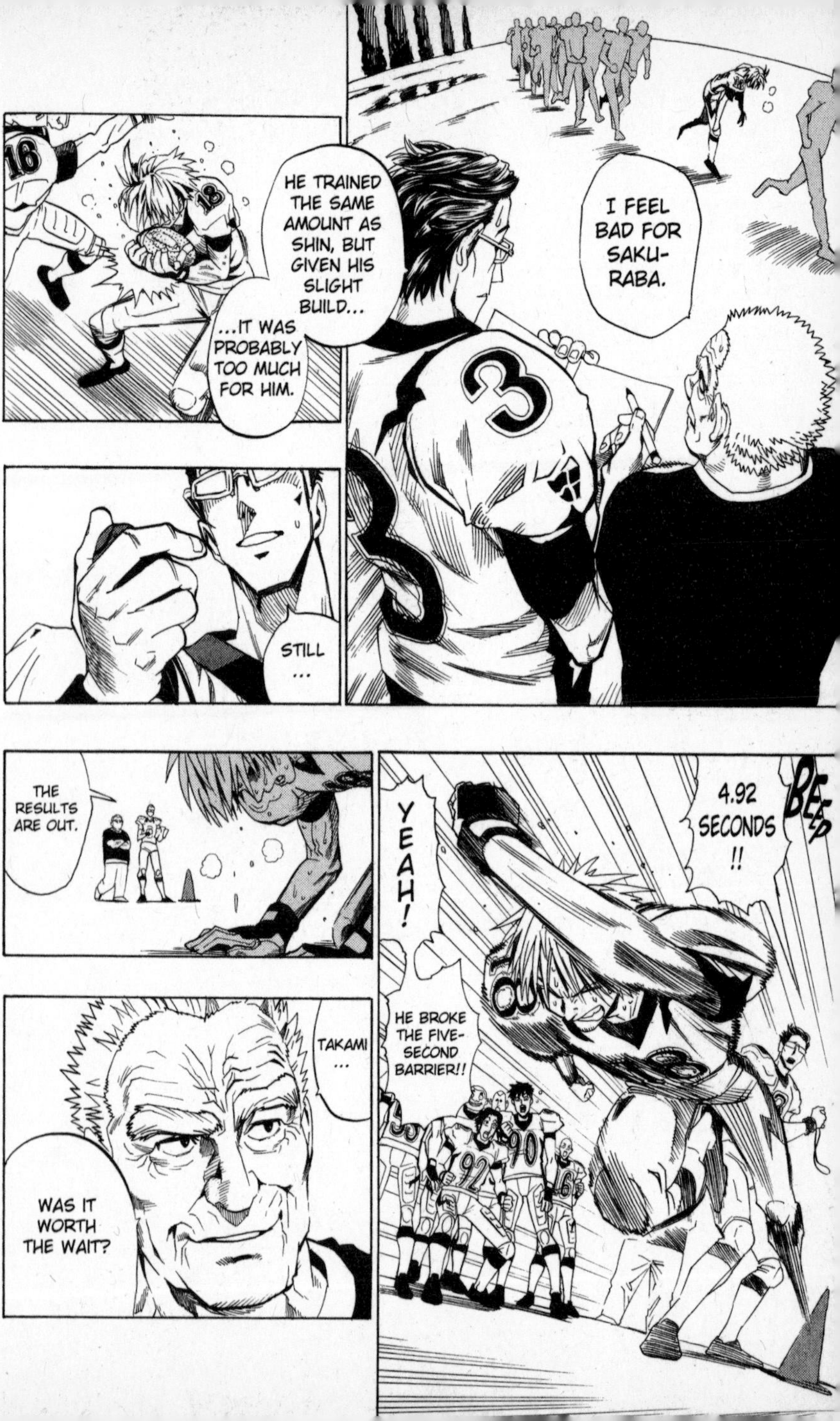
I FEEL BAD FOR SAKU-RABA.
HE TRAINED THE SAME AMOUNT AS SHIN, BUT GIVEN HIS SLIGHT BUILD...
...IT WAS PROBABLY TOO MUCH FOR HIM.
STILL ...
BEEP
4.92 SECONDS !!
YEAH!
HE BROKE THE FIVE-SECOND BARRIER!!
THE RESULTS ARE OUT.
TAKAMI ...
WAS IT WORTH THE WAIT?

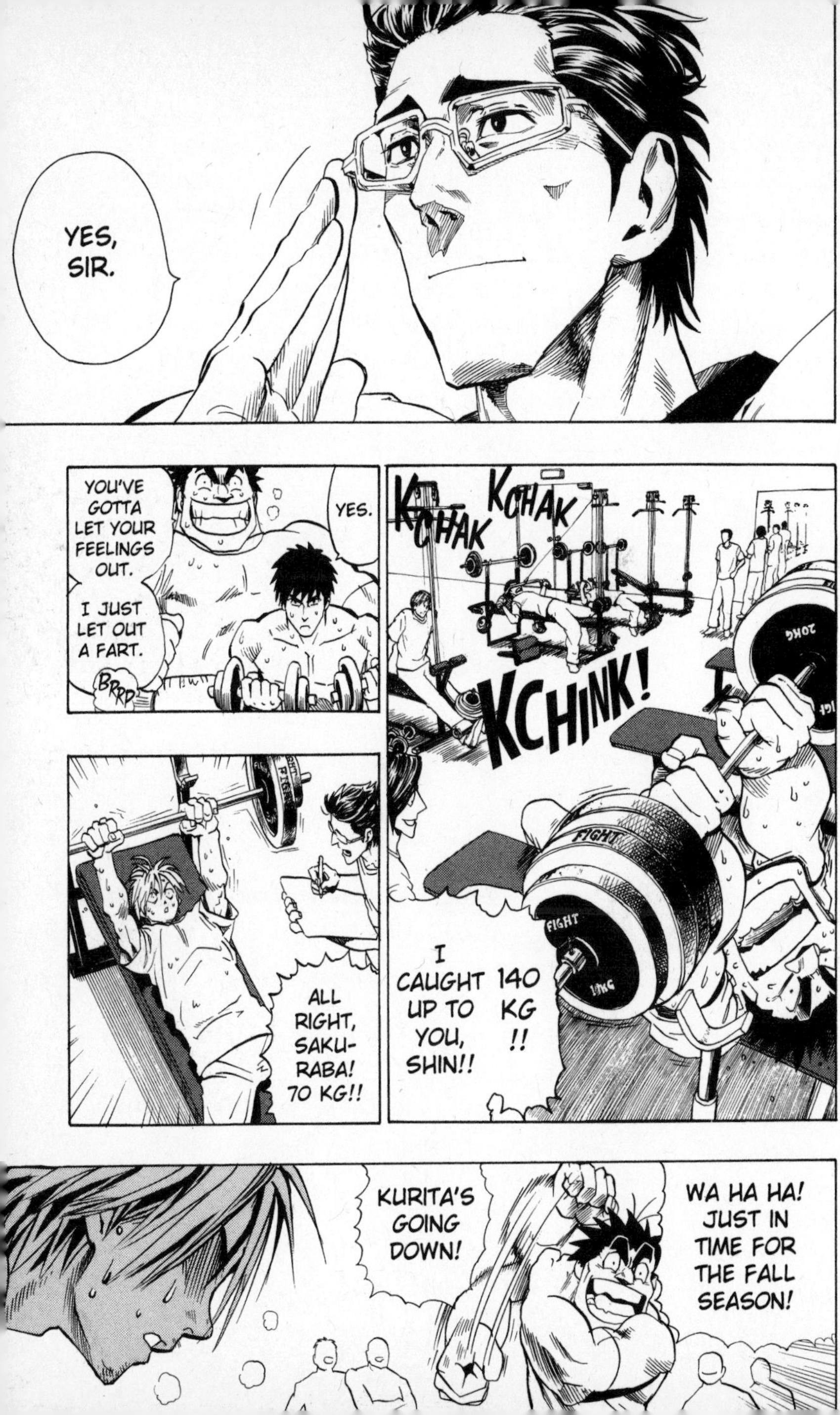
YES, SIR.
KCHAK
KCHAK
KCHINK!
140 KG!!
I CAUGHT UP TO YOU, SHIN!!
YES.
YOU'VE GOTTA LET YOUR FEELINGS OUT.
I JUST LET OUT A FART.
BRRD
ALL RIGHT, SAKU-RABA! 70 KG!!
WA HA HA! JUST IN TIME FOR THE FALL SEASON!
KURITA'S GOING DOWN!

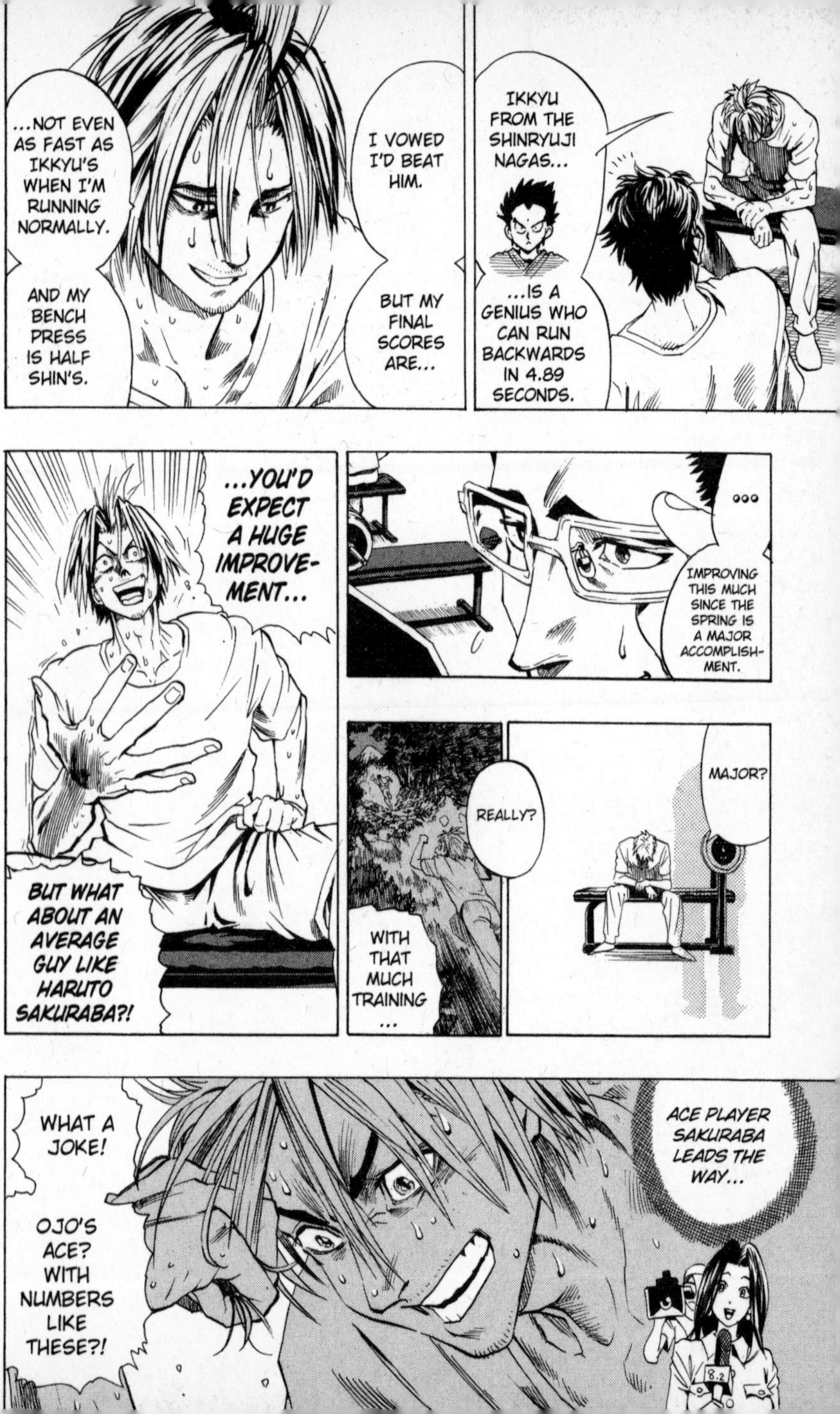
IKKYU FROM THE SHINRYUJI NAGAS...
...IS A GENIUS WHO CAN RUN BACKWARDS IN 4.89 SECONDS.
I VOWED I'D BEAT HIM.
BUT MY FINAL SCORES ARE...
...NOT EVEN AS FAST AS IKKYU'S WHEN I'M RUNNING NORMALLY.
AND MY BENCH PRESS IS HALF SHIN'S.
...
IMPROVING THIS MUCH SINCE THE SPRING IS A MAJOR ACCOMPLISHMENT.
MAJOR?
REALLY?
WITH THAT MUCH TRAINING...
...YOU'D EXPECT A HUGE IMPROVEMENT...
BUT WHAT ABOUT AN AVERAGE GUY LIKE HARUTO SAKURABA?!
ACE PLAYER SAKURABA LEADS THE WAY...
WHAT A JOKE!
OJO'S ACE? WITH NUMBERS LIKE THESE?!

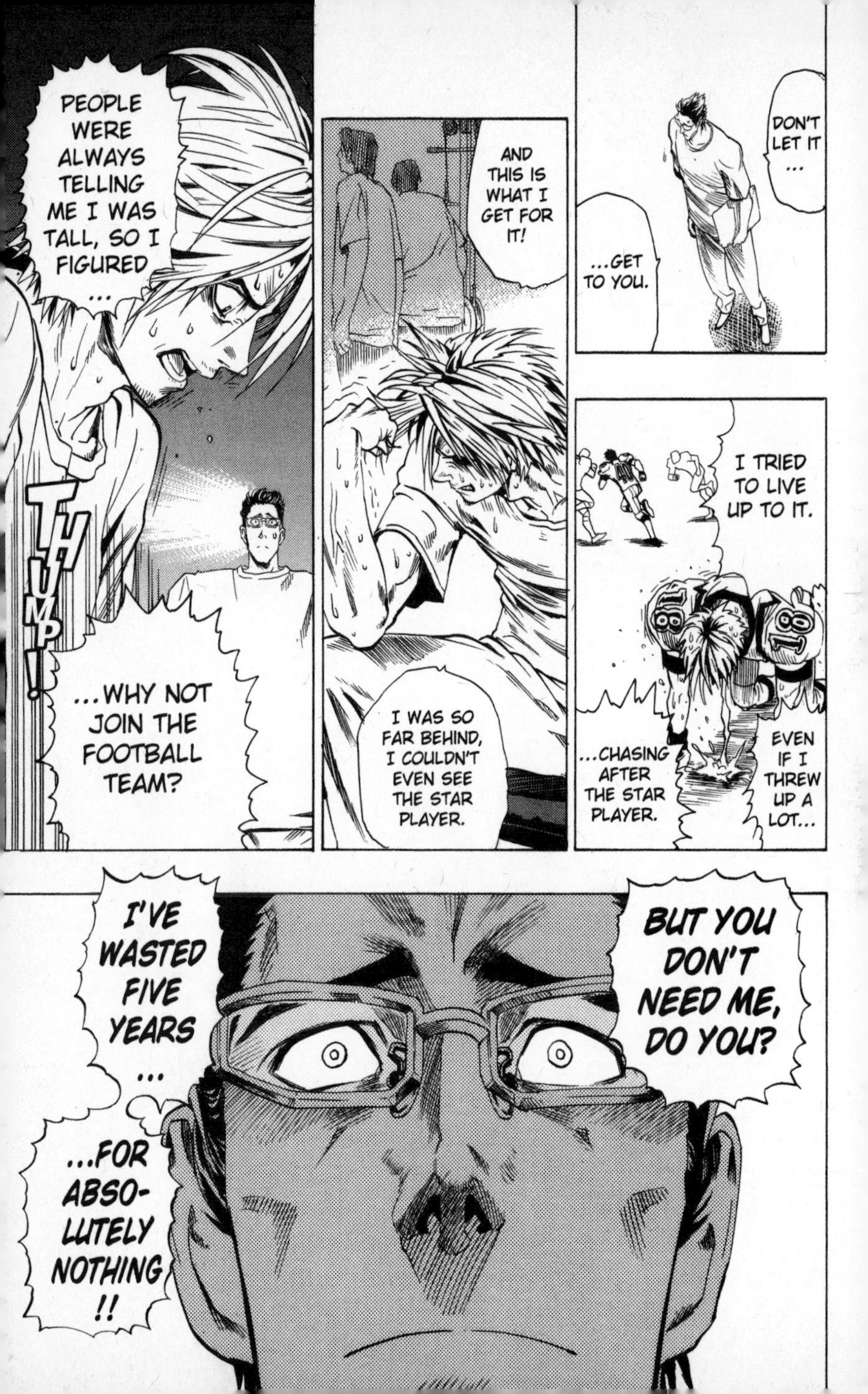
DON'T LET IT ...
...GET TO YOU.
I TRIED TO LIVE UP TO IT.
EVEN IF I THREW UP A LOT...
...CHASING AFTER THE STAR PLAYER.
AND THIS IS WHAT I GET FOR IT!
I WAS SO FAR BEHIND, I COULDN'T EVEN SEE THE STAR PLAYER.
PEOPLE WERE ALWAYS TELLING ME I WAS TALL, SO I FIGURED ...
THUMP!
...WHY NOT JOIN THE FOOTBALL TEAM?
BUT YOU DON'T NEED ME, DO YOU?
I'VE WASTED FIVE YEARS ...
...FOR ABSO-LUTELY NOTHING !!

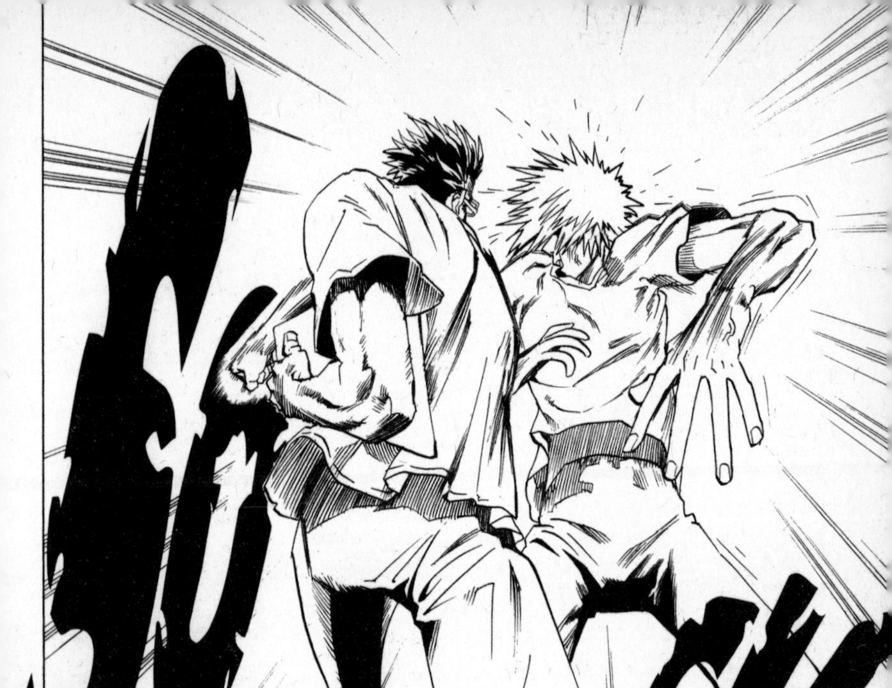
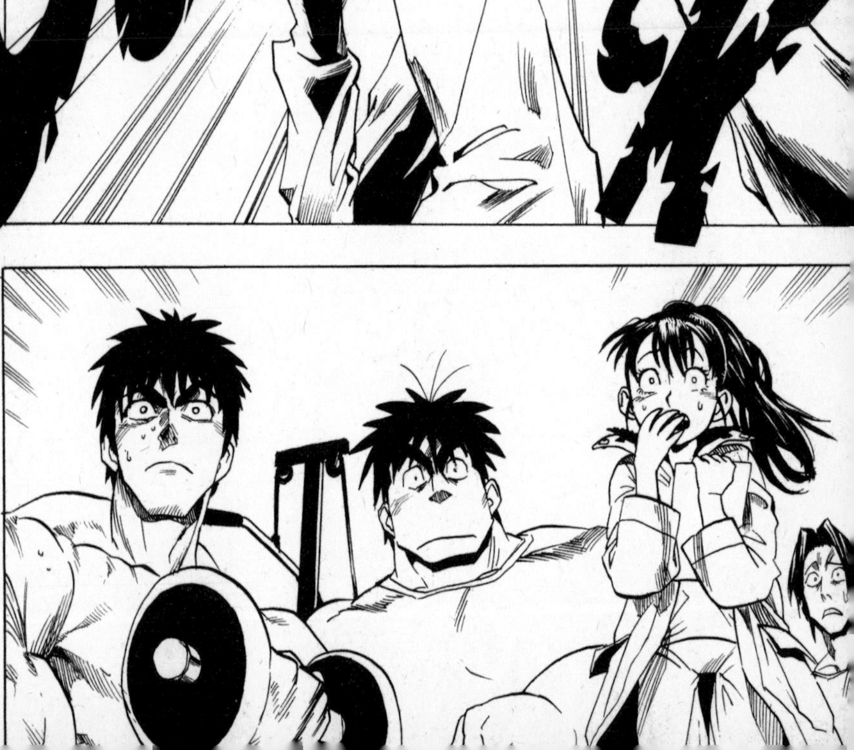

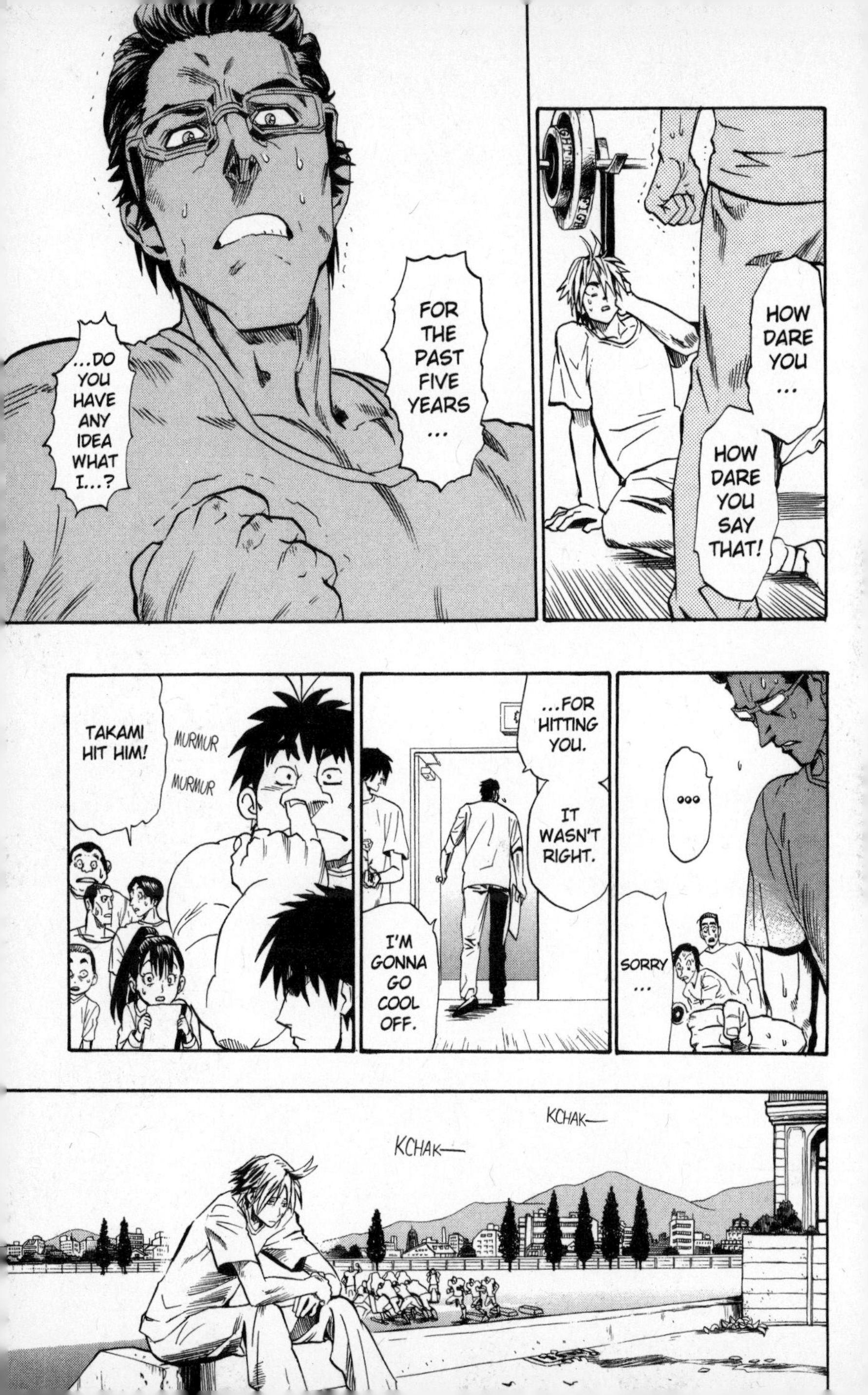
HOW DARE YOU...
HOW DARE YOU SAY THAT!
FOR THE PAST FIVE YEARS...
...DO YOU HAVE ANY IDEA WHAT I...?
...
SORRY...
...FOR HITTING YOU.
IT WASN'T RIGHT.
I'M GONNA GO COOL OFF.
MURMUR
MURMUR
TAKAMI HIT HIM!
KCHAK—
KCHAK—

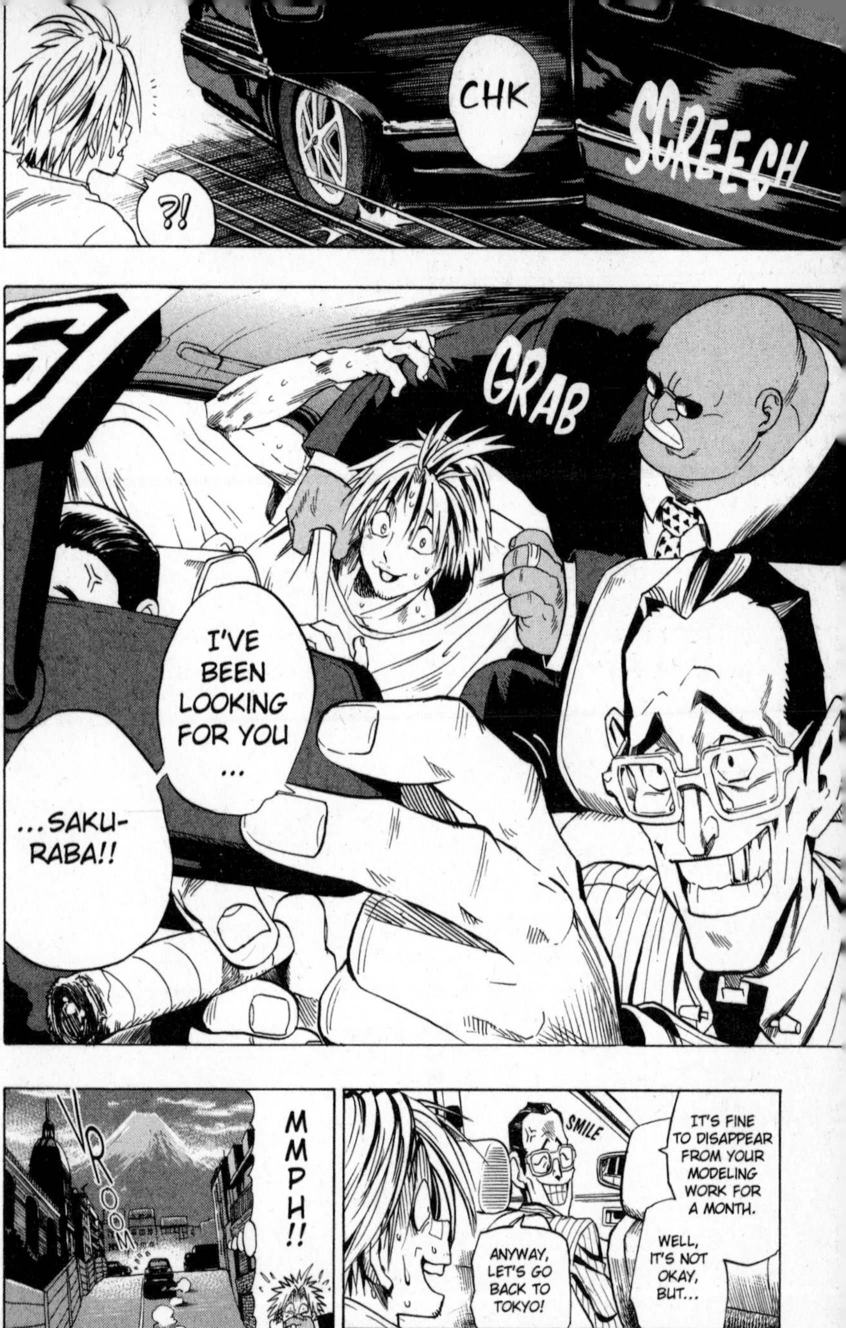
SCREECH
CHK
?!
GRAB
I'VE BEEN LOOKING FOR YOU ...
...SAKU-RABA!!
IT'S FINE TO DISAPPEAR FROM YOUR MODELING WORK FOR A MONTH.
SMILE
WELL, IT'S NOT OKAY, BUT...
ANYWAY, LET'S GO BACK TO TOKYO!
MMPH!!
VROOM

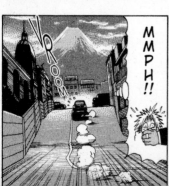

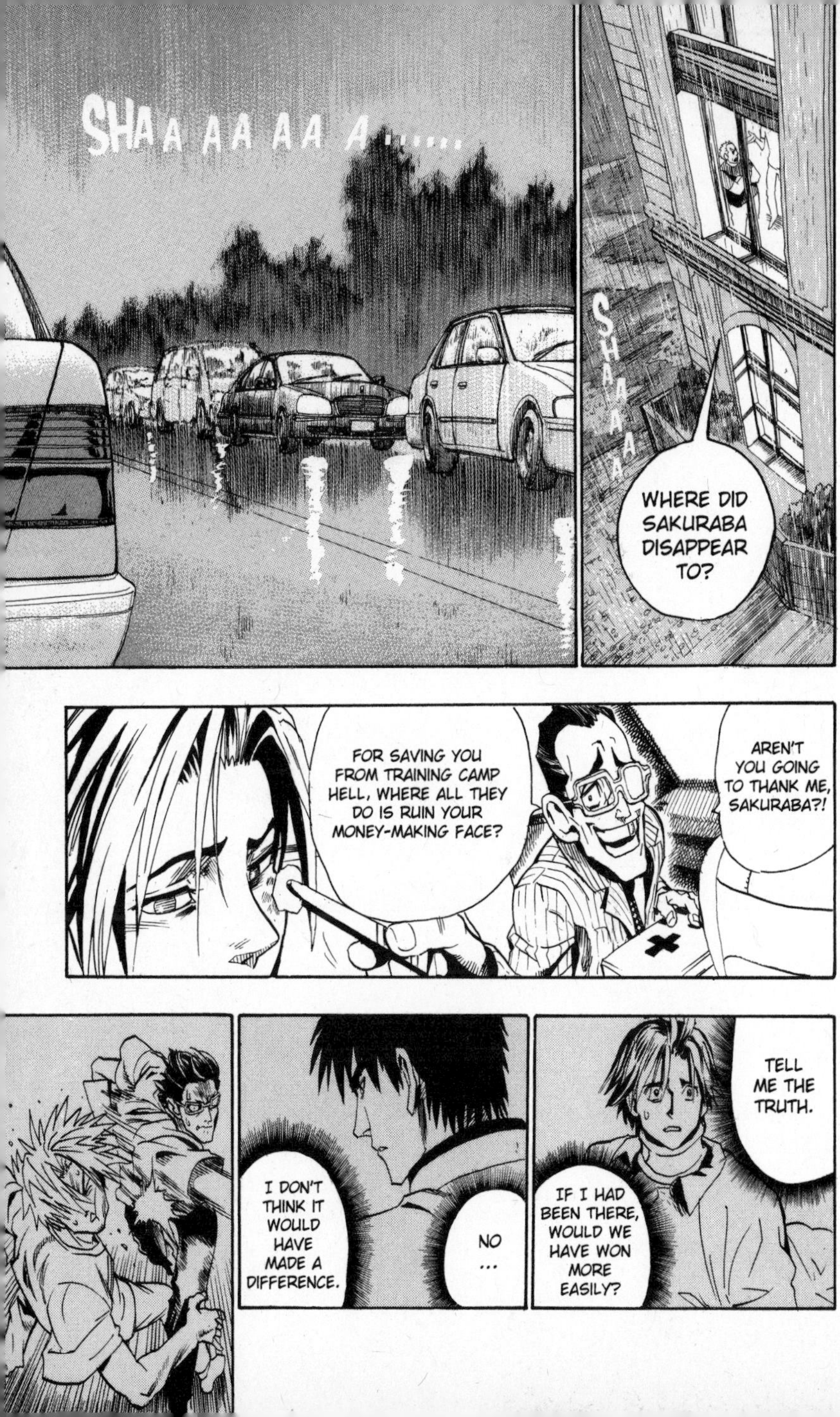
SHAAAA
WHERE DID SAKURABA DISAPPEAR TO?
SHAAAAAA......
AREN'T YOU GOING TO THANK ME, SAKURABA?!
FOR SAVING YOU FROM TRAINING CAMP HELL, WHERE ALL THEY DO IS RUIN YOUR MONEY-MAKING FACE?
TELL ME THE TRUTH.
IF I HAD BEEN THERE, WOULD WE HAVE WON MORE EASILY?
NO ...
I DON'T THINK IT WOULD HAVE MADE A DIFFERENCE.

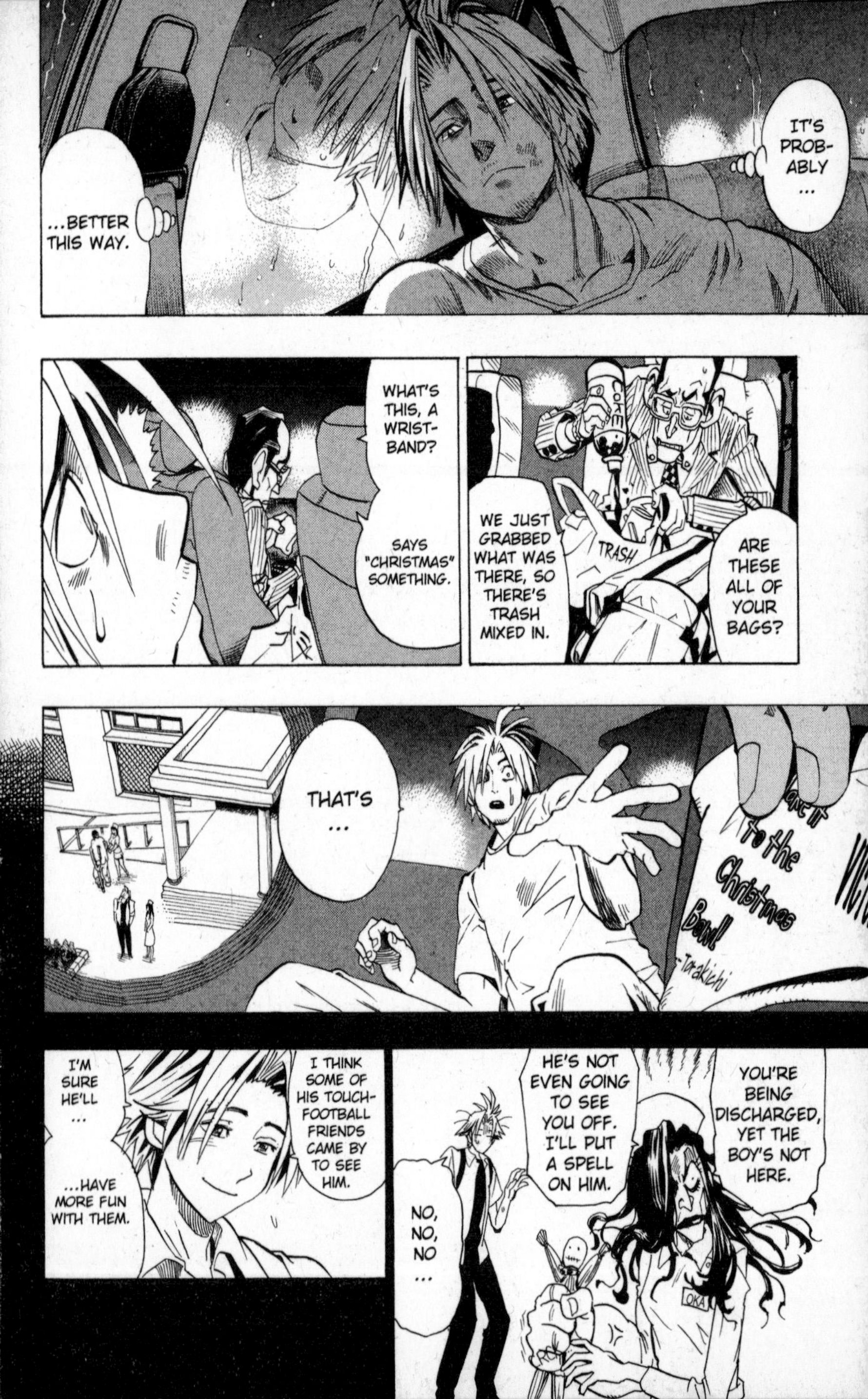
IT'S PROBABLY ...
...BETTER THIS WAY.
ARE THESE ALL OF YOUR BAGS?
COKE
TRASH
WE JUST GRABBED WHAT WAS THERE, SO THERE'S TRASH MIXED IN.
WHAT'S THIS, A WRIST-BAND?
SAYS "CHRISTMAS" SOMETHING.
to the Christmas Bowl!
-Torakichi
THAT'S ...
YOU'RE BEING DISCHARGED, YET THE BOY'S NOT HERE.
HE'S NOT EVEN GOING TO SEE YOU OFF. I'LL PUT A SPELL ON HIM.
OKA
NO, NO, NO ...
I THINK SOME OF HIS TOUCH-FOOTBALL FRIENDS CAME BY TO SEE HIM.
I'M SURE HE'LL ...
...HAVE MORE FUN WITH THEM.

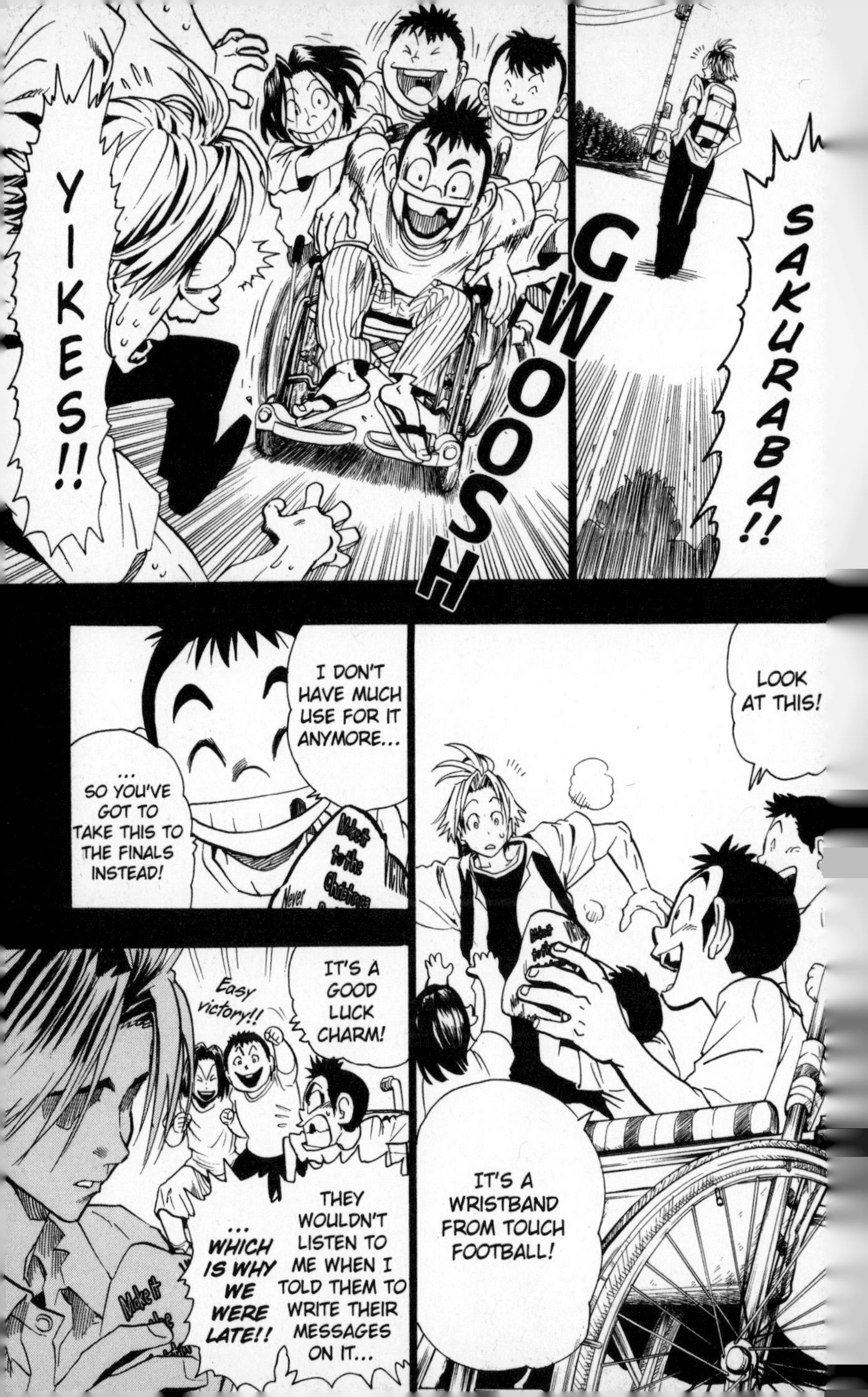
SAKURABA!!
GWOOSH
YIKES!!
LOOK AT THIS!
IT'S A WRISTBAND FROM TOUCH FOOTBALL!
I DON'T HAVE MUCH USE FOR IT ANYMORE...
... SO YOU'VE GOT TO TAKE THIS TO THE FINALS INSTEAD!
IT'S A GOOD LUCK CHARM!
Easy victory!!
THEY WOULDN'T LISTEN TO ME WHEN I TOLD THEM TO WRITE THEIR MESSAGES ON IT...
... WHICH IS WHY WE WERE LATE!!

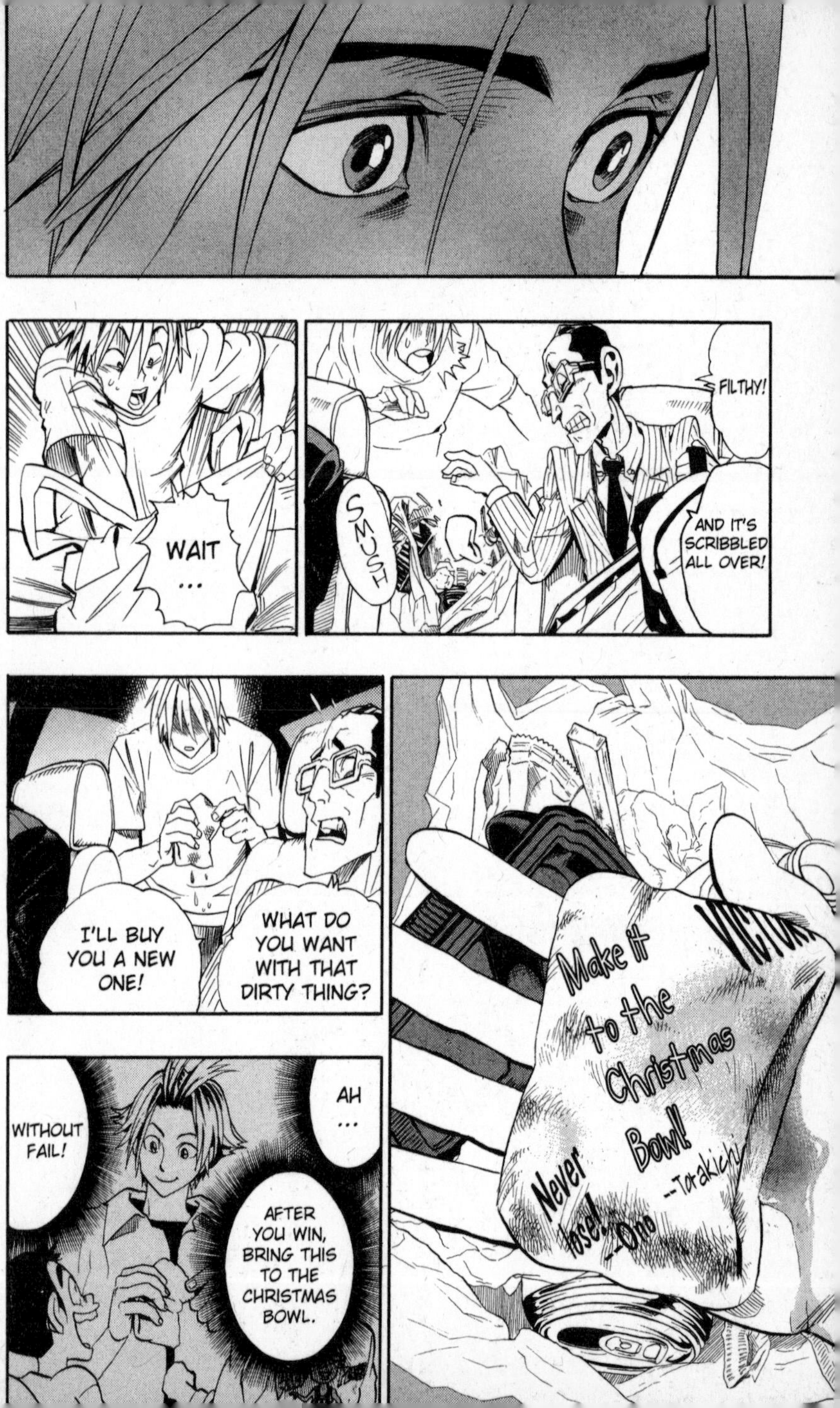
FILTHY!
AND IT'S SCRIBBLED ALL OVER!
SMUSH
WAIT ...
Make it to the Christmas Bowl!
Never lose!
--Torakichi
--Ono
WHAT DO YOU WANT WITH THAT DIRTY THING?
I'LL BUY YOU A NEW ONE!
AH ...
AFTER YOU WIN, BRING THIS TO THE CHRISTMAS BOWL.
WITHOUT FAIL!

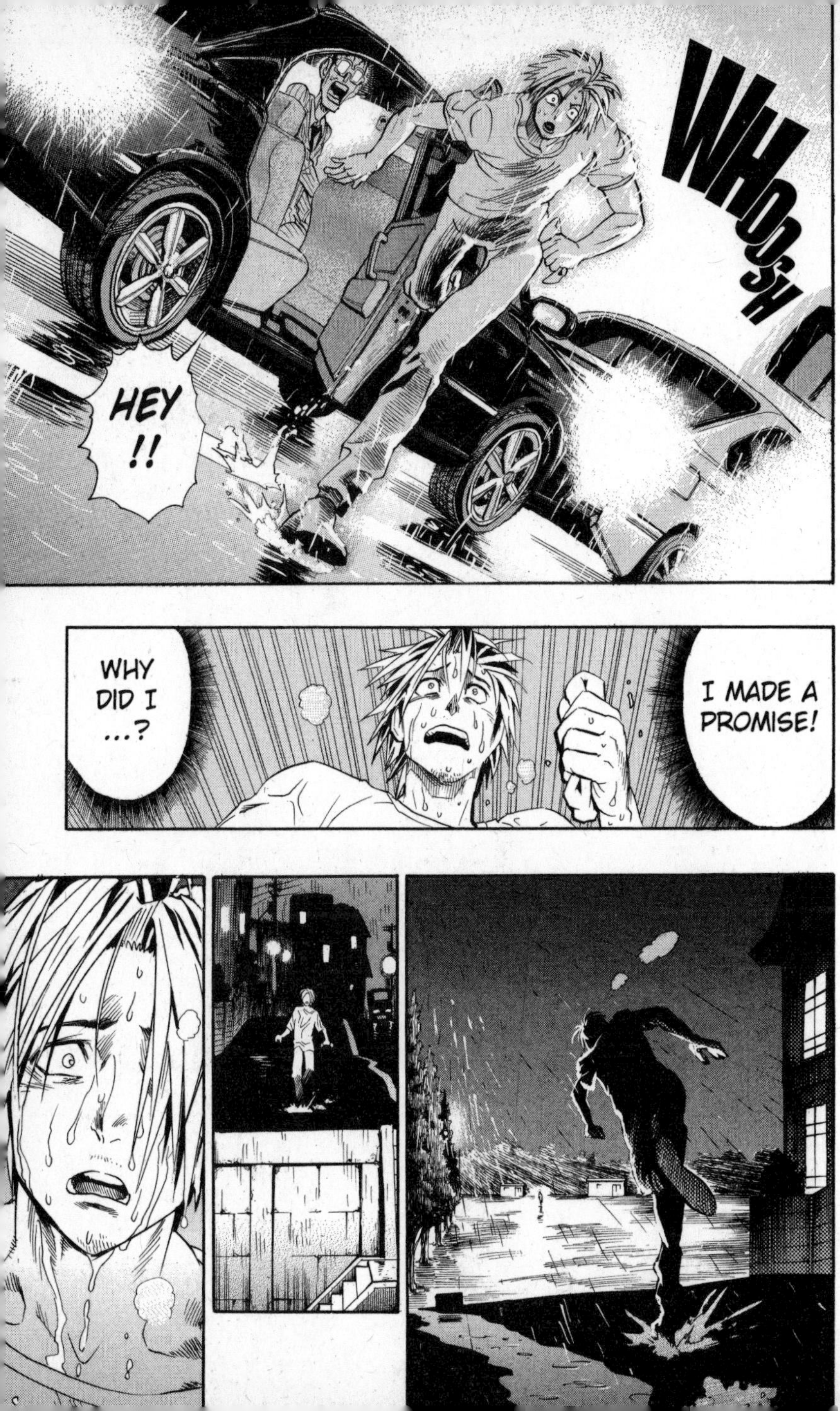
WHOOSH
HEY !!
I MADE A PROMISE!
WHY DID I ...?

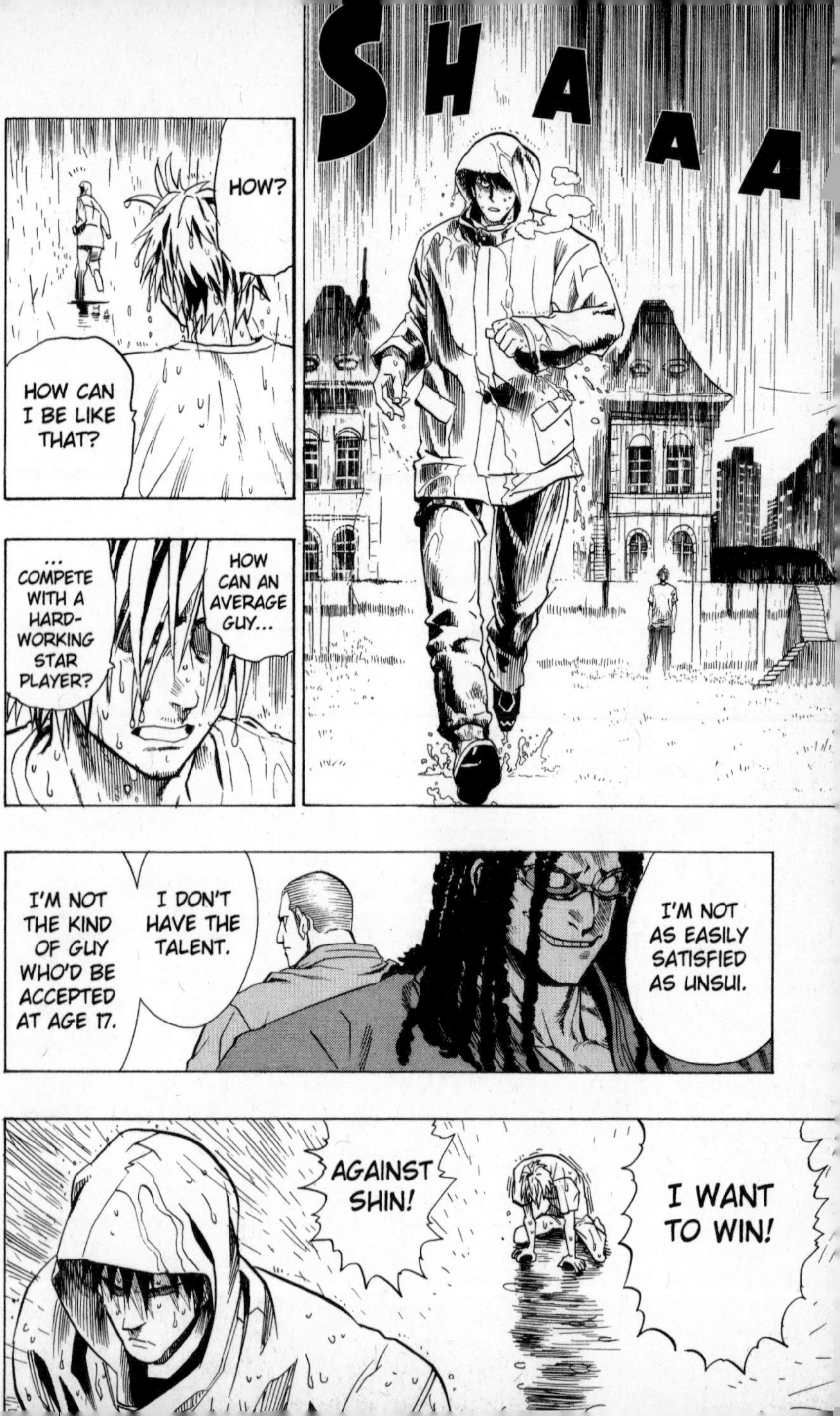
SHAAAA
HOW?
HOW CAN I BE LIKE THAT?
HOW CAN AN AVERAGE GUY...
... COMPETE WITH A HARD-WORKING STAR PLAYER?
I'M NOT AS EASILY SATISFIED AS UNSUI.
I DON'T HAVE THE TALENT.
I'M NOT THE KIND OF GUY WHO'D BE ACCEPTED AT AGE 17.
I WANT TO WIN!
AGAINST SHIN!

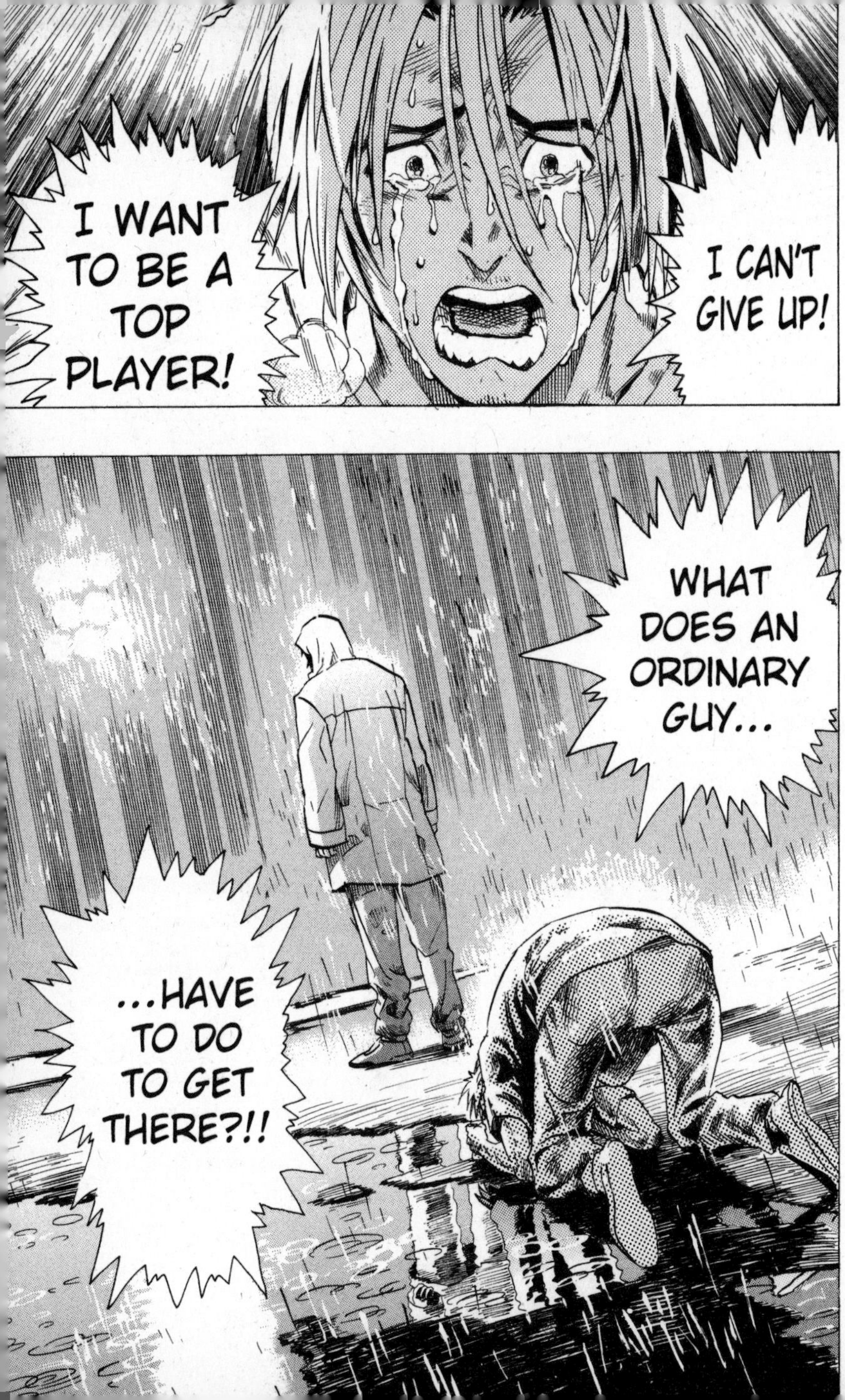
I CAN'T GIVE UP!
I WANT TO BE A TOP PLAYER!
WHAT DOES AN ORDINARY GUY...
...HAVE TO DO TO GET THERE?!!

OJO WHITE KNIGHTS STARTING LINEUP ROSTER

OFFENSE

| 3 | Quarterback |

Ichiro Takami

Power ▬▬
Speed ▬▬
Technique ▬▬▬▬▬▬

| 16 | Tight end |

Hikaru Itadaki

Power ▬▬▬▬
Speed ▬▬▬
Technique ▬▬▬

| 18 | Receiver |

Haruto Sakuraba

Power ▬▬▬
Speed ▬▬▬▬▬
Technique ▬▬

| 83 | Receiver |

Shun Kanzaki

Power ▬▬
Speed ▬▬▬▬▬
Technique ▬▬▬

| 32 | Running Back |

Keisuke Nekoyama

Power ▬▬
Speed ▬▬▬▬
Technique ▬▬▬

| 38 | Running Back |

Shoichi Mayumura

Power ▬▬
Speed ▬▬▬▬
Technique ▬▬

| 60 | Lineman |

Makoto Otawara

Power ▬▬▬▬▬
Speed ▬▬▬
Technique ▬▬

| 52 | Lineman |

Reiji Kagamido

Power ▬▬▬▬
Speed ▬▬
Technique ▬▬▬▬▬

| 62 | Lineman |

Atsuo Iwabana

Power ▬▬▬▬
Speed ▬
Technique ▬▬▬▬

| 78 | Lineman |

Yoshinori Agota

Power ▬▬▬▬
Speed ▬▬
Technique ▬▬▬

| 57 | Lineman |

Eiji Suzuki

Power ▬▬▬▬
Speed ▬▬▬
Technique ▬▬▬

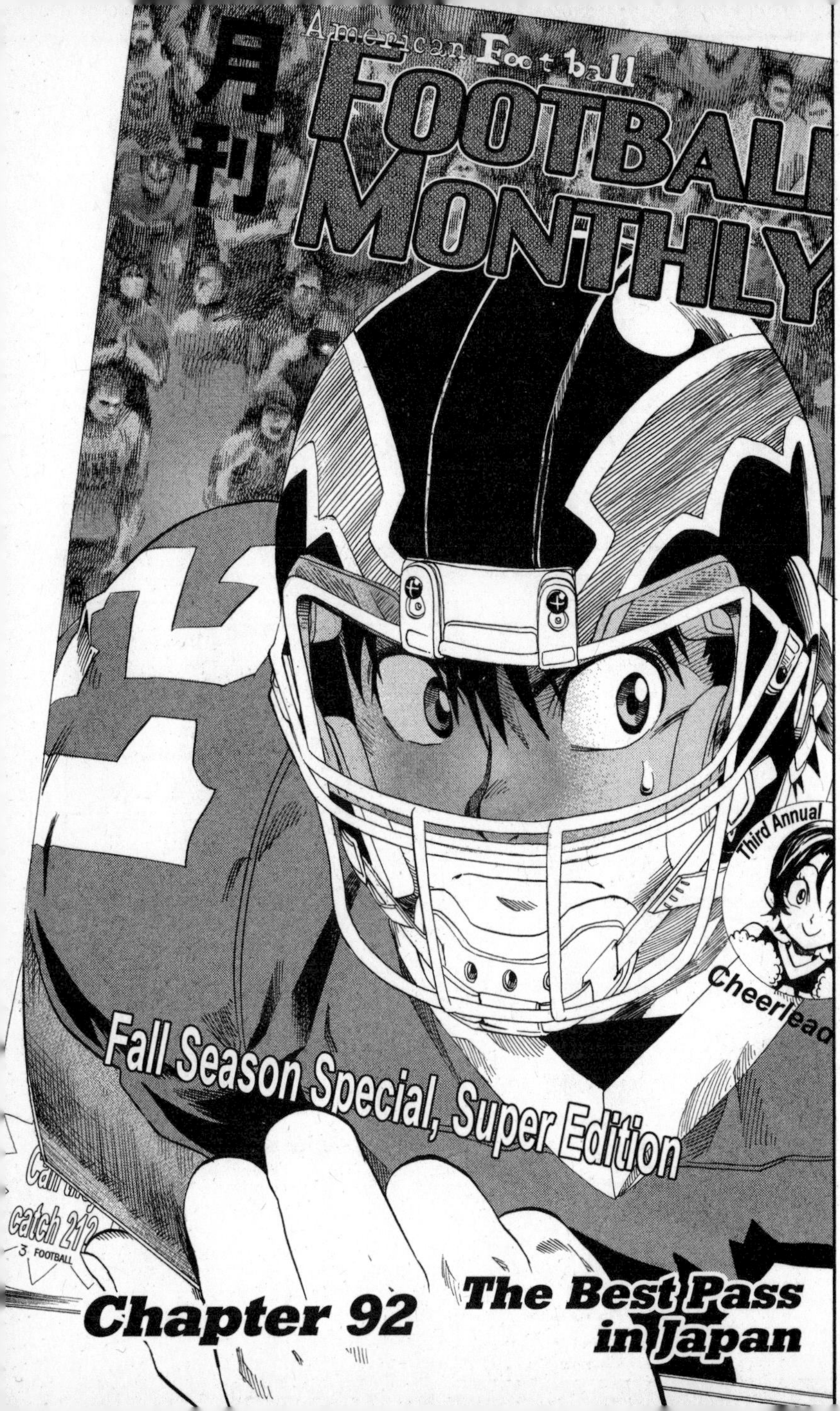
月刊
American Football
FOOTBALL MONTHLY
Third Annual
Cheerlead
Fall Season Special, Super Edition
3 FOOTBALL
Chapter 92
The Best Pass in Japan

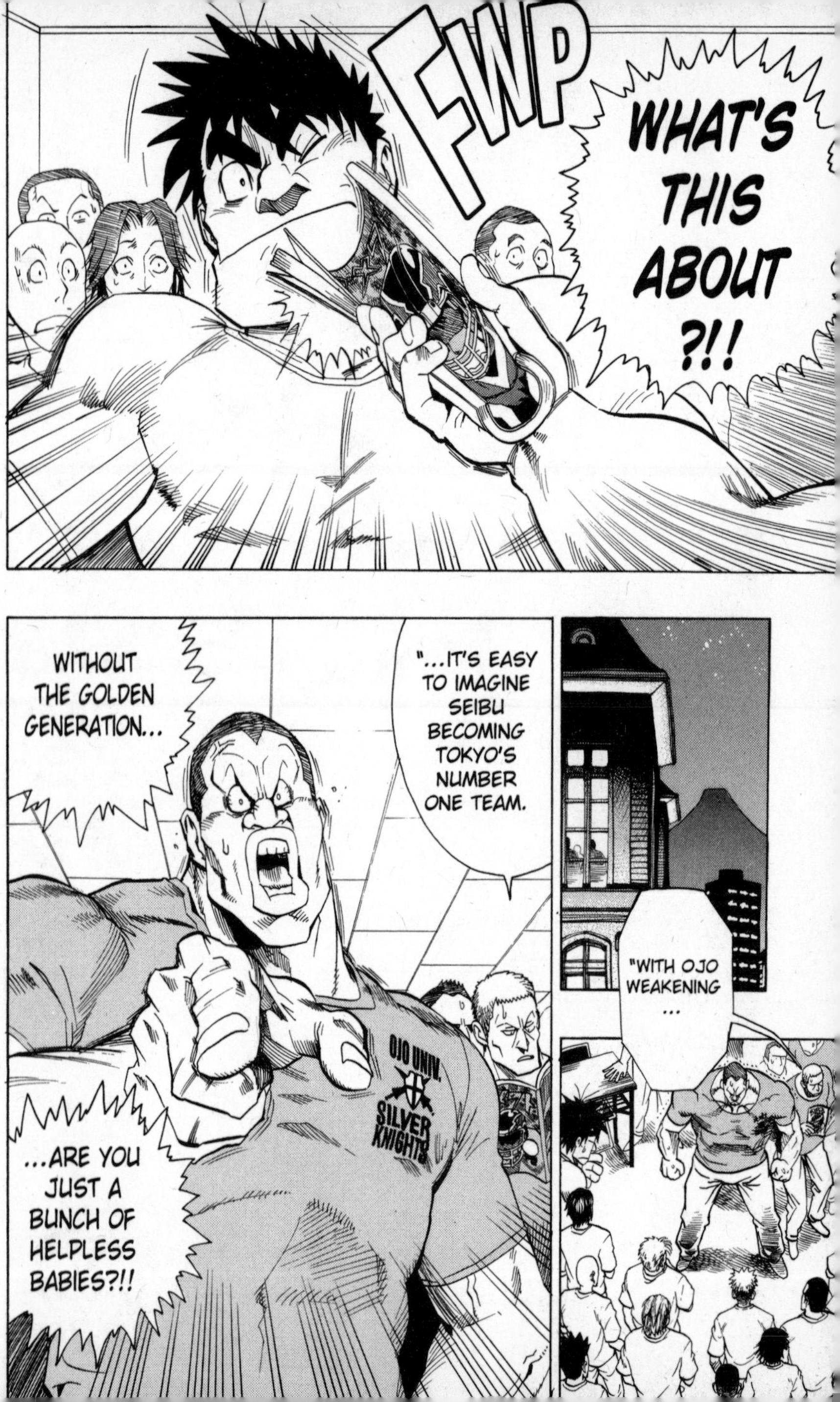
WHAT'S THIS ABOUT ?!!
FWP
"WITH OJO WEAKENING ...
"...IT'S EASY TO IMAGINE SEIBU BECOMING TOKYO'S NUMBER ONE TEAM.
WITHOUT THE GOLDEN GENERATION...
OJO UNIV. SILVER KNIGHTS
...ARE YOU JUST A BUNCH OF HELPLESS BABIES?!!

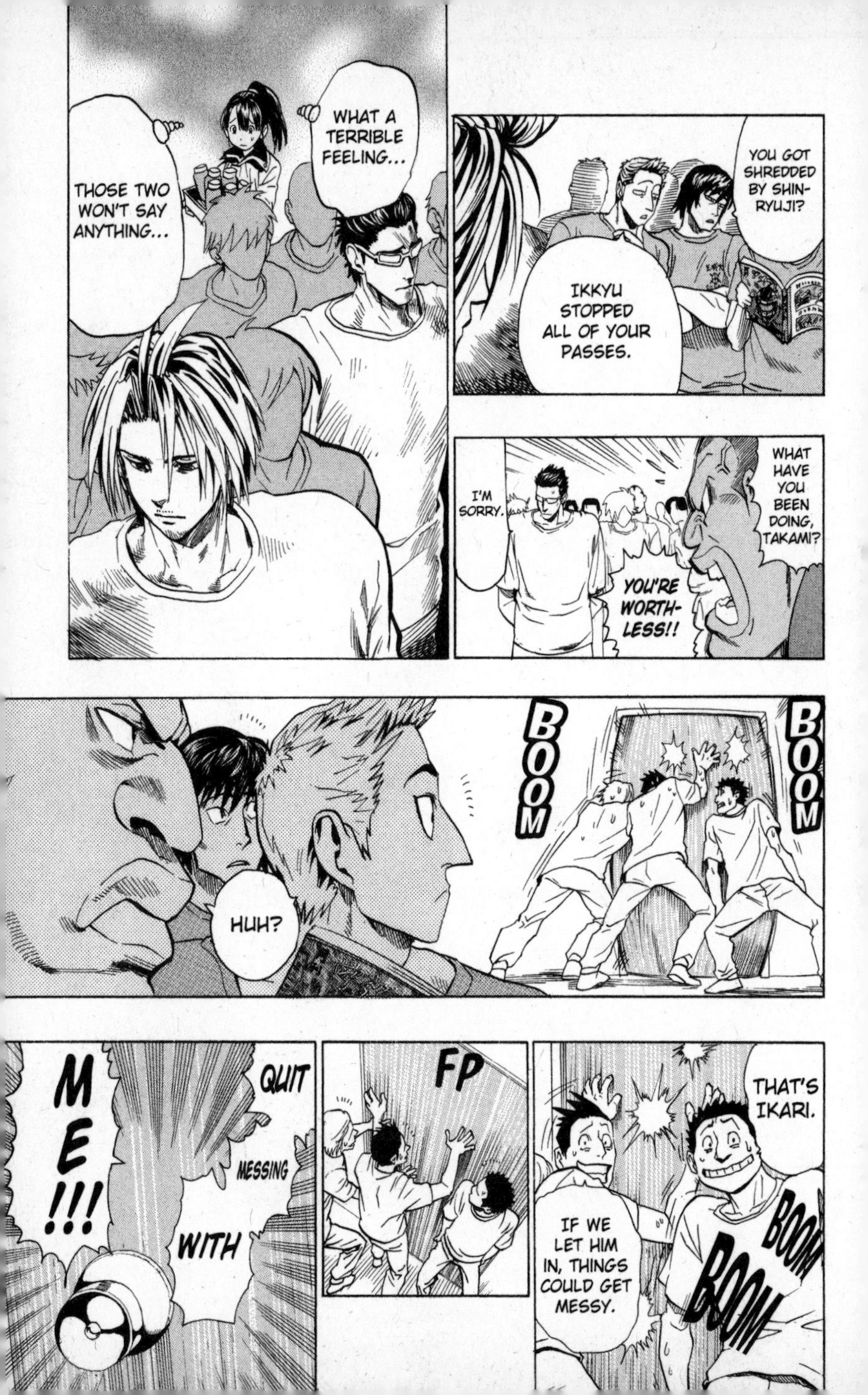
YOU GOT SHREDDED BY SHIN-RYUJI?
IKKYU STOPPED ALL OF YOUR PASSES.
WHAT HAVE YOU BEEN DOING, TAKAMI?
YOU'RE WORTHLESS!!
I'M SORRY.
WHAT A TERRIBLE FEELING...
THOSE TWO WON'T SAY ANYTHING...
BOOM
BOOM
HUH?
THAT'S IKARI.
IF WE LET HIM IN, THINGS COULD GET MESSY.
BOOM
BOOM
FP
QUIT MESSING WITH ME!!!

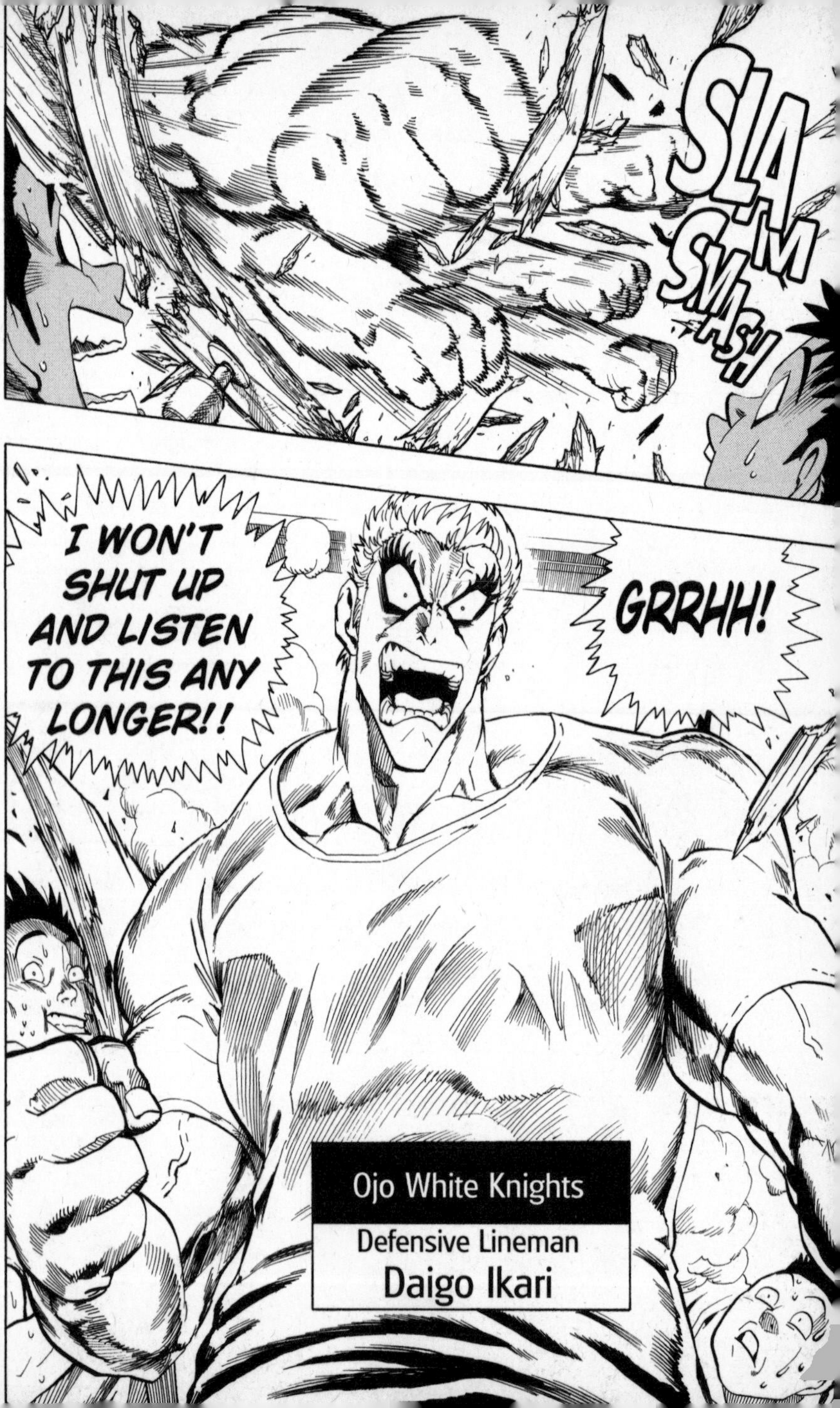
SLAM
SMASH!!
GRRHH!
I WON'T SHUT UP AND LISTEN TO THIS ANY LONGER!!
Ojo White Knights
Defensive Lineman
Daigo Ikari

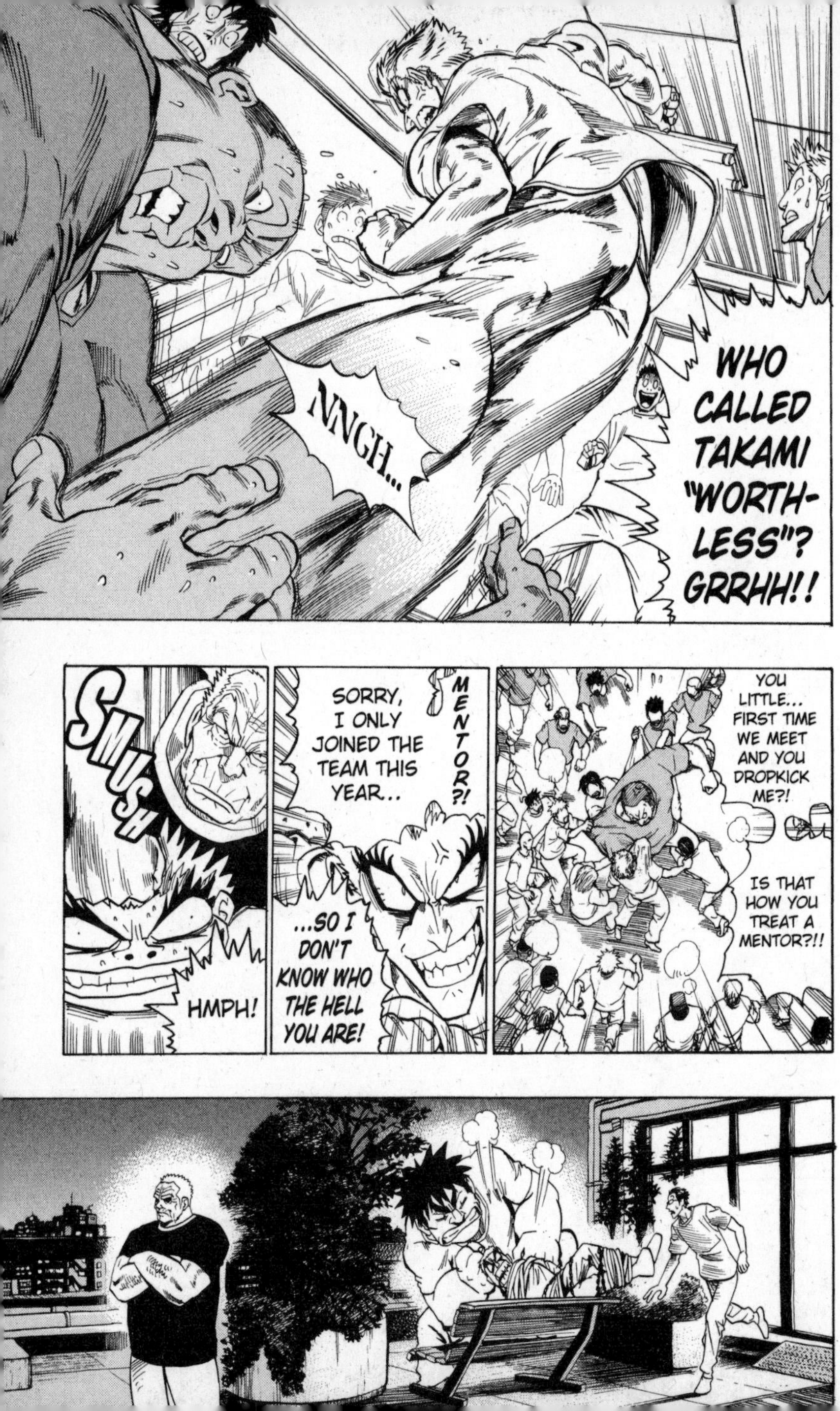
WHO CALLED TAKAMI "WORTH-LESS"? GRRHH!!
NNGH...
YOU LITTLE... FIRST TIME WE MEET AND YOU DROPKICK ME?!
IS THAT HOW YOU TREAT A MENTOR?!!
MENTOR?!
SORRY, I ONLY JOINED THE TEAM THIS YEAR...
...SO I DON'T KNOW WHO THE HELL YOU ARE!
SMUSH
HMPH!

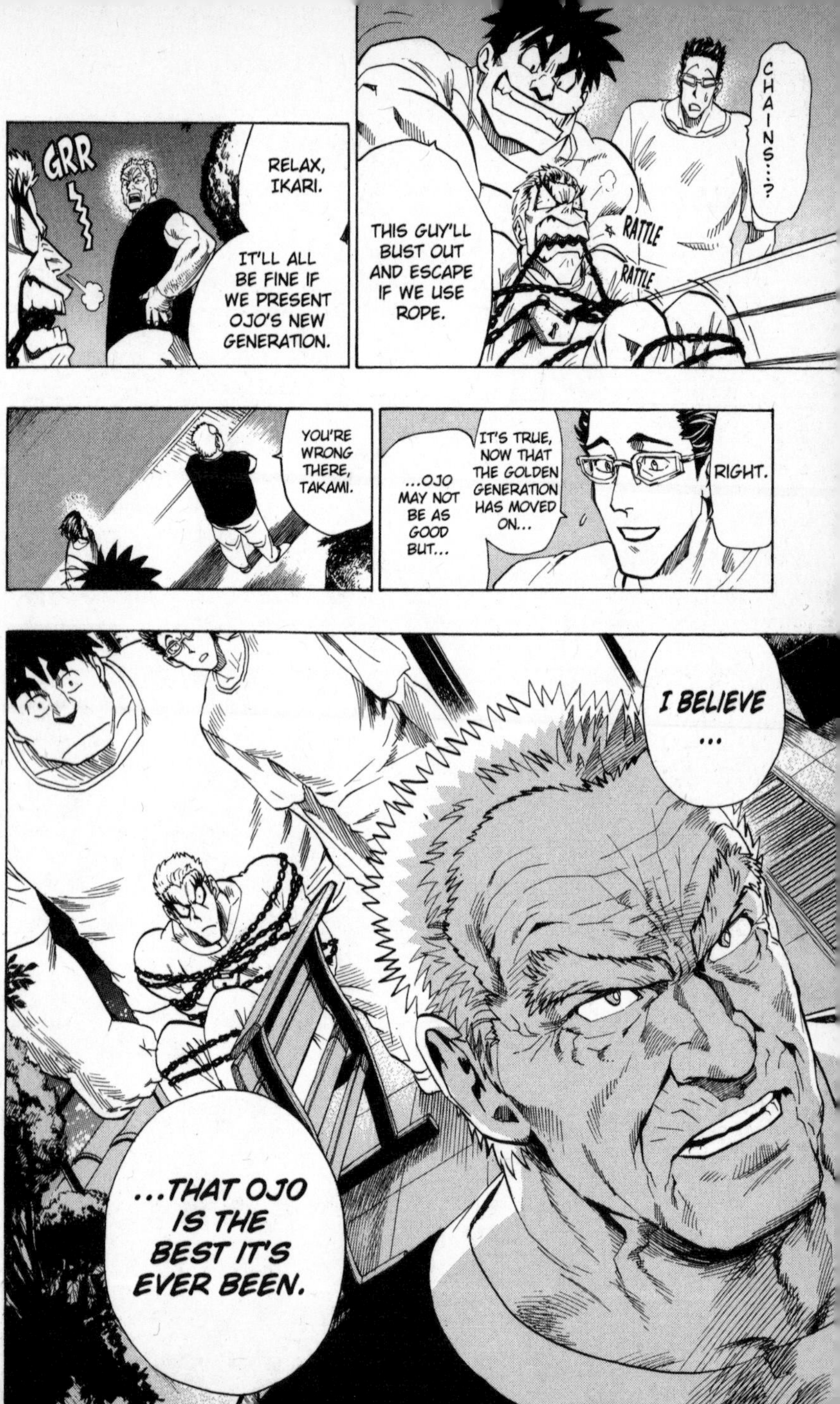
CHAINS...?
RATTLE
RATTLE
THIS GUY'LL BUST OUT AND ESCAPE IF WE USE ROPE.
RELAX, IKARI.
IT'LL ALL BE FINE IF WE PRESENT OJO'S NEW GENERATION.
GRR
RIGHT.
IT'S TRUE, NOW THAT THE GOLDEN GENERATION HAS MOVED ON...
...OJO MAY NOT BE AS GOOD BUT...
YOU'RE WRONG THERE, TAKAMI.
I BELIEVE ...
...THAT OJO IS THE BEST IT'S EVER BEEN.

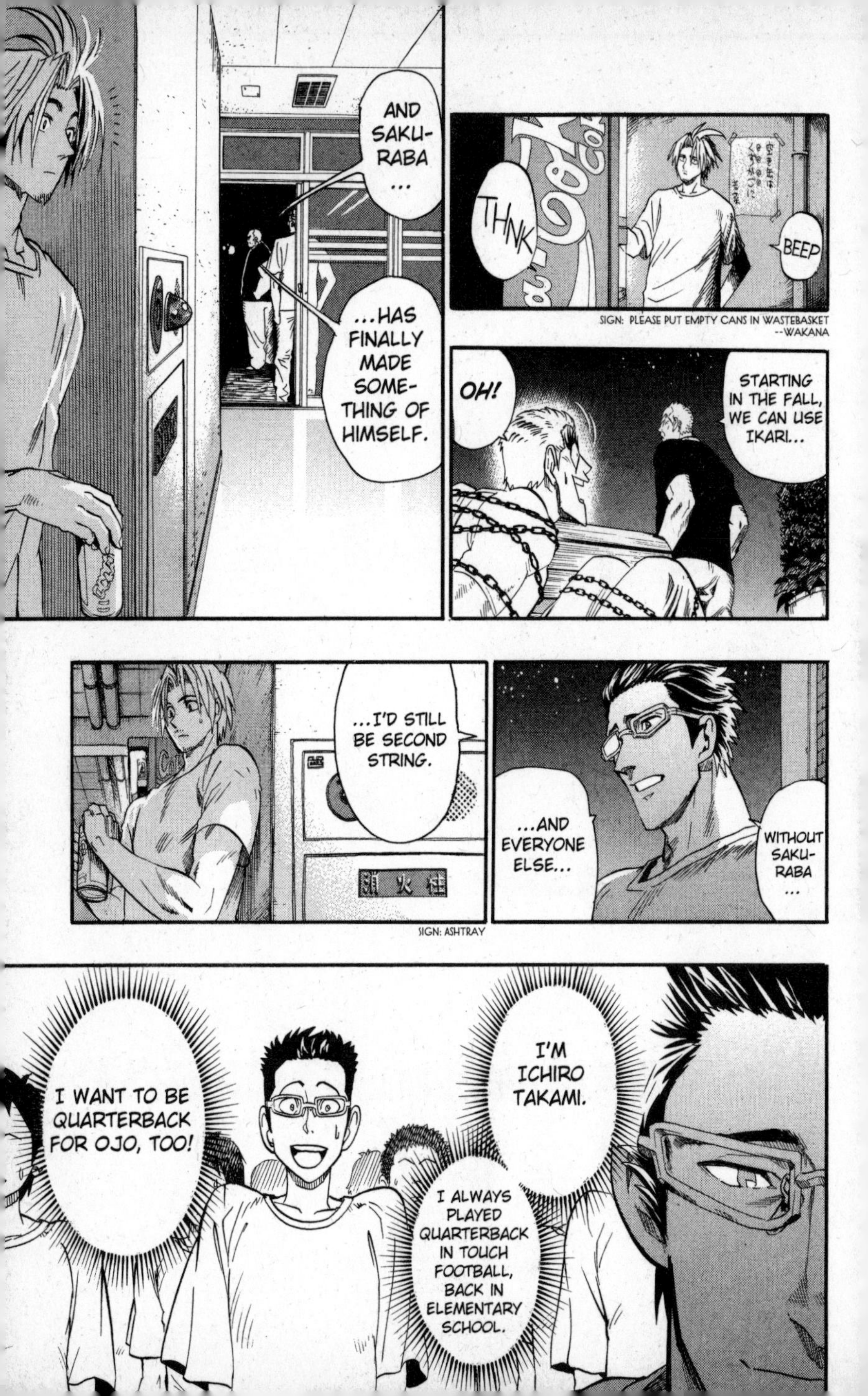
BEEP
THNK
SIGN: PLEASE PUT EMPTY CANS IN WASTEBASKET --WAKANA
STARTING IN THE FALL, WE CAN USE IKARI...
OH!
AND SAKU-RABA ...
...HAS FINALLY MADE SOME-THING OF HIMSELF.
WITHOUT SAKU-RABA ...
...AND EVERYONE ELSE...
...I'D STILL BE SECOND STRING.
SIGN: ASHTRAY
I'M ICHIRO TAKAMI.
I ALWAYS PLAYED QUARTERBACK IN TOUCH FOOTBALL, BACK IN ELEMENTARY SCHOOL.
I WANT TO BE QUARTERBACK FOR OJO, TOO!

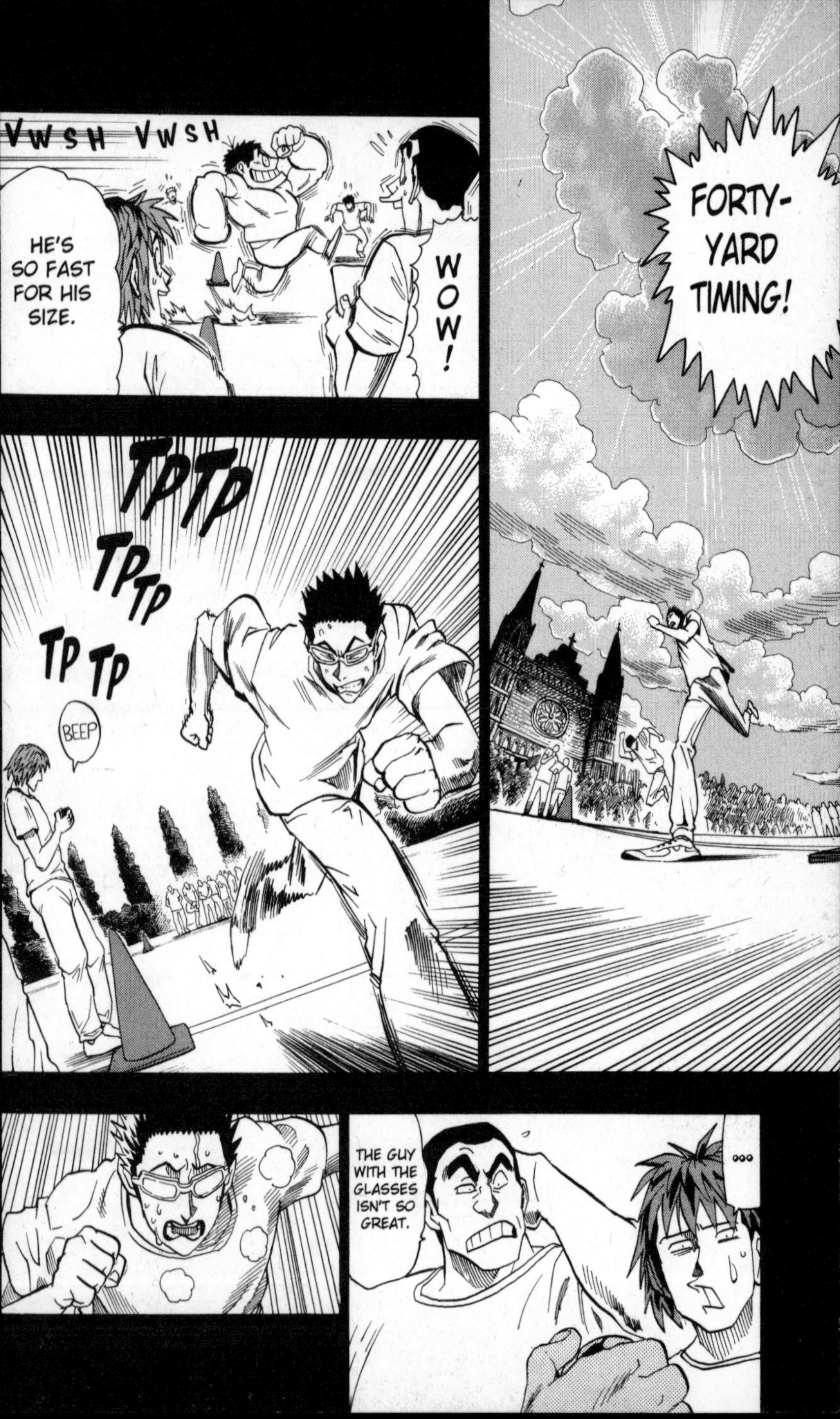
FORTY-YARD TIMING!
VWSH VWSH
HE'S SO FAST FOR HIS SIZE.
WOW!
TPTP
TPTP
TP TP
BEEP
...
THE GUY WITH THE GLASSES ISN'T SO GREAT.

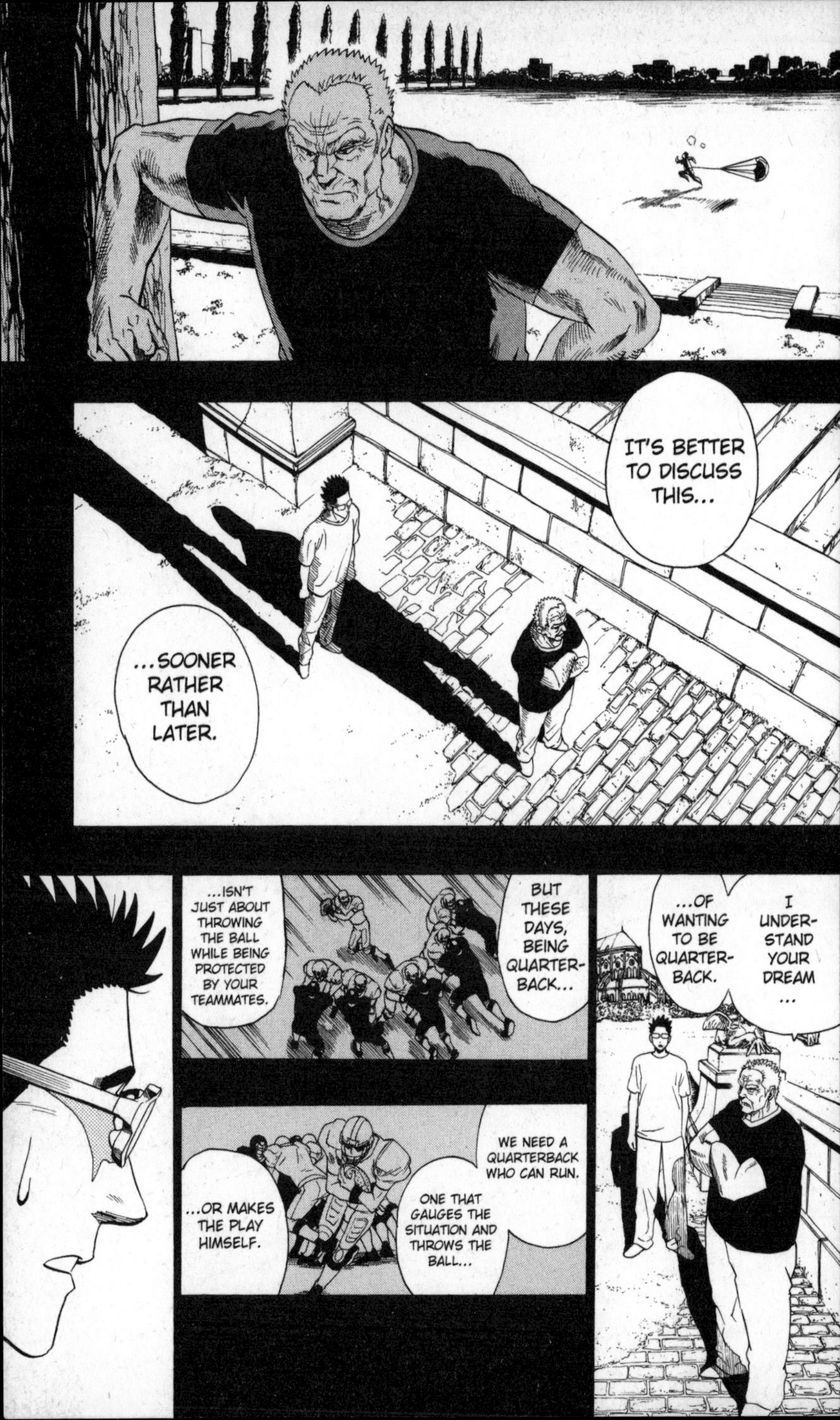

IT'S BETTER TO DISCUSS THIS...
...SOONER RATHER THAN LATER.
I UNDERSTAND YOUR DREAM...
...OF WANTING TO BE QUARTERBACK.
BUT THESE DAYS, BEING QUARTERBACK...
...ISN'T JUST ABOUT THROWING THE BALL WHILE BEING PROTECTED BY YOUR TEAMMATES.
WE NEED A QUARTERBACK WHO CAN RUN.
ONE THAT GAUGES THE SITUATION AND THROWS THE BALL...
...OR MAKES THE PLAY HIMSELF.

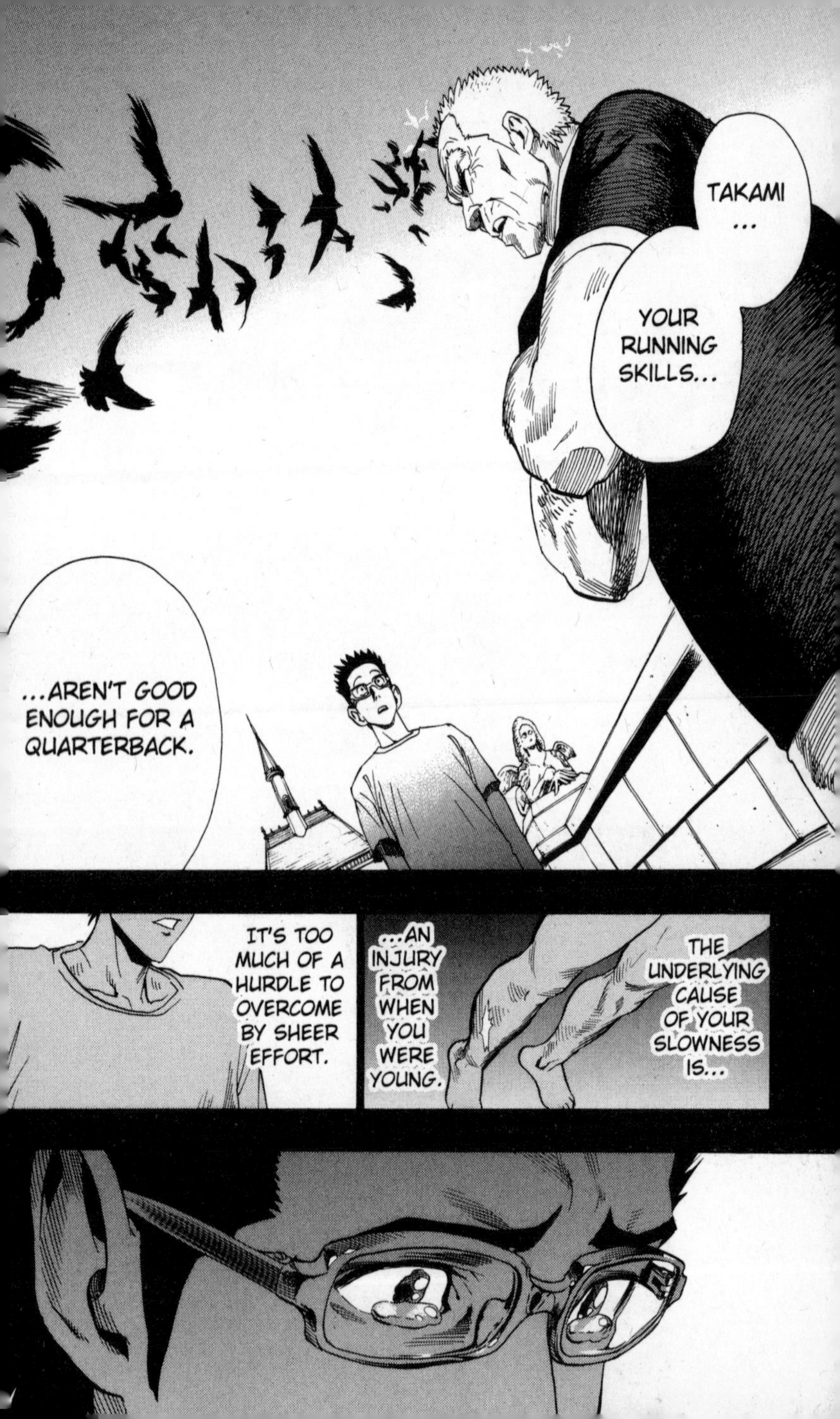
TAKAMI ...
YOUR RUNNING SKILLS...
...AREN'T GOOD ENOUGH FOR A QUARTERBACK.
THE UNDERLYING CAUSE OF YOUR SLOWNESS IS...
...AN INJURY FROM WHEN YOU WERE YOUNG.
IT'S TOO MUCH OF A HURDLE TO OVERCOME BY SHEER EFFORT.

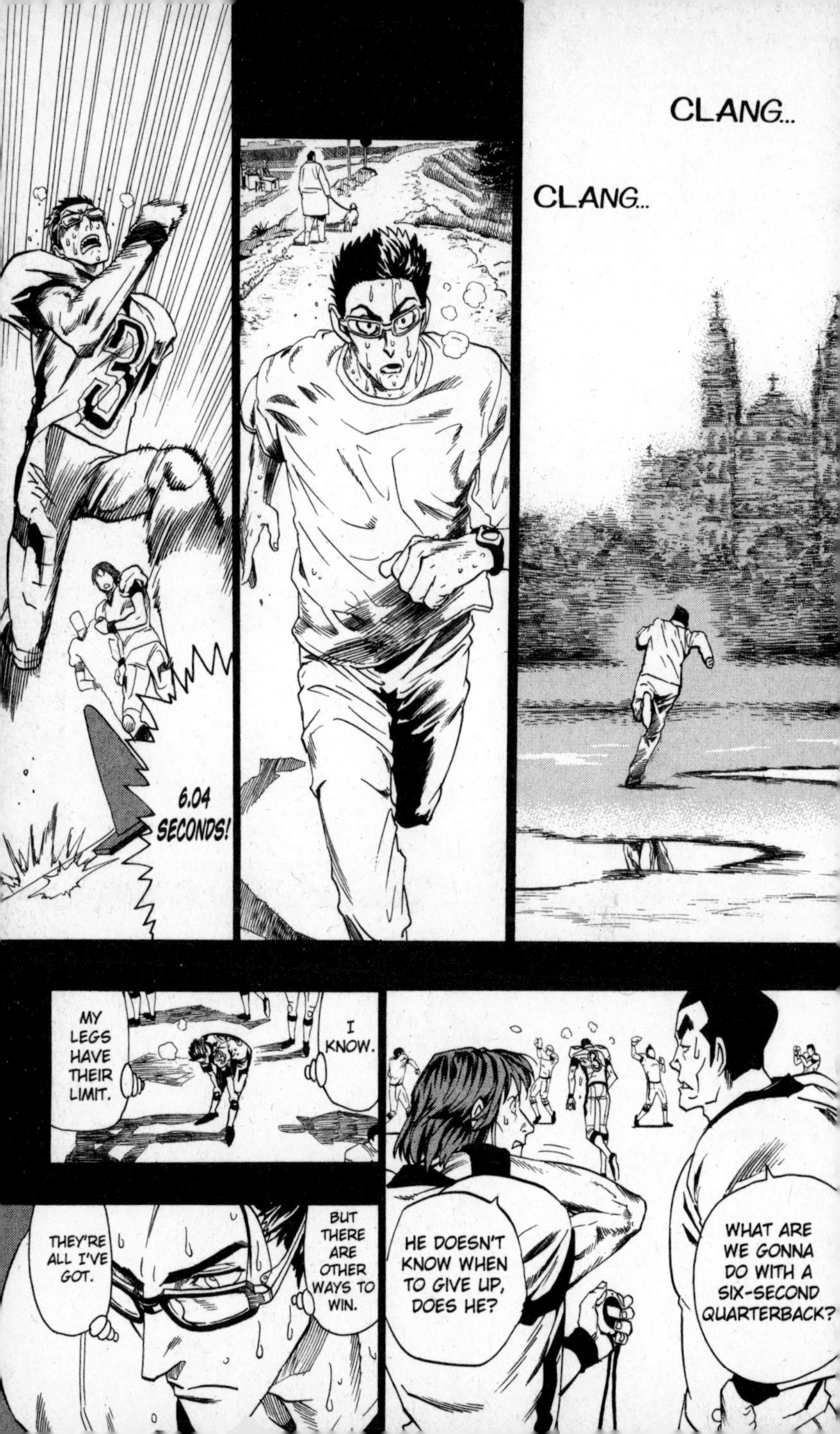
CLANG...
CLANG...
6.04 SECONDS!
WHAT ARE WE GONNA DO WITH A SIX-SECOND QUARTERBACK?
HE DOESN'T KNOW WHEN TO GIVE UP, DOES HE?
I KNOW.
MY LEGS HAVE THEIR LIMIT.
BUT THERE ARE OTHER WAYS TO WIN.
THEY'RE ALL I'VE GOT.

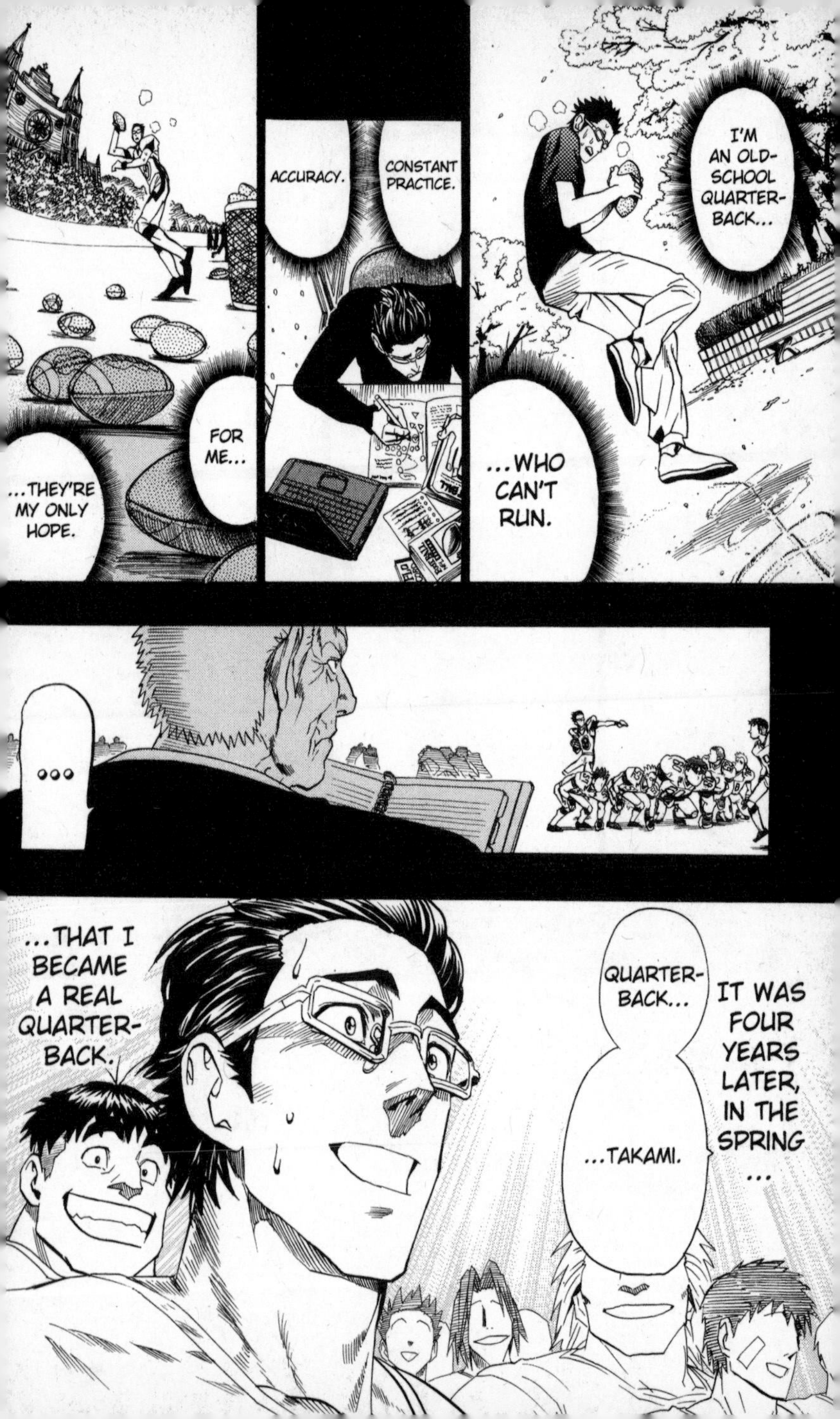
I'M AN OLD-SCHOOL QUARTER-BACK...
...WHO CAN'T RUN.
CONSTANT PRACTICE.
ACCURACY.
FOR ME...
...THEY'RE MY ONLY HOPE.
...
IT WAS FOUR YEARS LATER, IN THE SPRING...
QUARTER-BACK...
...TAKAMI.
...THAT I BECAME A REAL QUARTER-BACK.

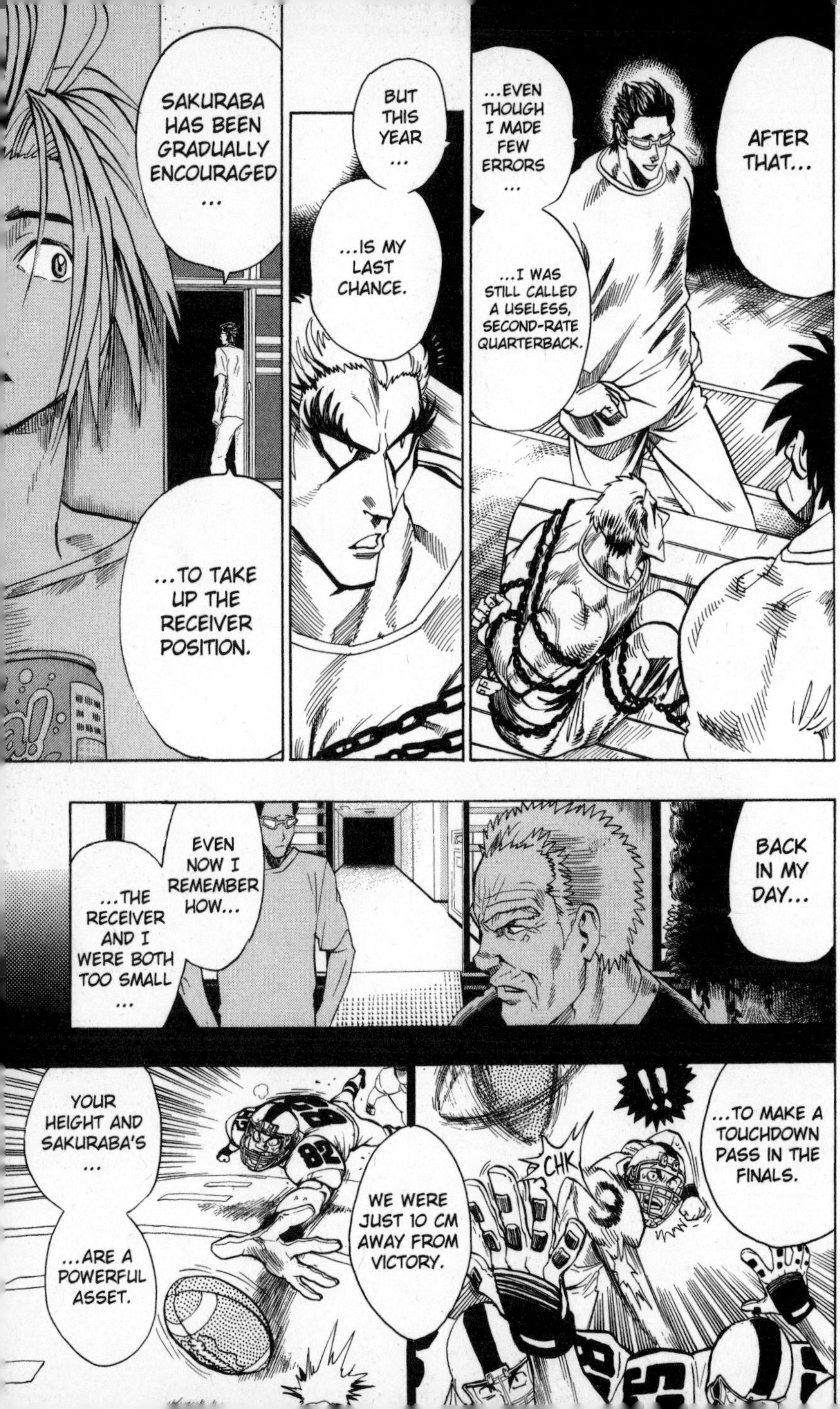
AFTER THAT...
...EVEN THOUGH I MADE FEW ERRORS...
...I WAS STILL CALLED A USELESS, SECOND-RATE QUARTERBACK.
BUT THIS YEAR...
...IS MY LAST CHANCE.
SAKURABA HAS BEEN GRADUALLY ENCOURAGED...
...TO TAKE UP THE RECEIVER POSITION.
BACK IN MY DAY...
EVEN NOW I REMEMBER HOW...
...THE RECEIVER AND I WERE BOTH TOO SMALL...
...TO MAKE A TOUCHDOWN PASS IN THE FINALS.
CHK
WE WERE JUST 10 CM AWAY FROM VICTORY.
YOUR HEIGHT AND SAKURABA'S...
...ARE A POWERFUL ASSET.

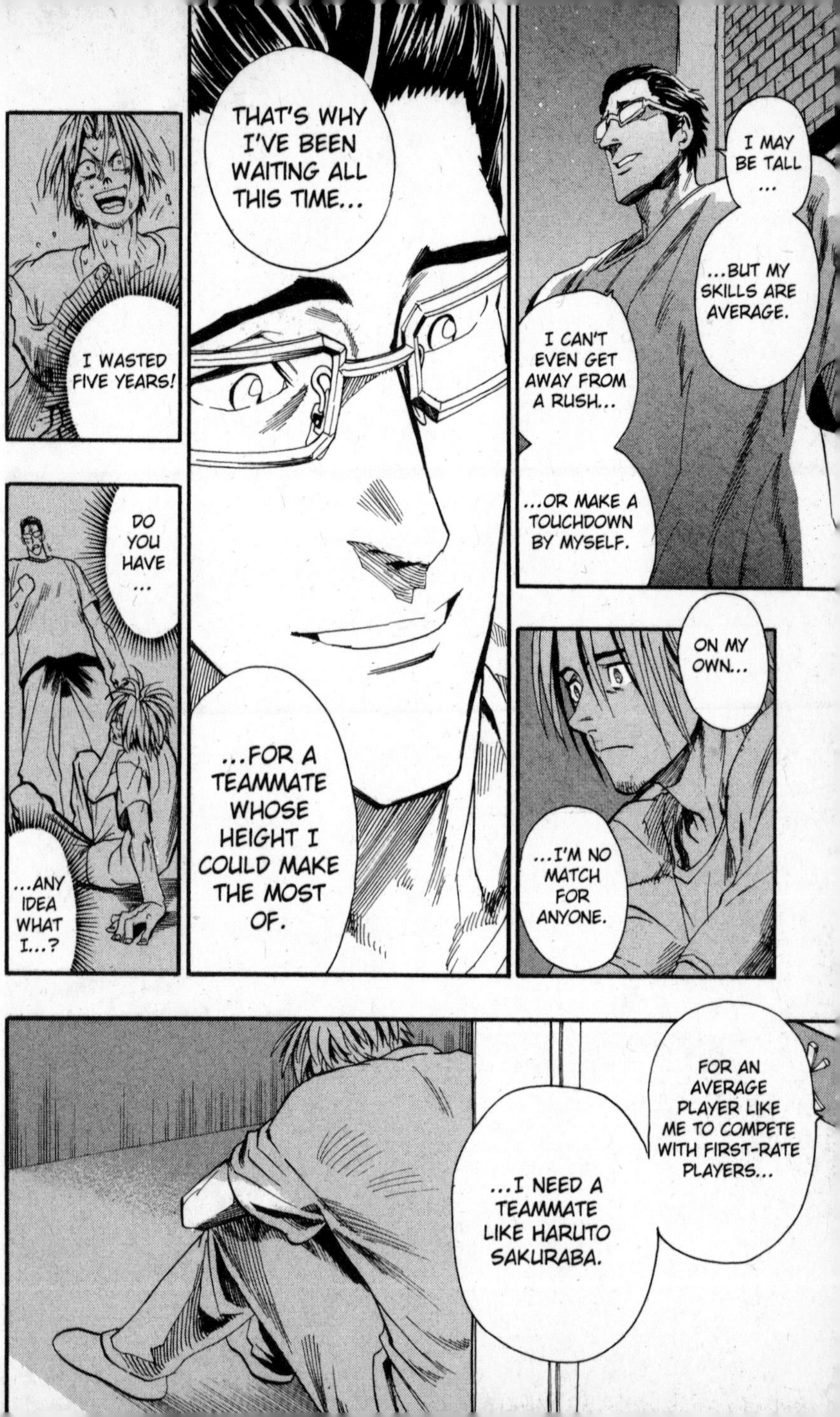
I MAY BE TALL...
...BUT MY SKILLS ARE AVERAGE.
I CAN'T EVEN GET AWAY FROM A RUSH...
...OR MAKE A TOUCHDOWN BY MYSELF.
ON MY OWN...
...I'M NO MATCH FOR ANYONE.
THAT'S WHY I'VE BEEN WAITING ALL THIS TIME...
...FOR A TEAMMATE WHOSE HEIGHT I COULD MAKE THE MOST OF.
I WASTED FIVE YEARS!
DO YOU HAVE...
...ANY IDEA WHAT I...?
FOR AN AVERAGE PLAYER LIKE ME TO COMPETE WITH FIRST-RATE PLAYERS...
...I NEED A TEAMMATE LIKE HARUTO SAKURABA.

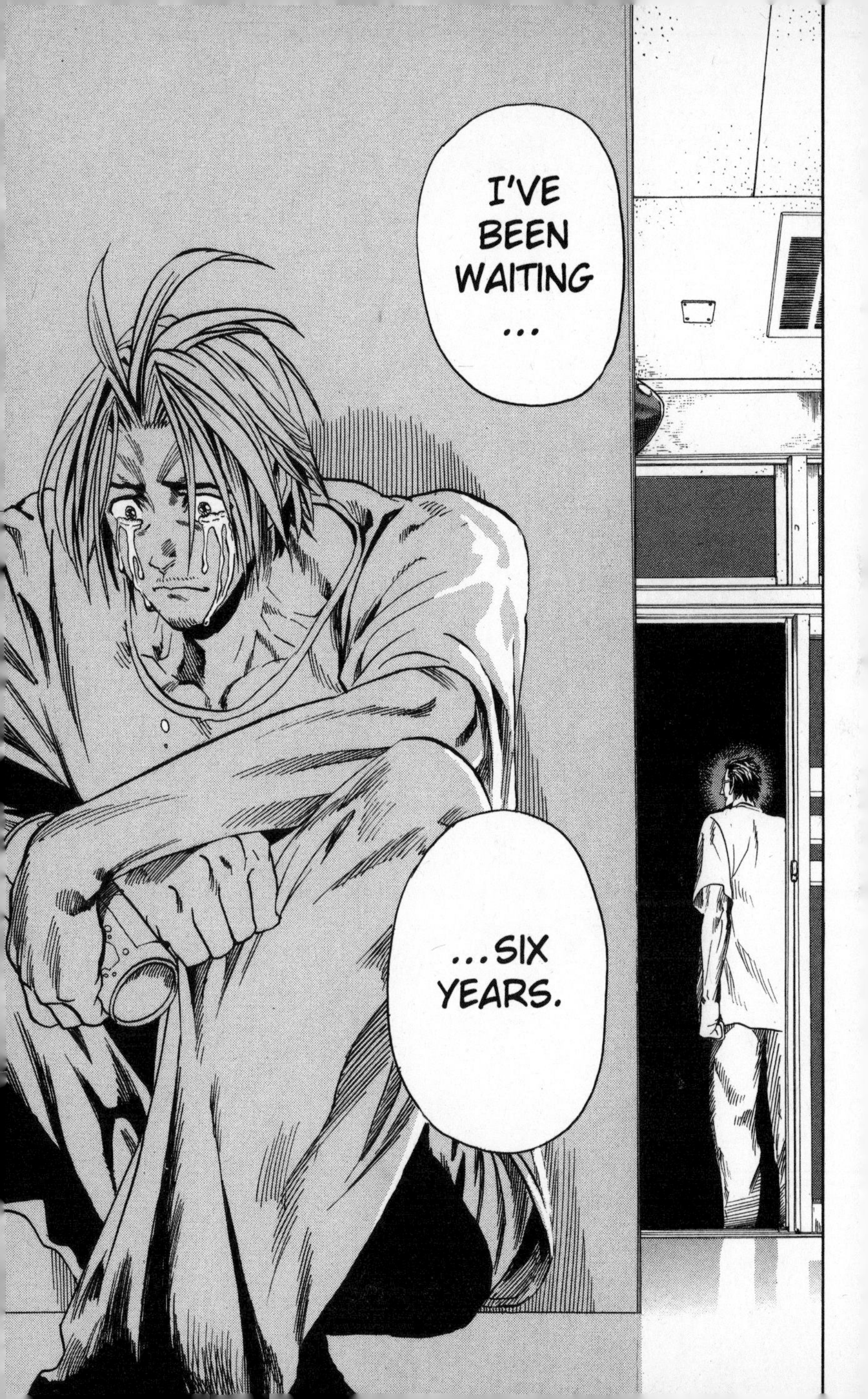
I'VE BEEN WAITING ...
...SIX YEARS.

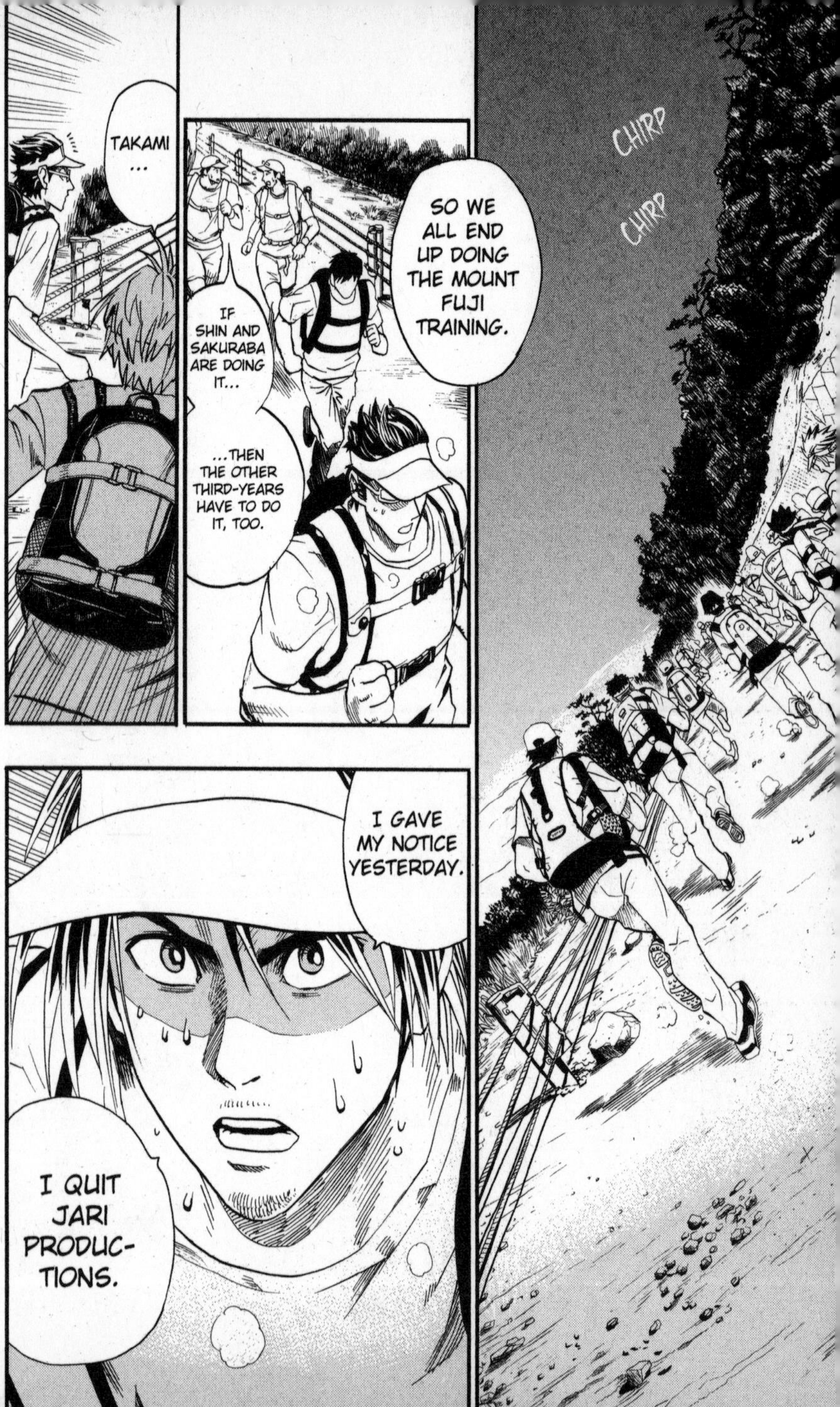
CHIRP
CHIRP
SO WE ALL END UP DOING THE MOUNT FUJI TRAINING.
IF SHIN AND SAKURABA ARE DOING IT...
...THEN THE OTHER THIRD-YEARS HAVE TO DO IT, TOO.
TAKAMI...
I GAVE MY NOTICE YESTERDAY.
I QUIT JARI PRODUCTIONS.

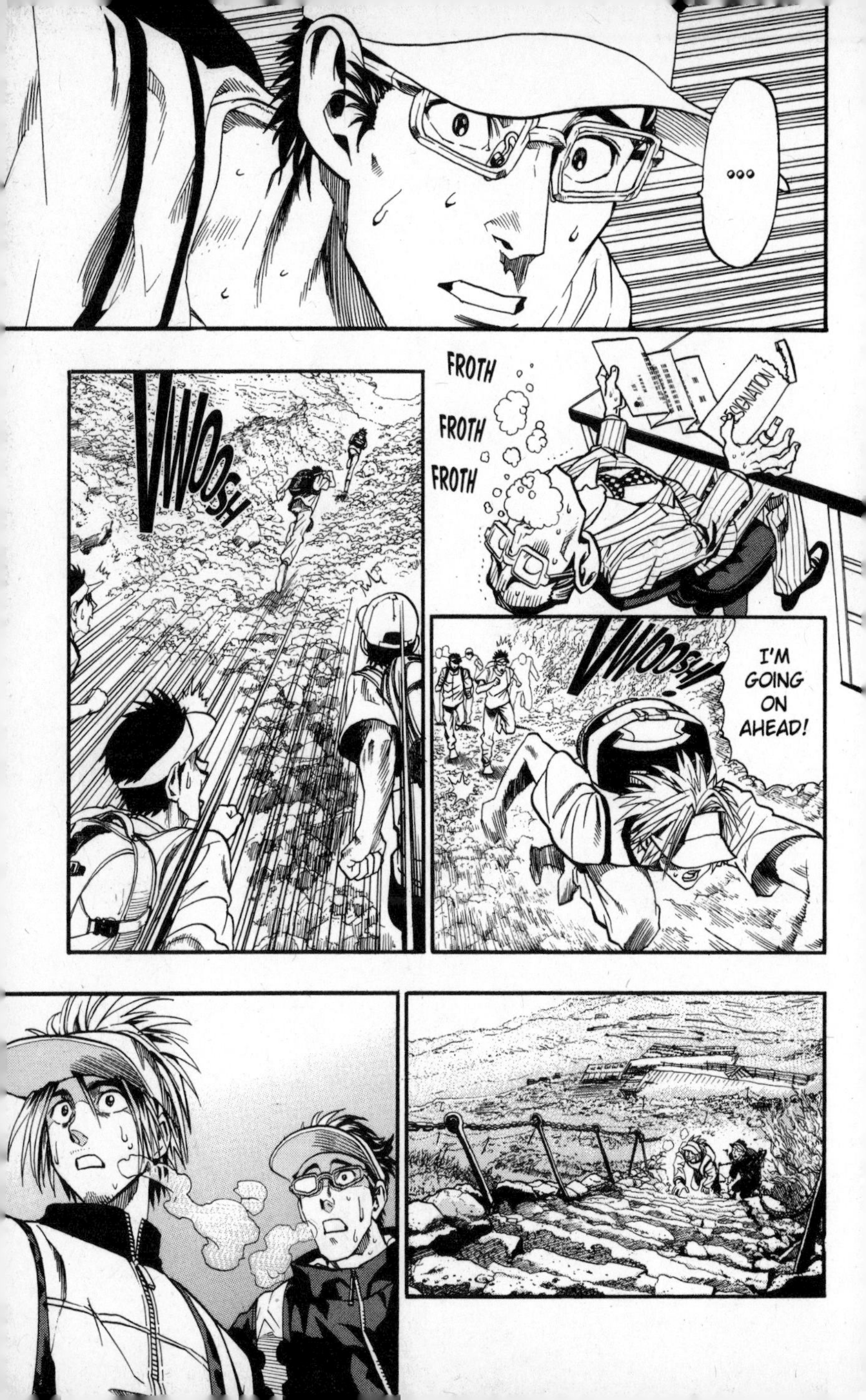
...
FROTH
FROTH
FROTH
VWOOSH!
I'M GOING ON AHEAD!
VWOOSH

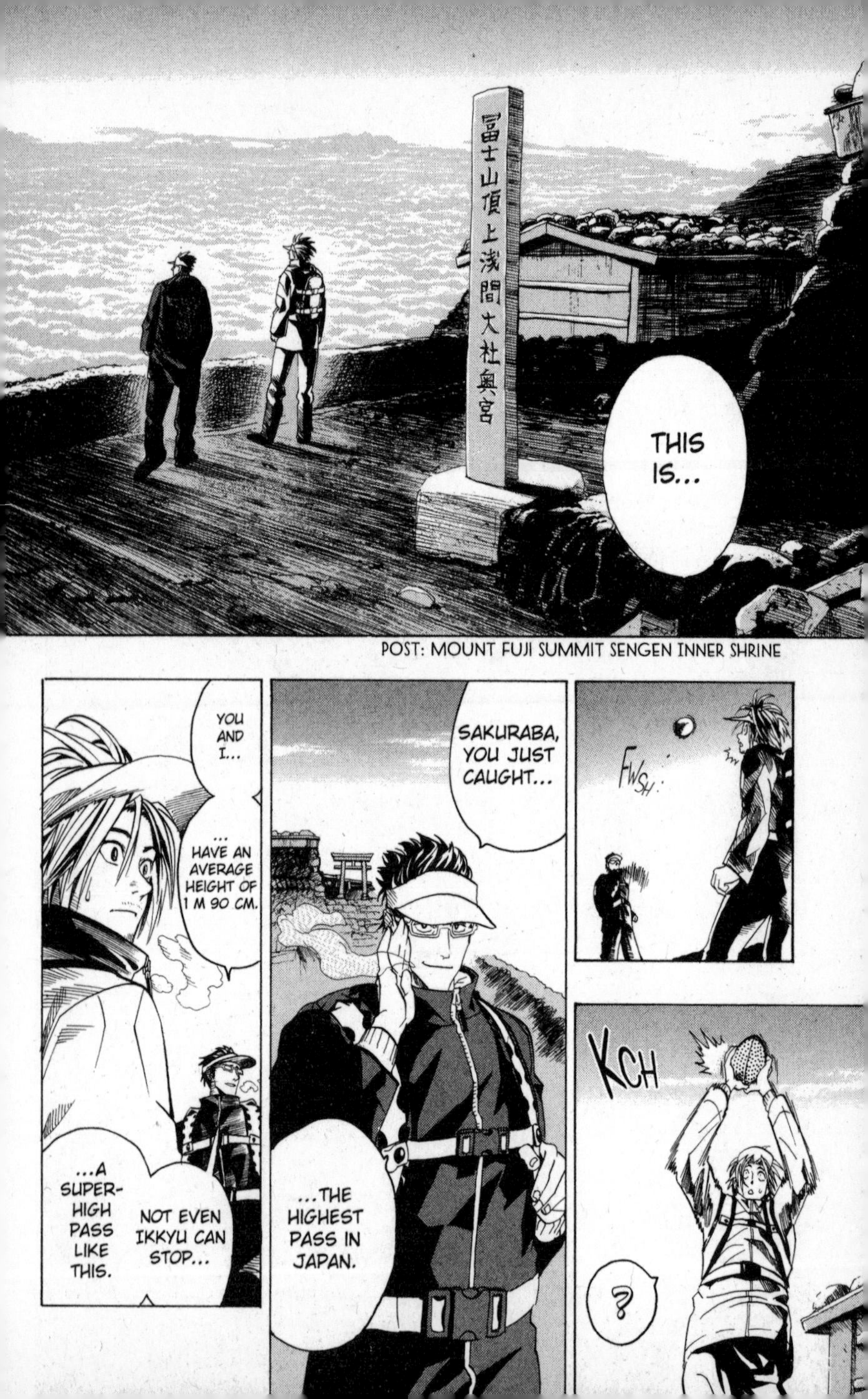
冨士山頂上浅間大社奥宮
THIS IS...
POST: MOUNT FUJI SUMMIT SENGEN INNER SHRINE
FWSH
KCH
?
SAKURABA, YOU JUST CAUGHT...
...THE HIGHEST PASS IN JAPAN.
YOU AND I...
...HAVE AN AVERAGE HEIGHT OF 1 M 90 CM.
NOT EVEN IKKYU CAN STOP...
...A SUPER-HIGH PASS LIKE THIS.

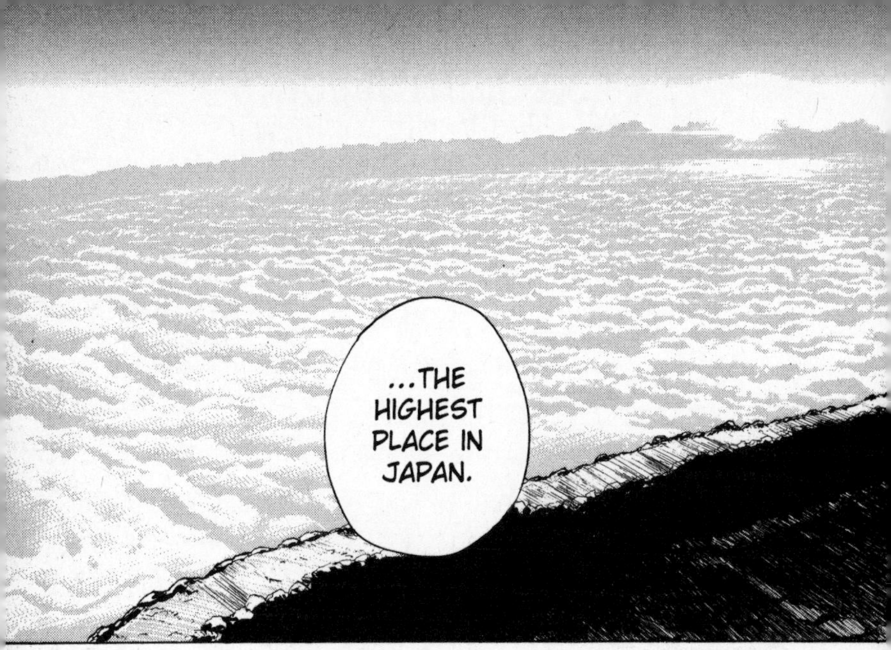
...THE HIGHEST PLACE IN JAPAN.
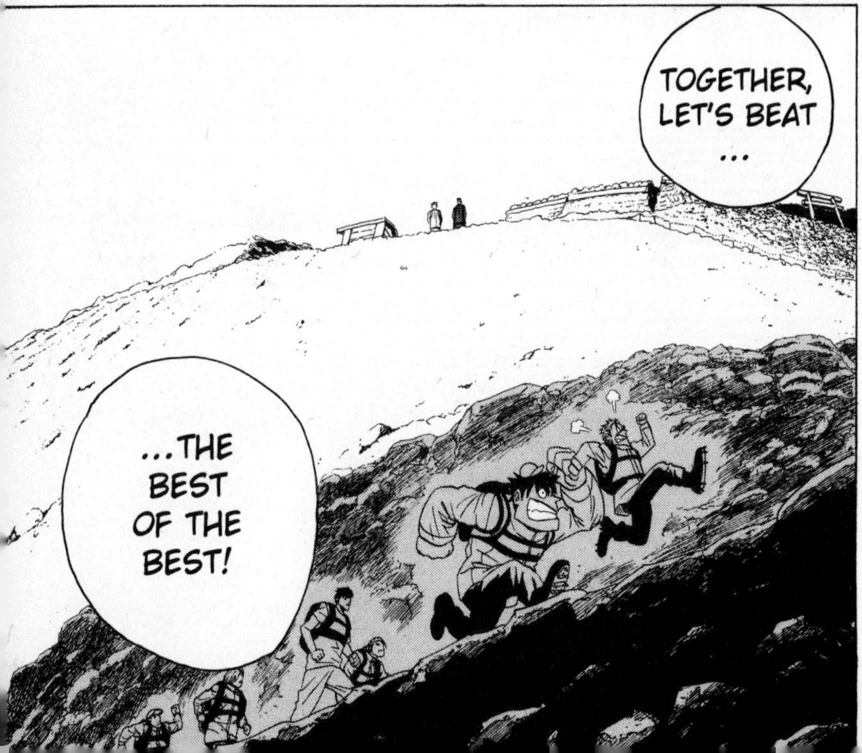
TOGETHER, LET'S BEAT ...
...THE BEST OF THE BEST!

40	Linebacker

Seijuro Shin

Power
Speed
Technique

35	Linebacker

Kyohei Yakumaru

Power
Speed
Technique

51	Linebacker

Takaya Gushiken

Power
Speed
Technique

22	Cornerback

Rintaro Tsuyashima

Power
Speed
Technique

25	Cornerback

Hiroyuki Iguchi

Power
Speed
Technique

15	Safety

Tadashi Tsurime

Power
Speed
Technique

33	Safety

Sota Nakawaki

Power
Speed
Technique

60	Lineman

Makoto Otawara

Power
Speed
Technique

66	Lineman

Daigo Ikari

Power
Speed **?**
Technique

92	Lineman

Naoki Uemura

Power
Speed
Technique

70	Lineman

Yorihiro Watanabe

Power
Speed
Technique

Chapter 93
A Binding Oath

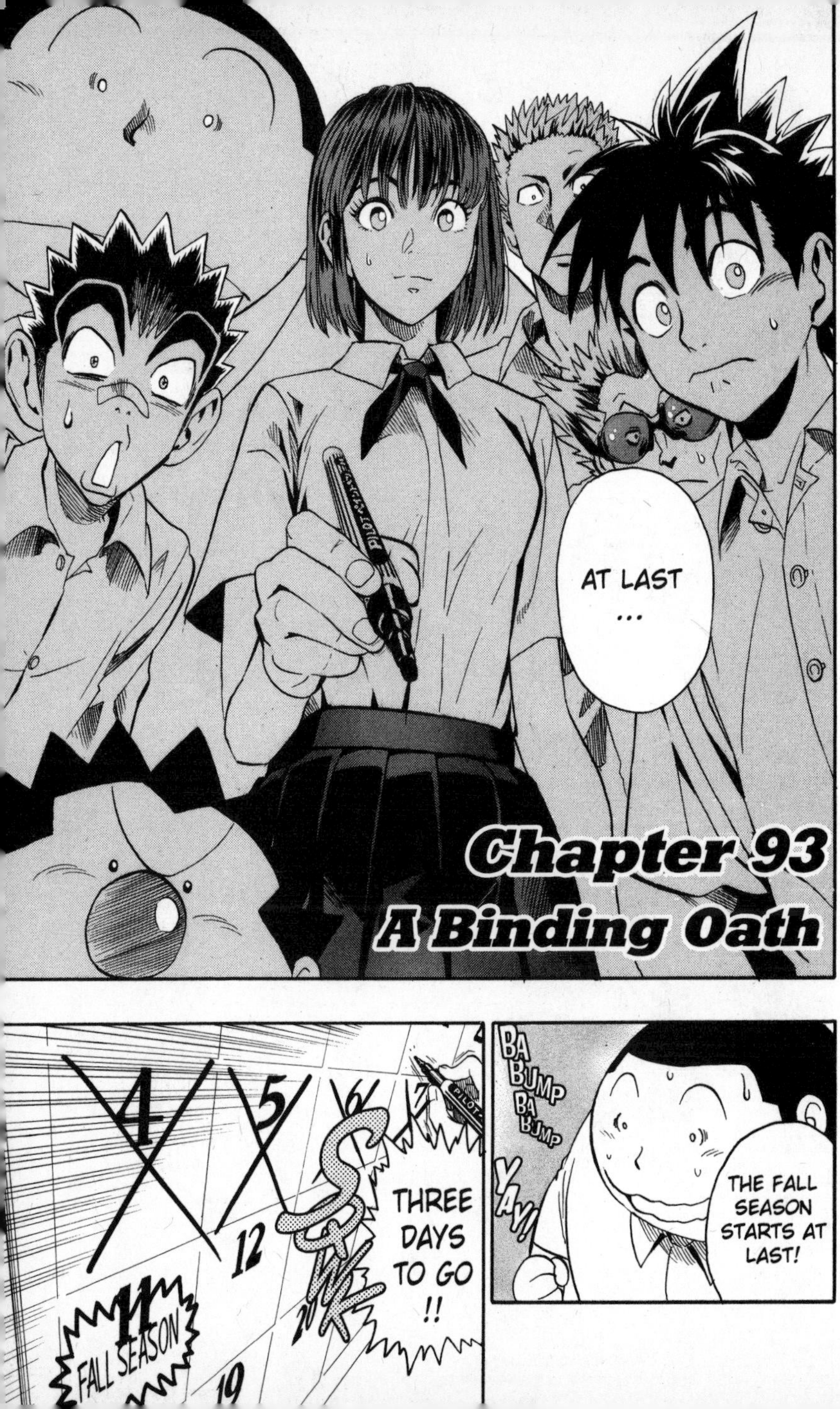
AT LAST ...
BA BUMP BA BUMP
YAY!
THE FALL SEASON STARTS AT LAST!
THREE DAYS TO GO !!
FALL SEASON

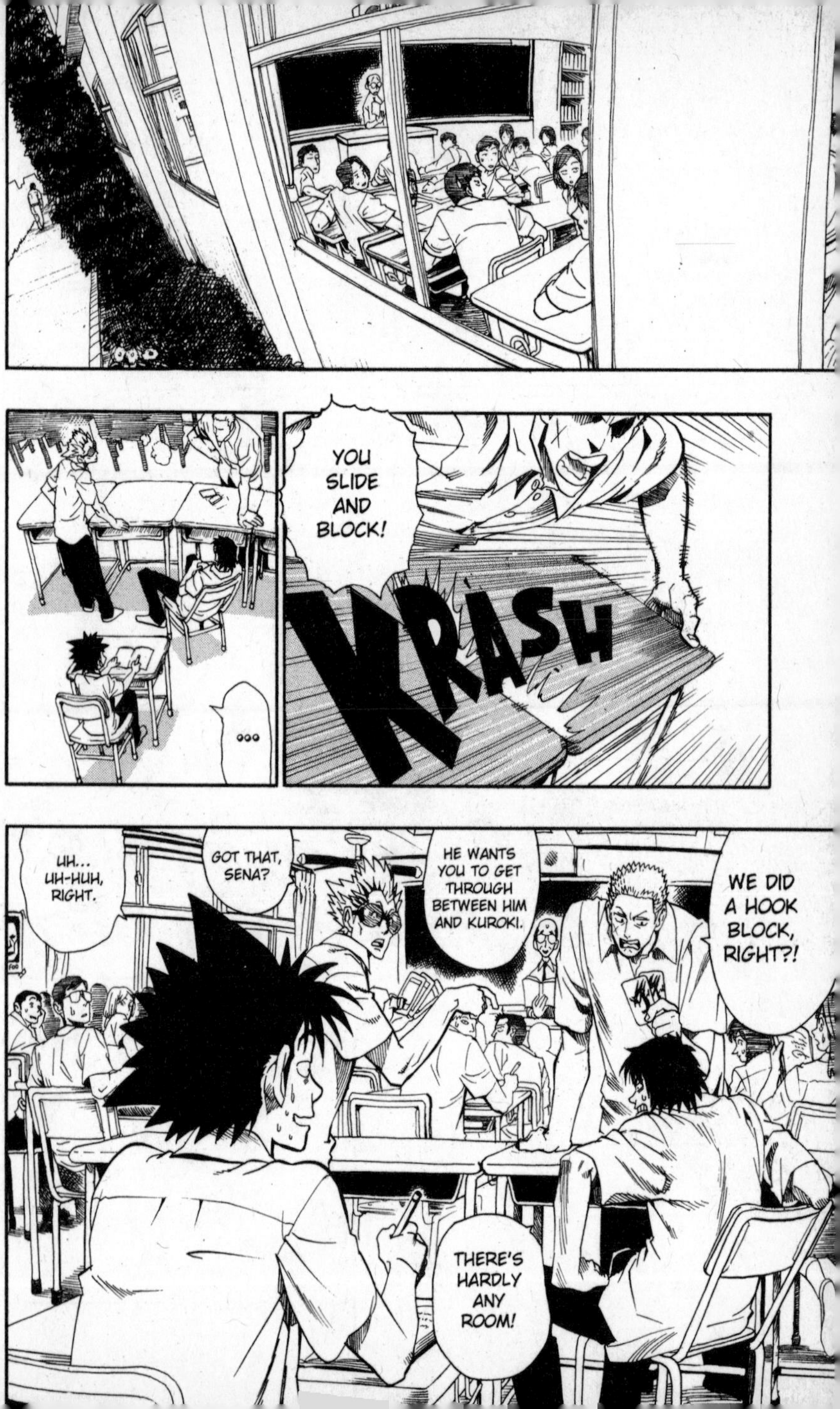

YOU SLIDE AND BLOCK!
KRASH
...
WE DID A HOOK BLOCK, RIGHT?!
HE WANTS YOU TO GET THROUGH BETWEEN HIM AND KUROKI.
GOT THAT, SENA?
UH... UH-HUH, RIGHT.
THERE'S HARDLY ANY ROOM!

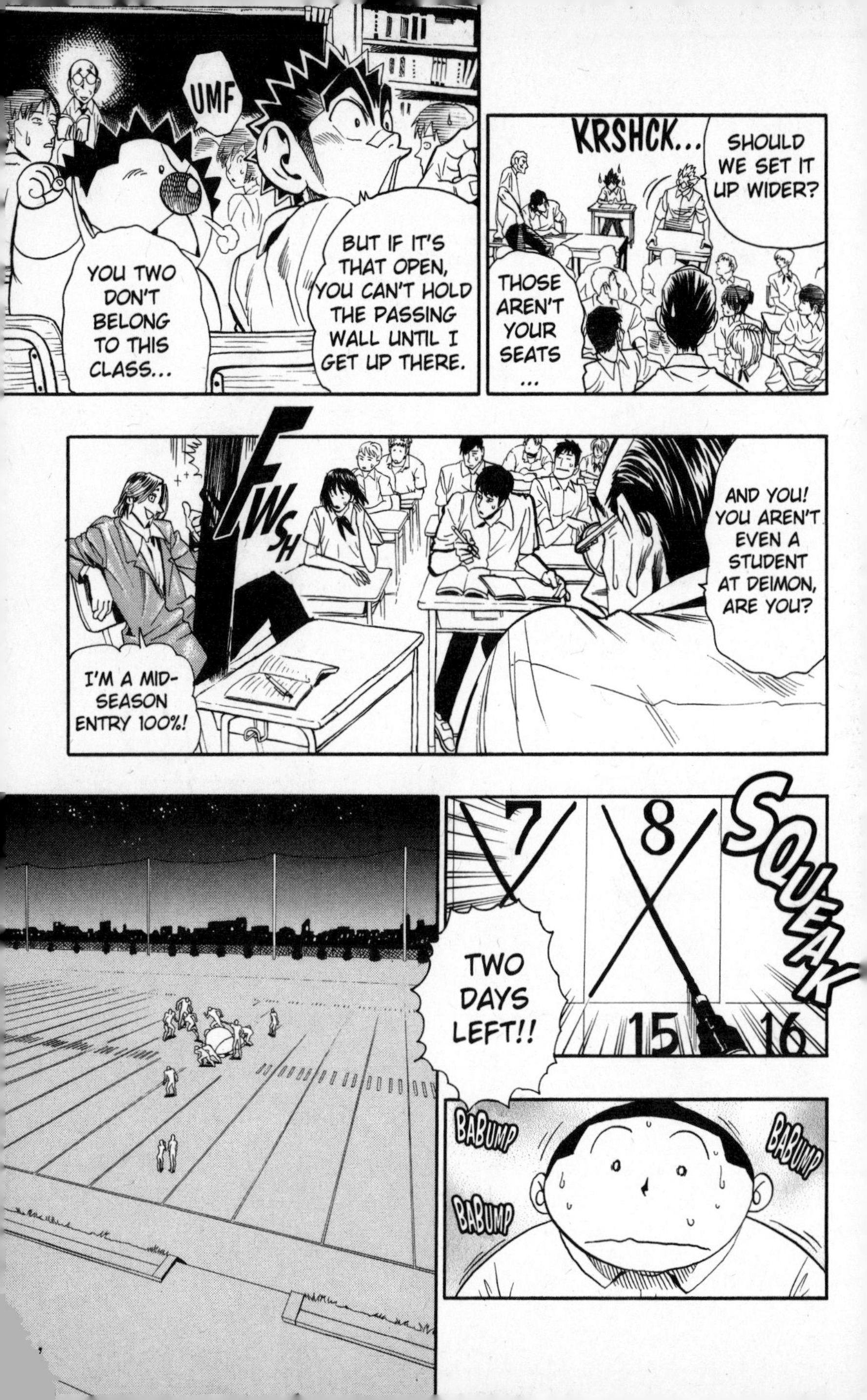
SHOULD WE SET IT UP WIDER?
KRSHCK...
THOSE AREN'T YOUR SEATS...
UMF
BUT IF IT'S THAT OPEN, YOU CAN'T HOLD THE PASSING WALL UNTIL I GET UP THERE.
YOU TWO DON'T BELONG TO THIS CLASS...
AND YOU! YOU AREN'T EVEN A STUDENT AT DEIMON, ARE YOU?
FWSH
I'M A MID-SEASON ENTRY 100%!
SQUEAK
7
8
15
16
TWO DAYS LEFT!!
BABUMP
BABUMP
BABUMP

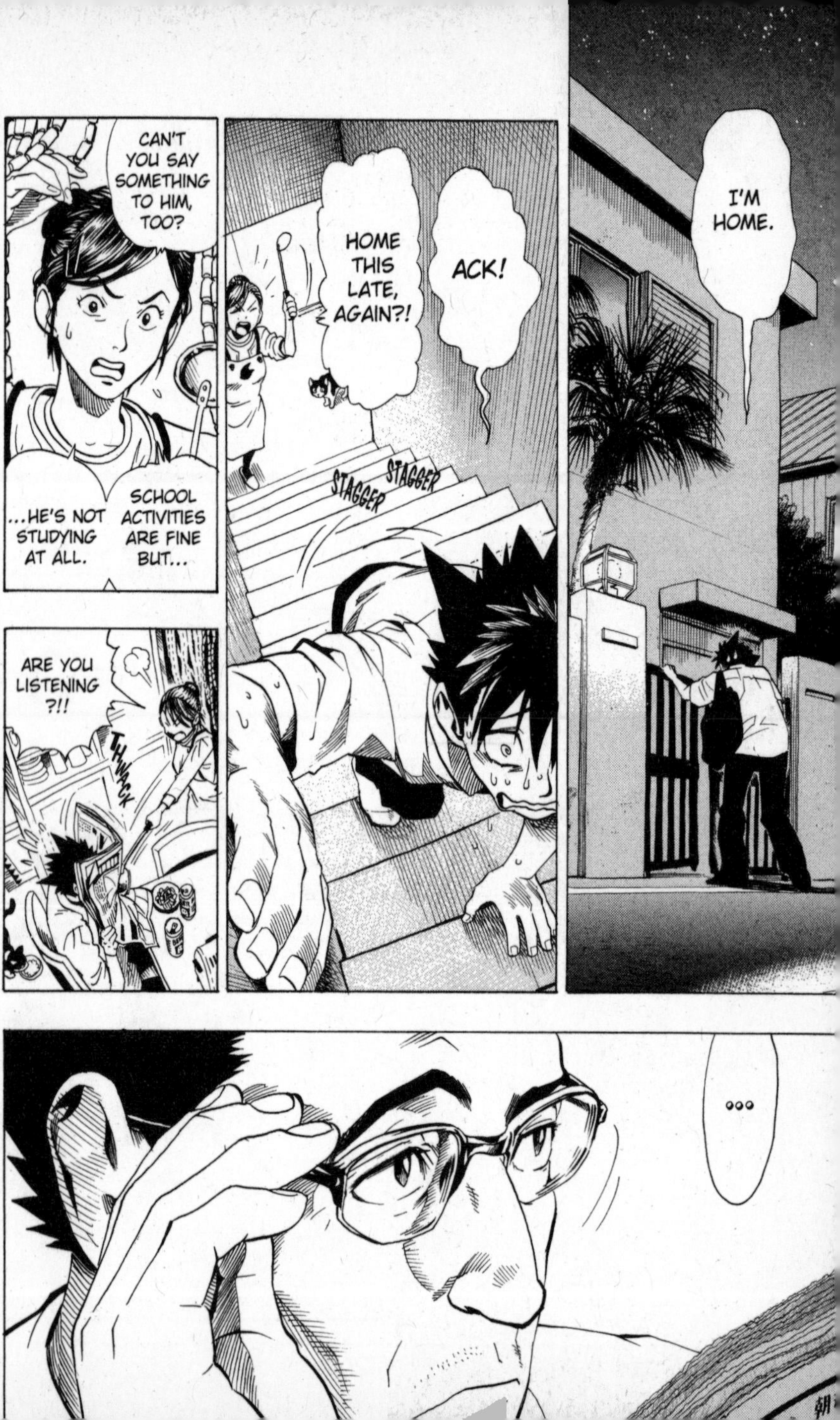

I'M HOME.
ACK!
HOME THIS LATE, AGAIN?!
STAGGER
STAGGER
CAN'T YOU SAY SOMETHING TO HIM, TOO?
SCHOOL ACTIVITIES ARE FINE BUT...
...HE'S NOT STUDYING AT ALL.
ARE YOU LISTENING ?!!
THWACK
...

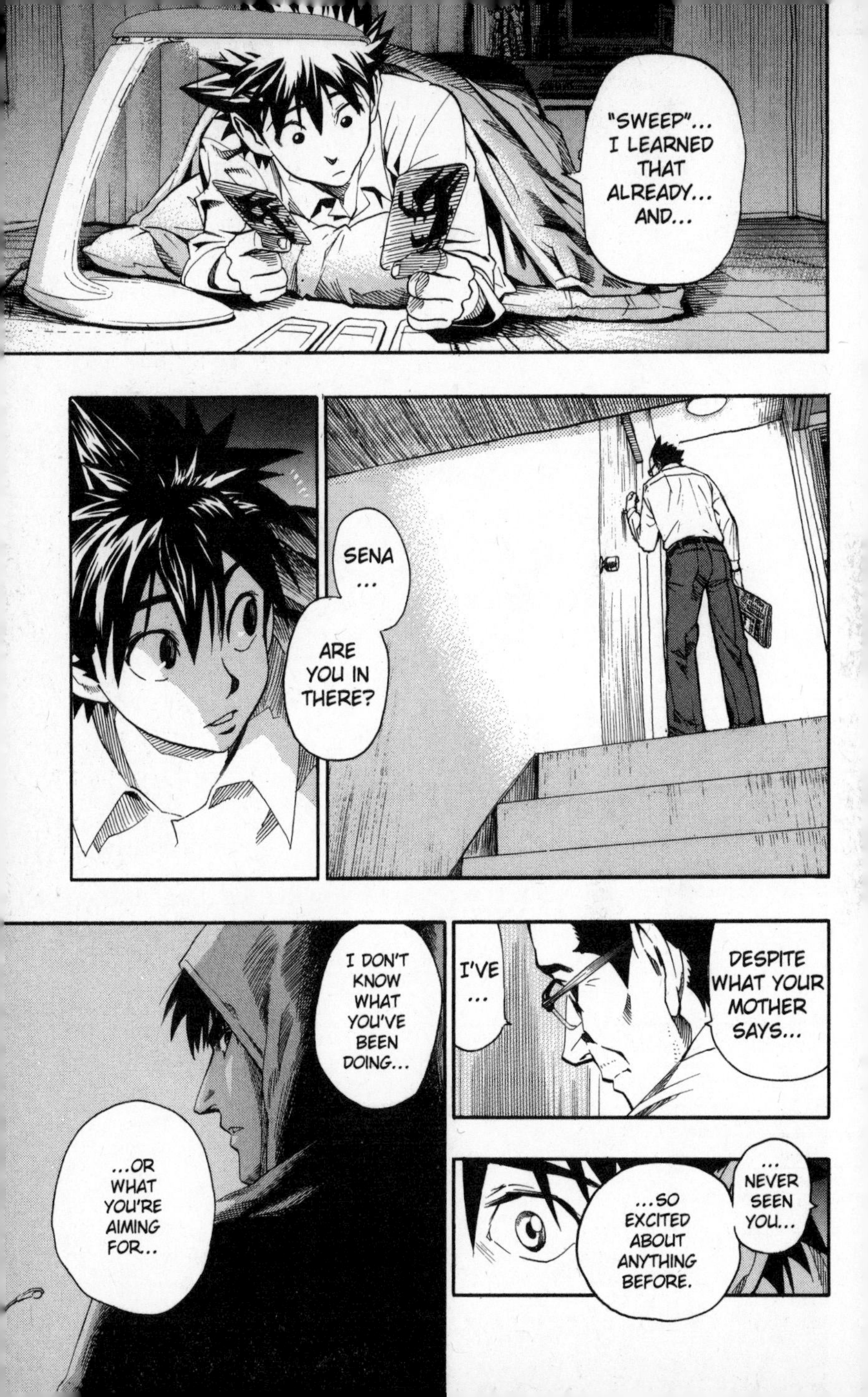
"SWEEP"... I LEARNED THAT ALREADY... AND...
SENA ...
ARE YOU IN THERE?
DESPITE WHAT YOUR MOTHER SAYS...
I'VE ...
... NEVER SEEN YOU...
...SO EXCITED ABOUT ANYTHING BEFORE.
I DON'T KNOW WHAT YOU'VE BEEN DOING...
...OR WHAT YOU'RE AIMING FOR...

...BUT AS YOUR FATHER, I'M BEHIND YOU.

FOLLOW IT THROUGH TO THE END!

...

I WILL.

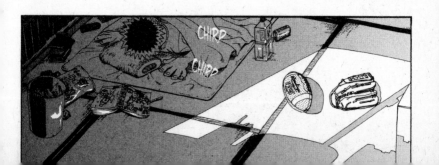

CHIRP

CHIRP

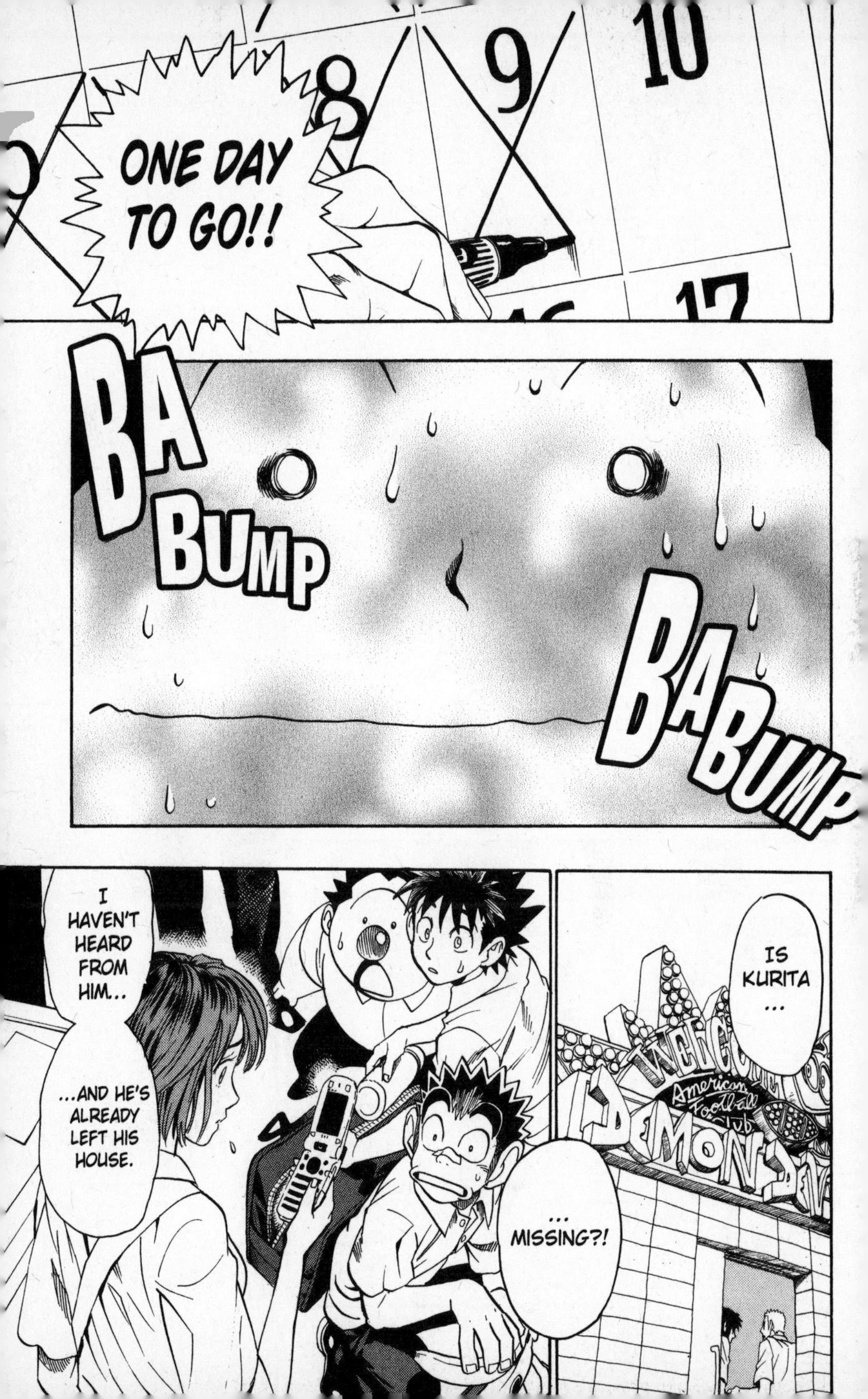
ONE DAY TO GO!!
BA BUMP
BA BUMP
BA BUMP
IS KURITA ...
... MISSING?!
I HAVEN'T HEARD FROM HIM...
...AND HE'S ALREADY LEFT HIS HOUSE.
American Football Club

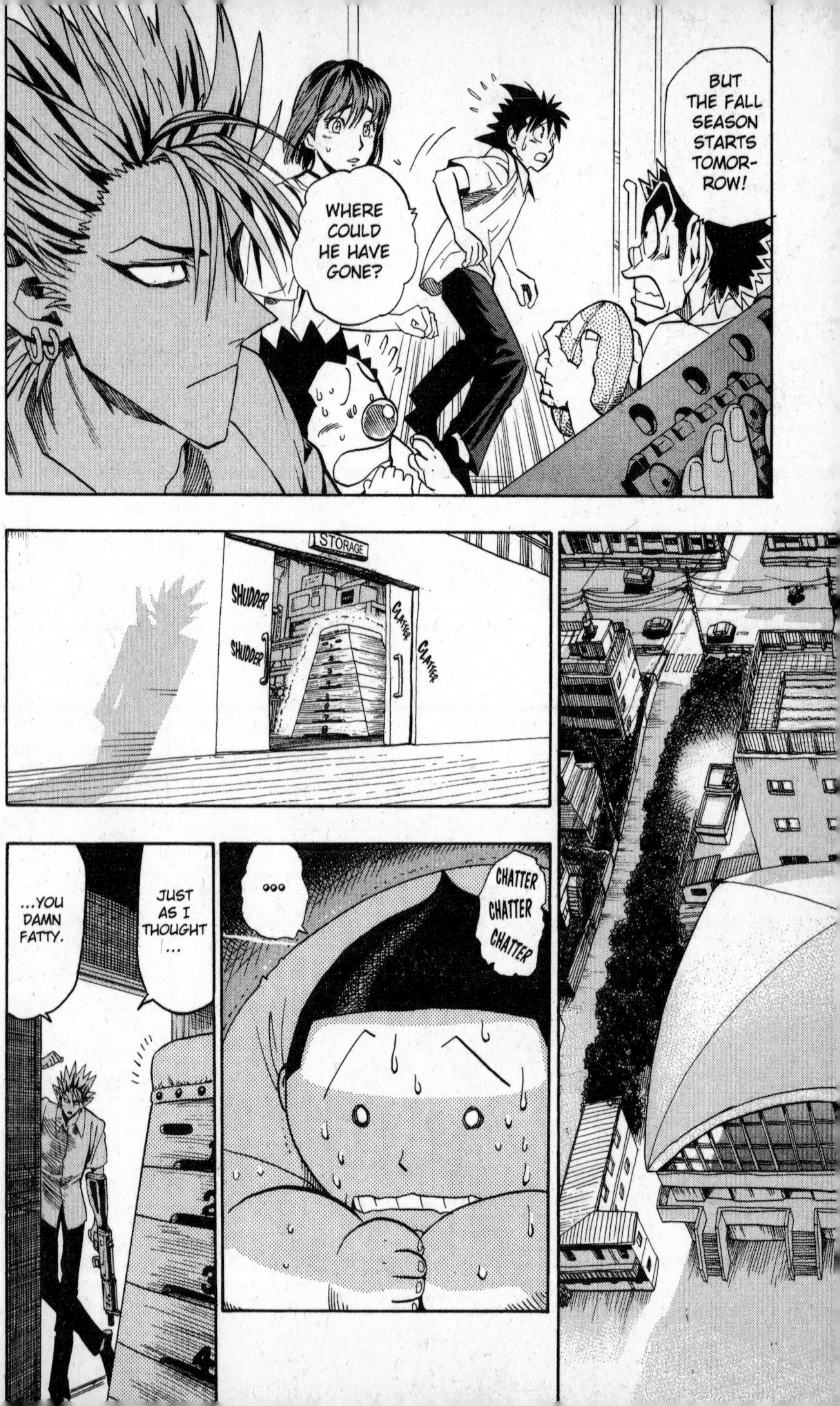
BUT THE FALL SEASON STARTS TOMOR-ROW!
WHERE COULD HE HAVE GONE?
STORAGE
CLATTER
CLATTER
SHUDDER
SHUDDER
CHATTER
CHATTER
CHATTER
...
JUST AS I THOUGHT ...
...YOU DAMN FATTY.

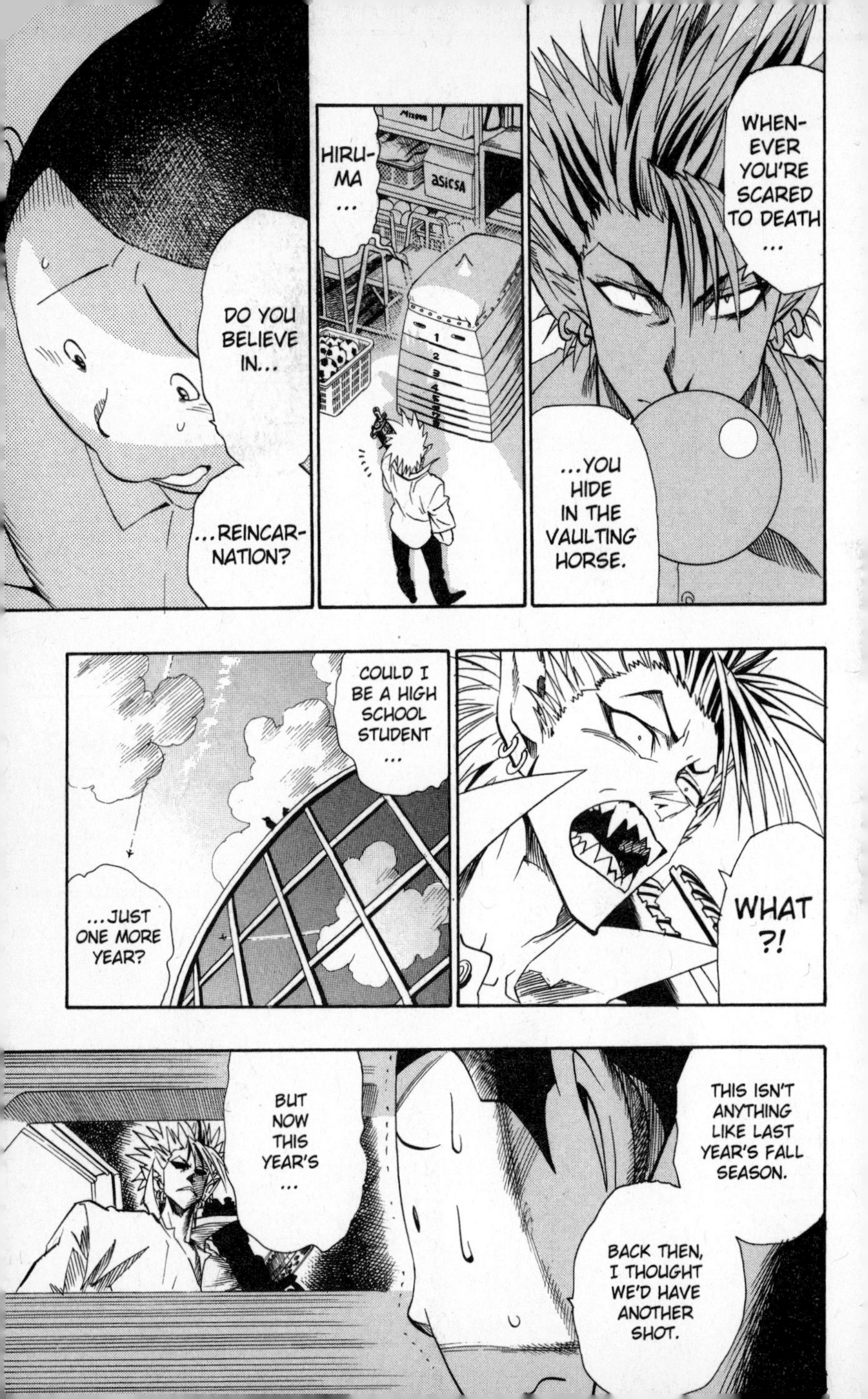
WHEN-EVER YOU'RE SCARED TO DEATH...
...YOU HIDE IN THE VAULTING HORSE.
HIRU-MA...
DO YOU BELIEVE IN...
...REINCAR-NATION?
WHAT?!
COULD I BE A HIGH SCHOOL STUDENT...
...JUST ONE MORE YEAR?
THIS ISN'T ANYTHING LIKE LAST YEAR'S FALL SEASON.
BACK THEN, I THOUGHT WE'D HAVE ANOTHER SHOT.
BUT NOW THIS YEAR'S...

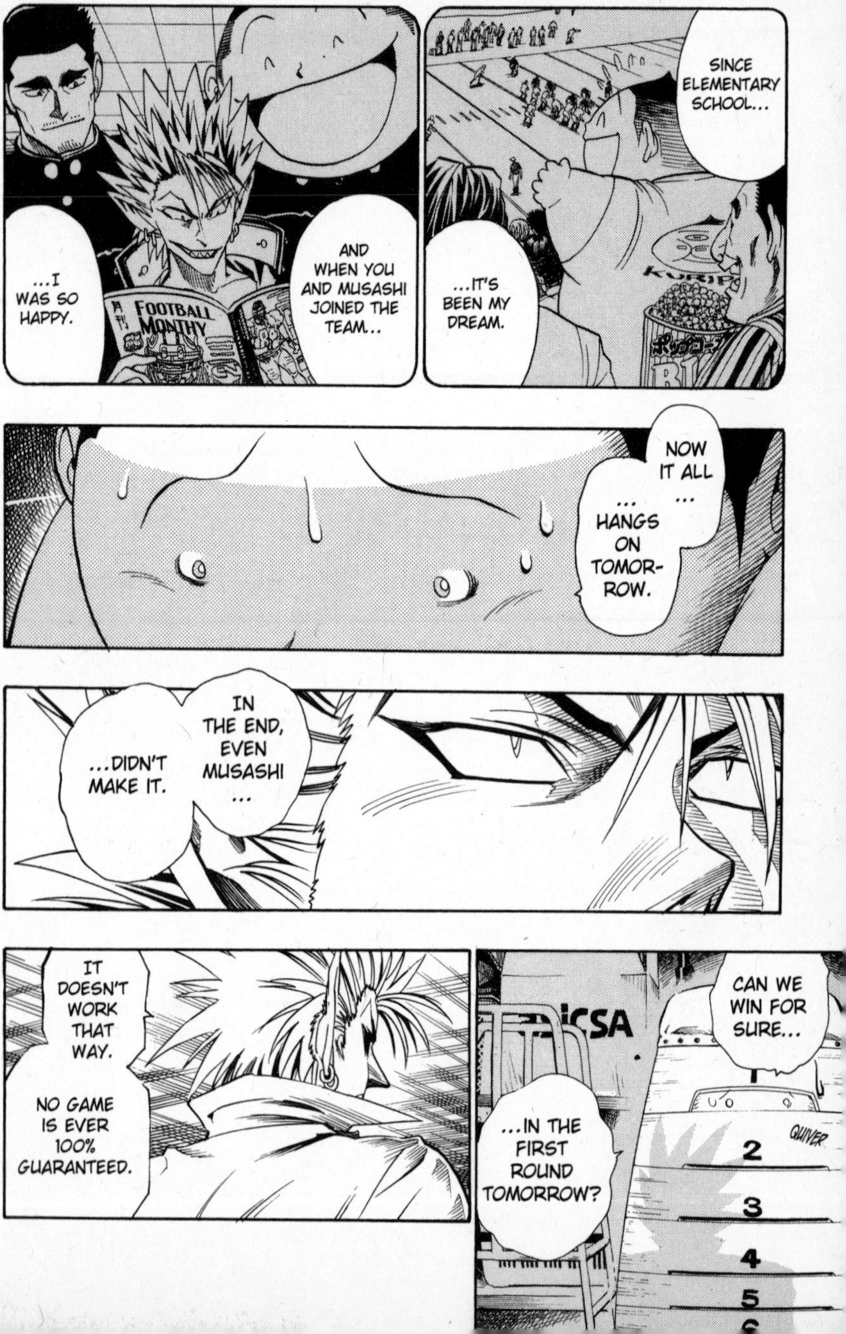
SINCE ELEMENTARY SCHOOL...
...IT'S BEEN MY DREAM.
AND WHEN YOU AND MUSASHI JOINED THE TEAM...
...I WAS SO HAPPY.
FOOTBALL MONTHY
NOW IT ALL ... ... HANGS ON TOMORROW.
IN THE END, EVEN MUSASHI ...
...DIDN'T MAKE IT.
CAN WE WIN FOR SURE...
...IN THE FIRST ROUND TOMORROW?
QUIVER
IT DOESN'T WORK THAT WAY.
NO GAME IS EVER 100% GUARANTEED.

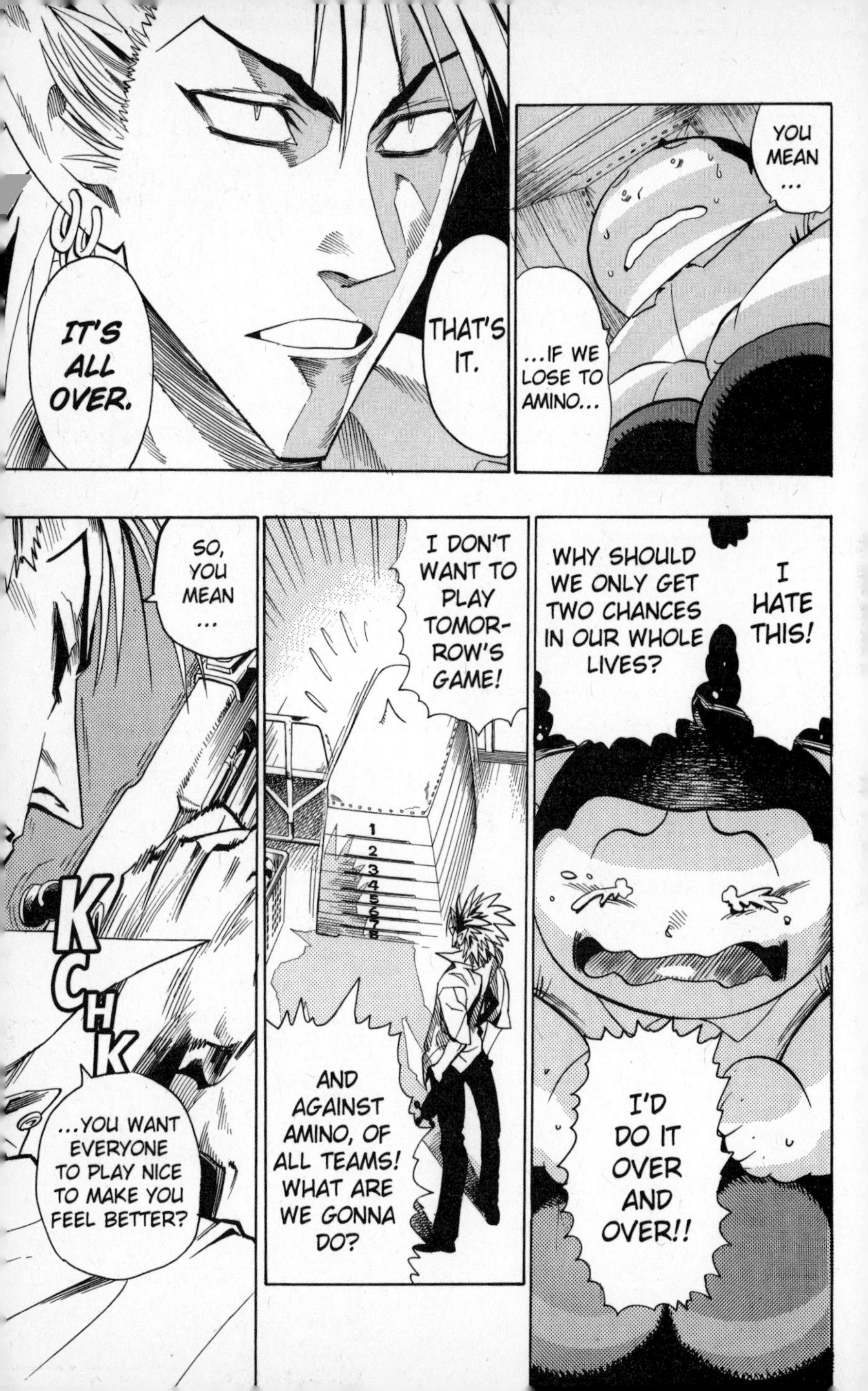
YOU MEAN ...
...IF WE LOSE TO AMINO...
THAT'S IT.
IT'S ALL OVER.
I HATE THIS!
WHY SHOULD WE ONLY GET TWO CHANCES IN OUR WHOLE LIVES?
I'D DO IT OVER AND OVER!!
I DON'T WANT TO PLAY TOMORROW'S GAME!
AND AGAINST AMINO, OF ALL TEAMS! WHAT ARE WE GONNA DO?
SO, YOU MEAN ...
KCHK
...YOU WANT EVERYONE TO PLAY NICE TO MAKE YOU FEEL BETTER?

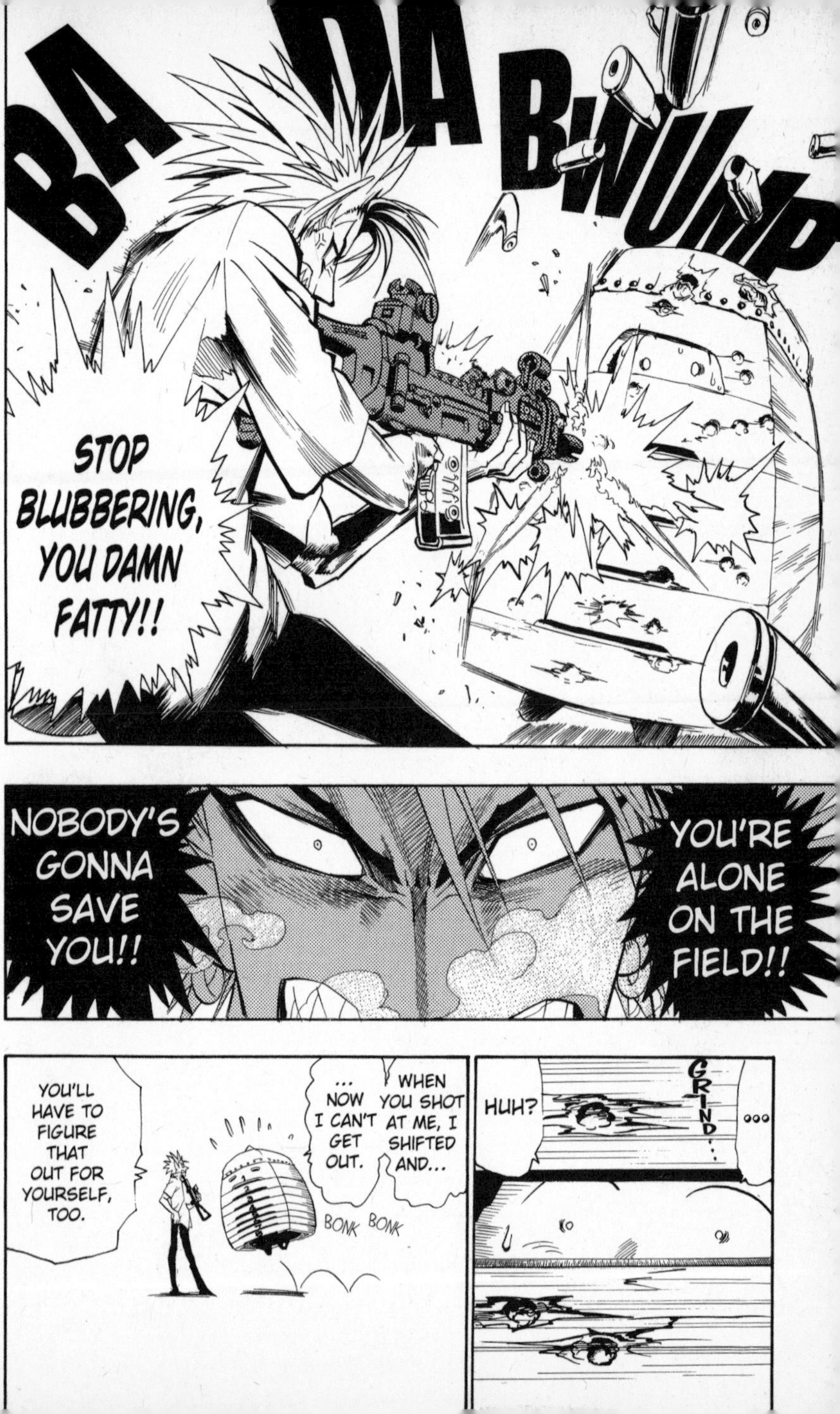
BA DA BWUMP
STOP BLUBBERING, YOU DAMN FATTY!!
YOU'RE ALONE ON THE FIELD!!
NOBODY'S GONNA SAVE YOU!!
GRIND...
...
HUH?
WHEN YOU SHOT AT ME, I SHIFTED AND...
... NOW I CAN'T GET OUT.
BONK BONK
YOU'LL HAVE TO FIGURE THAT OUT FOR YOURSELF, TOO.

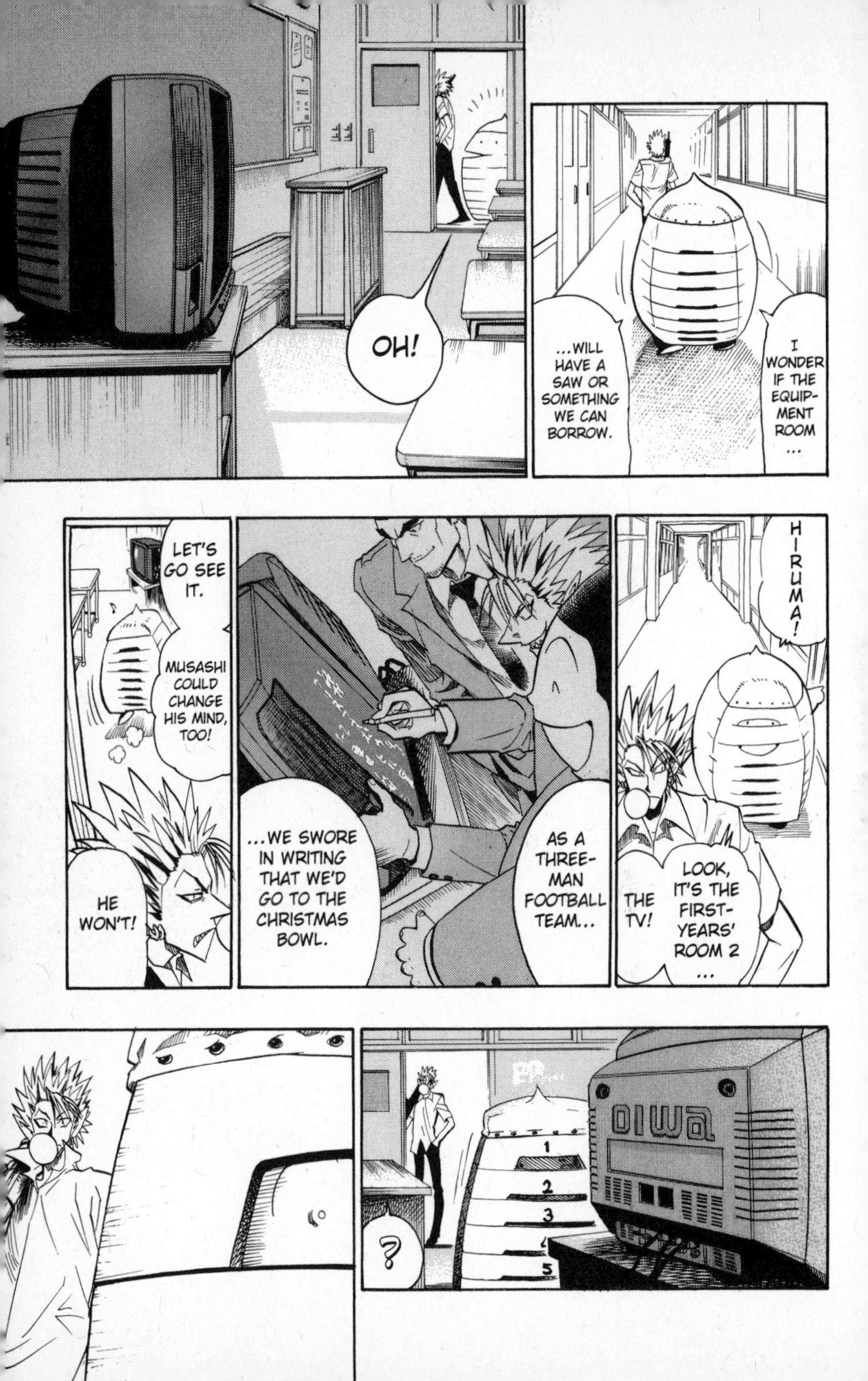
I WONDER IF THE EQUIPMENT ROOM...
...WILL HAVE A SAW OR SOMETHING WE CAN BORROW.
OH!
HIRUMA!
LOOK, IT'S THE FIRST-YEARS' ROOM 2...
THE TV!
AS A THREE-MAN FOOTBALL TEAM...
...WE SWORE IN WRITING THAT WE'D GO TO THE CHRISTMAS BOWL.
LET'S GO SEE IT.
MUSASHI COULD CHANGE HIS MIND, TOO!
HE WON'T!
oiwa
?

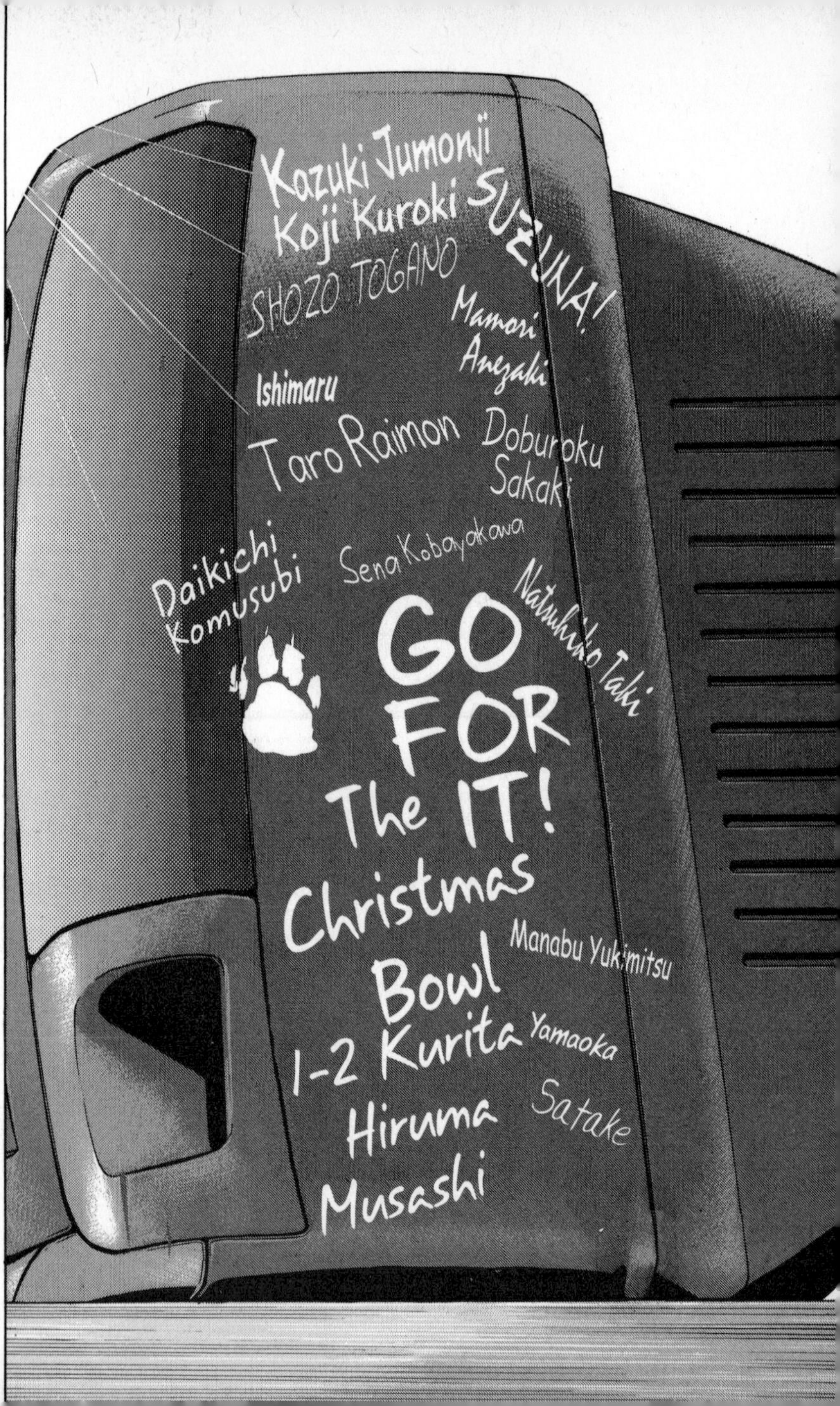
Kazuki Jumonji
Koji Kuroki
SUZUNA!
SHOZO TOGANO
Mamori Anezaki
Ishimaru
Taro Raimon
Doburoku Sakaki
Daikichi Komusubi
Sena Kobayakawa
Natsuhiko Taki
GO FOR The IT! Christmas Bowl
Manabu Yukimitsu
1-2 Kurita
Yamaoka
Hiruma
Satake
Musashi

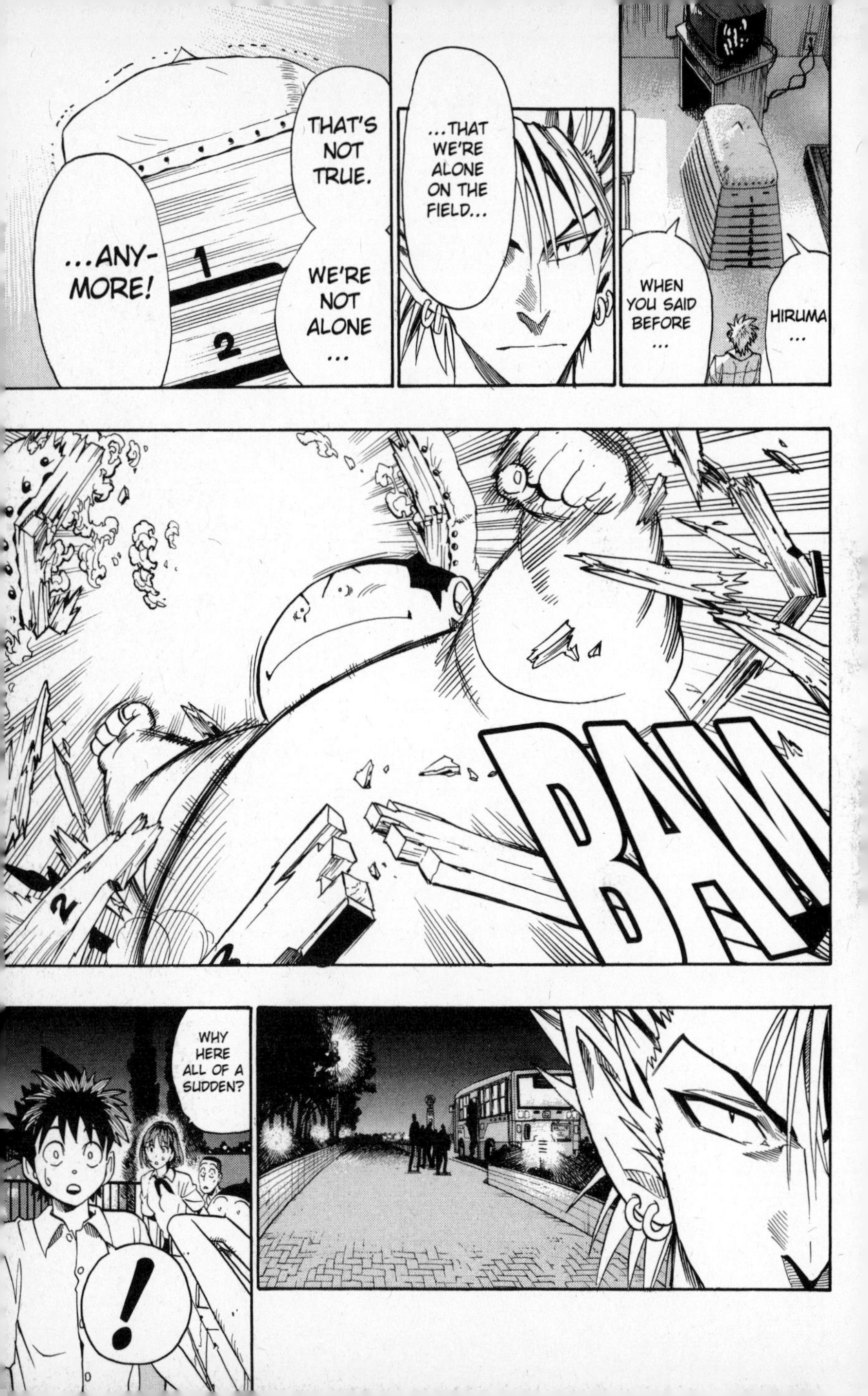
HIRUMA ...
WHEN YOU SAID BEFORE ...
...THAT WE'RE ALONE ON THE FIELD...
THAT'S NOT TRUE.
WE'RE NOT ALONE ...
...ANY-MORE!
BAM
WHY HERE ALL OF A SUDDEN?
!

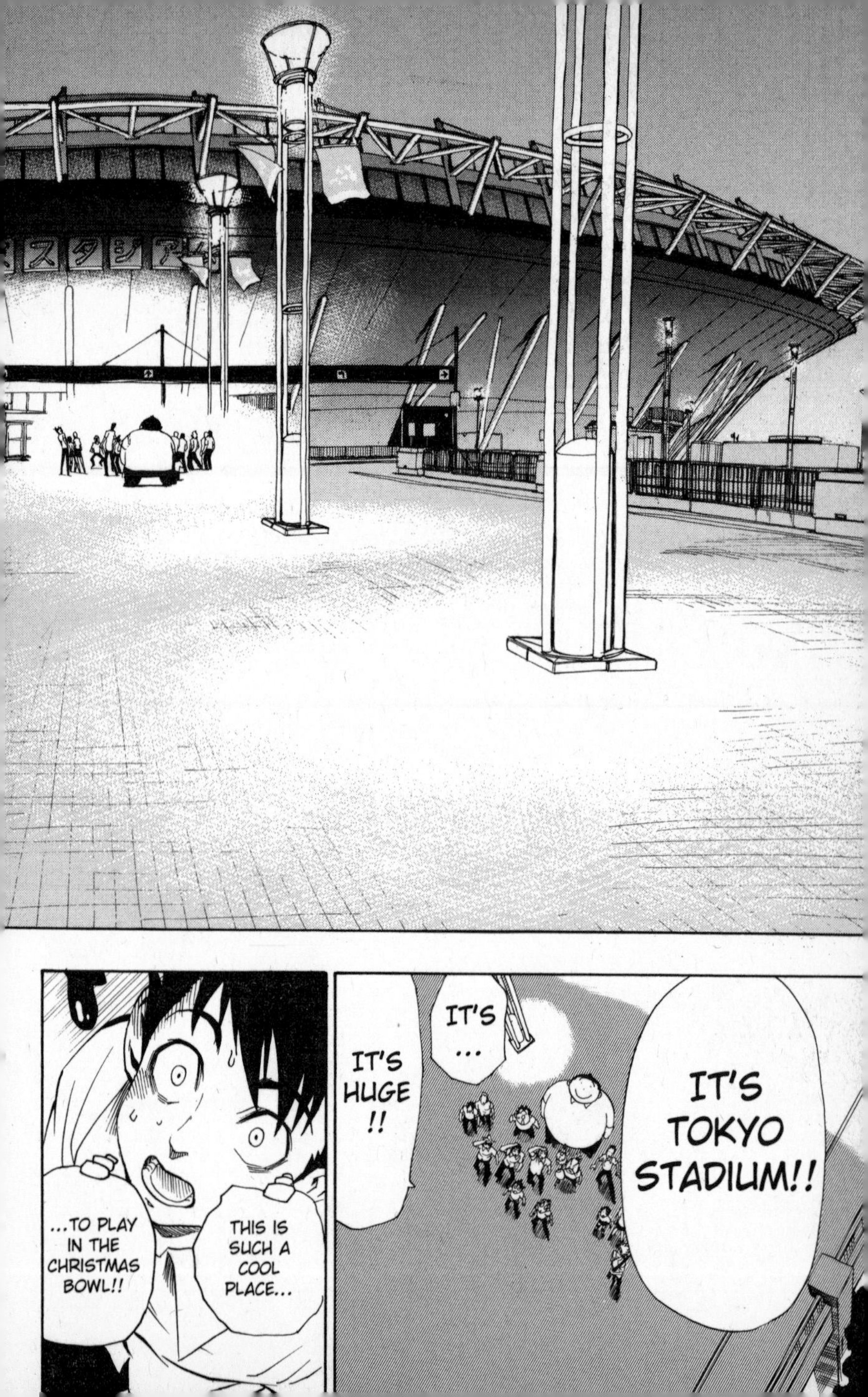
IT'S TOKYO STADIUM!!
IT'S ...
IT'S HUGE !!
THIS IS SUCH A COOL PLACE...
...TO PLAY IN THE CHRISTMAS BOWL!!

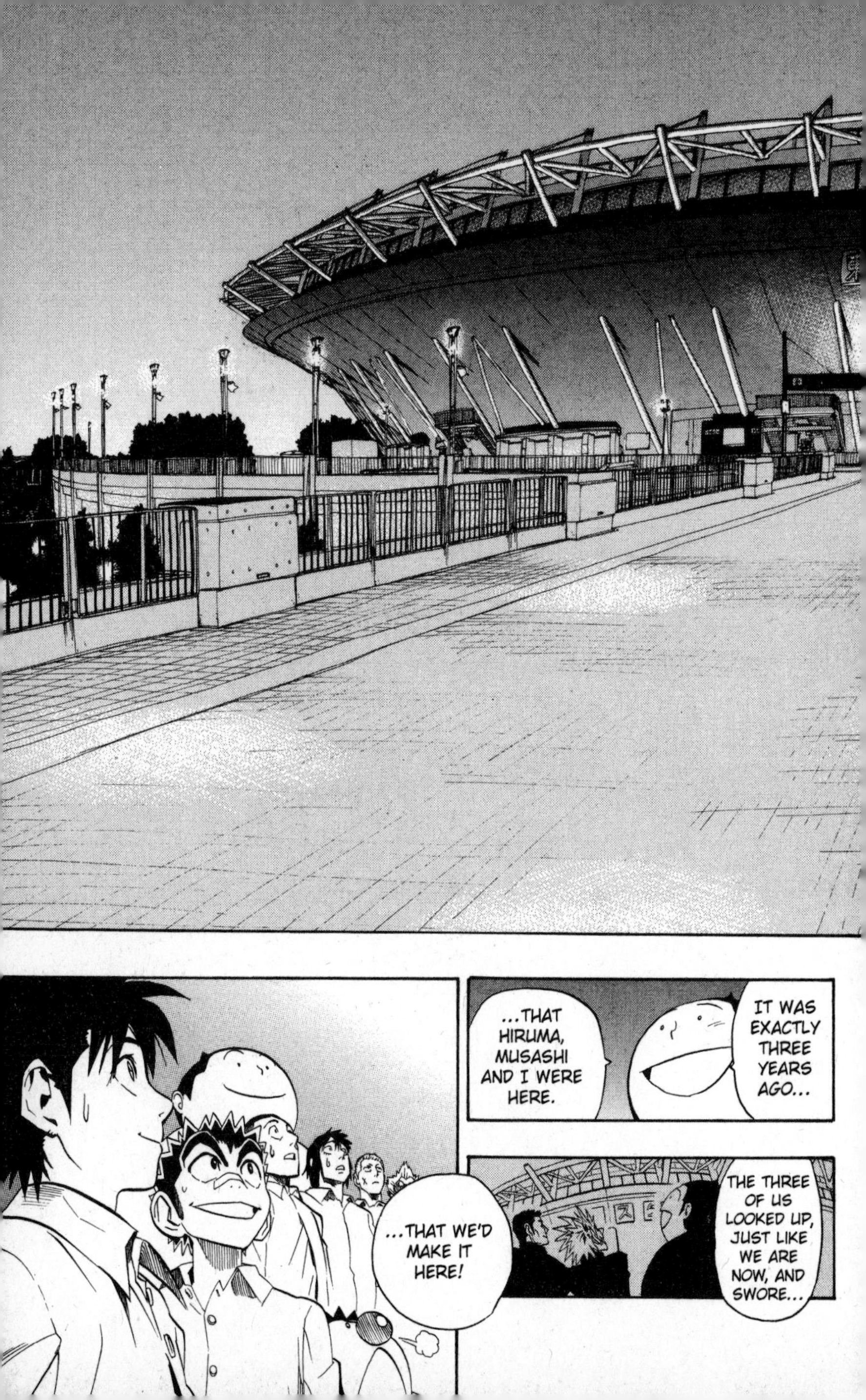
IT WAS EXACTLY THREE YEARS AGO...
...THAT HIRUMA, MUSASHI AND I WERE HERE.
THE THREE OF US LOOKED UP, JUST LIKE WE ARE NOW, AND SWORE...
...THAT WE'D MAKE IT HERE!

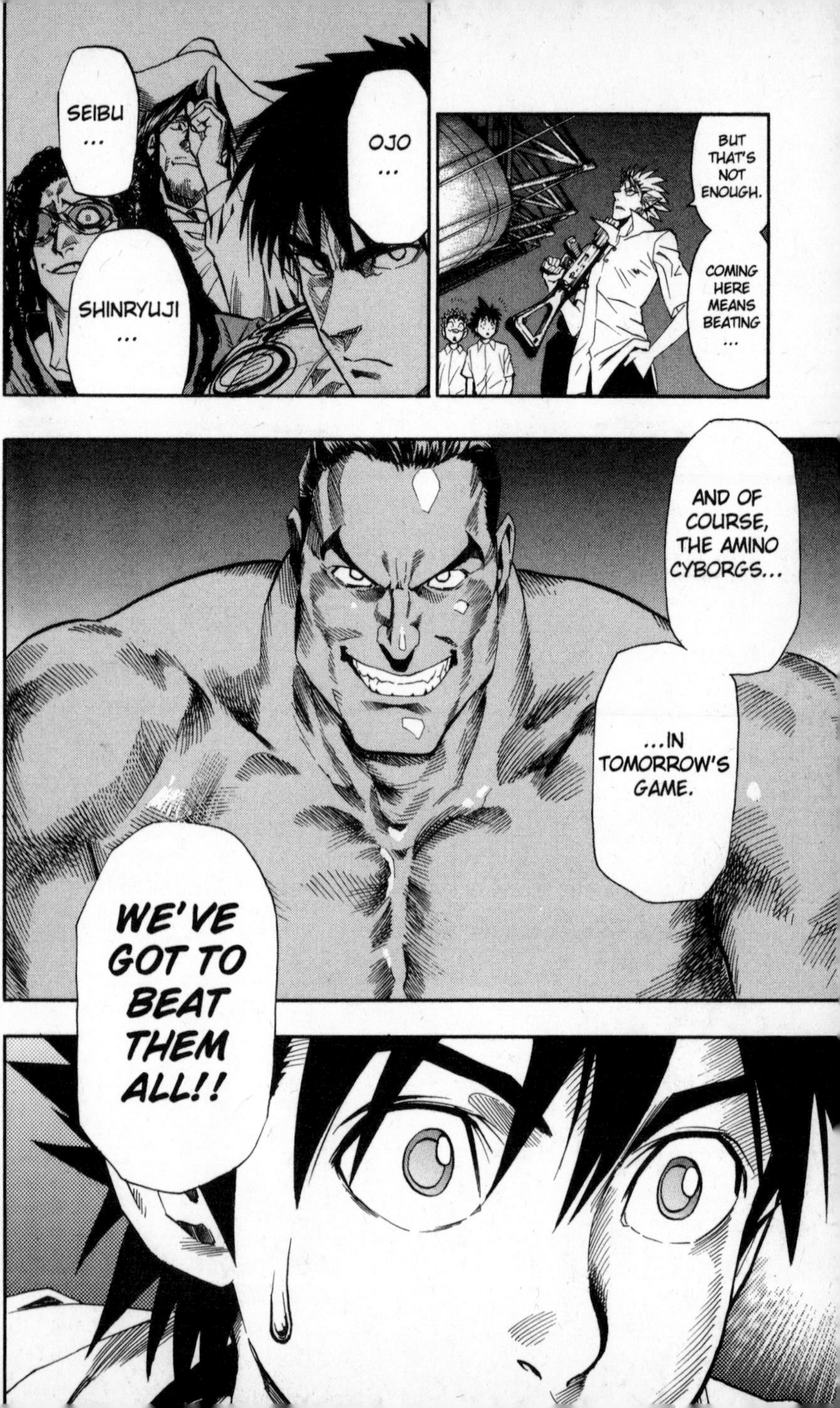
BUT THAT'S NOT ENOUGH.
COMING HERE MEANS BEATING ...
OJO ...
SEIBU ...
SHINRYUJI ...
AND OF COURSE, THE AMINO CYBORGS...
...IN TOMORROW'S GAME.
WE'VE GOT TO BEAT THEM ALL!!

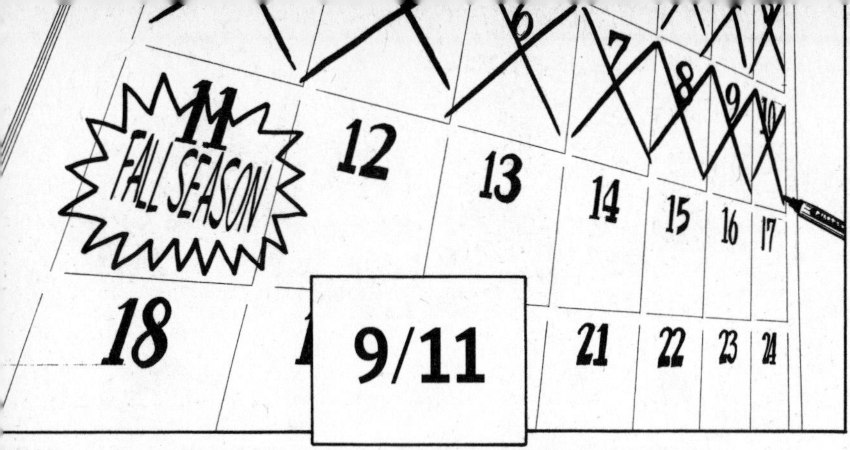
11
FALL SEASON
12
13
14
15
16
17
18
21
22
23
24
9/11
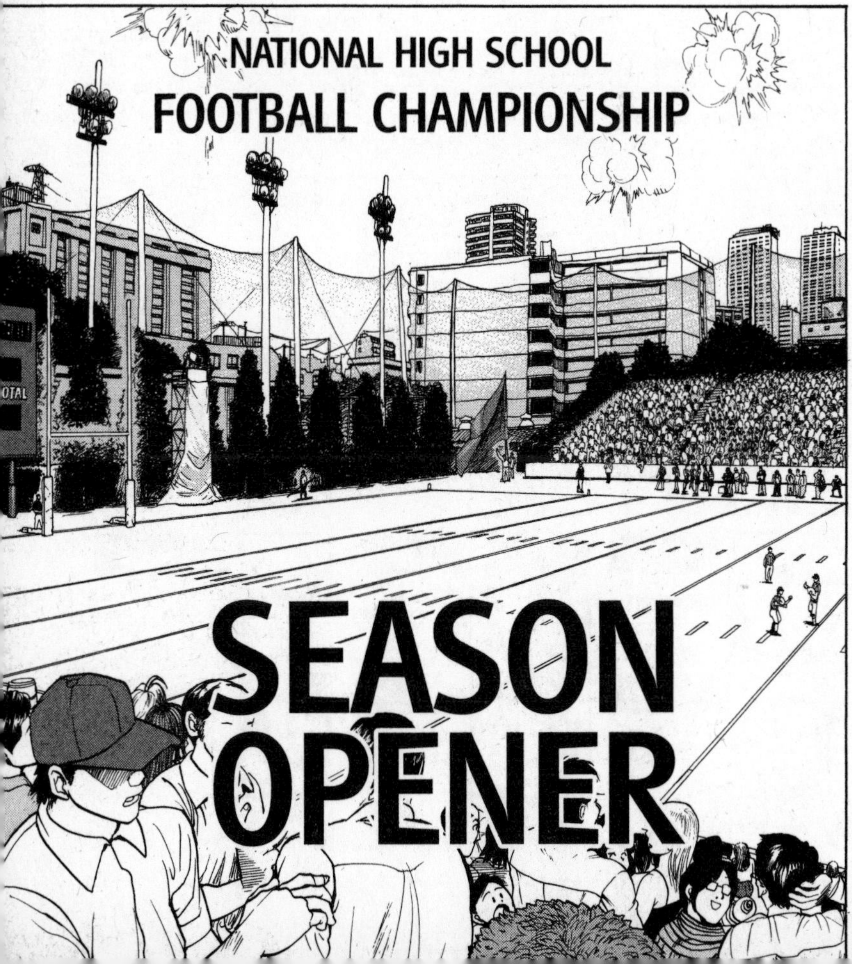
NATIONAL HIGH SCHOOL FOOTBALL CHAMPIONSHIP
SEASON OPENER

Devil Bat 021

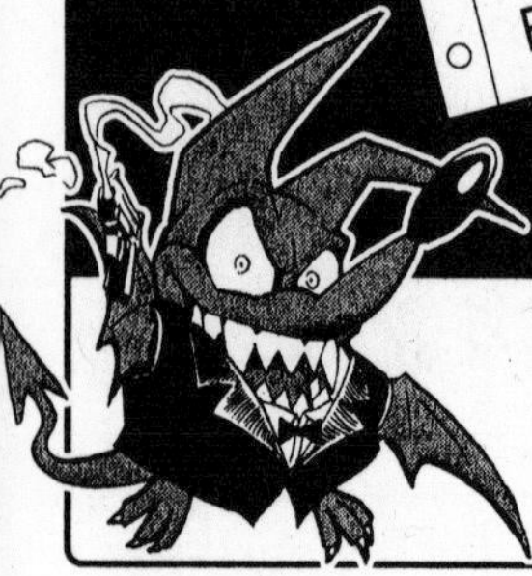

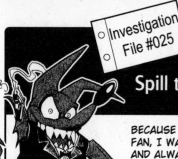

Investigation File #025

Spill the manager's secrets!

BECAUSE I'M A HUGE DEVIL BATS FAN, I WANT TO BECOME MANAGER AND ALWAYS HAVE PROVISIONS ON HAND. TELL ME WHAT TO BRING TO MAKE EVERYONE HAPPY!

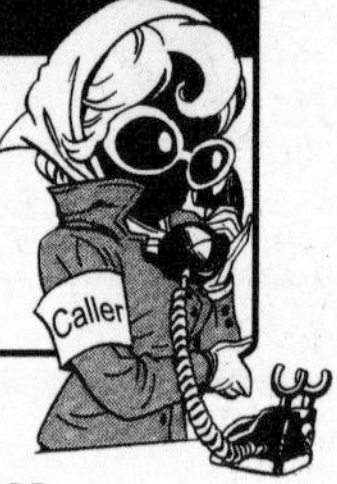
Caller

No name given

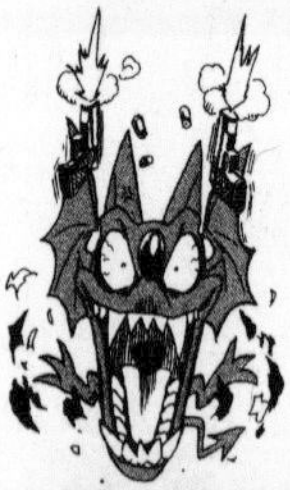

HERE'S ANOTHER ONE WHO WANTS ALL KINDS OF INFORMATION! IF THE LIST FOR OJO'S PLAYERS WASN'T BAD ENOUGH, THIS VOLUME SEEMS TO CALL FOR A WHOLE LOT OF RESEARCH, DAMN IT!

Provisions That Would Keep Them Happy (At a Glance)

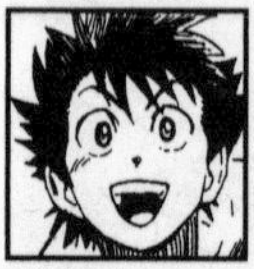	Sena	Tape for preventing injuries
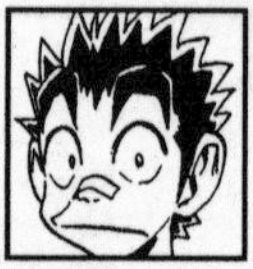	Monta	Bananas
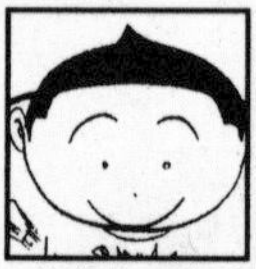	Kurita	If it's food, he'll eat it.
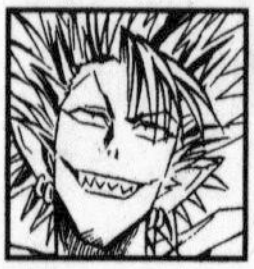	Hiruma	Slaves
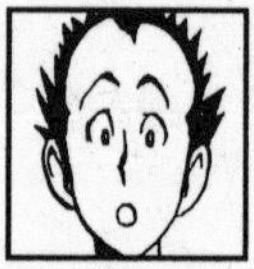	Yukimitsu	Sports drinks
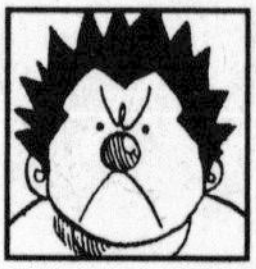	Komusubi	Rice balls
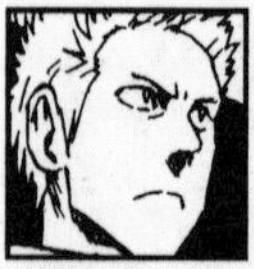	Jumonji	Lemon slices in honey
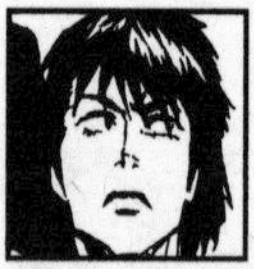	Kuroki	Break time
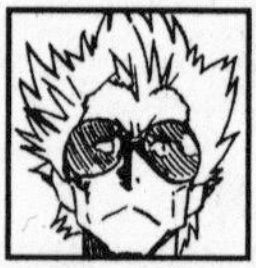	Togano	Manga
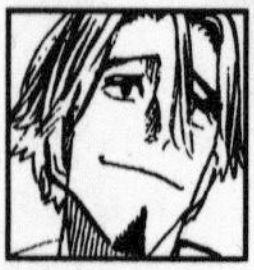	Taki	Applause
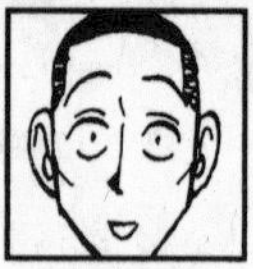	Ishimaru	Good feelings
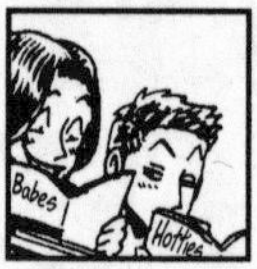 Babes Hotties	Satake & Yamaoka	Underpants

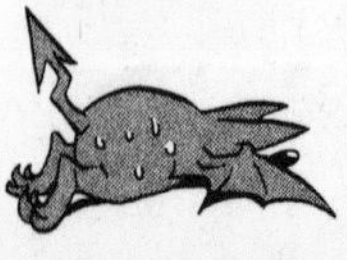

HUF HUF, I'M TIRED...
I WON'T COLLECT ANY MORE DATA, DAMN YOU!

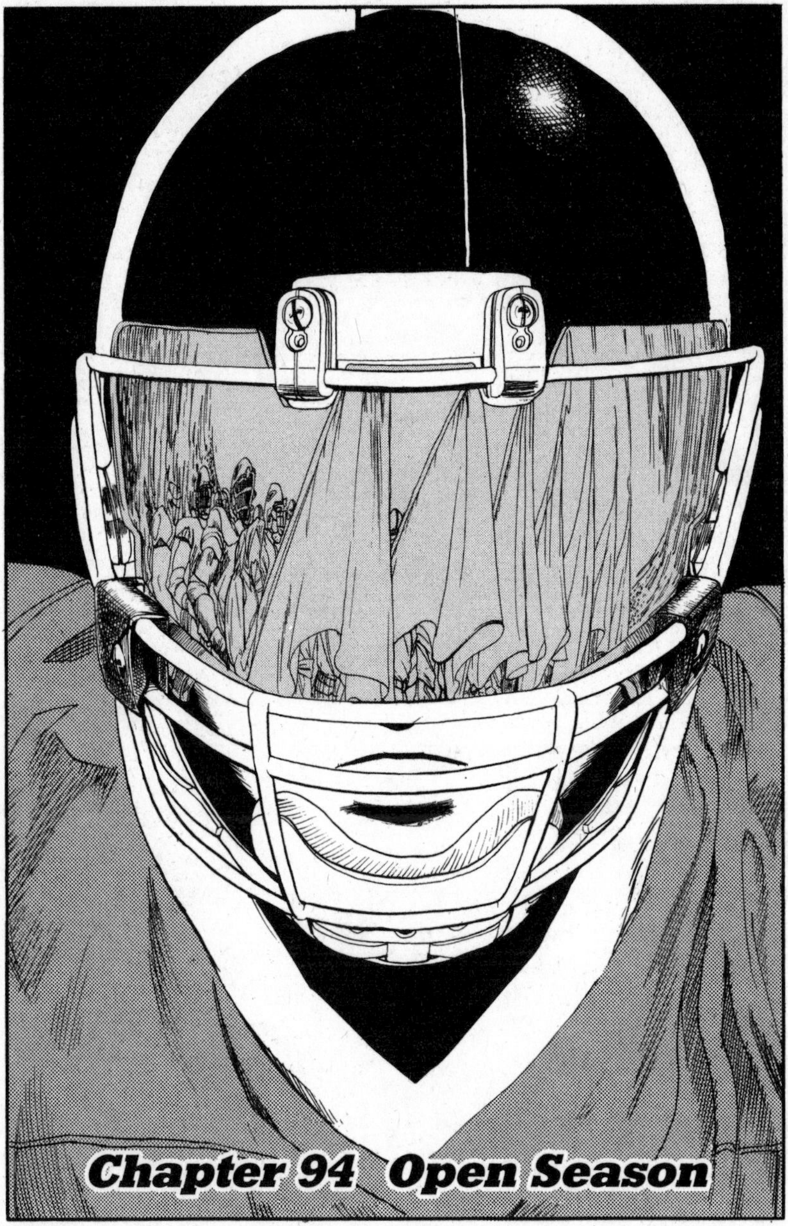

Chapter 94 Open Season

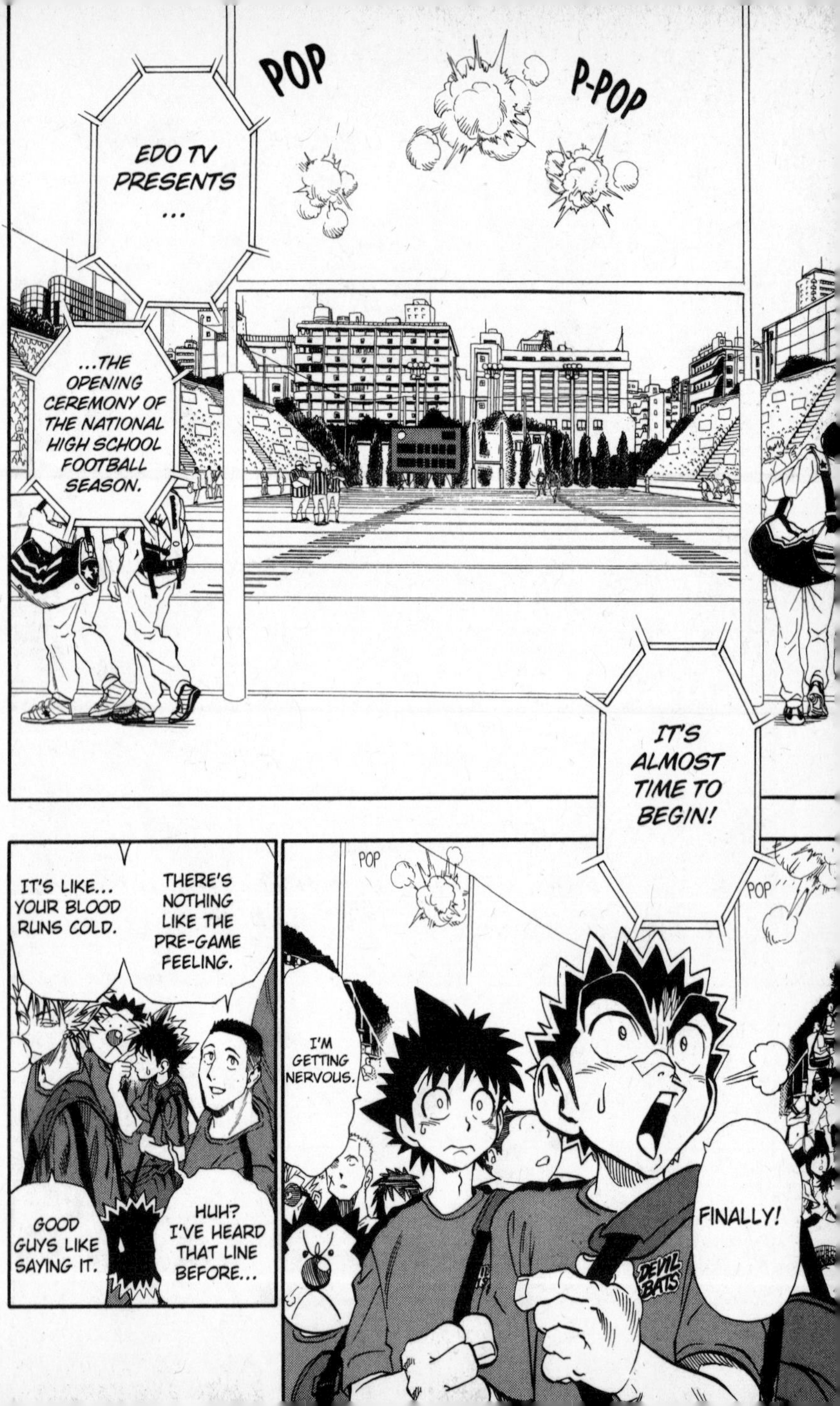
P-POP
POP
EDO TV PRESENTS ...
...THE OPENING CEREMONY OF THE NATIONAL HIGH SCHOOL FOOTBALL SEASON.
IT'S ALMOST TIME TO BEGIN!
POP
POP
FINALLY!
I'M GETTING NERVOUS.
THERE'S NOTHING LIKE THE PRE-GAME FEELING.
IT'S LIKE... YOUR BLOOD RUNS COLD.
HUH? I'VE HEARD THAT LINE BEFORE...
GOOD GUYS LIKE SAYING IT.

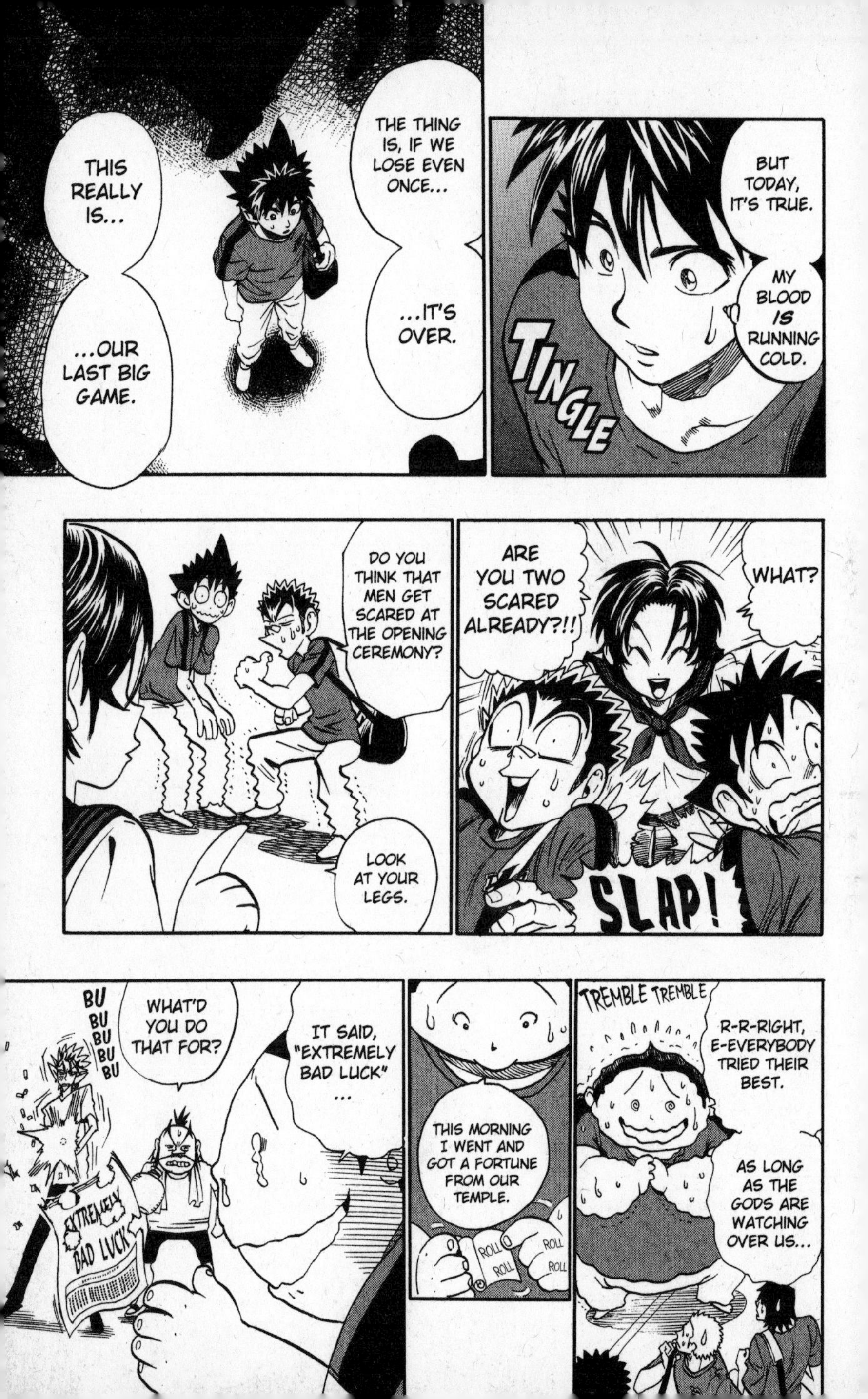
BUT TODAY, IT'S TRUE.
MY BLOOD IS RUNNING COLD.
TINGLE
THE THING IS, IF WE LOSE EVEN ONCE...
...IT'S OVER.
THIS REALLY IS...
...OUR LAST BIG GAME.
WHAT?
ARE YOU TWO SCARED ALREADY?!!
SLAP!
DO YOU THINK THAT MEN GET SCARED AT THE OPENING CEREMONY?
LOOK AT YOUR LEGS.
TREMBLE TREMBLE
R-R-RIGHT, E-EVERYBODY TRIED THEIR BEST.
AS LONG AS THE GODS ARE WATCHING OVER US...
THIS MORNING I WENT AND GOT A FORTUNE FROM OUR TEMPLE.
ROLL ROLL ROLL ROLL
IT SAID, "EXTREMELY BAD LUCK"...
WHAT'D YOU DO THAT FOR?
BU BU BU BU BU
EXTREMELY BAD LUCK

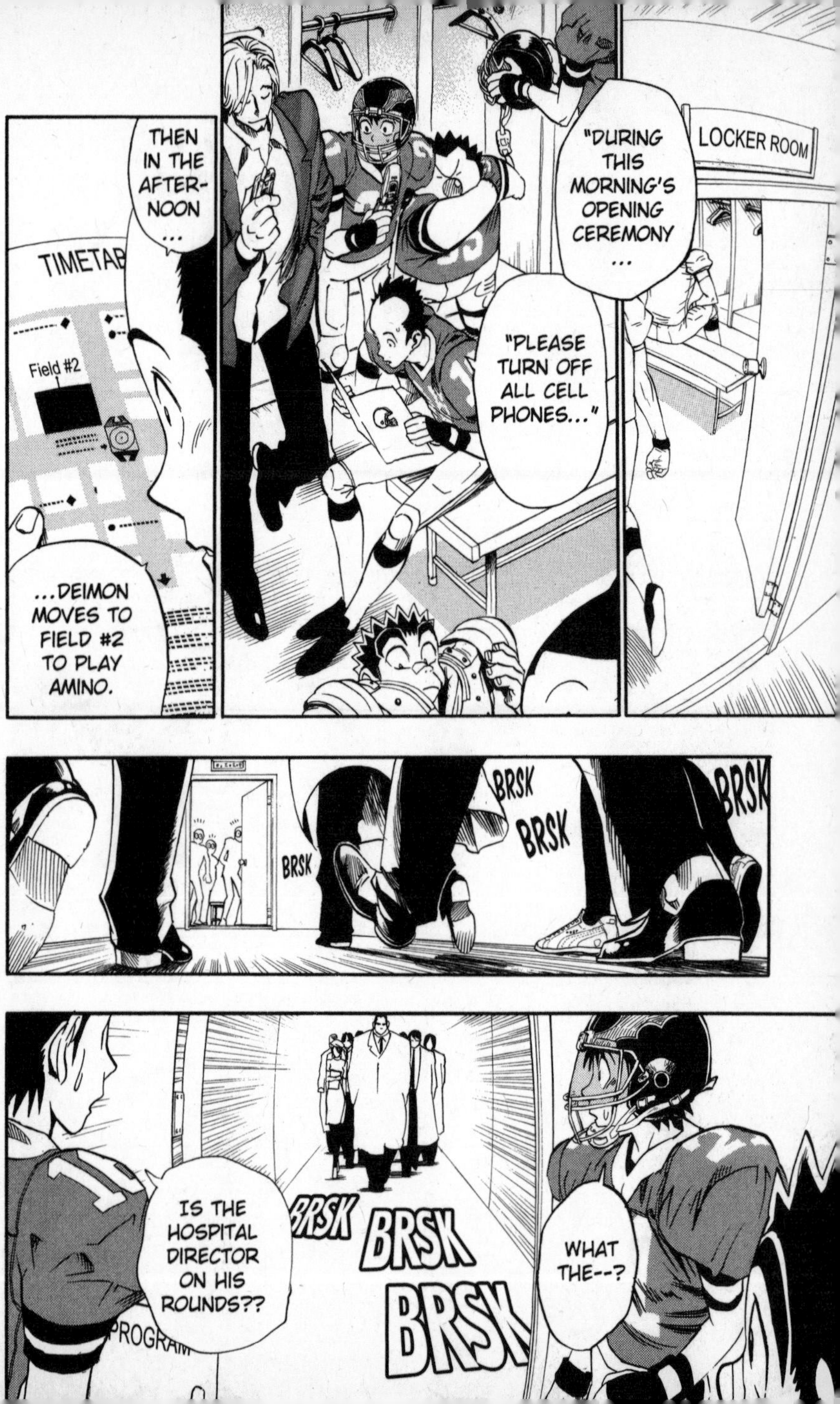
LOCKER ROOM
"DURING THIS MORNING'S OPENING CEREMONY ...
"PLEASE TURN OFF ALL CELL PHONES..."
THEN IN THE AFTERNOON ...
TIMETAB
Field #2
...DEIMON MOVES TO FIELD #2 TO PLAY AMINO.
BRSK
BRSK
BRSK
BRSK
WHAT THE--?
BRSK
BRSK
BRSK
IS THE HOSPITAL DIRECTOR ON HIS ROUNDS??
PROGRAM

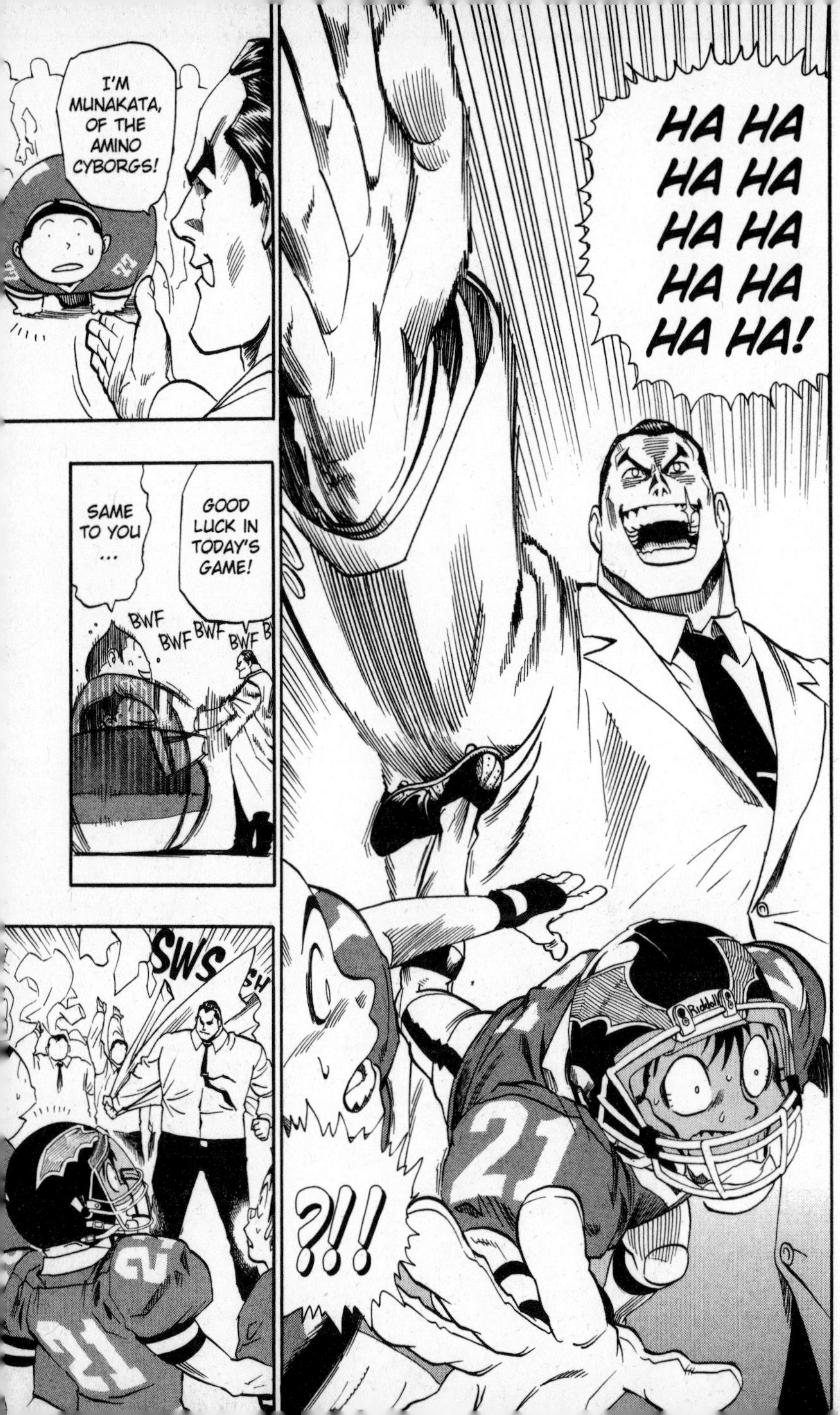
HA HA HA HA HA HA HA HA HA HA!
?!!
I'M MUNAKATA, OF THE AMINO CYBORGS!
GOOD LUCK IN TODAY'S GAME!
SAME TO YOU ...
BWF BWF BWF BWF
SWS

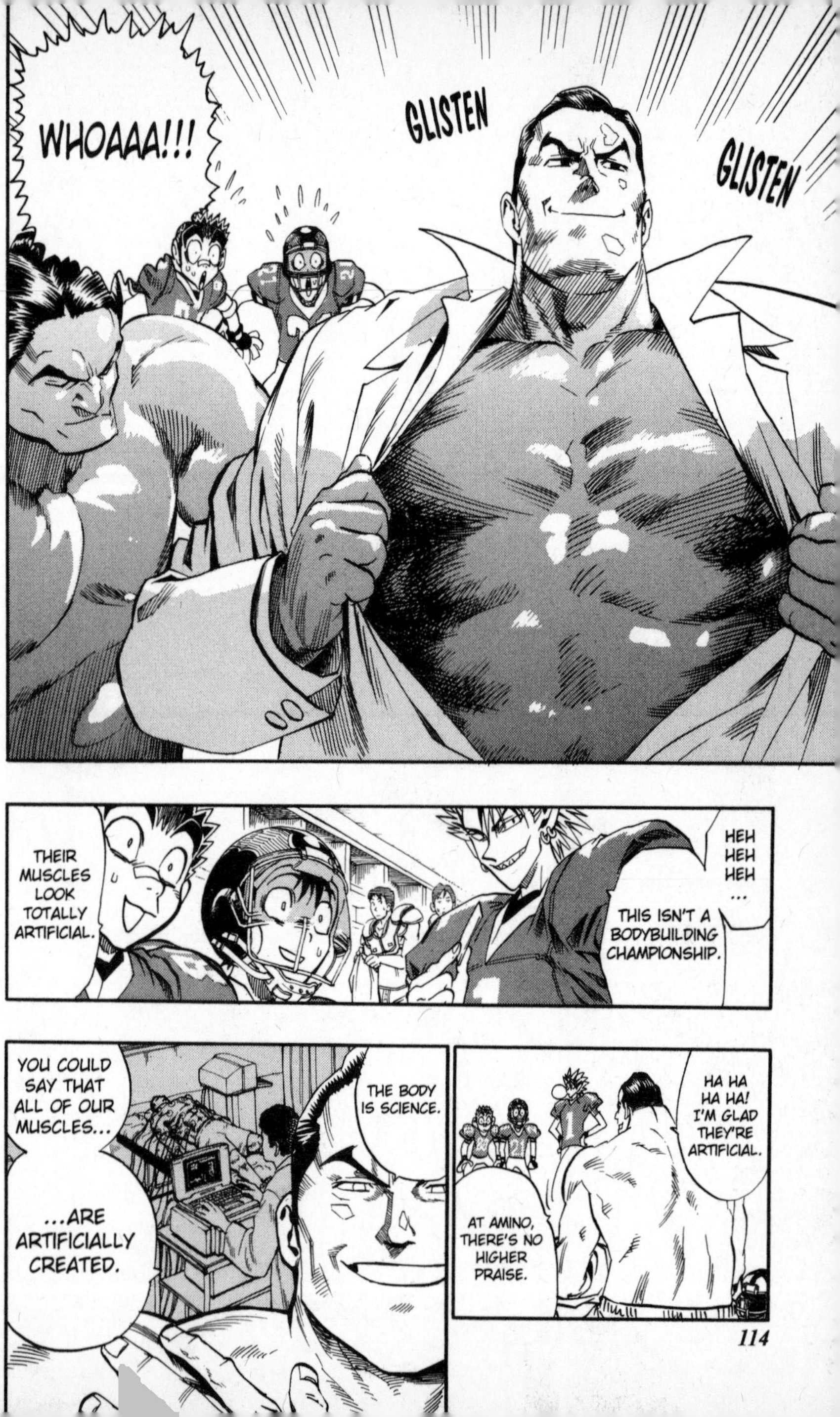
GLISTEN
GLISTEN
WHOAAA!!!
HEH HEH HEH...
THIS ISN'T A BODYBUILDING CHAMPIONSHIP.
THEIR MUSCLES LOOK TOTALLY ARTIFICIAL.
HA HA HA HA! I'M GLAD THEY'RE ARTIFICIAL.
AT AMINO, THERE'S NO HIGHER PRAISE.
THE BODY IS SCIENCE.
YOU COULD SAY THAT ALL OF OUR MUSCLES...
...ARE ARTIFICIALLY CREATED.

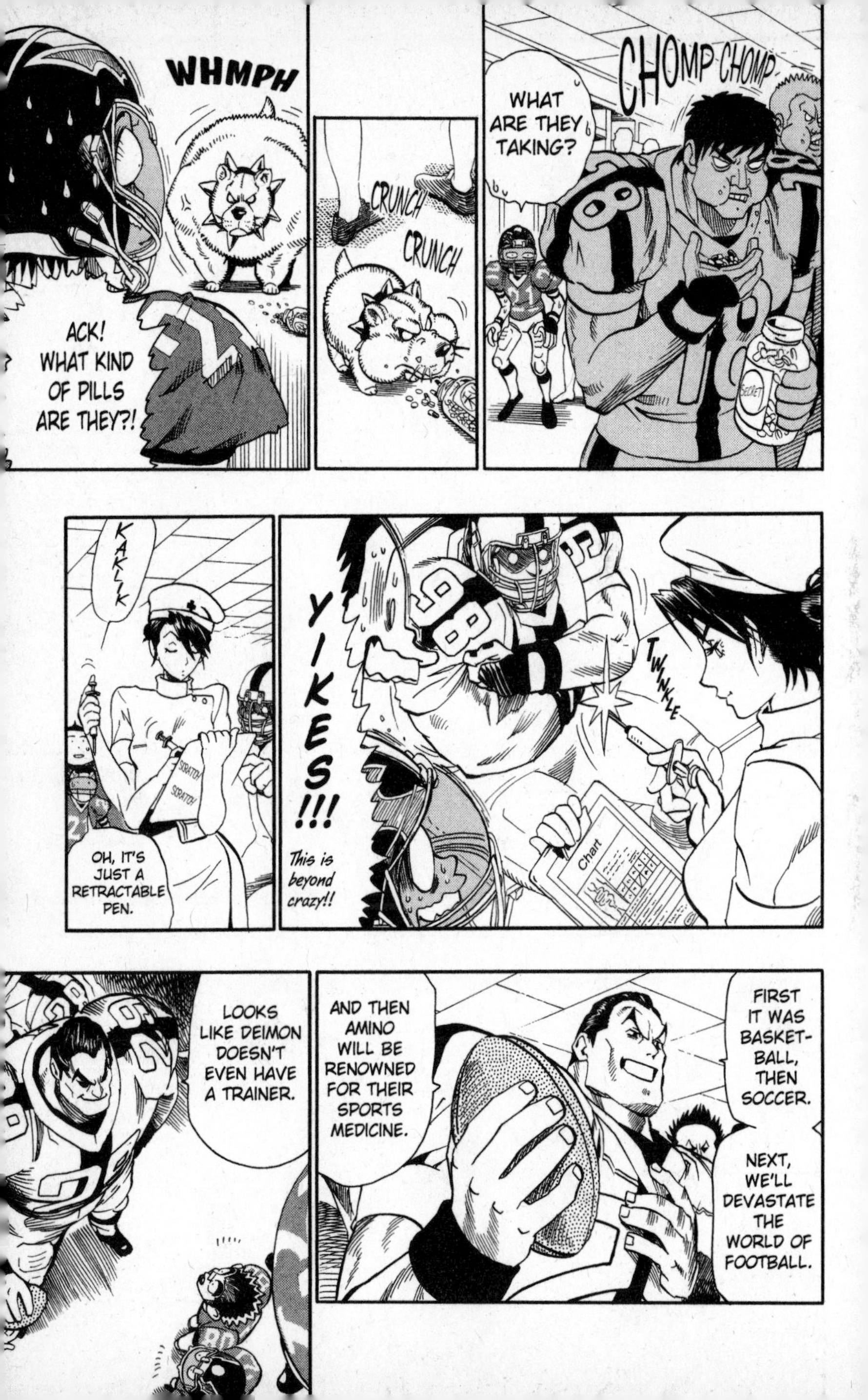
CHOMP CHOMP
WHAT ARE THEY TAKING?
CRUNCH
CRUNCH
WHMPH
ACK! WHAT KIND OF PILLS ARE THEY?!
TWINKLE
Chart
YIKES!!!
This is beyond crazy!!
KAKLIK
SCRATCH
SCRATCH
OH, IT'S JUST A RETRACTABLE PEN.
FIRST IT WAS BASKET-BALL, THEN SOCCER.
NEXT, WE'LL DEVASTATE THE WORLD OF FOOTBALL.
AND THEN AMINO WILL BE RENOWNED FOR THEIR SPORTS MEDICINE.
LOOKS LIKE DEIMON DOESN'T EVEN HAVE A TRAINER.

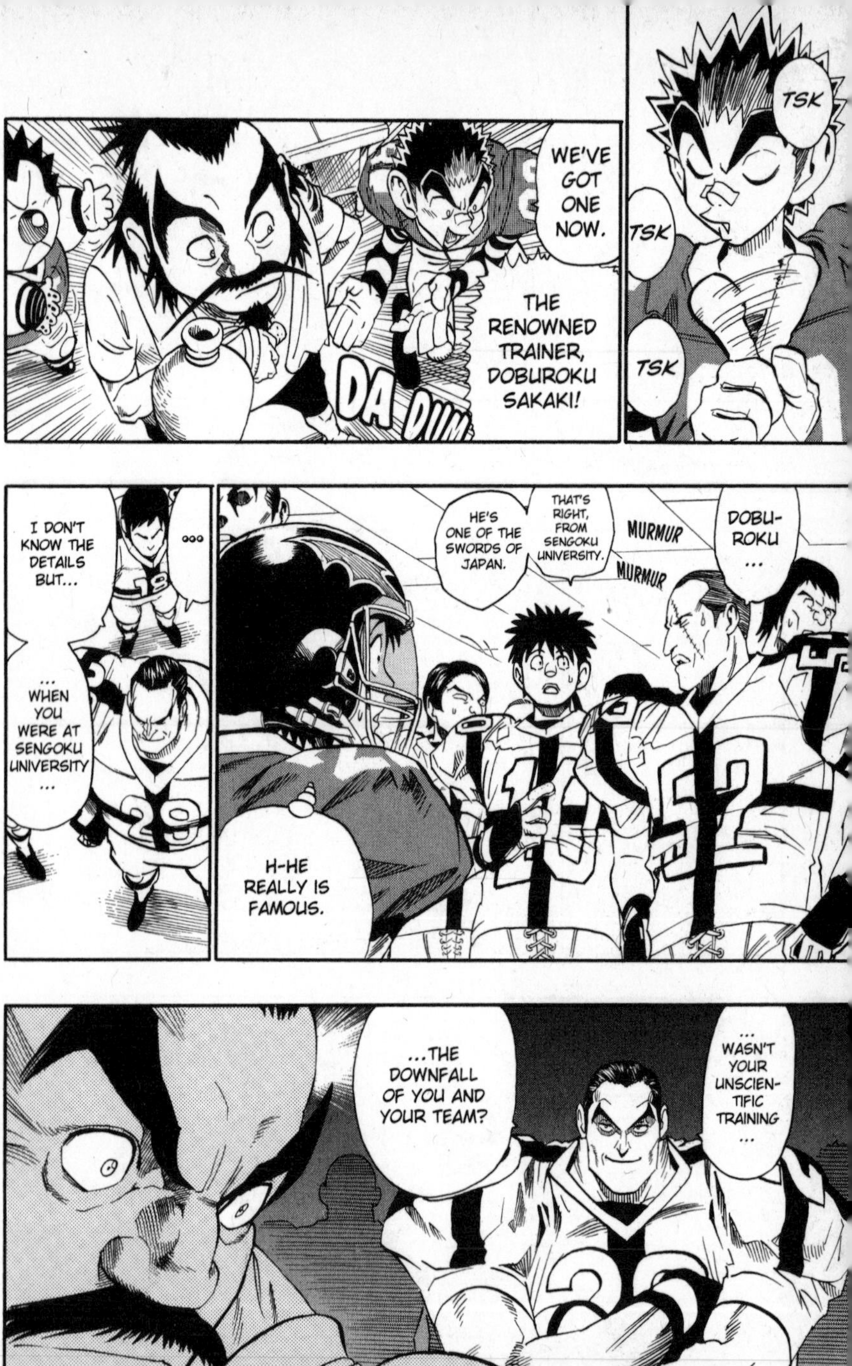
TSK
TSK
TSK
WE'VE GOT ONE NOW.
THE RENOWNED TRAINER, DOBUROKU SAKAKI!
DA DUM
DOBU-ROKU ...
MURMUR
MURMUR
THAT'S RIGHT, FROM SENGOKU UNIVERSITY.
HE'S ONE OF THE SWORDS OF JAPAN.
H-HE REALLY IS FAMOUS.
...
I DON'T KNOW THE DETAILS BUT...
... WHEN YOU WERE AT SENGOKU UNIVERSITY ...
... WASN'T YOUR UNSCIEN-TIFIC TRAINING ...
...THE DOWNFALL OF YOU AND YOUR TEAM?

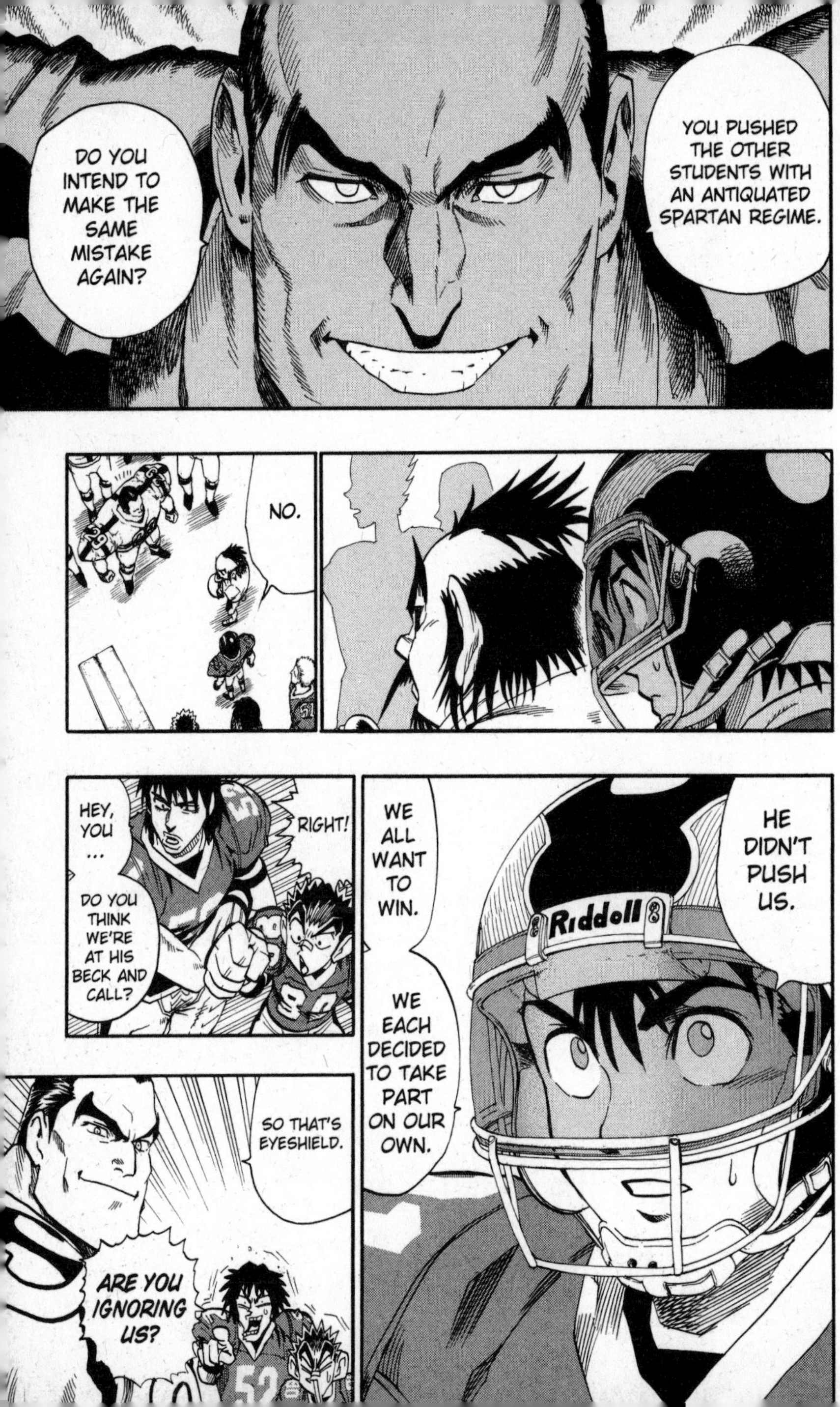
YOU PUSHED THE OTHER STUDENTS WITH AN ANTIQUATED SPARTAN REGIME.
DO YOU INTEND TO MAKE THE SAME MISTAKE AGAIN?
NO.
HE DIDN'T PUSH US.
Riddoll
WE ALL WANT TO WIN.
WE EACH DECIDED TO TAKE PART ON OUR OWN.
RIGHT!
HEY, YOU ...
DO YOU THINK WE'RE AT HIS BECK AND CALL?
SO THAT'S EYESHIELD.
ARE YOU IGNORING US?

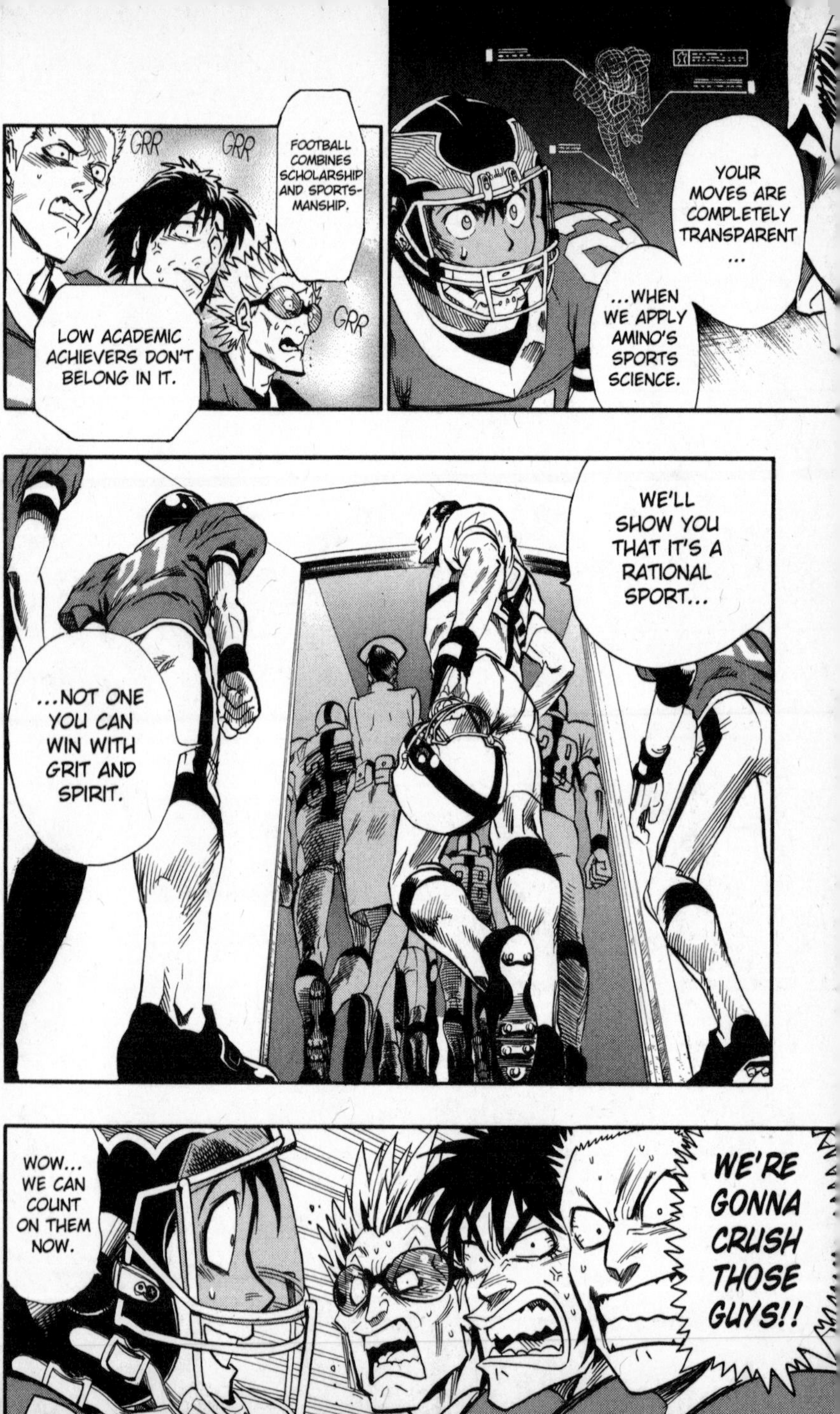
YOUR MOVES ARE COMPLETELY TRANSPARENT ...
...WHEN WE APPLY AMINO'S SPORTS SCIENCE.
FOOTBALL COMBINES SCHOLARSHIP AND SPORTS-MANSHIP.
GRR
GRR
GRR
LOW ACADEMIC ACHIEVERS DON'T BELONG IN IT.
WE'LL SHOW YOU THAT IT'S A RATIONAL SPORT...
...NOT ONE YOU CAN WIN WITH GRIT AND SPIRIT.
WE'RE GONNA CRUSH THOSE GUYS!!
WOW... WE CAN COUNT ON THEM NOW.

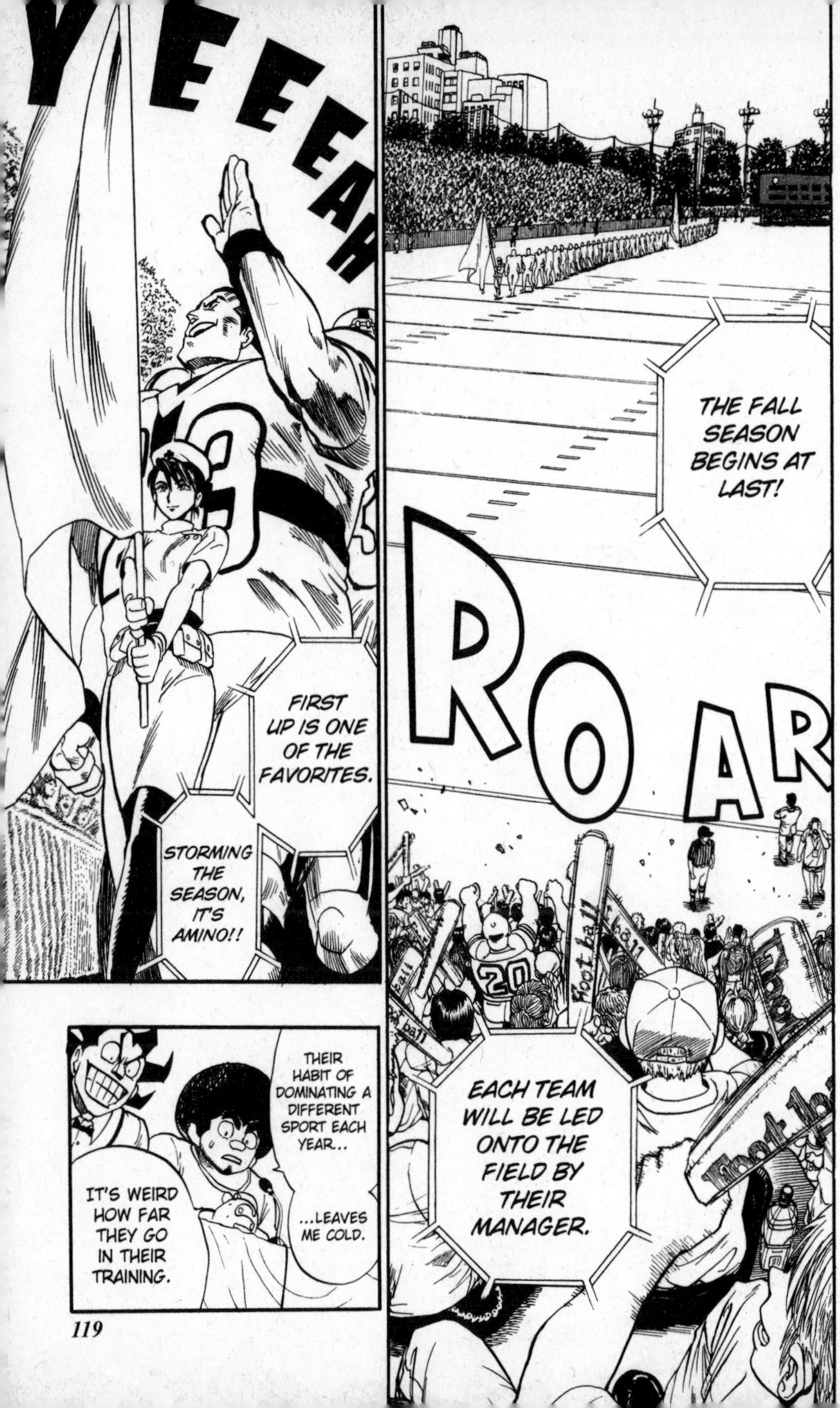
THE FALL SEASON BEGINS AT LAST!
ROAR
EACH TEAM WILL BE LED ONTO THE FIELD BY THEIR MANAGER.
YEEEAH
FIRST UP IS ONE OF THE FAVORITES.
STORMING THE SEASON, IT'S AMINO!!
THEIR HABIT OF DOMINATING A DIFFERENT SPORT EACH YEAR...
...LEAVES ME COLD.
IT'S WEIRD HOW FAR THEY GO IN THEIR TRAINING.

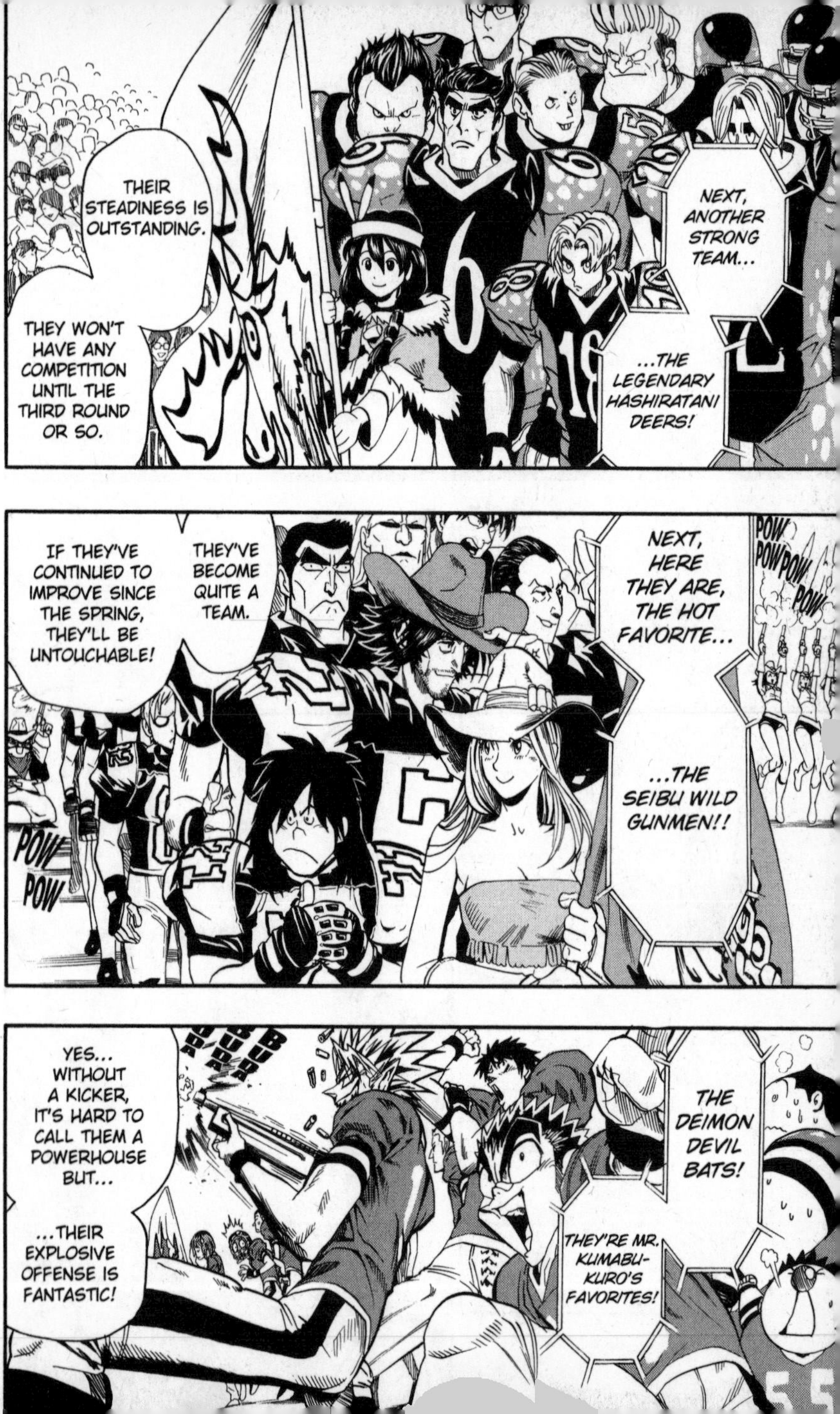
NEXT, ANOTHER STRONG TEAM...
...THE LEGENDARY HASHIRATANI DEERS!
THEIR STEADINESS IS OUTSTANDING.
THEY WON'T HAVE ANY COMPETITION UNTIL THE THIRD ROUND OR SO.
POW POW POW POW
NEXT, HERE THEY ARE, THE HOT FAVORITE...
...THE SEIBU WILD GUNMEN!!
THEY'VE BECOME QUITE A TEAM.
IF THEY'VE CONTINUED TO IMPROVE SINCE THE SPRING, THEY'LL BE UNTOUCHABLE!
POW POW
THE DEIMON DEVIL BATS!
THEY'RE MR. KUMABUKURO'S FAVORITES!
YES... WITHOUT A KICKER, IT'S HARD TO CALL THEM A POWERHOUSE BUT...
...THEIR EXPLOSIVE OFFENSE IS FANTASTIC!

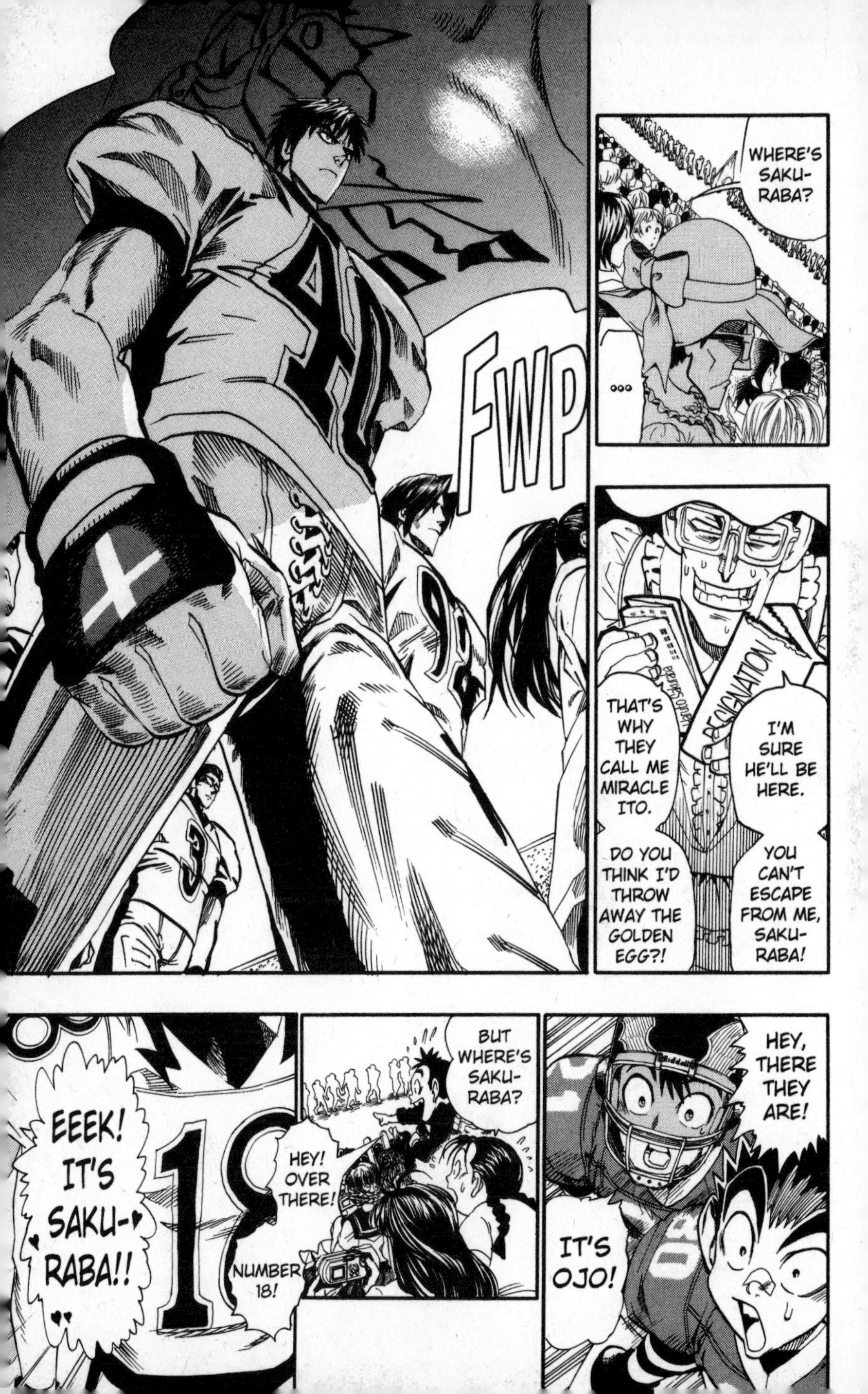
WHERE'S SAKU-RABA?
...
RESIGNATION
I'M SURE HE'LL BE HERE.
THAT'S WHY THEY CALL ME MIRACLE ITO.
YOU CAN'T ESCAPE FROM ME, SAKU-RABA!
DO YOU THINK I'D THROW AWAY THE GOLDEN EGG?!
FWP
HEY, THERE THEY ARE!
IT'S OJO!
BUT WHERE'S SAKU-RABA?
HEY! OVER THERE!
NUMBER 18!
EEEK! IT'S SAKU-RABA!!

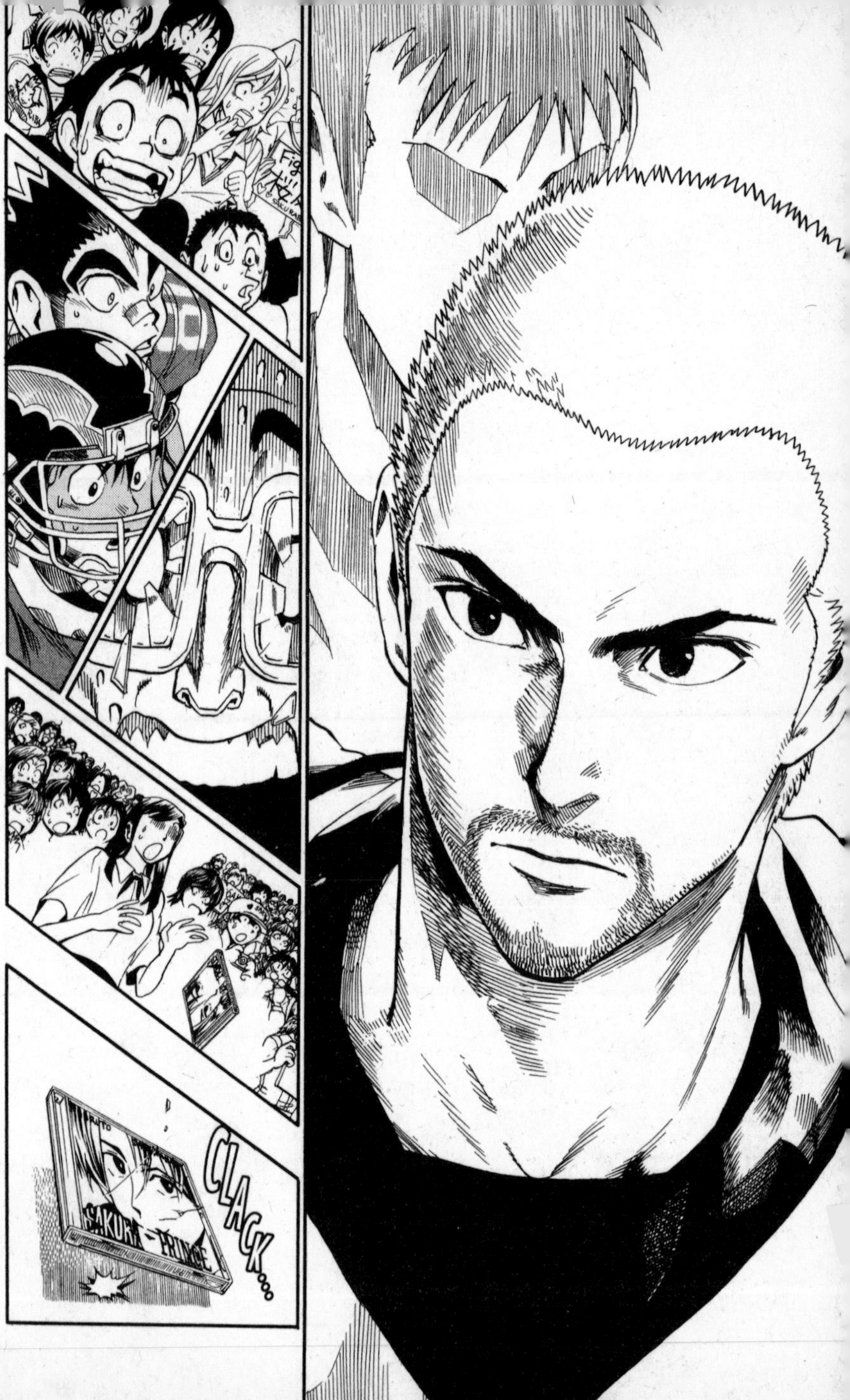
SAKURA PRINCE
CLACK...

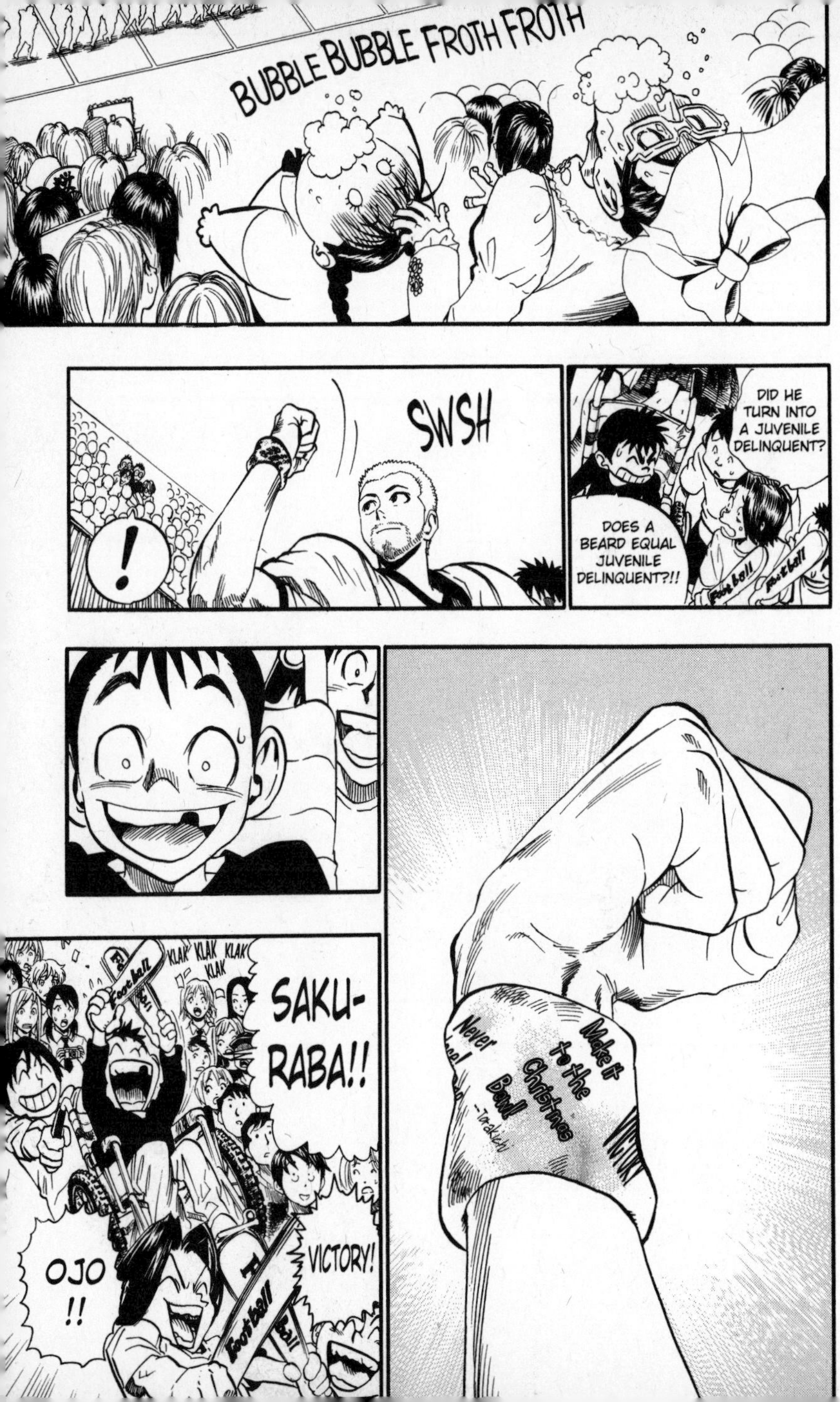
BUBBLE BUBBLE FROTH FROTH
DID HE TURN INTO A JUVENILE DELINQUENT?
DOES A BEARD EQUAL JUVENILE DELINQUENT?!!
SWSH
!
Make it to the Christmas Bowl
Never
KLAK KLAK KLAK KLAK
SAKU-RABA!!
VICTORY!
OJO !!
Football

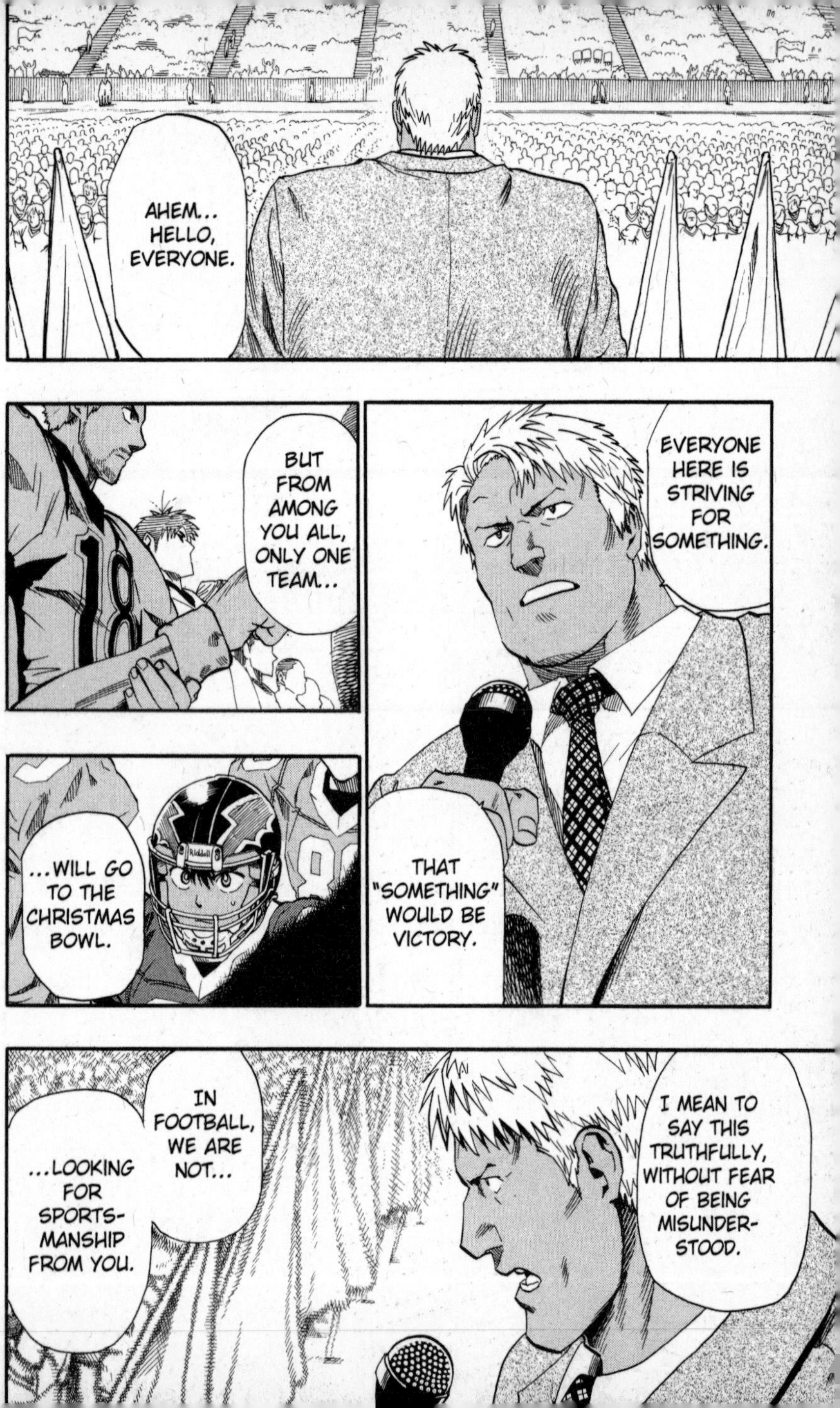
AHEM... HELLO, EVERYONE.
EVERYONE HERE IS STRIVING FOR SOMETHING.
THAT "SOMETHING" WOULD BE VICTORY.
BUT FROM AMONG YOU ALL, ONLY ONE TEAM...
...WILL GO TO THE CHRISTMAS BOWL.
I MEAN TO SAY THIS TRUTHFULLY, WITHOUT FEAR OF BEING MISUNDER-STOOD.
IN FOOTBALL, WE ARE NOT...
...LOOKING FOR SPORTS-MANSHIP FROM YOU.

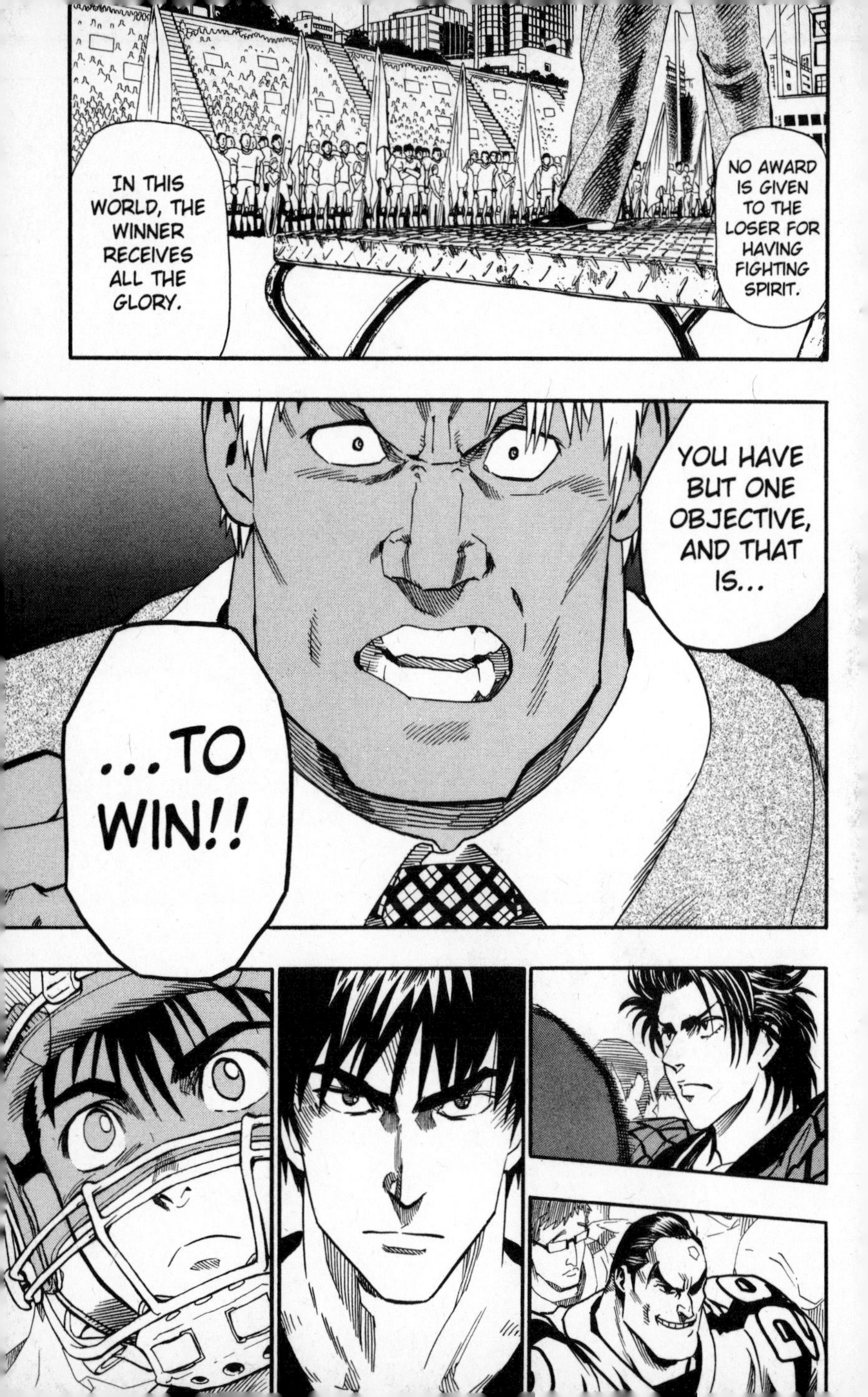
NO AWARD IS GIVEN TO THE LOSER FOR HAVING FIGHTING SPIRIT.
IN THIS WORLD, THE WINNER RECEIVES ALL THE GLORY.
YOU HAVE BUT ONE OBJECTIVE, AND THAT IS...
...TO WIN!!

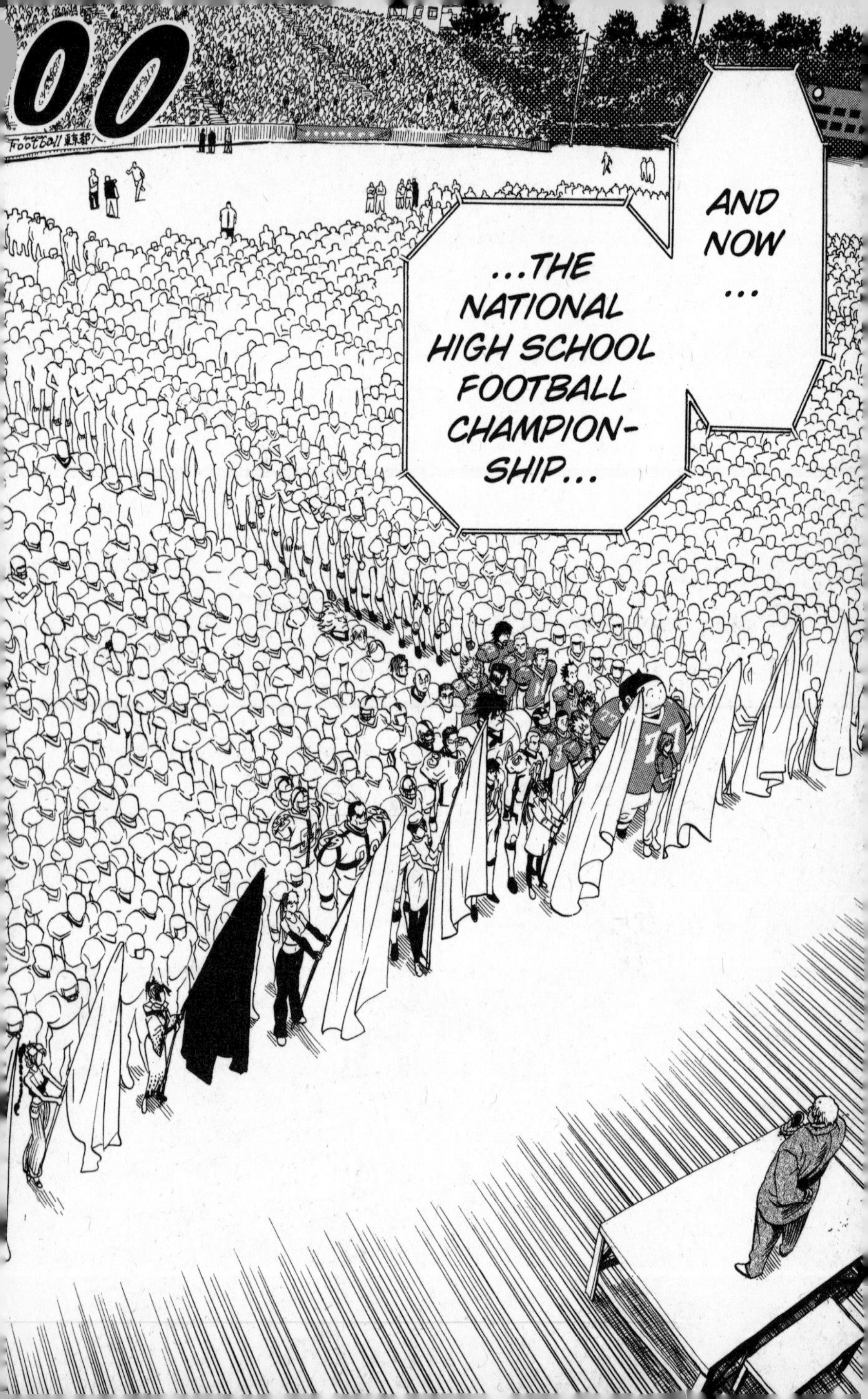
AND NOW ...
...THE NATIONAL HIGH SCHOOL FOOTBALL CHAMPION-SHIP...

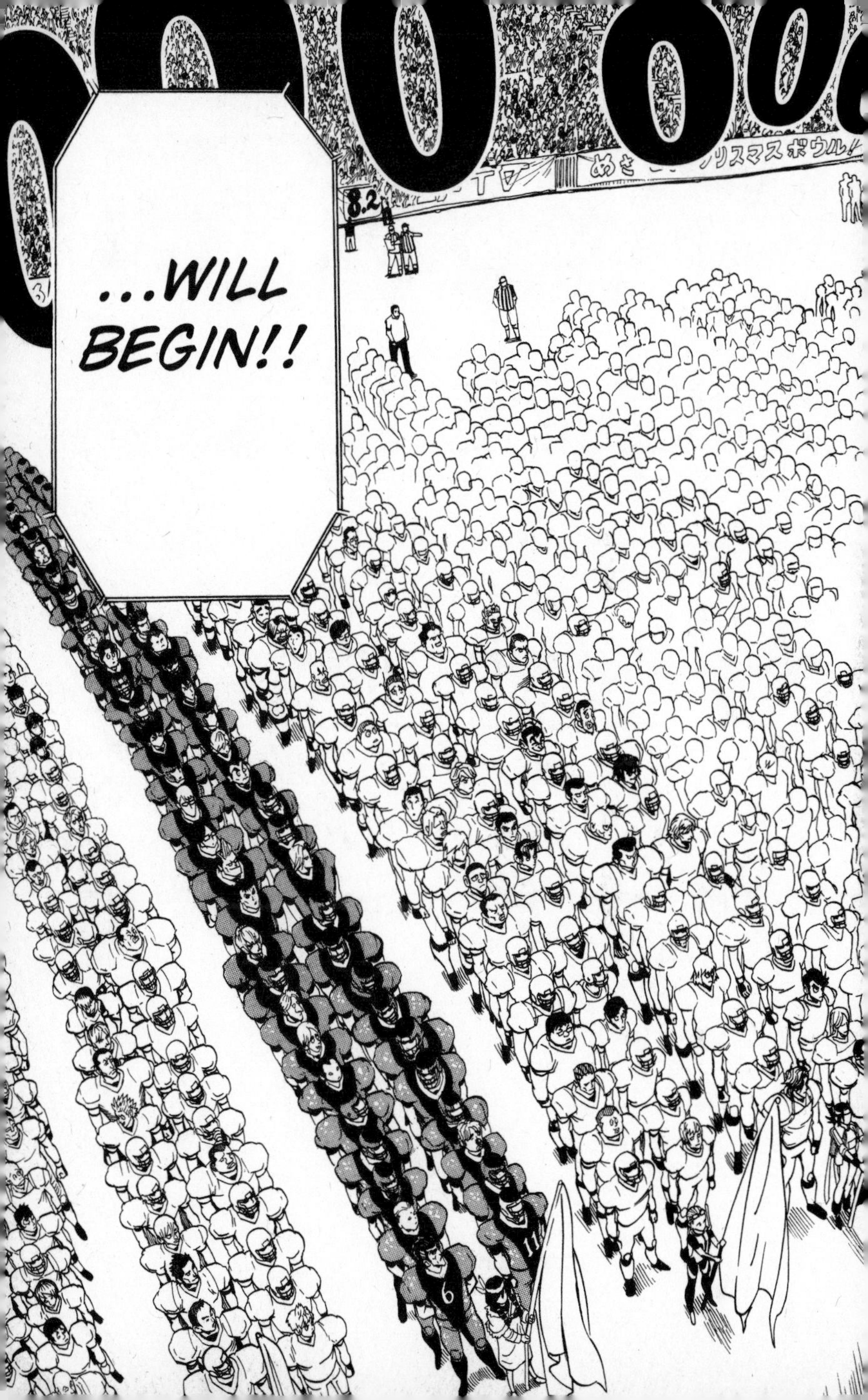
...WILL BEGIN!!
8.2

Eyeshield 21 Survey Corner **Devil Bat 021**

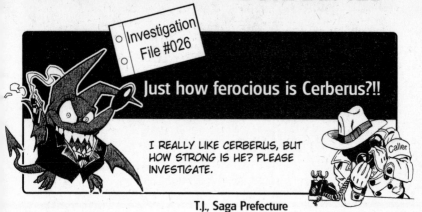

Investigation File #026

Just how ferocious is Cerberus?!!

I REALLY LIKE CERBERUS, BUT HOW STRONG IS HE? PLEASE INVESTIGATE.

Caller

T.J., Saga Prefecture

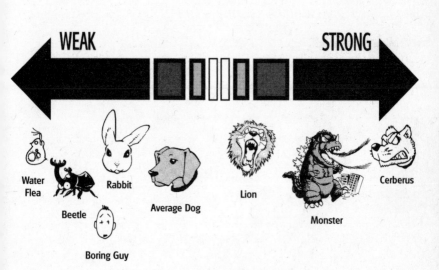

WEAK
STRONG
Water Flea
Beetle
Rabbit
Boring Guy
Average Dog
Lion
Monster
Cerberus

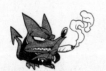

ABOUT THIS STRONG.

Chapter 95 Deimon's Worst Day

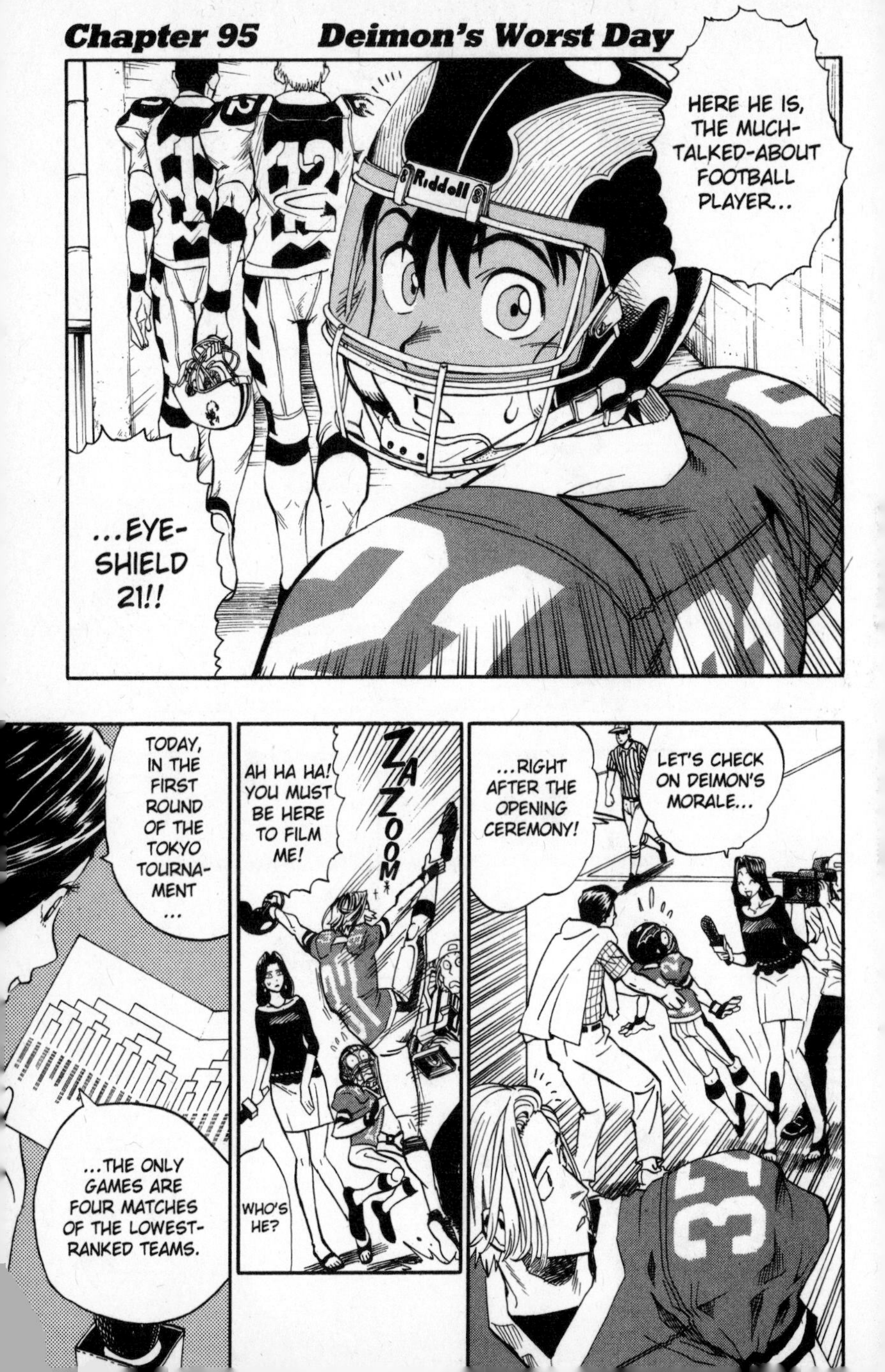
HERE HE IS, THE MUCH-TALKED-ABOUT FOOTBALL PLAYER...
...EYE-SHIELD 21!!
LET'S CHECK ON DEIMON'S MORALE...
...RIGHT AFTER THE OPENING CEREMONY!
AH HA HA! YOU MUST BE HERE TO FILM ME!
ZAZOOOM
WHO'S HE?
TODAY, IN THE FIRST ROUND OF THE TOKYO TOURNAMENT...
...THE ONLY GAMES ARE FOUR MATCHES OF THE LOWEST-RANKED TEAMS.

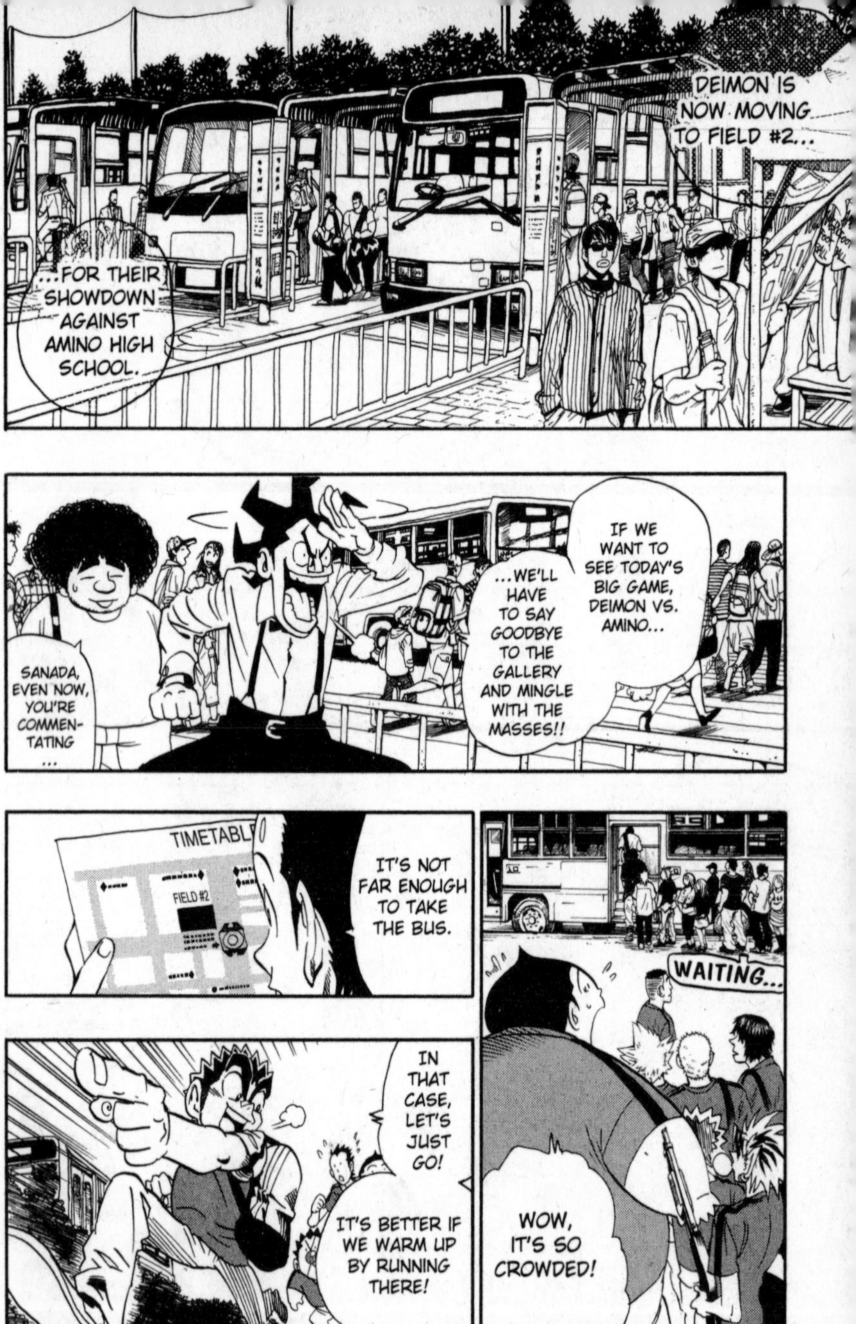
DEIMON IS NOW MOVING TO FIELD #2...
...FOR THEIR SHOWDOWN AGAINST AMINO HIGH SCHOOL.
IF WE WANT TO SEE TODAY'S BIG GAME, DEIMON VS. AMINO...
...WE'LL HAVE TO SAY GOODBYE TO THE GALLERY AND MINGLE WITH THE MASSES!!
SANADA, EVEN NOW, YOU'RE COMMENTATING...
WAITING...
WOW, IT'S SO CROWDED!
TIMETABLE
FIELD #2
IT'S NOT FAR ENOUGH TO TAKE THE BUS.
IN THAT CASE, LET'S JUST GO!
IT'S BETTER IF WE WARM UP BY RUNNING THERE!

READ THIS WAY

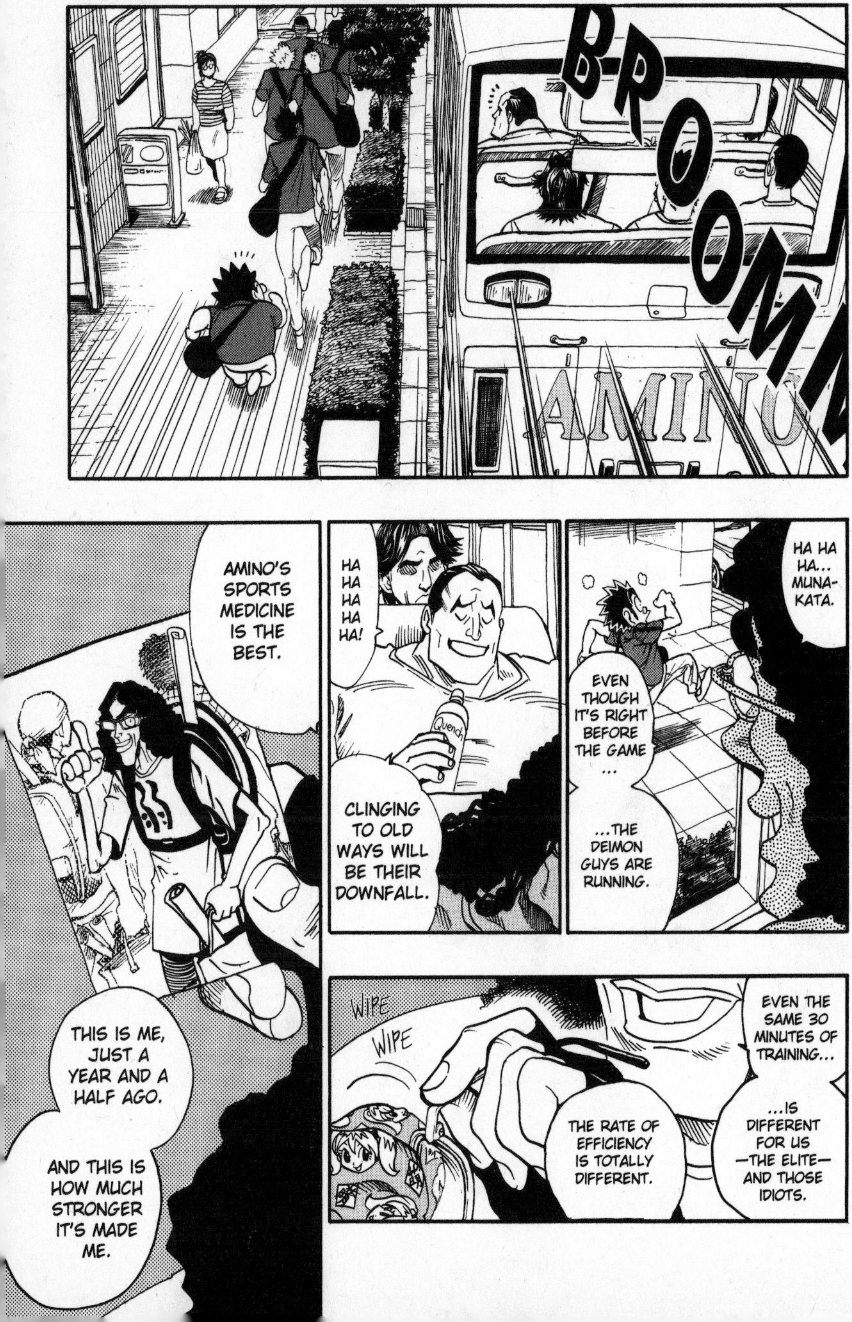
BROOOM
AMINO
HA HA HA... MUNAKATA.
EVEN THOUGH IT'S RIGHT BEFORE THE GAME...
...THE DEIMON GUYS ARE RUNNING.
HA HA HA HA HA!
Quench
CLINGING TO OLD WAYS WILL BE THEIR DOWNFALL.
EVEN THE SAME 30 MINUTES OF TRAINING...
...IS DIFFERENT FOR US —THE ELITE— AND THOSE IDIOTS.
THE RATE OF EFFICIENCY IS TOTALLY DIFFERENT.
WIPE
WIPE
AMINO'S SPORTS MEDICINE IS THE BEST.
THIS IS ME, JUST A YEAR AND A HALF AGO.
AND THIS IS HOW MUCH STRONGER IT'S MADE ME.

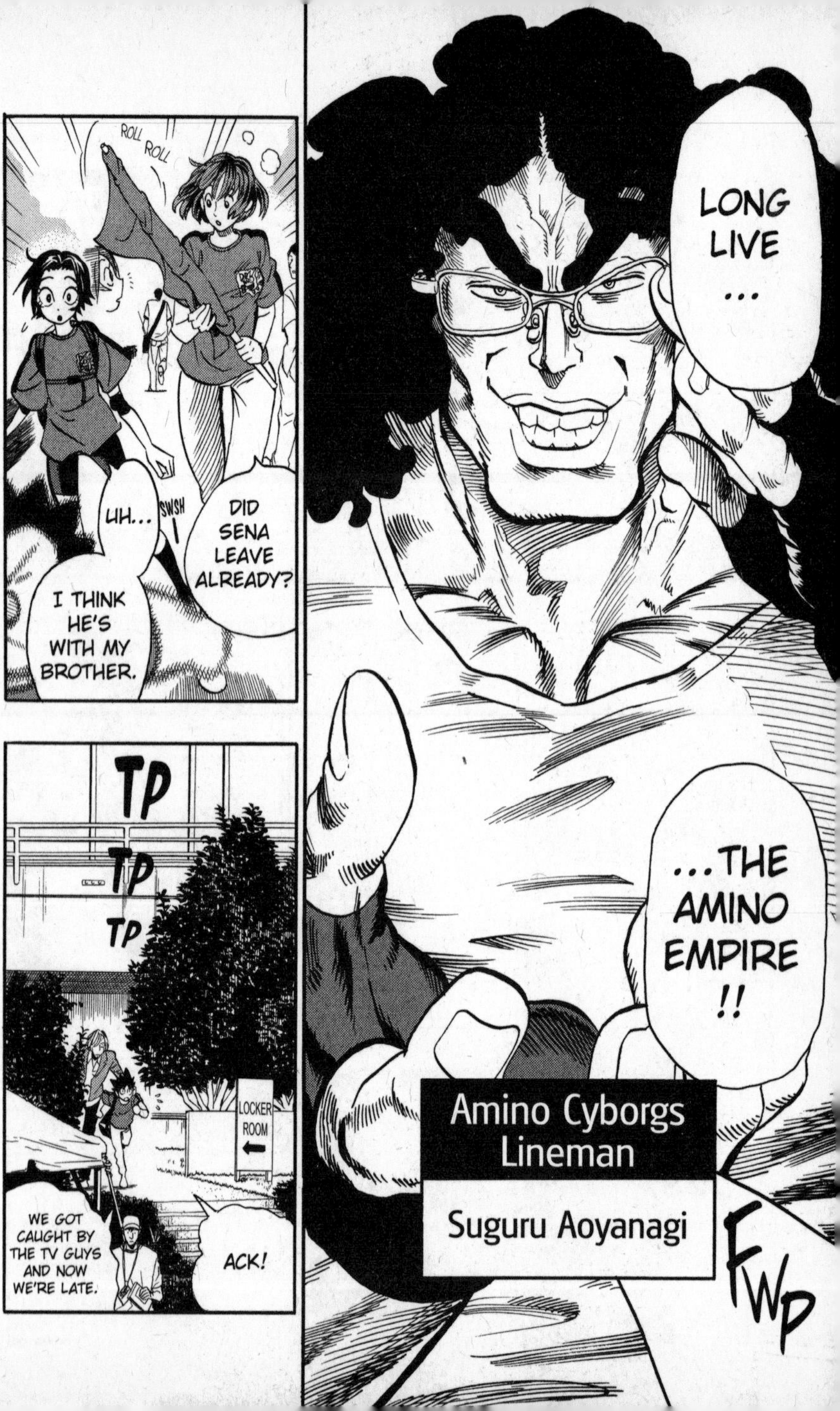
LONG LIVE ...
...THE AMINO EMPIRE!!
Amino Cyborgs Lineman
Suguru Aoyanagi
FWP
ROLL ROLL
DID SENA LEAVE ALREADY?
UH...
SWSH
I THINK HE'S WITH MY BROTHER.
TP
TP
TP
LOCKER ROOM
ACK!
WE GOT CAUGHT BY THE TV GUYS AND NOW WE'RE LATE.

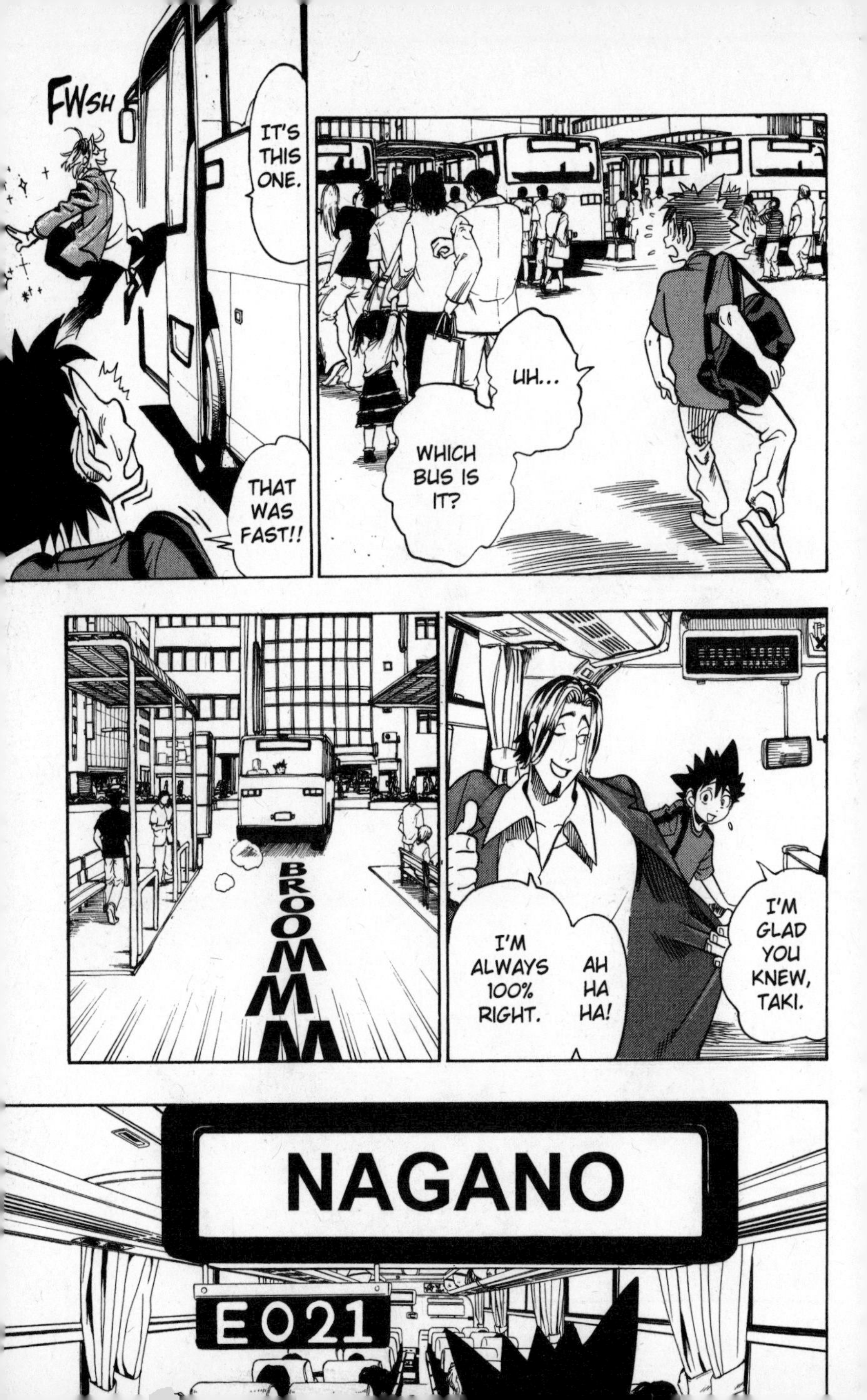
UH...
WHICH BUS IS IT?
IT'S THIS ONE.
FWSH
THAT WAS FAST!!
I'M GLAD YOU KNEW, TAKI.
AH HA HA!
I'M ALWAYS 100% RIGHT.
BROOMMM
NAGANO
E021

Chapter 95
Deimon's Worst Day

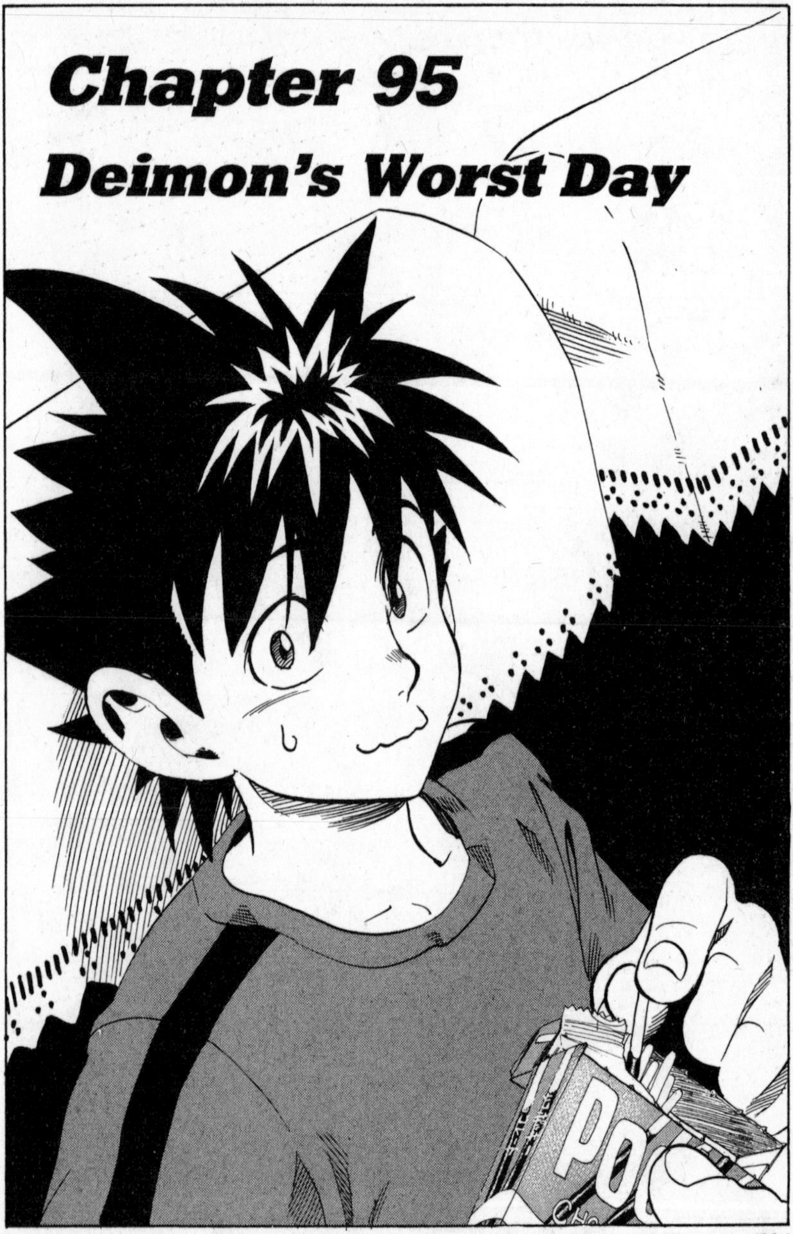

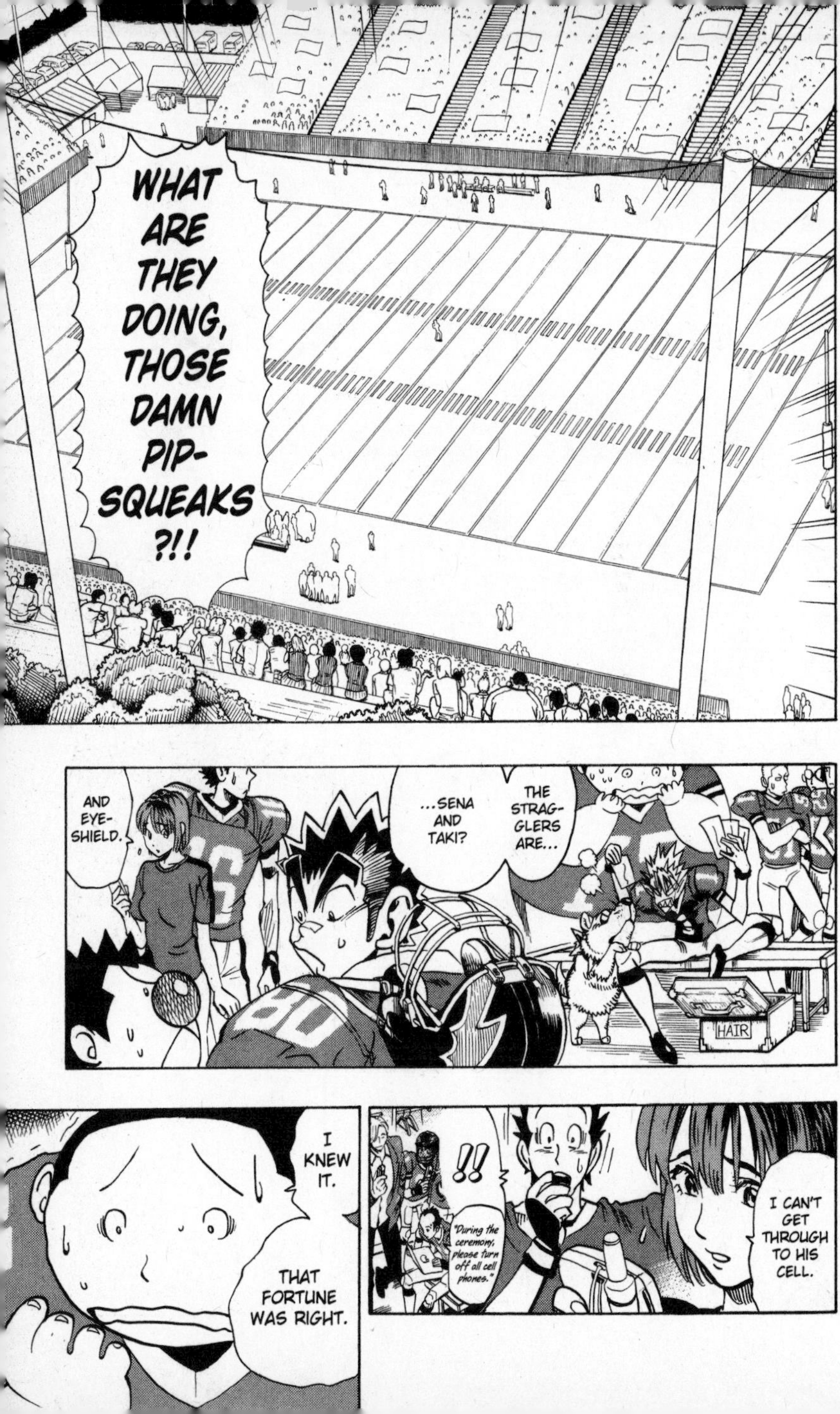
WHAT ARE THEY DOING, THOSE DAMN PIP-SQUEAKS?!!
THE STRAG-GLERS ARE...
...SENA AND TAKI?
AND EYE-SHIELD.
HAIR
I CAN'T GET THROUGH TO HIS CELL.
!!
"During the ceremony, please turn off all cell phones."
I KNEW IT.
THAT FORTUNE WAS RIGHT.

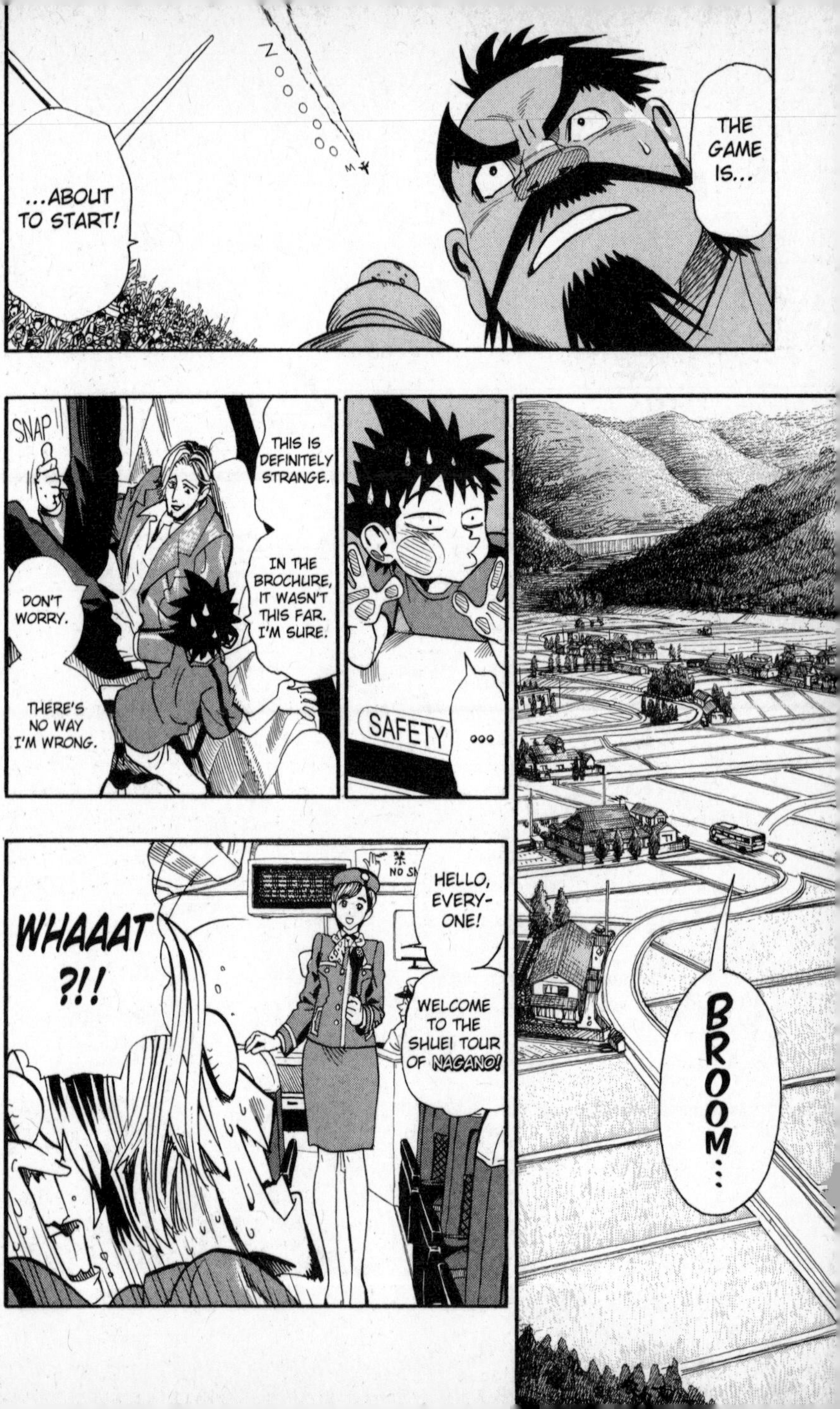
THE GAME IS...
...ABOUT TO START!
BROOM...
SAFETY
...
SNAP
THIS IS DEFINITELY STRANGE.
IN THE BROCHURE, IT WASN'T THIS FAR. I'M SURE.
DON'T WORRY.
THERE'S NO WAY I'M WRONG.
HELLO, EVERYONE!
WELCOME TO THE SHUEI TOUR OF NAGANO!
WHAAAT ?!!

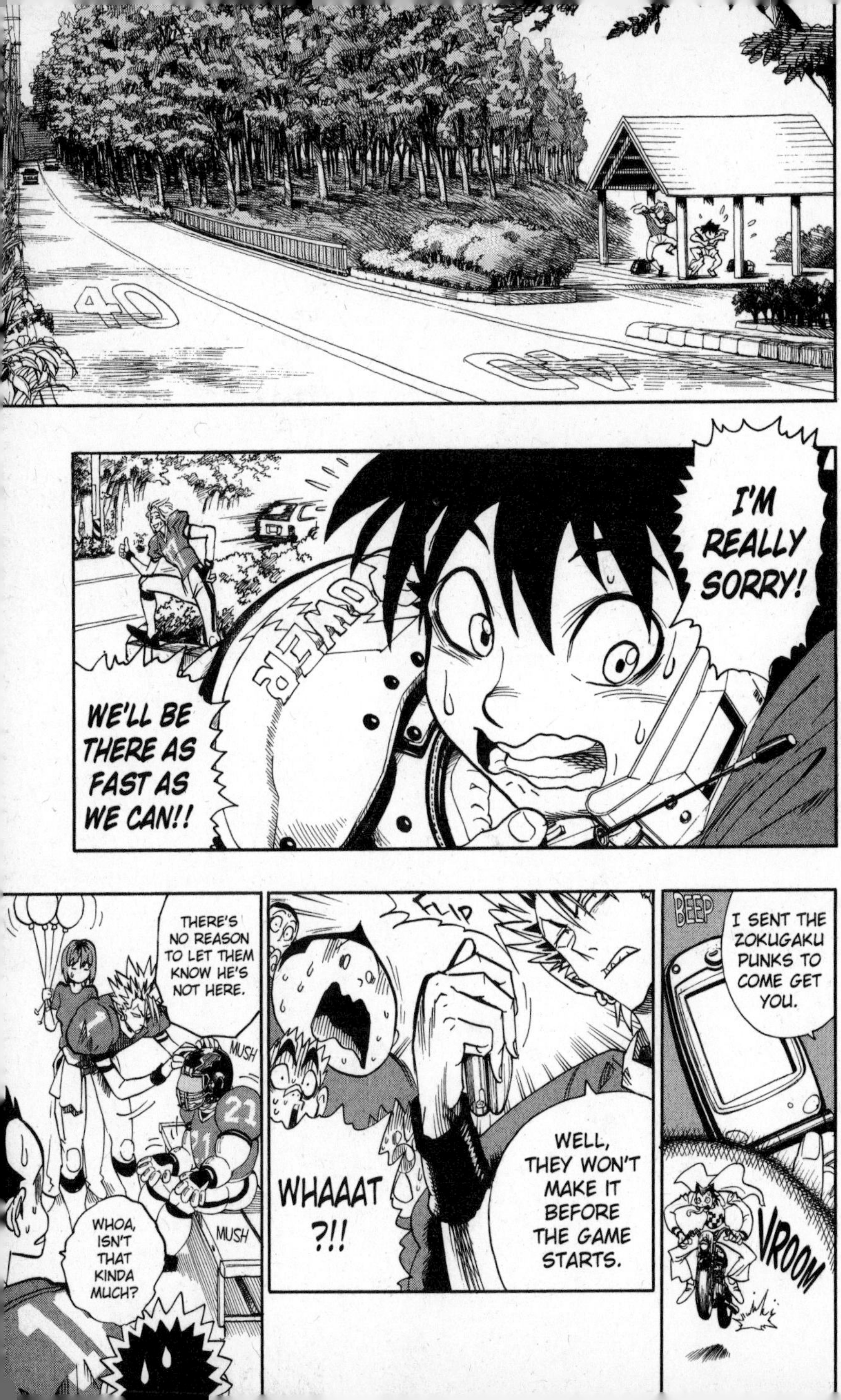
I'M REALLY SORRY!
WE'LL BE THERE AS FAST AS WE CAN!!
BEEP
I SENT THE ZOKUGAKU PUNKS TO COME GET YOU.
VROOM
FLIP
WELL, THEY WON'T MAKE IT BEFORE THE GAME STARTS.
WHAAAT ?!!
THERE'S NO REASON TO LET THEM KNOW HE'S NOT HERE.
MUSH
MUSH
WHOA, ISN'T THAT KINDA MUCH?

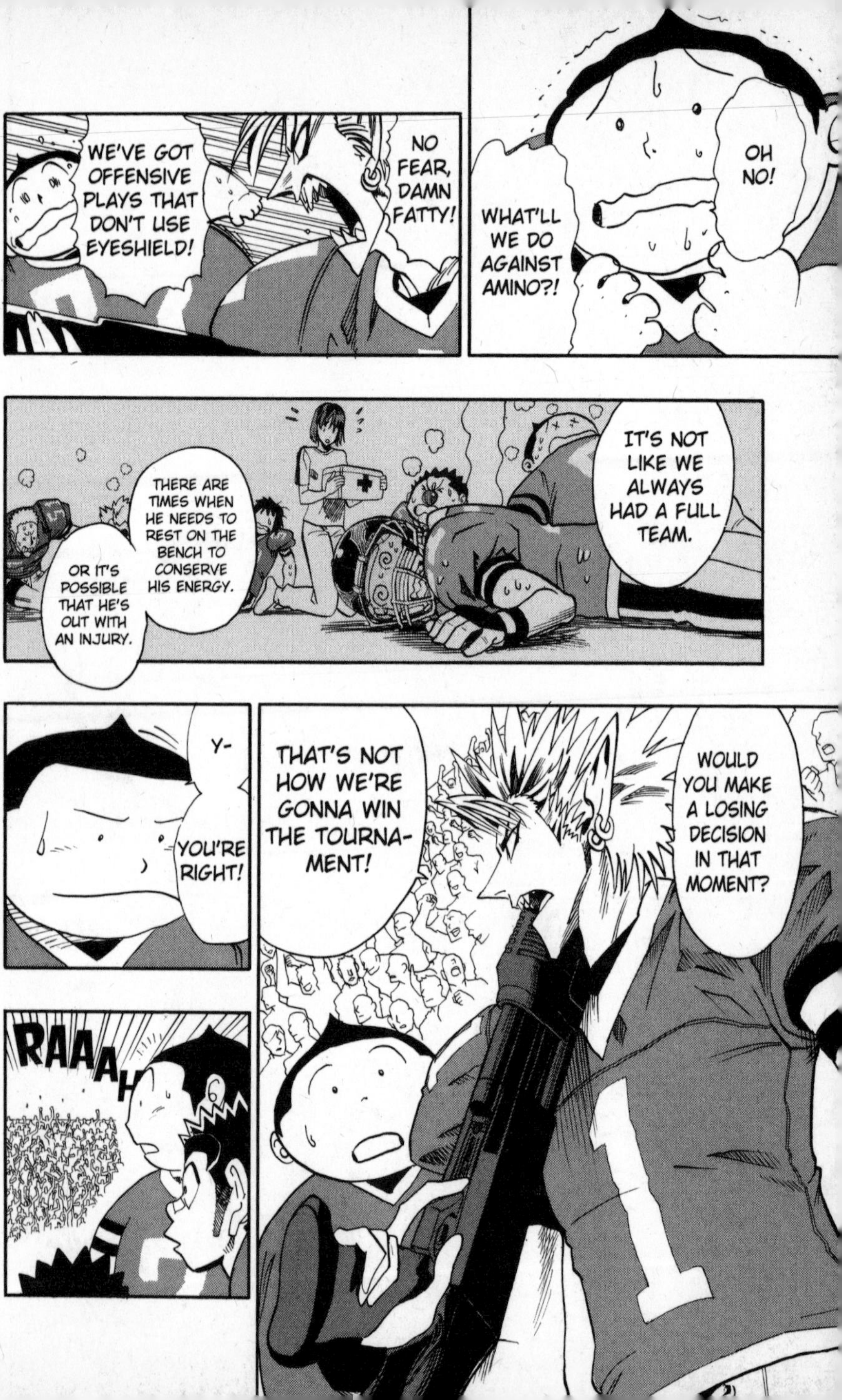
OH NO!
WHAT'LL WE DO AGAINST AMINO?!
NO FEAR, DAMN FATTY!
WE'VE GOT OFFENSIVE PLAYS THAT DON'T USE EYESHIELD!
IT'S NOT LIKE WE ALWAYS HAD A FULL TEAM.
THERE ARE TIMES WHEN HE NEEDS TO REST ON THE BENCH TO CONSERVE HIS ENERGY.
OR IT'S POSSIBLE THAT HE'S OUT WITH AN INJURY.
WOULD YOU MAKE A LOSING DECISION IN THAT MOMENT?
THAT'S NOT HOW WE'RE GONNA WIN THE TOURNA-MENT!
Y-
YOU'RE RIGHT!
RAAAH

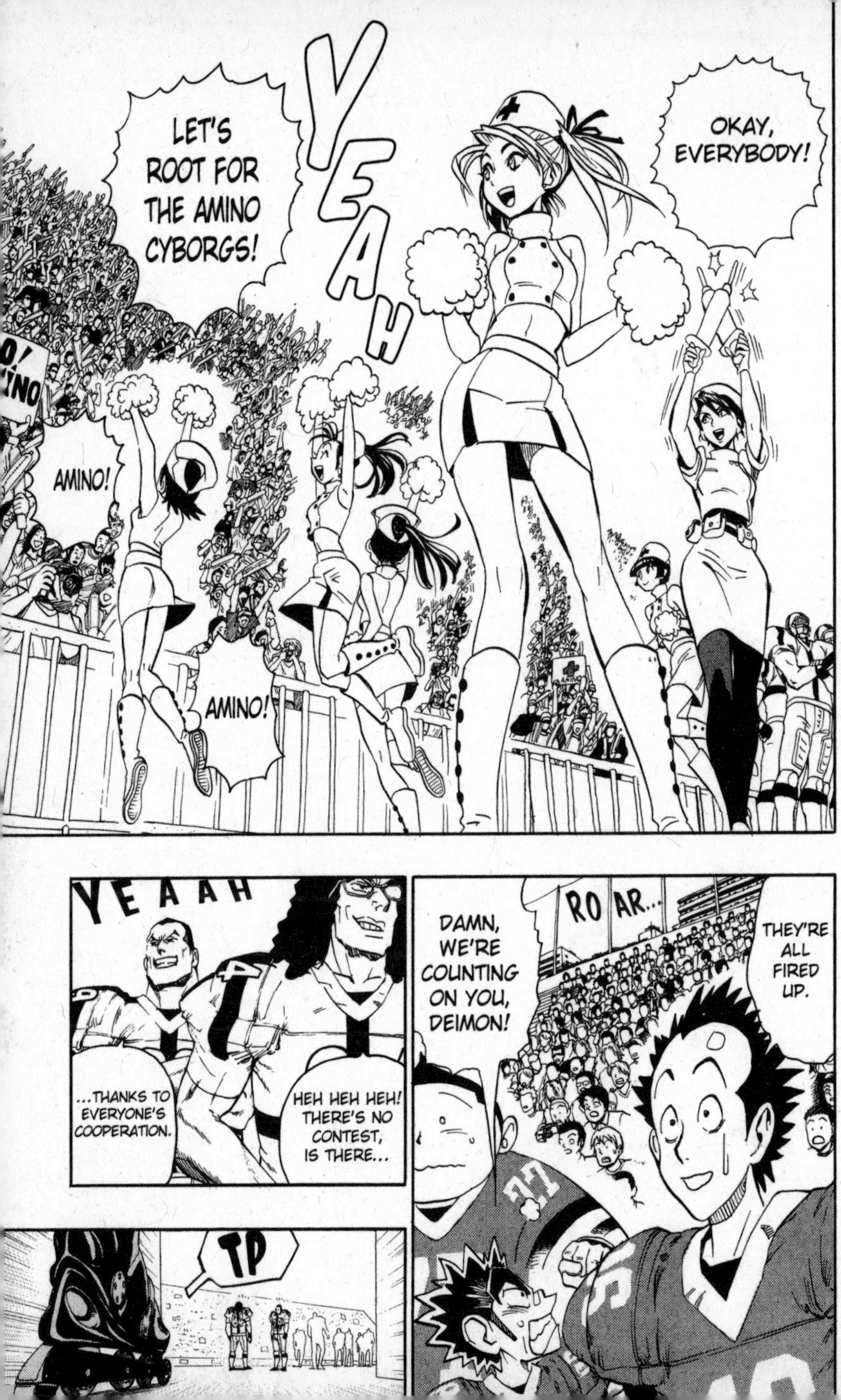
OKAY, EVERYBODY!
YEAH
LET'S ROOT FOR THE AMINO CYBORGS!
AMINO!
AMINO!
THEY'RE ALL FIRED UP.
RO AR...
DAMN, WE'RE COUNTING ON YOU, DEIMON!
YEAAH
HEH HEH HEH! THERE'S NO CONTEST, IS THERE...
...THANKS TO EVERYONE'S COOPERATION.
TP

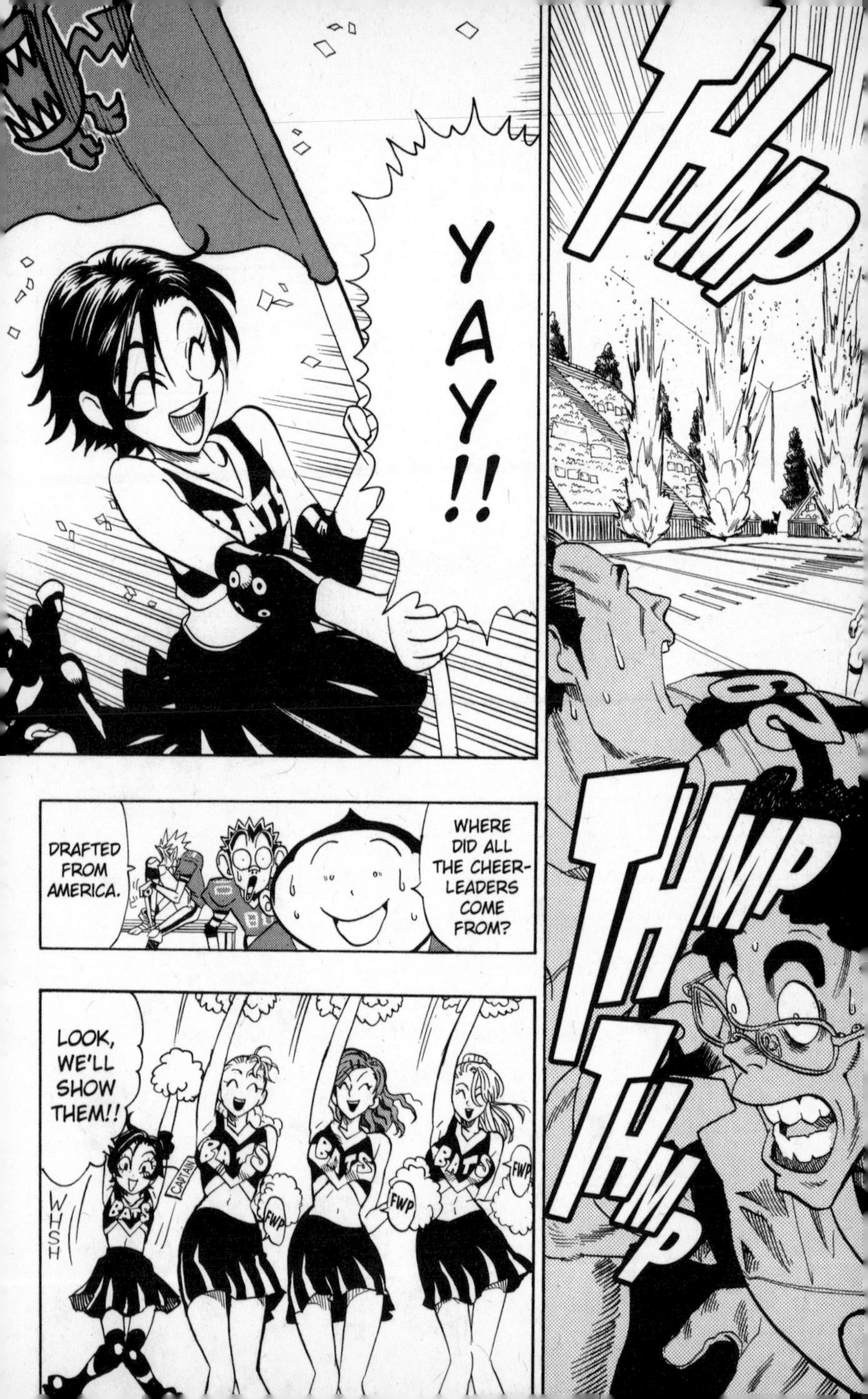
THMP
THMP
THMP
THMP
YAY!!
BATS
WHERE DID ALL THE CHEER-LEADERS COME FROM?
DRAFTED FROM AMERICA.
LOOK, WE'LL SHOW THEM!!
BATS
BATS
BATS
BATS
CAPTAIN
FWP
FWP
FWP
WHSH

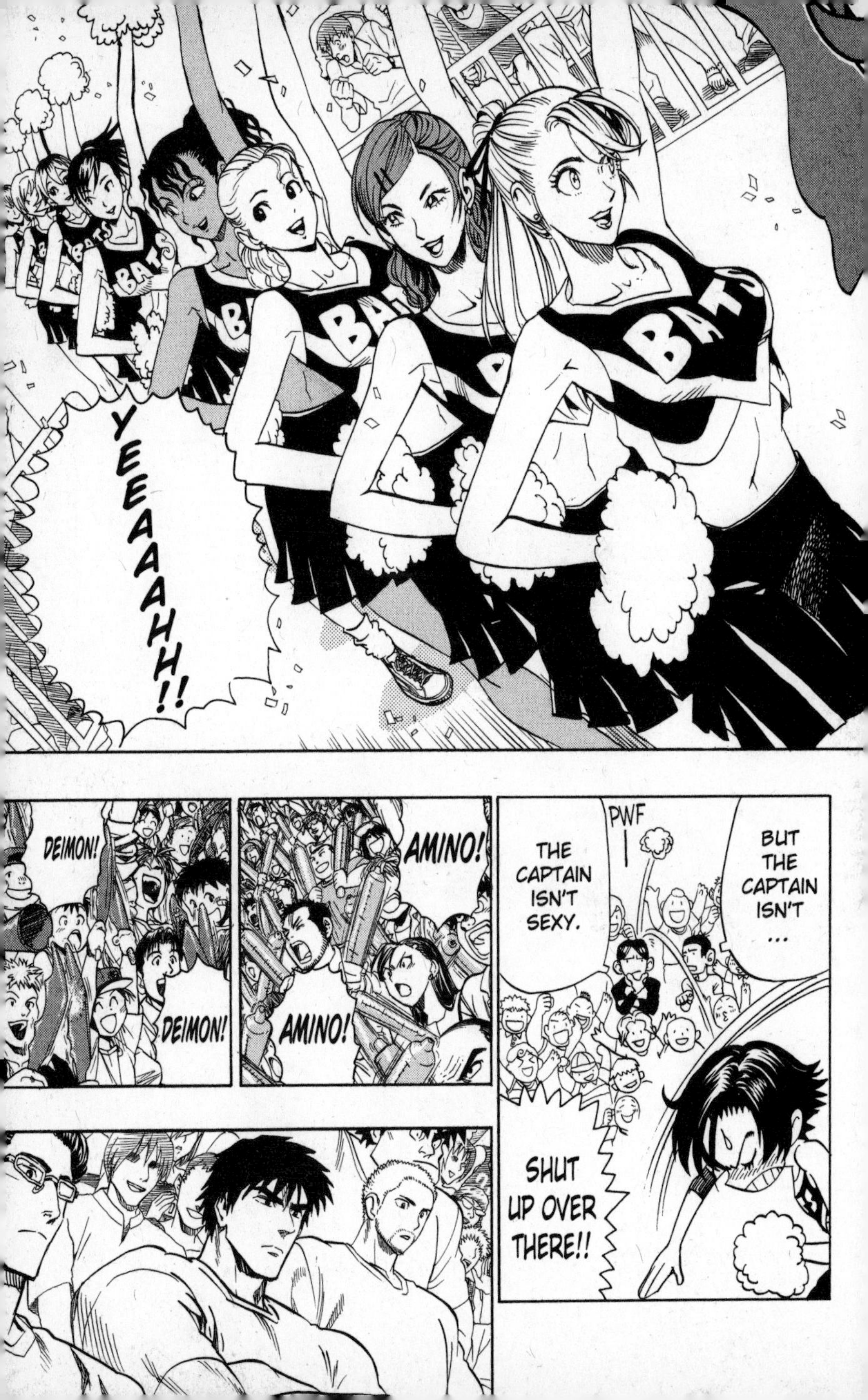
YEEAAAAHH!!
BUT THE CAPTAIN ISN'T ...
PWF
THE CAPTAIN ISN'T SEXY.
SHUT UP OVER THERE!!
AMINO!
AMINO!
DEIMON!
DEIMON!

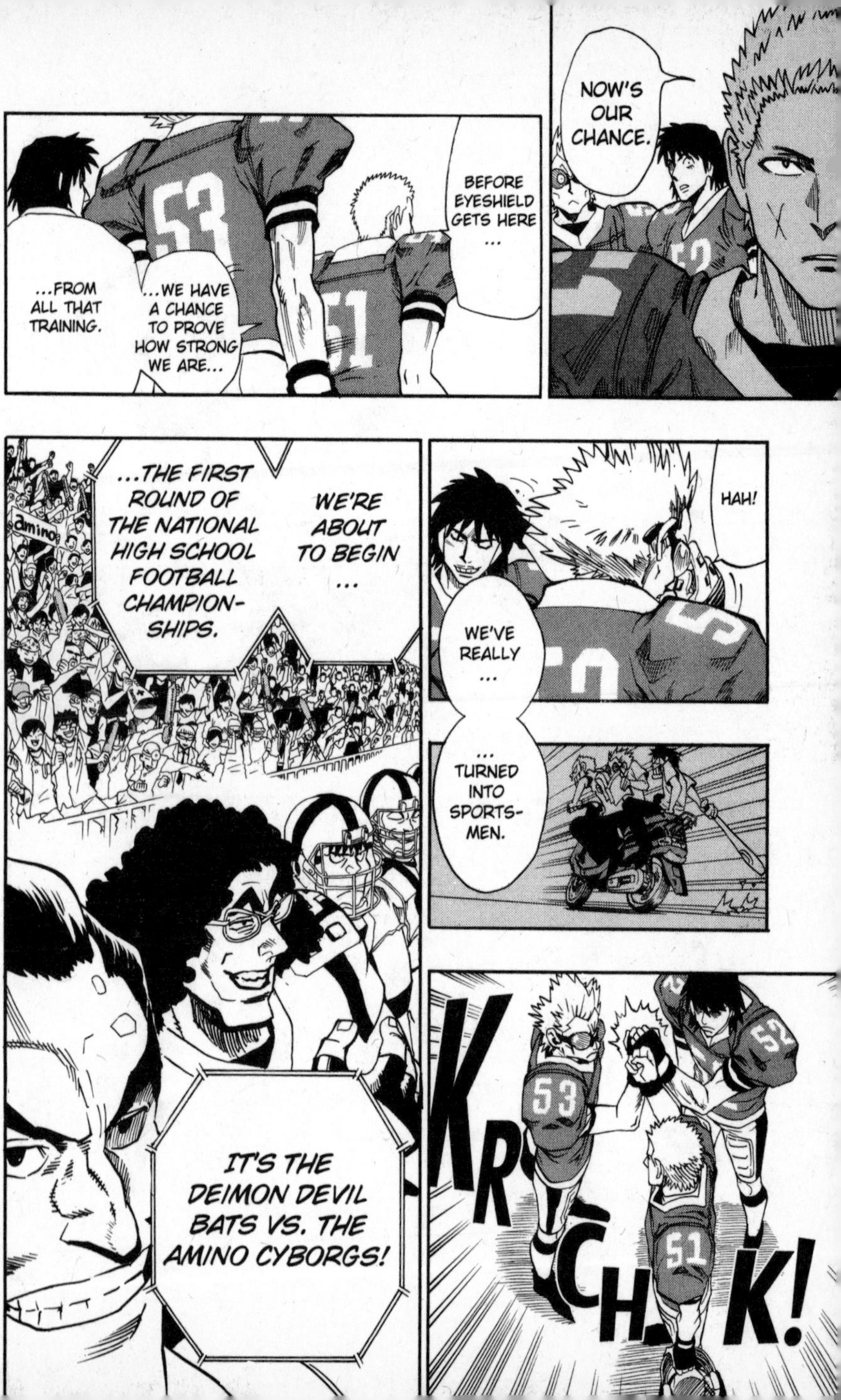
NOW'S OUR CHANCE.
BEFORE EYESHIELD GETS HERE ...
...WE HAVE A CHANCE TO PROVE HOW STRONG WE ARE...
...FROM ALL THAT TRAINING.
HAH!
WE'VE REALLY ...
... TURNED INTO SPORTS-MEN.
KRCHK!
WE'RE ABOUT TO BEGIN ...
...THE FIRST ROUND OF THE NATIONAL HIGH SCHOOL FOOTBALL CHAMPION-SHIPS.
amino
IT'S THE DEIMON DEVIL BATS VS. THE AMINO CYBORGS!

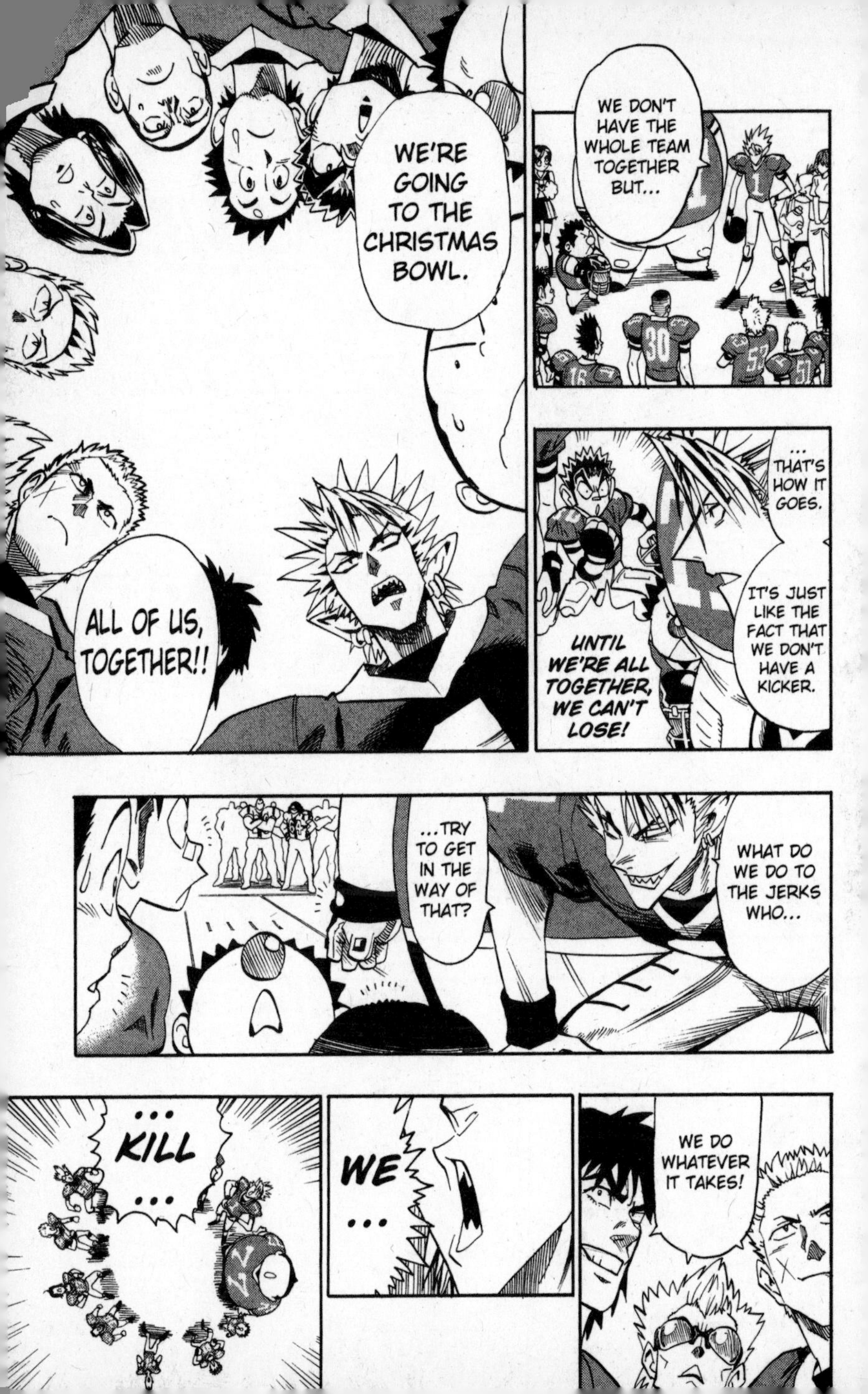
WE DON'T HAVE THE WHOLE TEAM TOGETHER BUT...
...THAT'S HOW IT GOES.
IT'S JUST LIKE THE FACT THAT WE DON'T HAVE A KICKER.
UNTIL WE'RE ALL TOGETHER, WE CAN'T LOSE!
WE'RE GOING TO THE CHRISTMAS BOWL.
ALL OF US, TOGETHER!!
WHAT DO WE DO TO THE JERKS WHO...
...TRY TO GET IN THE WAY OF THAT?
WE DO WHATEVER IT TAKES!
WE ...
... KILL ...

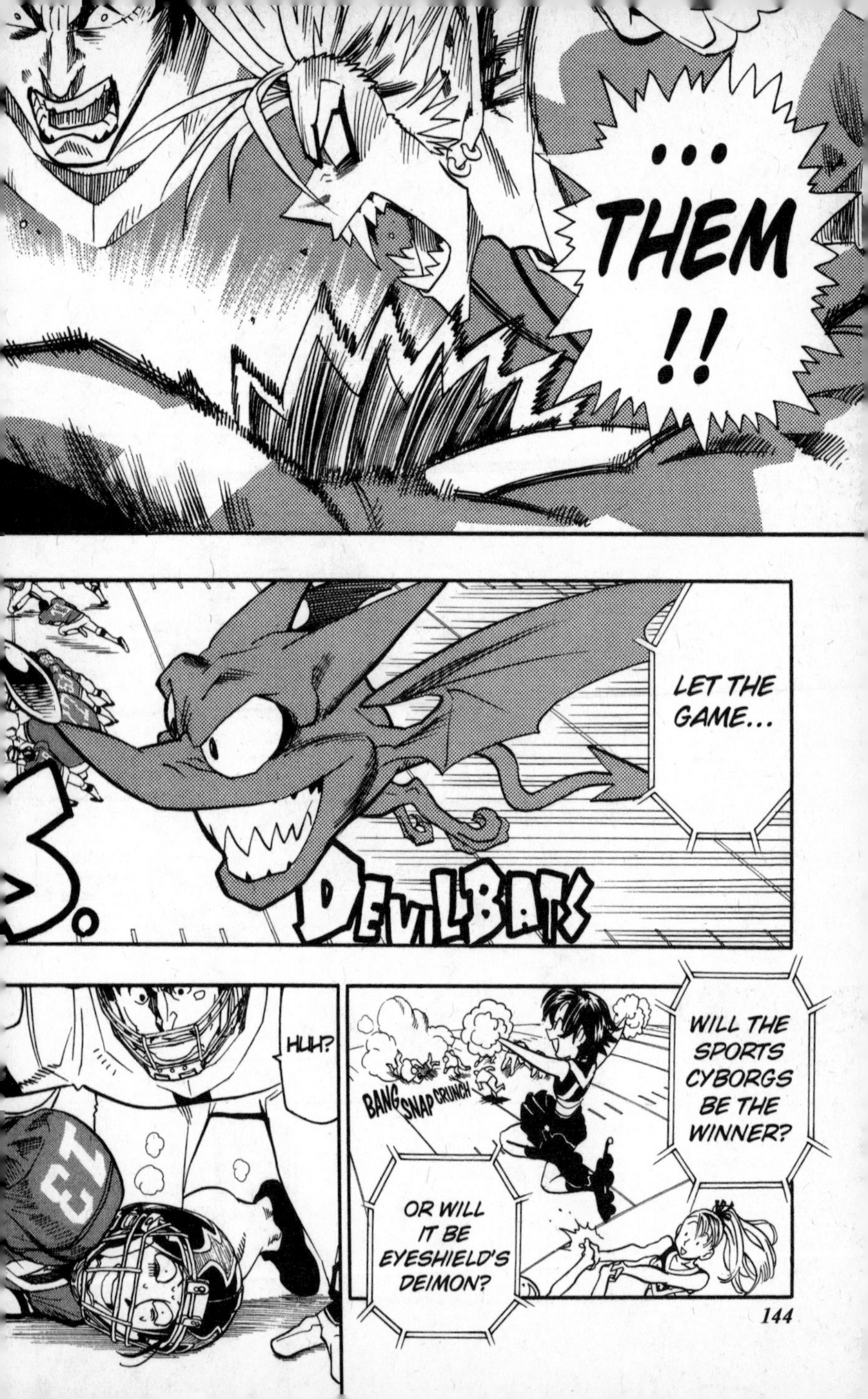
...THEM!!
LET THE GAME...
DEVILBATS
WILL THE SPORTS CYBORGS BE THE WINNER?
OR WILL IT BE EYESHIELD'S DEIMON?
BANG SNAP CRUNCH
HUH?

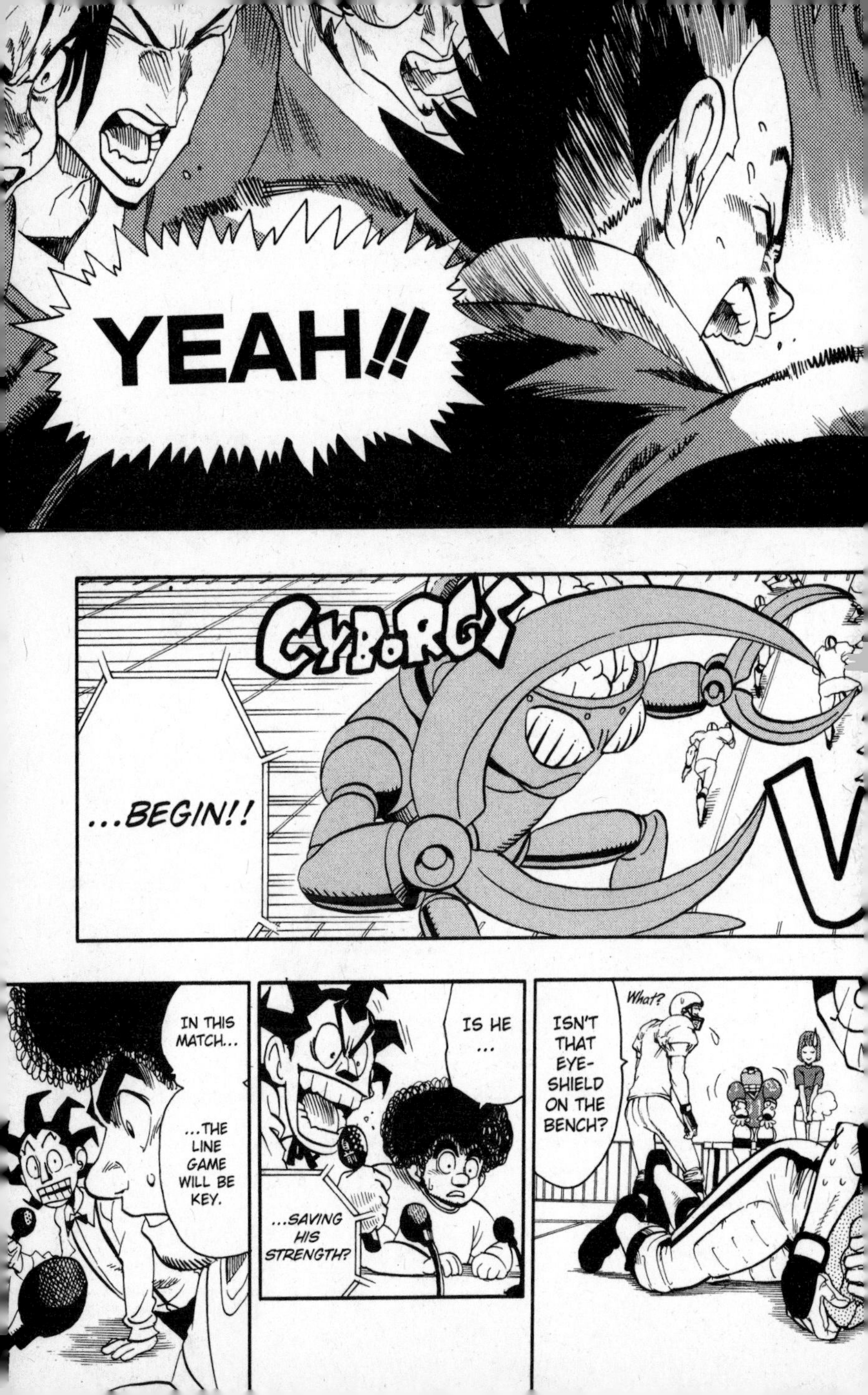
YEAH!!
CYBORGS
...BEGIN!!
What?
ISN'T THAT EYE-SHIELD ON THE BENCH?
IS HE ...
...SAVING HIS STRENGTH?
IN THIS MATCH...
...THE LINE GAME WILL BE KEY.

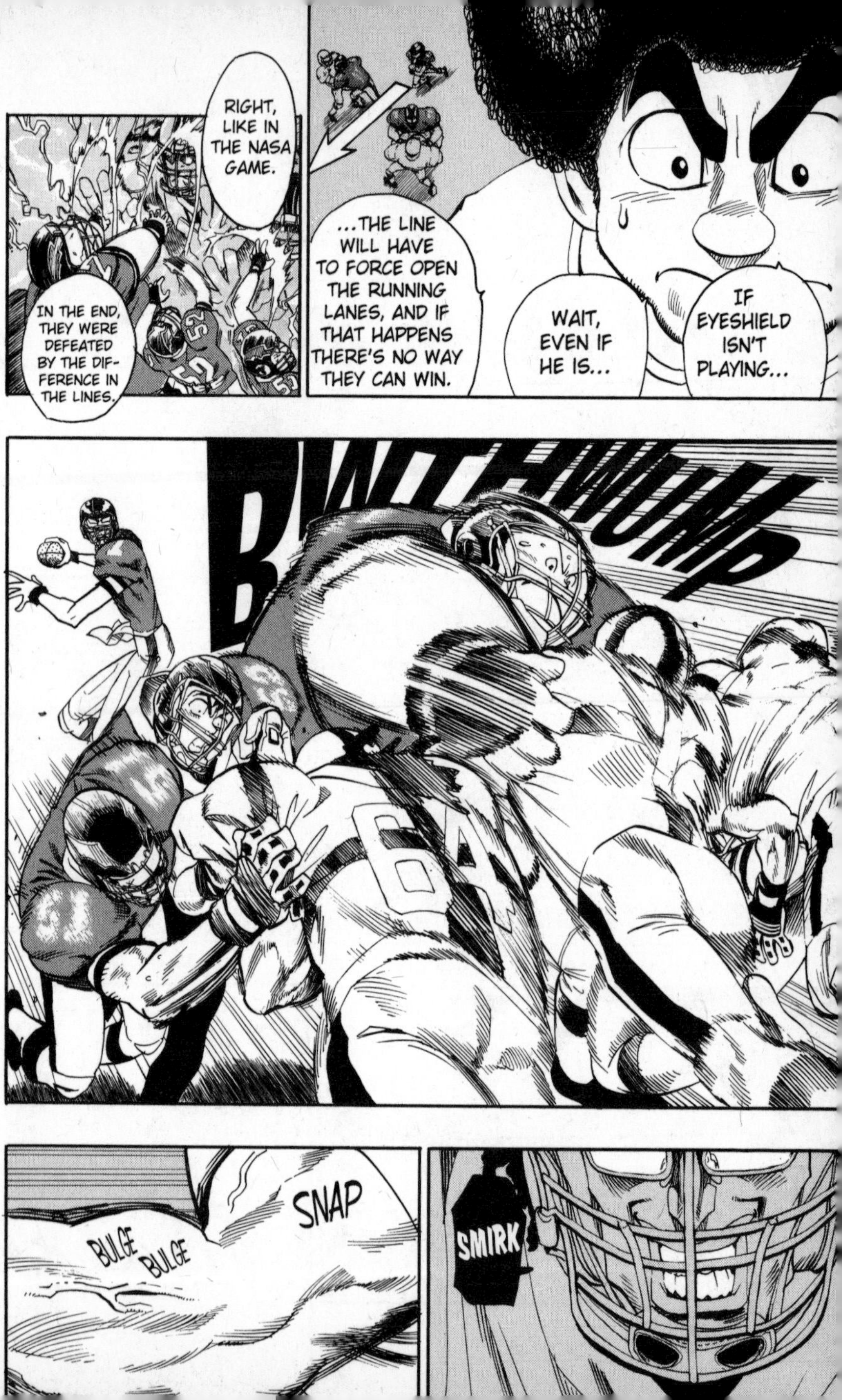
IF EYESHIELD ISN'T PLAYING...
WAIT, EVEN IF HE IS...
...THE LINE WILL HAVE TO FORCE OPEN THE RUNNING LANES, AND IF THAT HAPPENS THERE'S NO WAY THEY CAN WIN.
RIGHT, LIKE IN THE NASA GAME.
IN THE END, THEY WERE DEFEATED BY THE DIF- FERENCE IN THE LINES.
SMIRK
SNAP
BULGE BULGE

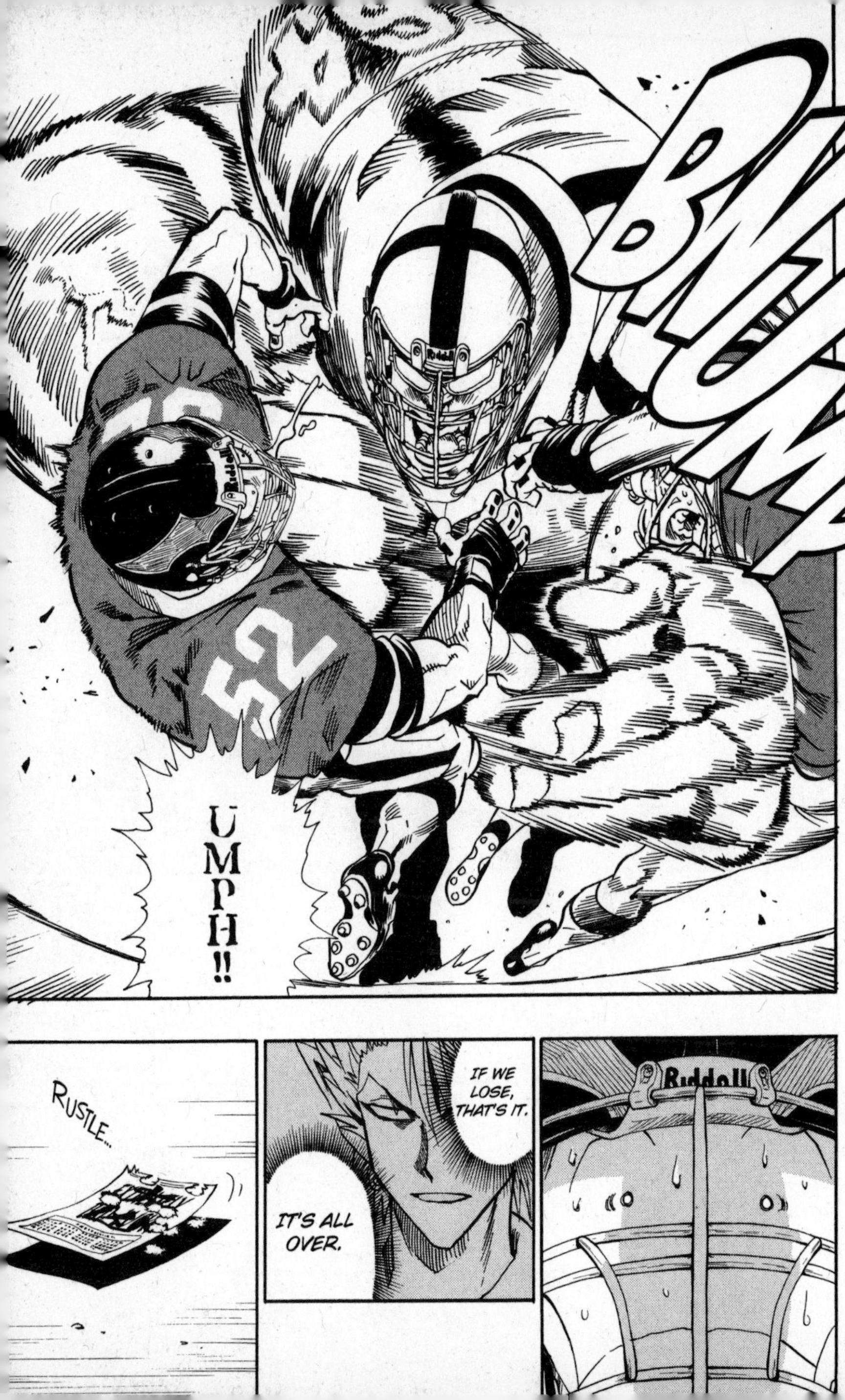
BWUMP
UMPH!!
IF WE LOSE, THAT'S IT.
IT'S ALL OVER.
RUSTLE...

Eyeshield 21 Survey Corner **Devil Bat 021**

Investigation File #027

At what age did Hiruma become interested in weapons? I'd like to know because I'd also like to own some.

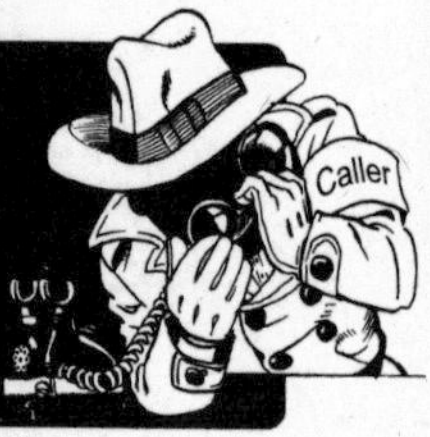
Caller

A.N., Tokyo

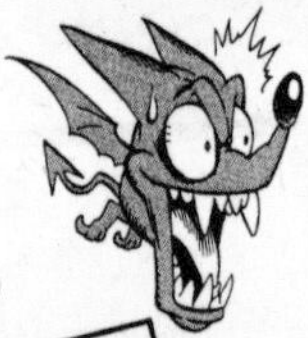

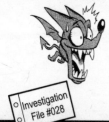

DON'T DO IT!!

Investigation File #028

Doburoku-sensei is pretty bald—has he tried using any hair growth products?

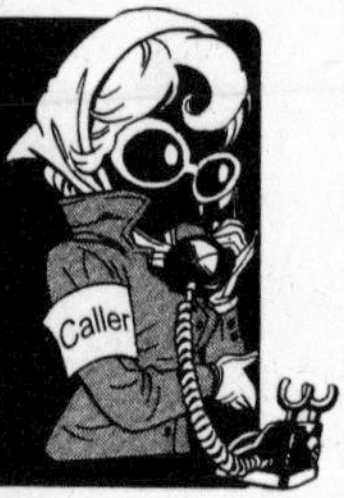
Caller

K.Y., Aichi Prefecture

THIS FEMALE CALLER EVEN DREW A PICTURE OF HIS BALD HEAD.

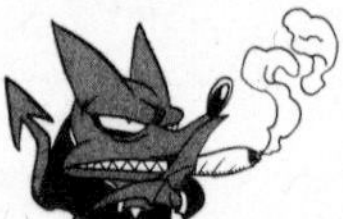

IS THAT ***REALLY*** WHAT YOU WANT TO KNOW?! OR DID YOU JUST WANT US TO PRINT YOUR LETTER? YOU CAN'T FOOL THIS DEVIL BAT.

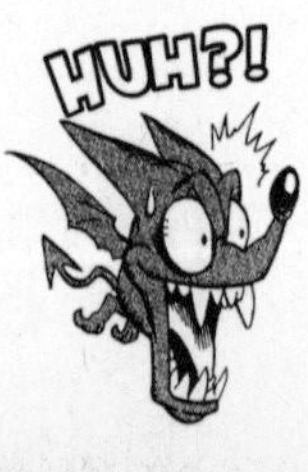
HUH?!

WAIT, YOU MANAGED TO GET YOUR WAY, DAMN YOU!!

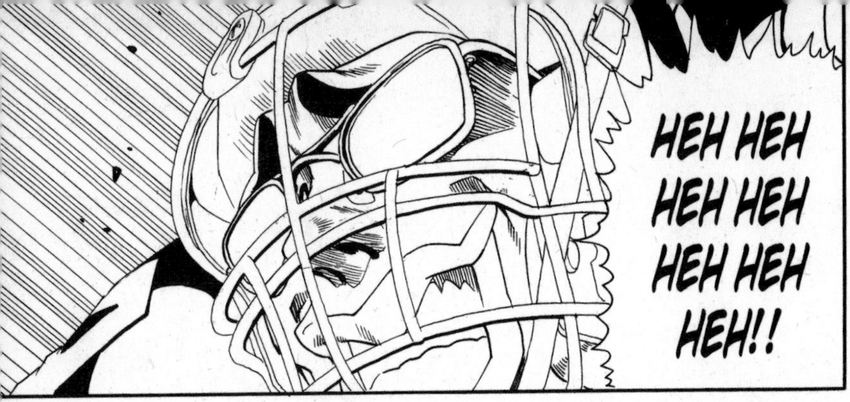
HEH HEH
HEH HEH
HEH HEH
HEH!!

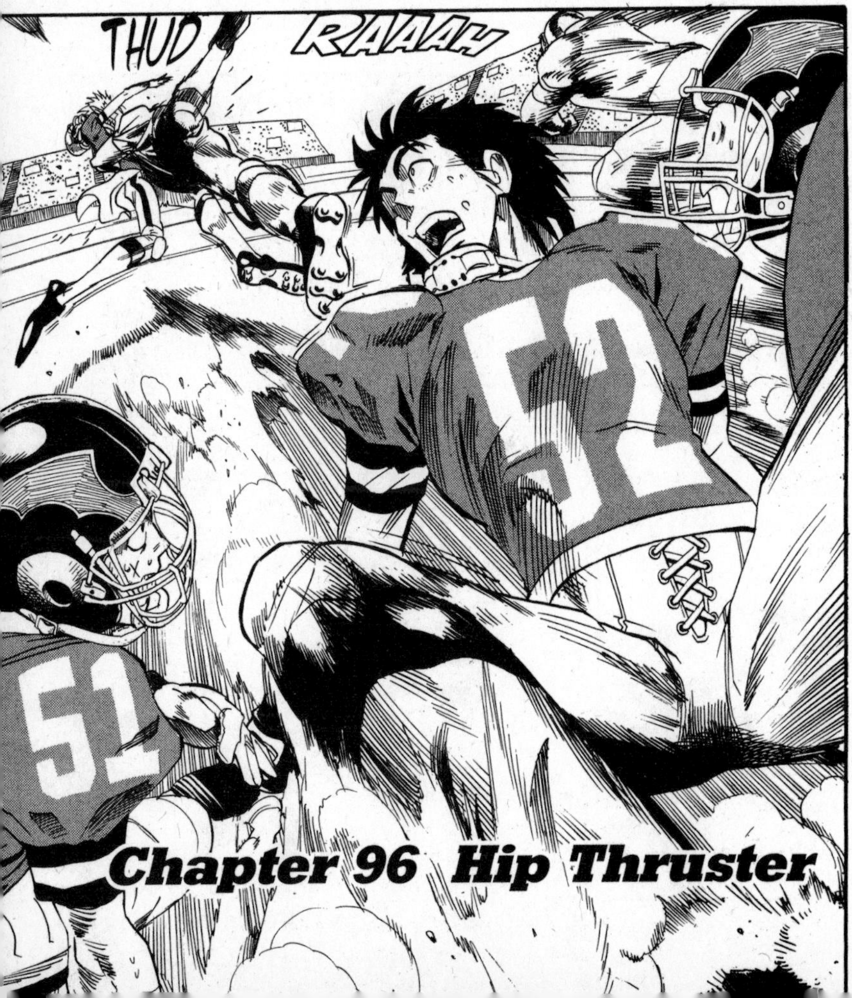
RAAAH
THUD
52
51
Chapter 96 Hip Thruster

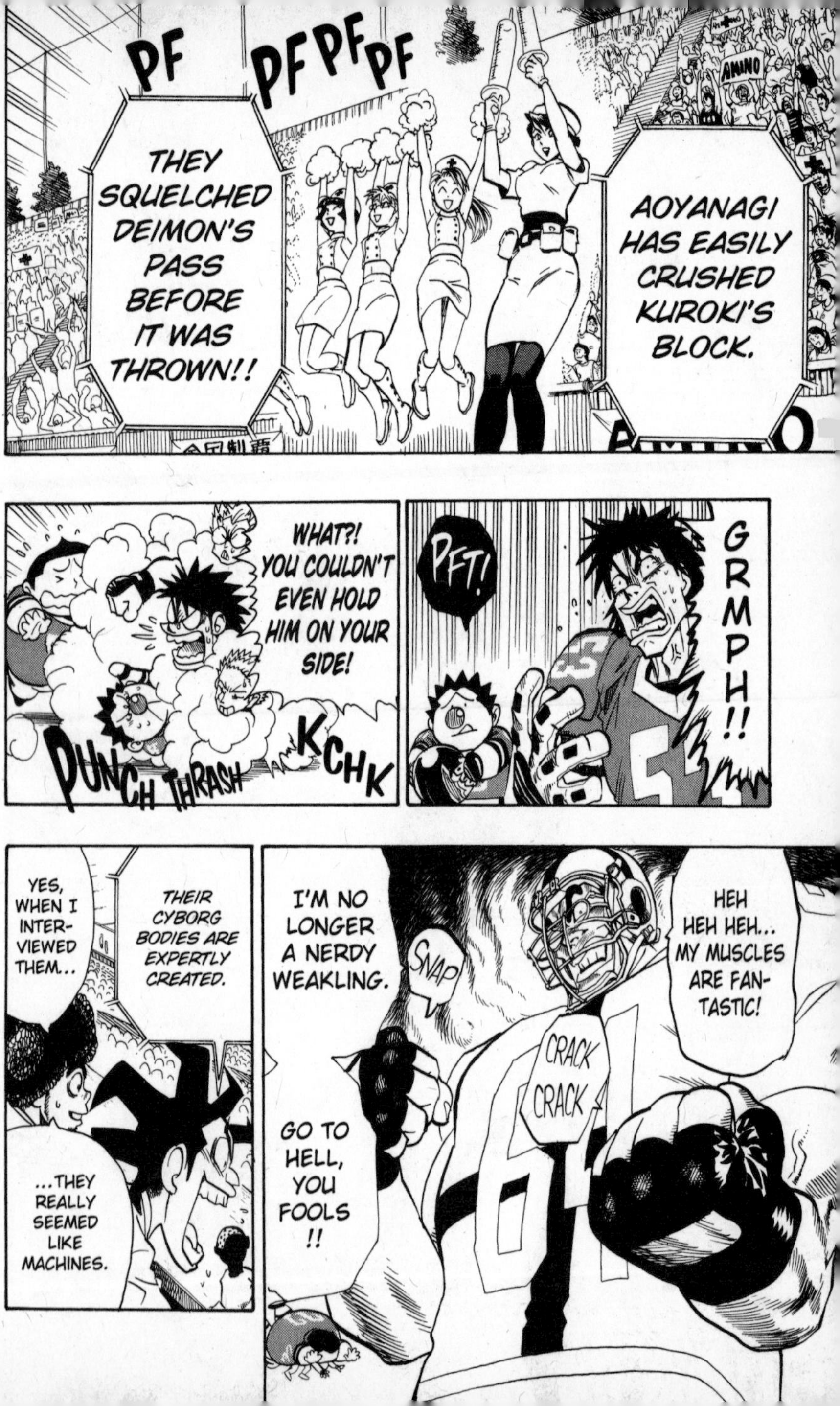
PF PF PF PF
AMINO
AOYANAGI HAS EASILY CRUSHED KUROKI'S BLOCK.
THEY SQUELCHED DEIMON'S PASS BEFORE IT WAS THROWN!!
PFT!
GRMPH!!
WHAT?! YOU COULDN'T EVEN HOLD HIM ON YOUR SIDE!
PUNCH THRASH
KCHK
HEH HEH HEH... MY MUSCLES ARE FAN-TASTIC!
CRACK CRACK
SNAP
I'M NO LONGER A NERDY WEAKLING.
GO TO HELL, YOU FOOLS!!
THEIR CYBORG BODIES ARE EXPERTLY CREATED.
YES, WHEN I INTER-VIEWED THEM...
...THEY REALLY SEEMED LIKE MACHINES.

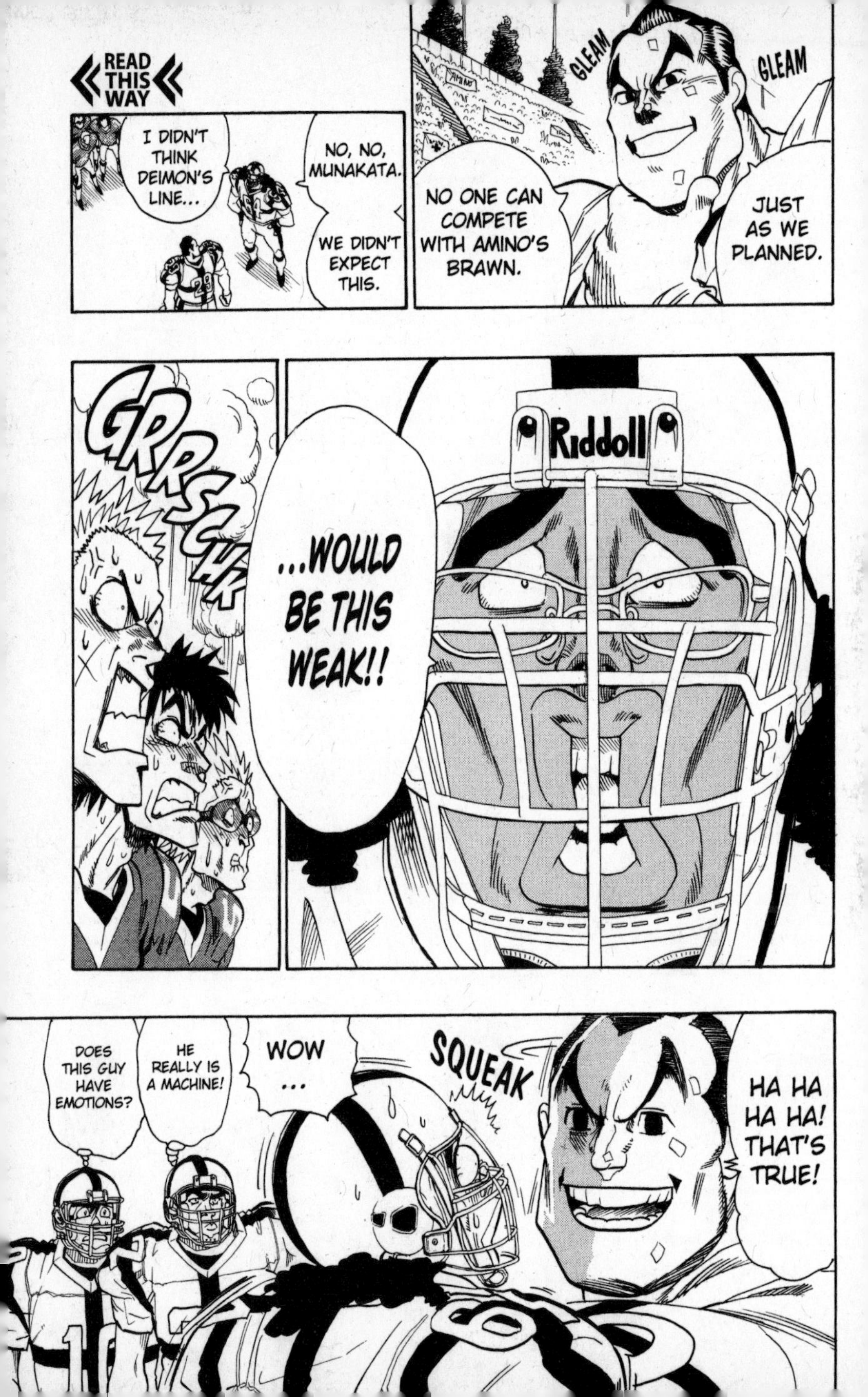
READ THIS WAY
GLEAM
GLEAM
JUST AS WE PLANNED.
NO ONE CAN COMPETE WITH AMINO'S BRAWN.
NO, NO, MUNAKATA.
WE DIDN'T EXPECT THIS.
I DIDN'T THINK DEIMON'S LINE...
Riddoll
...WOULD BE THIS WEAK!!
GRRSCHK
HA HA HA HA! THAT'S TRUE!
SQUEAK
WOW ...
HE REALLY IS A MACHINE!
DOES THIS GUY HAVE EMOTIONS?

PWF
PWF
PWF PWF

ROAR

WHOOAA
!!

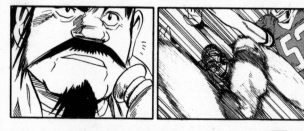

IT'S NO
GOOD!

AMINO
CRUSHED
THE LINE
AGAIN!!

THMP

BWFWSH

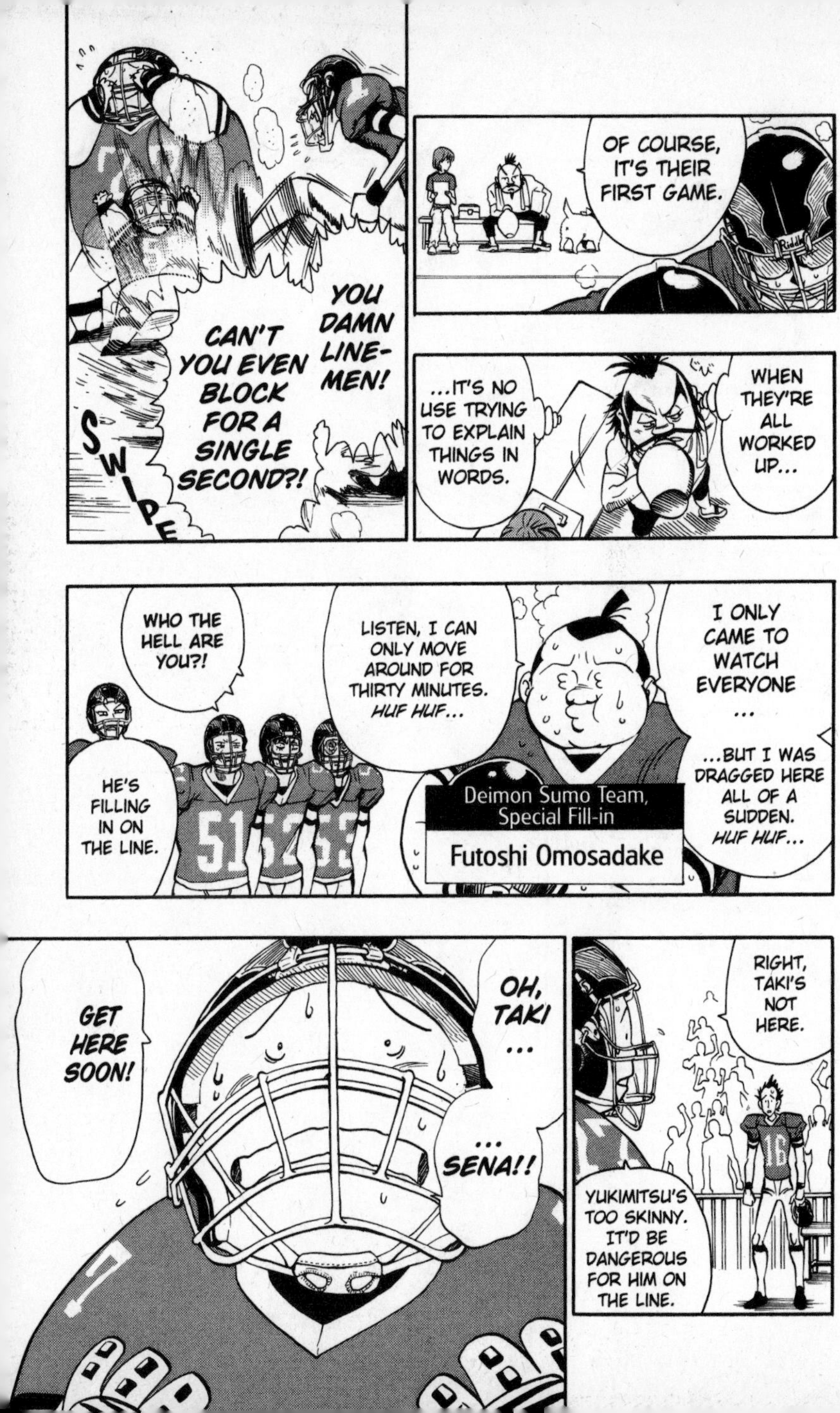
OF COURSE, IT'S THEIR FIRST GAME.
WHEN THEY'RE ALL WORKED UP...
...IT'S NO USE TRYING TO EXPLAIN THINGS IN WORDS.
YOU DAMN LINE-MEN!
CAN'T YOU EVEN BLOCK FOR A SINGLE SECOND?!
SWIPE
I ONLY CAME TO WATCH EVERYONE ...
...BUT I WAS DRAGGED HERE ALL OF A SUDDEN. HUF HUF...
Deimon Sumo Team, Special Fill-in
Futoshi Omosadake
LISTEN, I CAN ONLY MOVE AROUND FOR THIRTY MINUTES. HUF HUF...
WHO THE HELL ARE YOU?!
HE'S FILLING IN ON THE LINE.
RIGHT, TAKI'S NOT HERE.
YUKIMITSU'S TOO SKINNY. IT'D BE DANGEROUS FOR HIM ON THE LINE.
OH, TAKI ...
... SENA!!
GET HERE SOON!

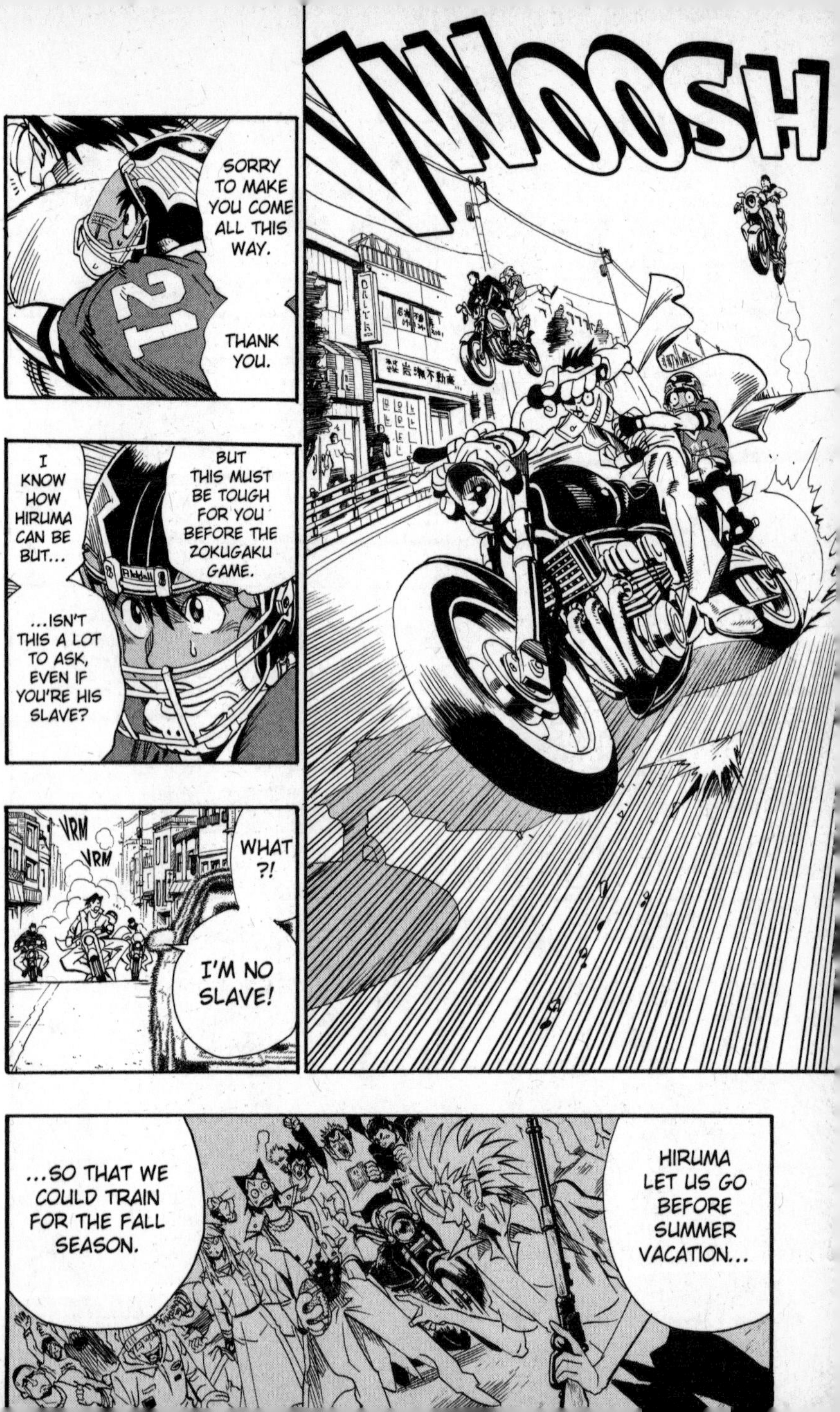
WOOSH
SORRY TO MAKE YOU COME ALL THIS WAY.
THANK YOU.
BUT THIS MUST BE TOUGH FOR YOU BEFORE THE ZOKUGAKU GAME.
I KNOW HOW HIRUMA CAN BE BUT...
...ISN'T THIS A LOT TO ASK, EVEN IF YOU'RE HIS SLAVE?
WHAT ?!
I'M NO SLAVE!
VRM
VRM
HIRUMA LET US GO BEFORE SUMMER VACATION...
...SO THAT WE COULD TRAIN FOR THE FALL SEASON.

READ THIS WAY

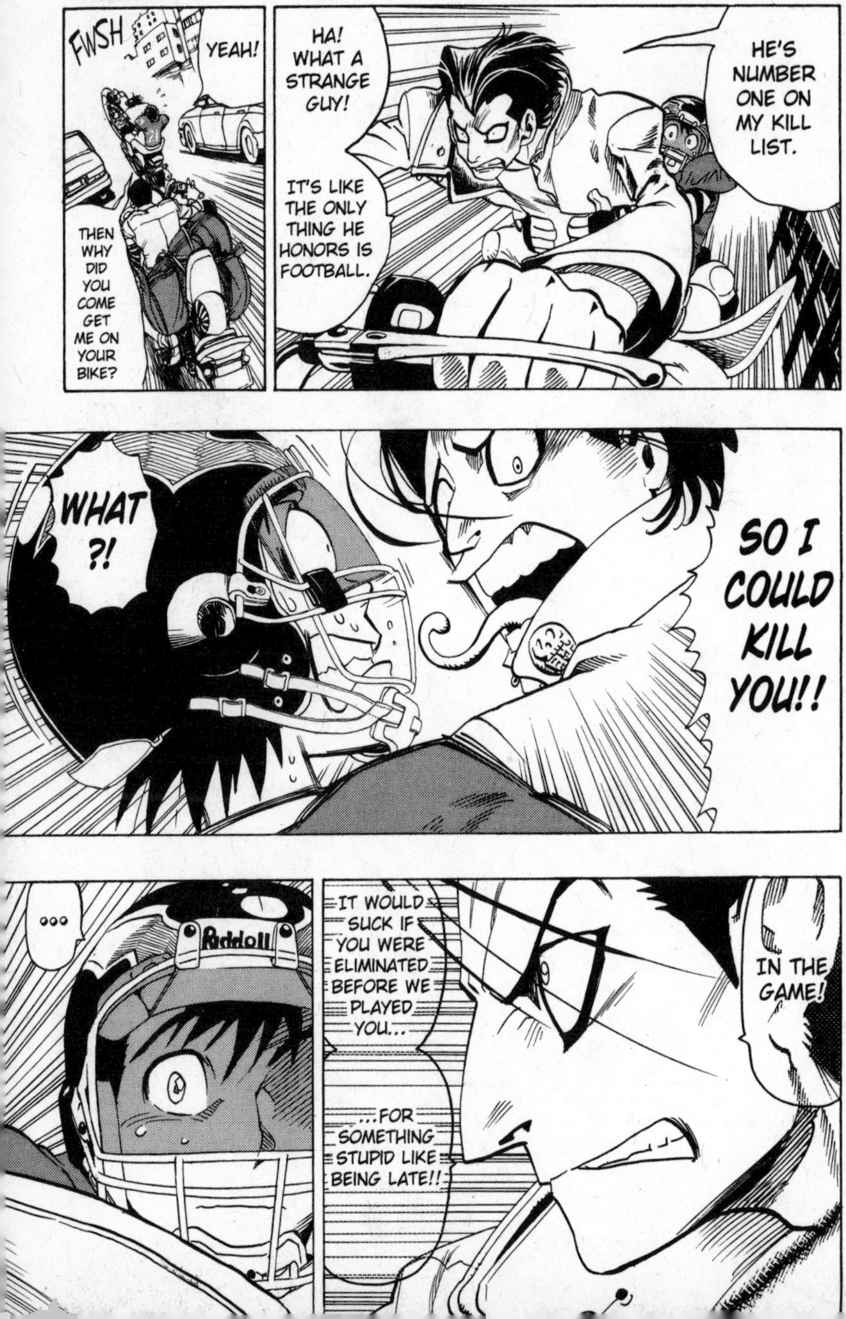
HE'S NUMBER ONE ON MY KILL LIST.
HA! WHAT A STRANGE GUY!
IT'S LIKE THE ONLY THING HE HONORS IS FOOTBALL.
YEAH!
FWSH
THEN WHY DID YOU COME GET ME ON YOUR BIKE?
SO I COULD KILL YOU!!
WHAT?!
IN THE GAME!
IT WOULD SUCK IF YOU WERE ELIMINATED BEFORE WE PLAYED YOU...
...FOR SOMETHING STUPID LIKE BEING LATE!!
...

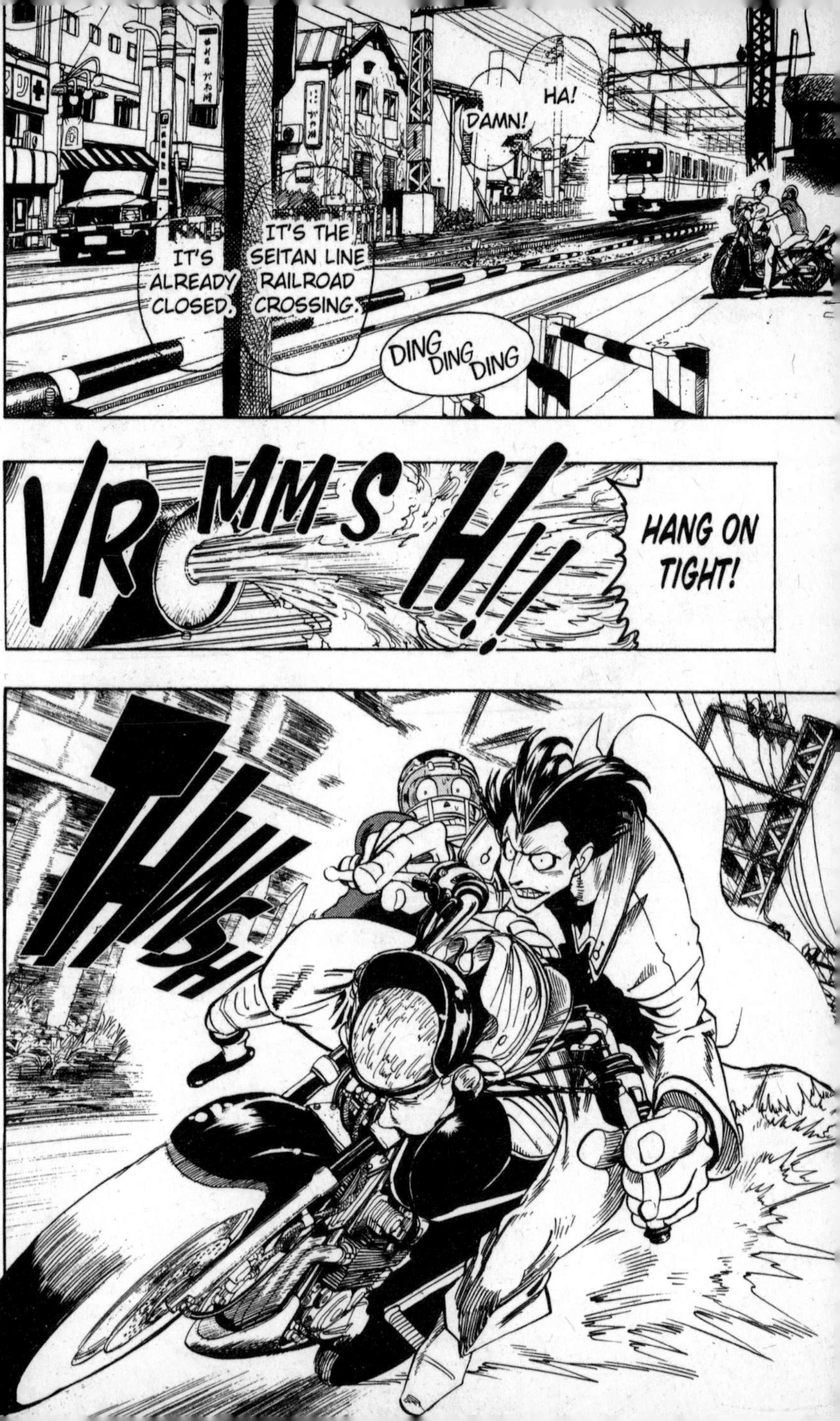
HA!
DAMN!
IT'S THE SEITAN LINE RAILROAD CROSSING.
DING DING DING
IT'S ALREADY CLOSED.
HANG ON TIGHT!
VRMMSH!!
THWSH!!

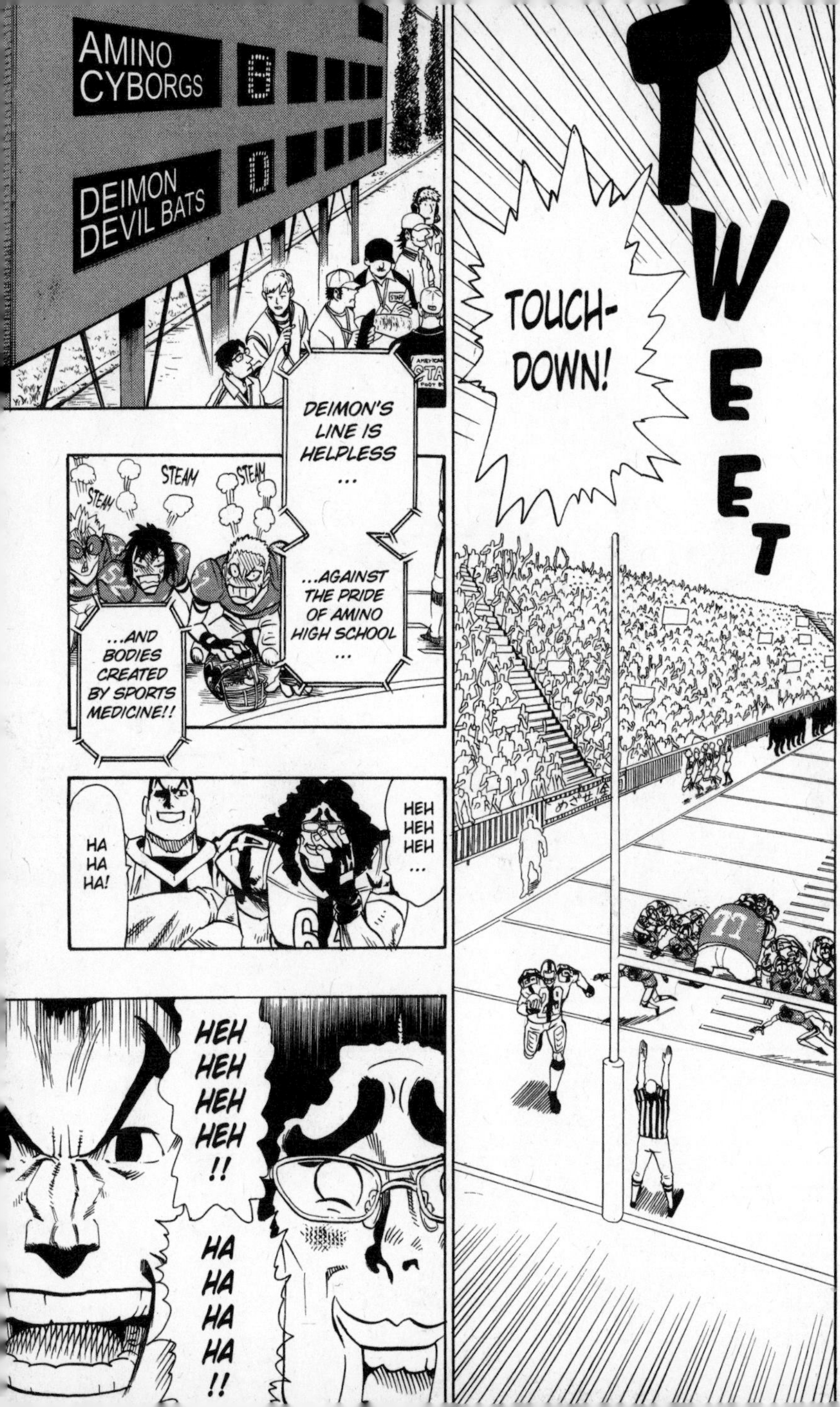
TWEET
TOUCH-DOWN!
AMINO CYBORGS 6
DEIMON DEVIL BATS 0
DEIMON'S LINE IS HELPLESS ...
...AGAINST THE PRIDE OF AMINO HIGH SCHOOL ...
...AND BODIES CREATED BY SPORTS MEDICINE!!
STEAM
STEAM
STEAM
HEH HEH HEH ...
HA HA HA!
HEH HEH HEH HEH !!
HA HA HA HA !!

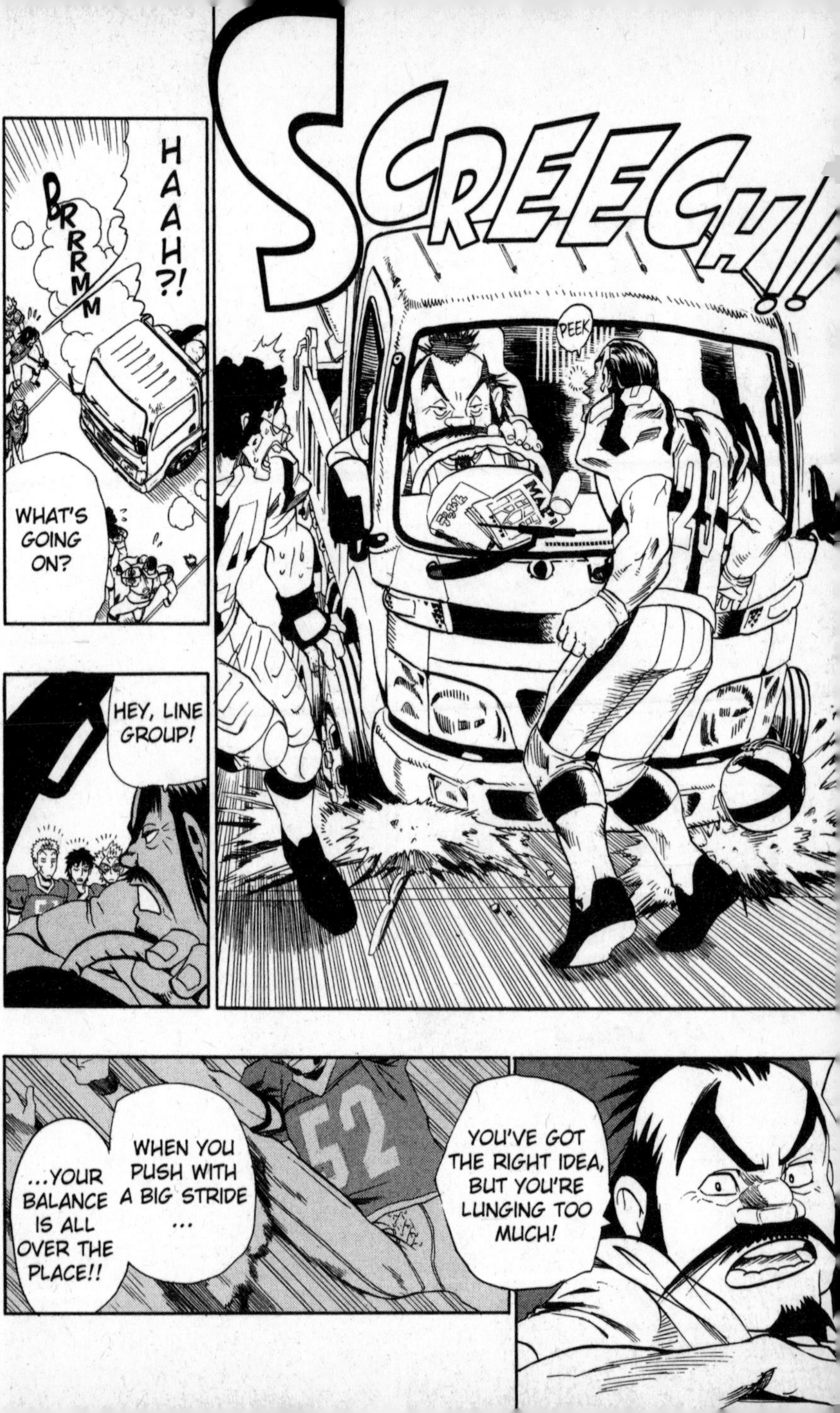
SCREECH!!!
PEEK
HAAAH?!
BRRRMM
WHAT'S GOING ON?
HEY, LINE GROUP!
YOU'VE GOT THE RIGHT IDEA, BUT YOU'RE LUNGING TOO MUCH!
WHEN YOU PUSH WITH A BIG STRIDE...
...YOUR BALANCE IS ALL OVER THE PLACE!!

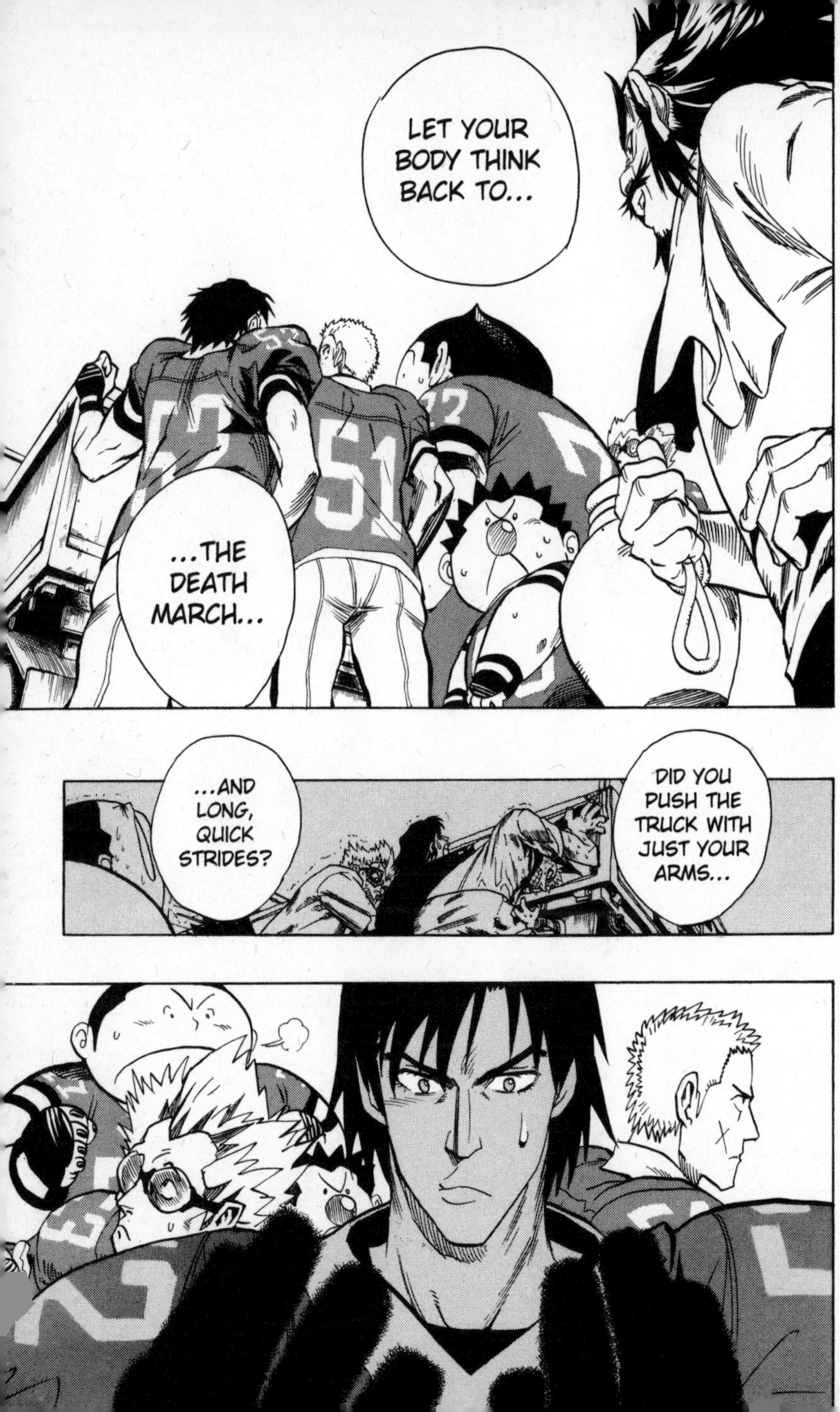
LET YOUR BODY THINK BACK TO...
...THE DEATH MARCH...
DID YOU PUSH THE TRUCK WITH JUST YOUR ARMS...
...AND LONG, QUICK STRIDES?

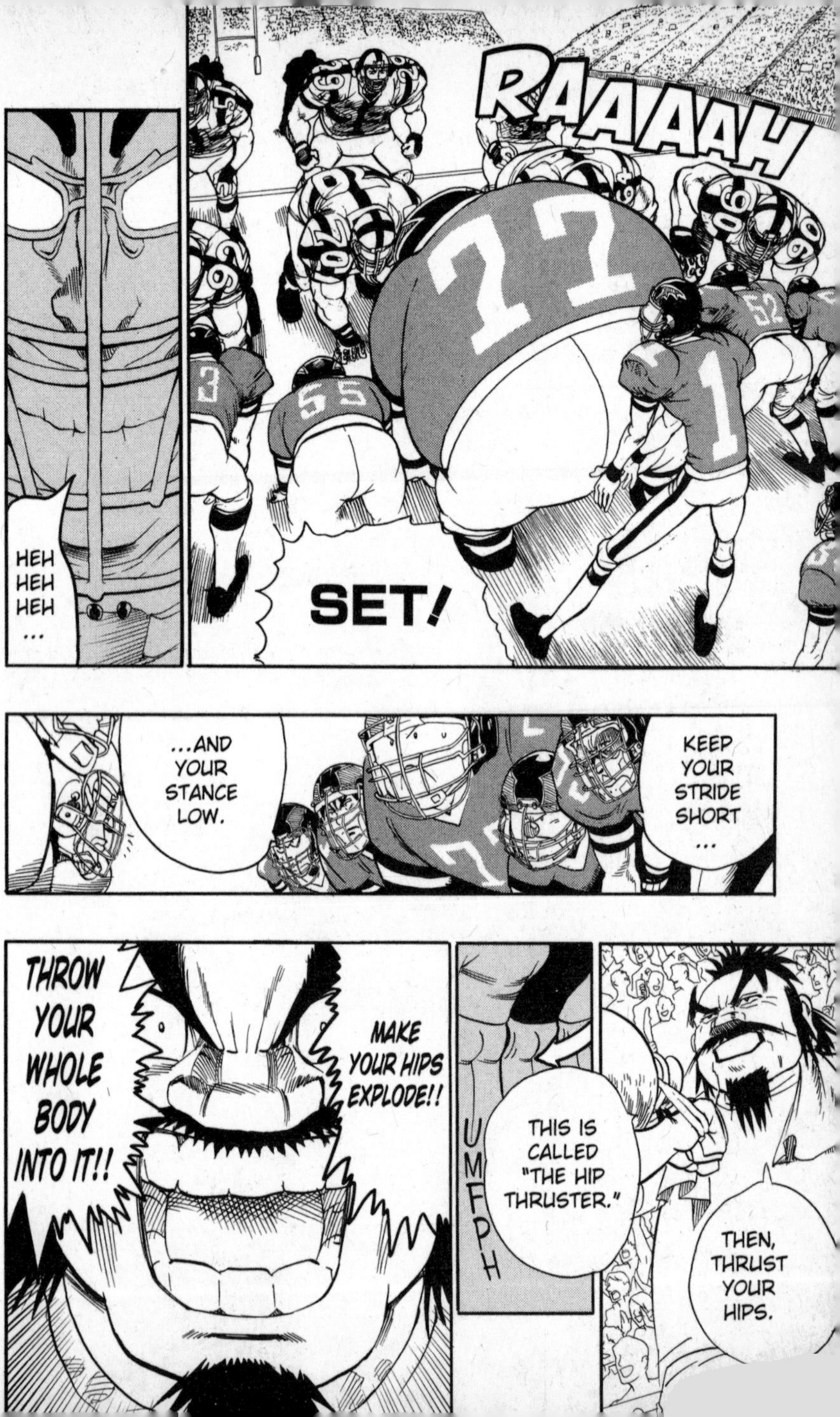
RAAAAH
SET!
HEH HEH HEH ...
KEEP YOUR STRIDE SHORT ...
...AND YOUR STANCE LOW.
THEN, THRUST YOUR HIPS.
THIS IS CALLED "THE HIP THRUSTER."
UMFPH
MAKE YOUR HIPS EXPLODE!!
THROW YOUR WHOLE BODY INTO IT!!

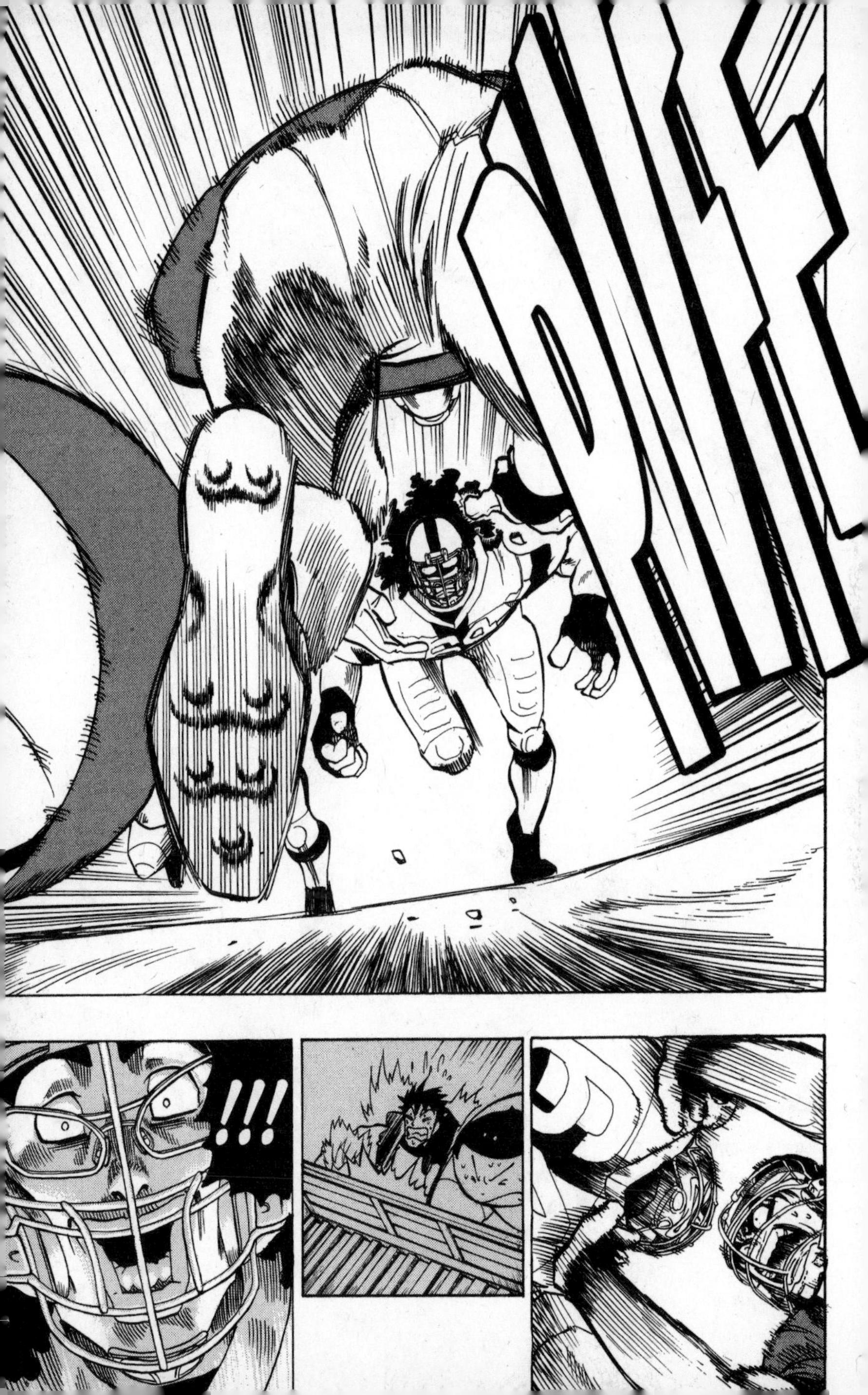
!!!

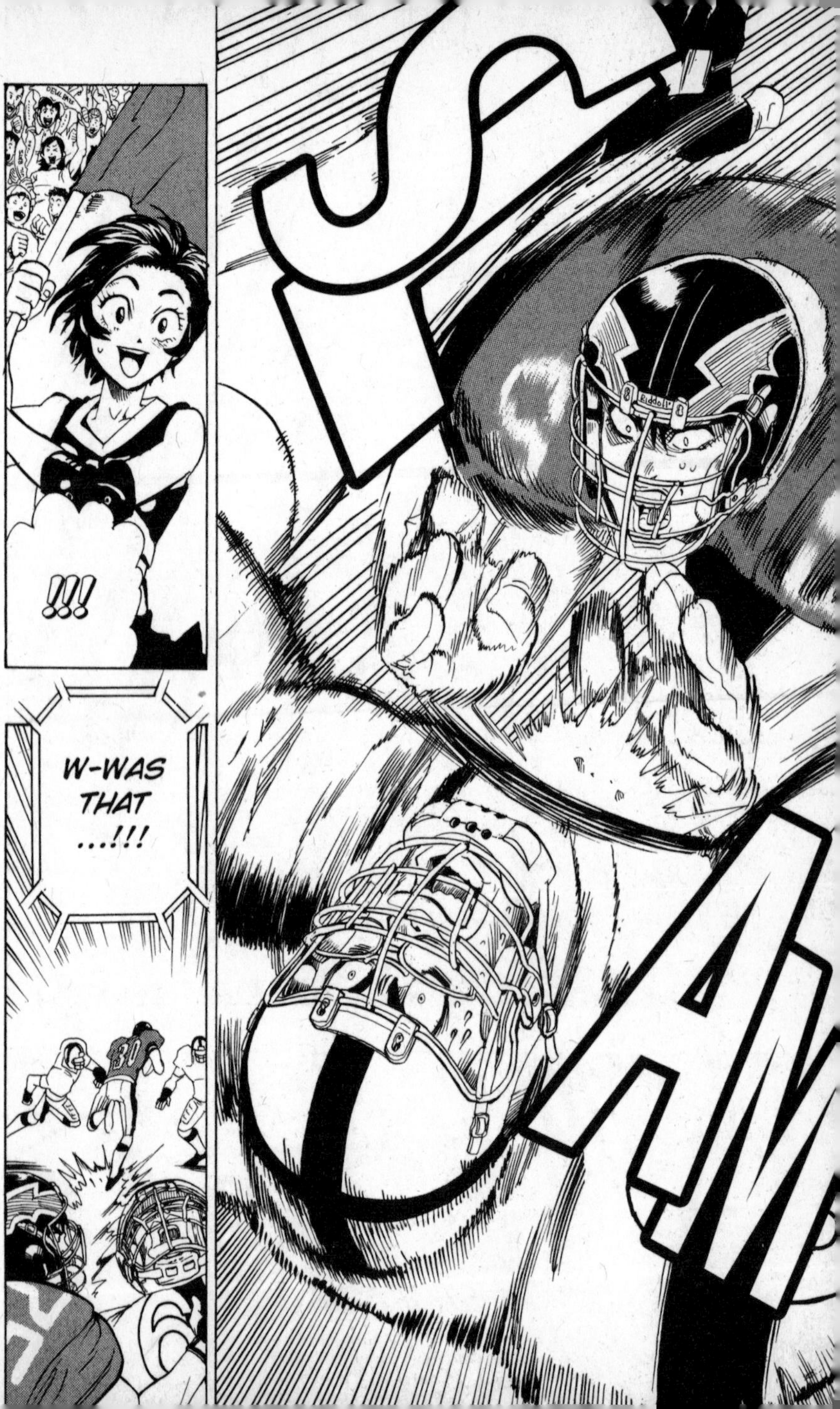
!!!
W-WAS THAT ...!!!

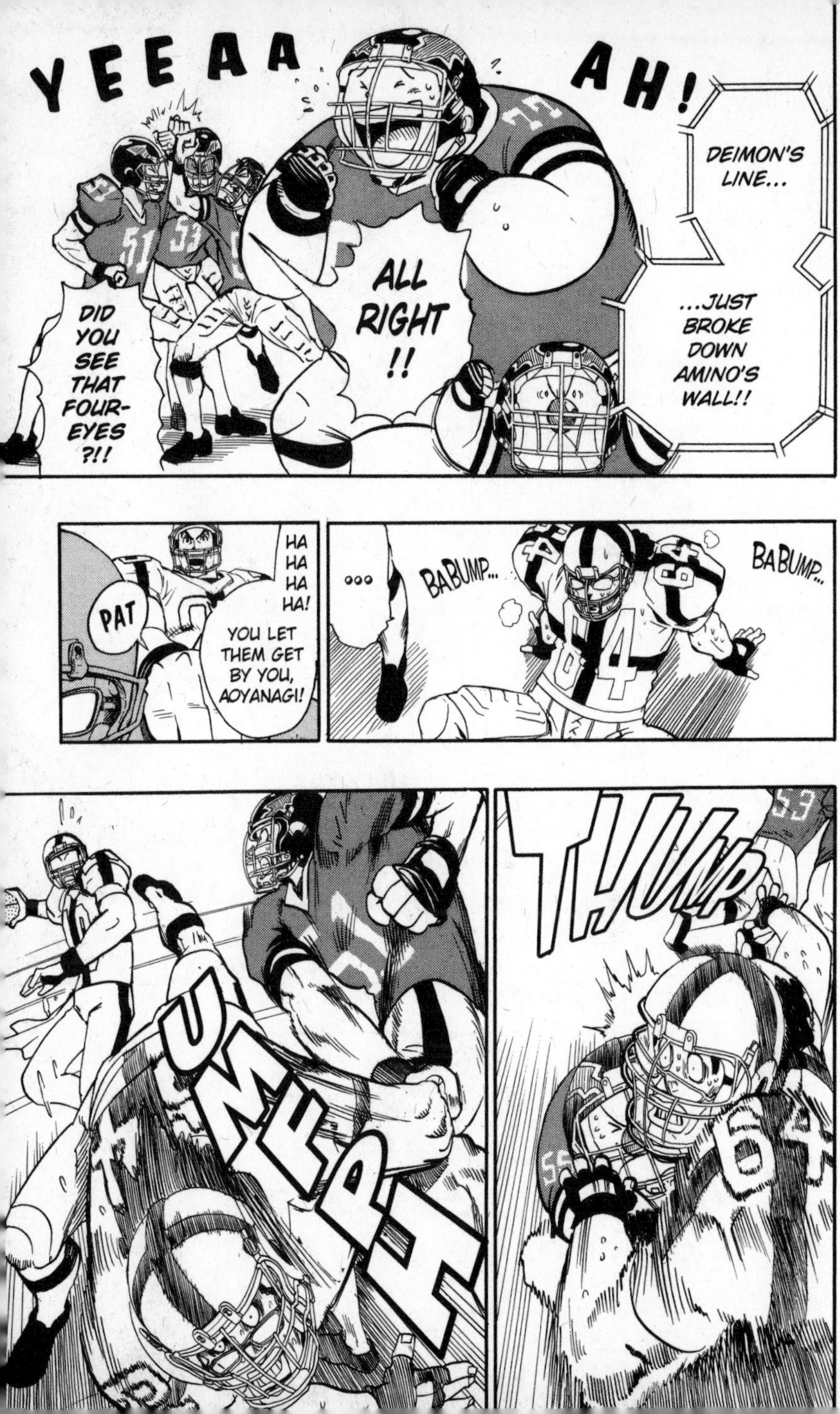
YEEAAAH!
DEIMON'S LINE...
...JUST BROKE DOWN AMINO'S WALL!!
ALL RIGHT!!
DID YOU SEE THAT FOUR-EYES?!!
BABUMP...
BABUMP...
...
HA HA HA HA!
YOU LET THEM GET BY YOU, AOYANAGI!
PAT
THUMP
UMPH

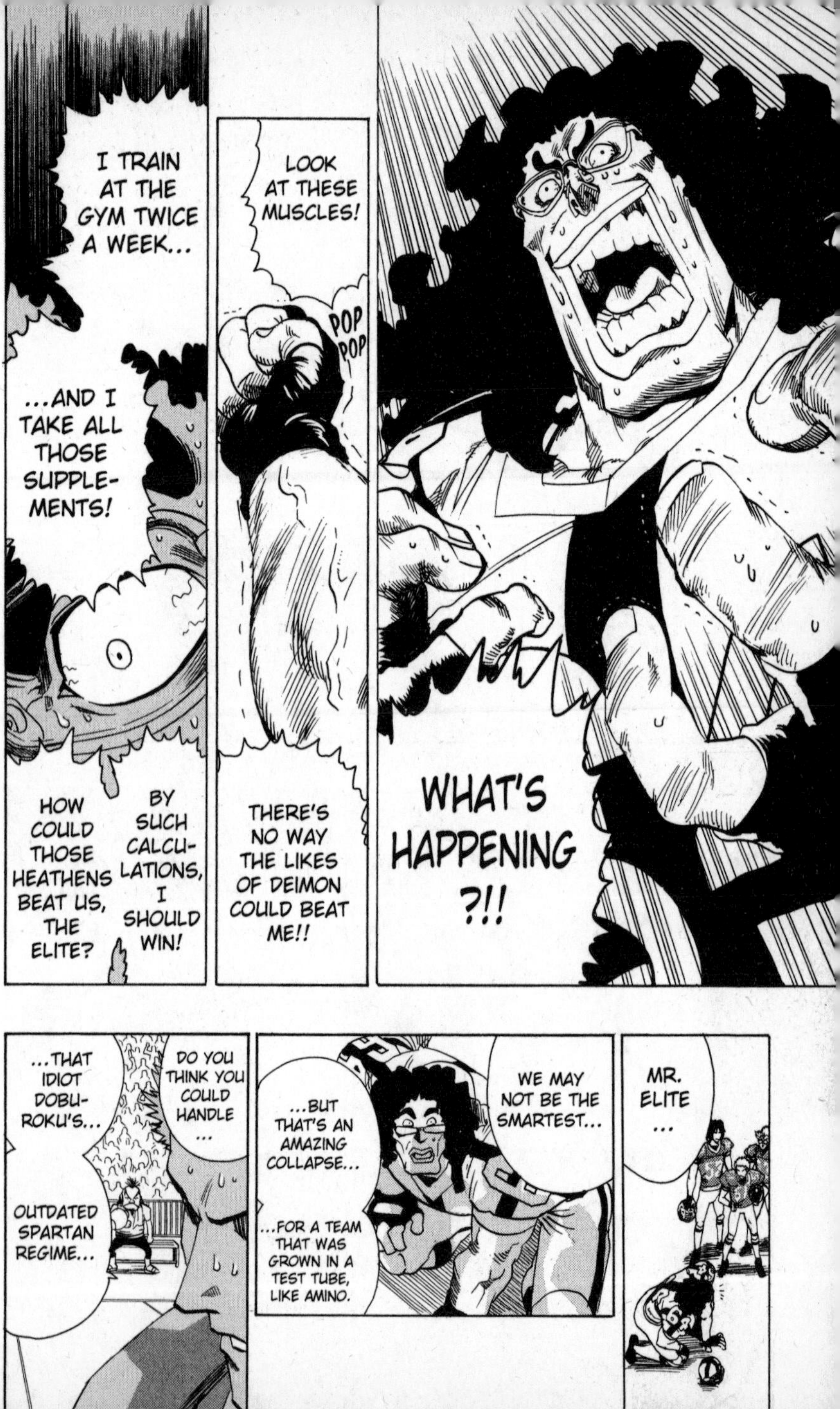
WHAT'S HAPPENING ?!!
LOOK AT THESE MUSCLES!
POP POP
THERE'S NO WAY THE LIKES OF DEIMON COULD BEAT ME!!
I TRAIN AT THE GYM TWICE A WEEK...
...AND I TAKE ALL THOSE SUPPLE- MENTS!
BY SUCH CALCU- LATIONS, I SHOULD WIN!
HOW COULD THOSE HEATHENS BEAT US, THE ELITE?
MR. ELITE ...
WE MAY NOT BE THE SMARTEST...
...BUT THAT'S AN AMAZING COLLAPSE...
...FOR A TEAM THAT WAS GROWN IN A TEST TUBE, LIKE AMINO.
DO YOU THINK YOU COULD HANDLE ...
...THAT IDIOT DOBU- ROKU'S...
OUTDATED SPARTAN REGIME...

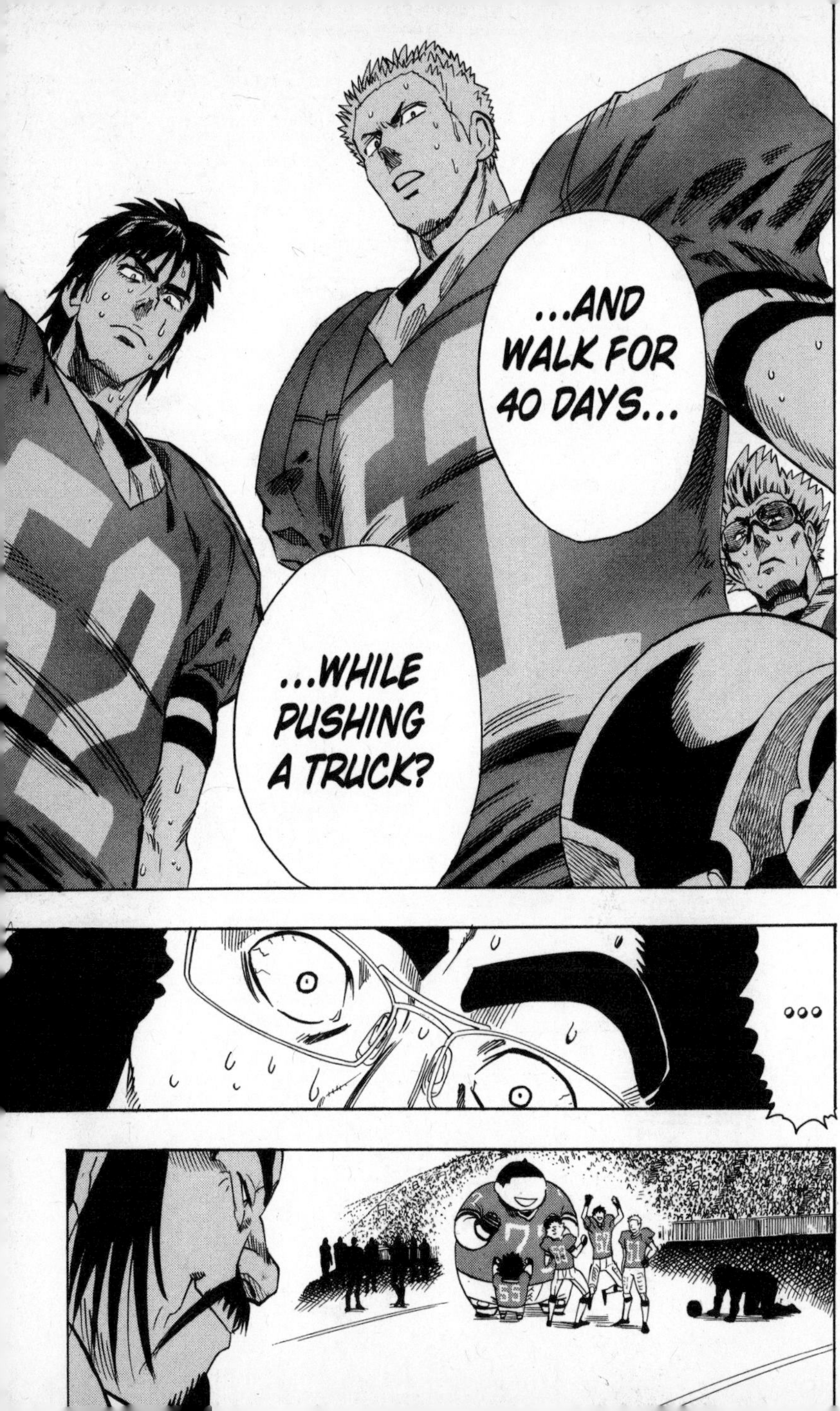
...AND WALK FOR 40 DAYS...
...WHILE PUSHING A TRUCK?
...

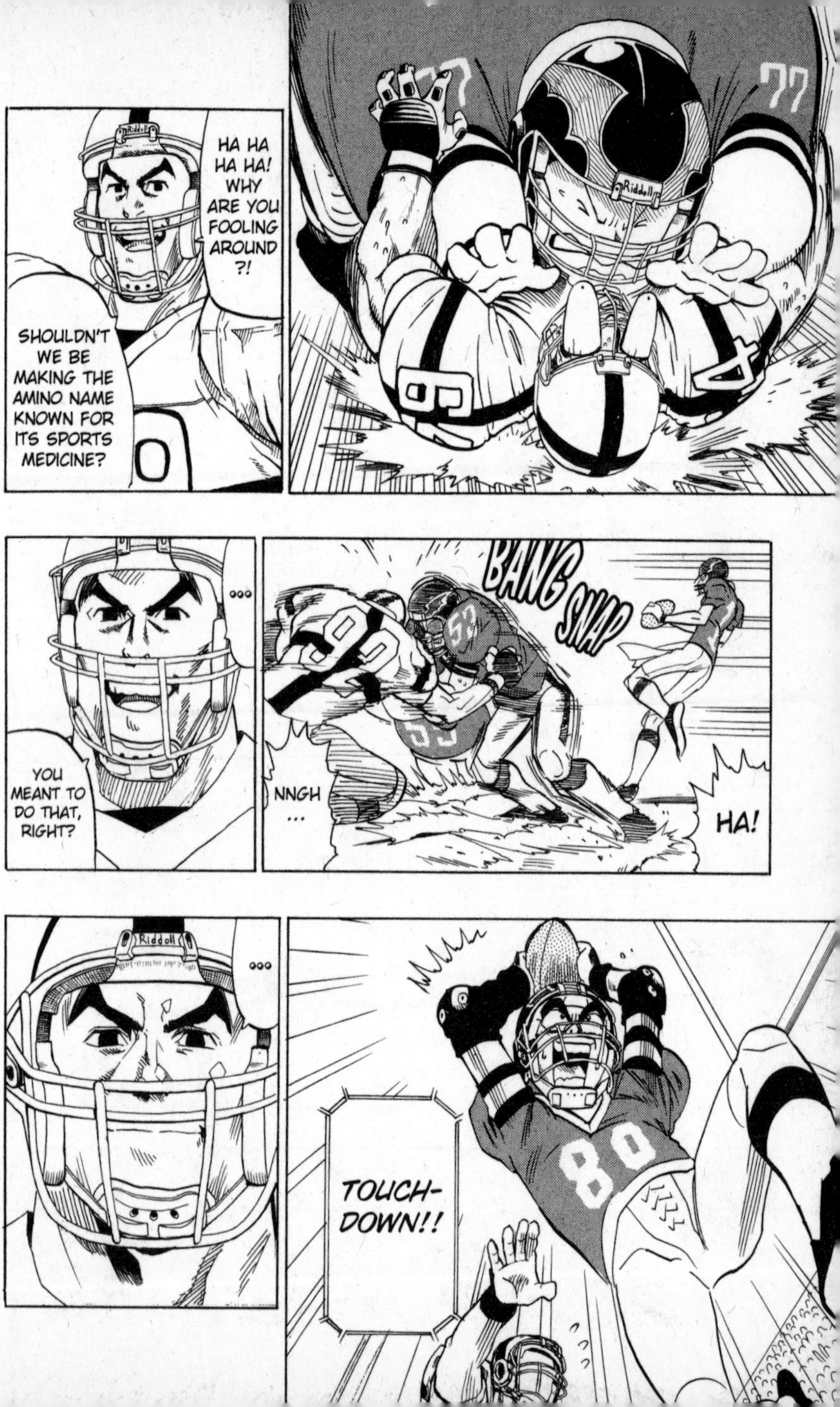
HA HA HA HA! WHY ARE YOU FOOLING AROUND ?!
SHOULDN'T WE BE MAKING THE AMINO NAME KNOWN FOR ITS SPORTS MEDICINE?
BANG SNAP
HA!
NNGH ...
...
YOU MEANT TO DO THAT, RIGHT?
TOUCH-DOWN!!
...

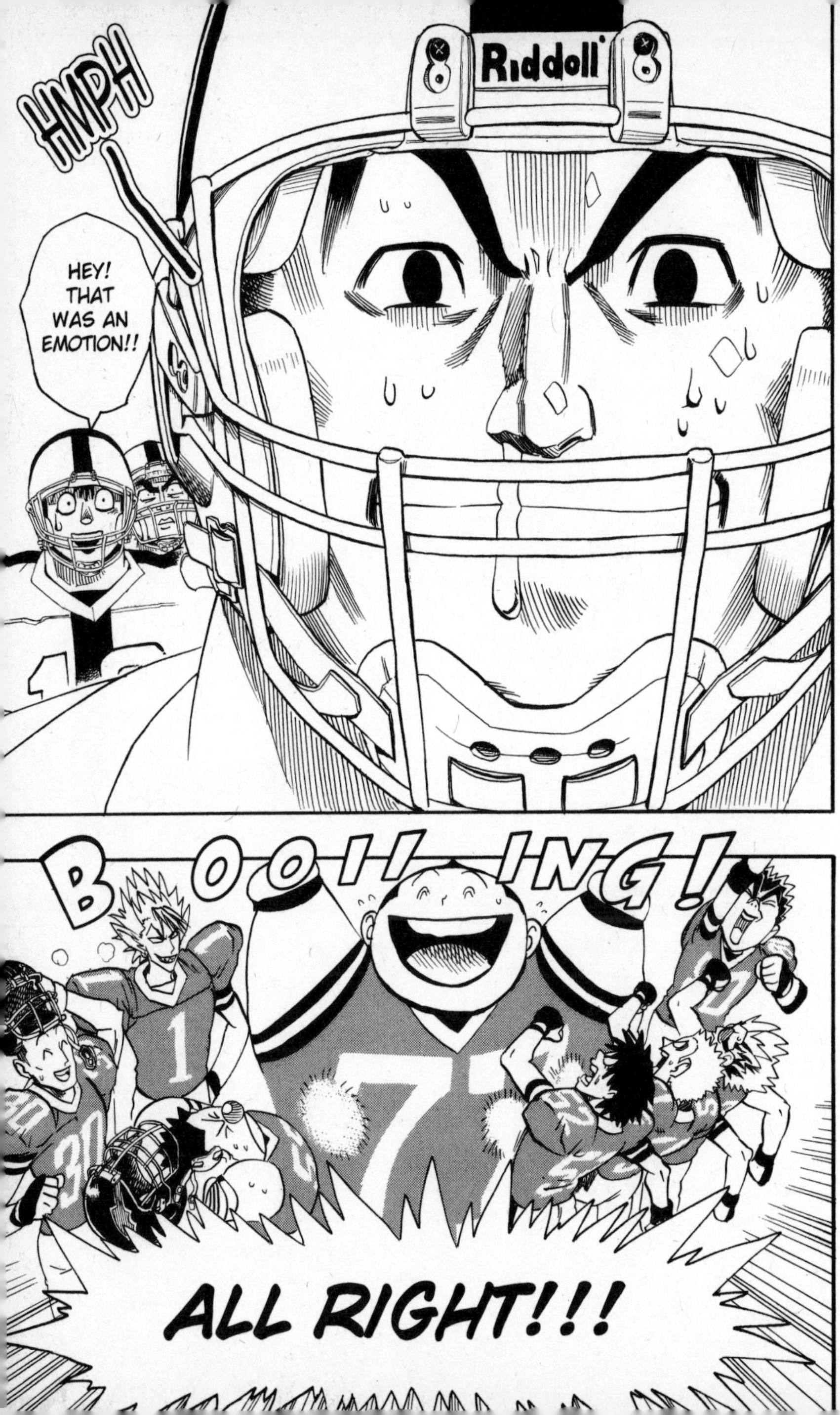

Riddoll
HMPH
HEY! THAT WAS AN EMOTION!!
BOOII ING!
ALL RIGHT!!!

Deluxe Biographies
of the Supporting Cast

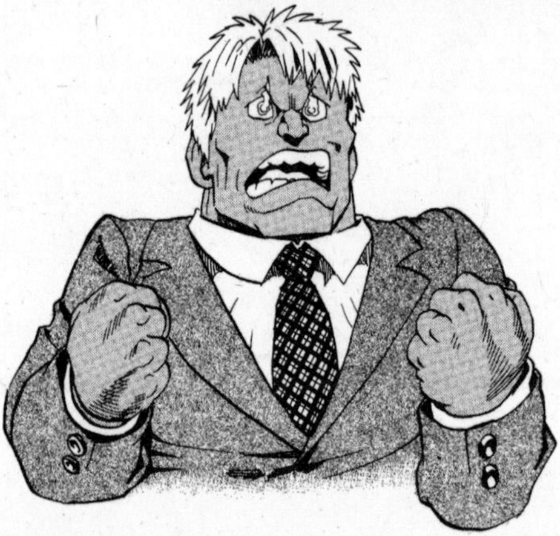

Director of the Football League

He's a pretty hot-blooded fellow. Even in winter, whatever room he's in doesn't need heating.

His book, *My Struggle: The Battle of Football*, was published by Sports Magazine Ltd.

Futoshi Omosadake

He's so incredibly lazy that he hates activity of any kind, which is how his body got to be this way.

He even hates to open his eyes, which is why he looks this way.

Lately, he hates even his own heartbeats. Of course, eating is the only thing he doesn't hate to do.

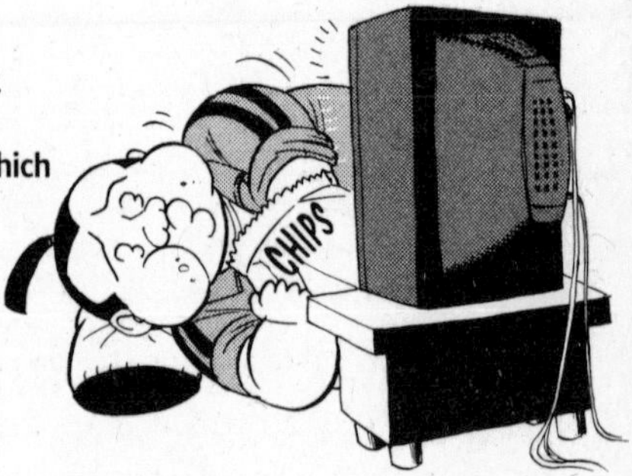
CHIPS

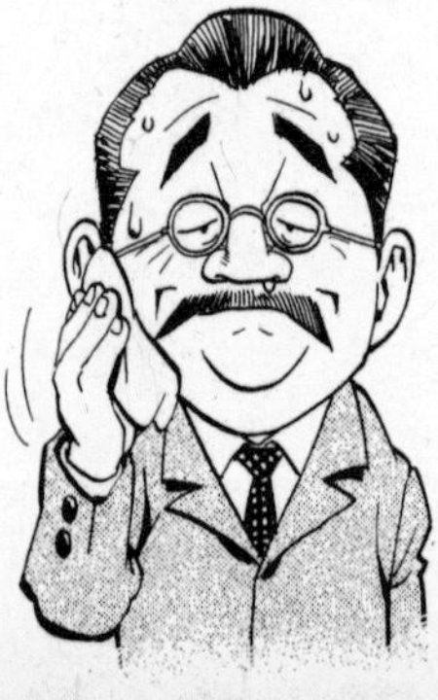

Deimon's Principal

One day, Hiruma said to him, "I've got some photos of you…" (you know how Hiruma is), and this stupid man incriminated himself by answering, "Uh, are you talking about my affair? What do you want to know?"

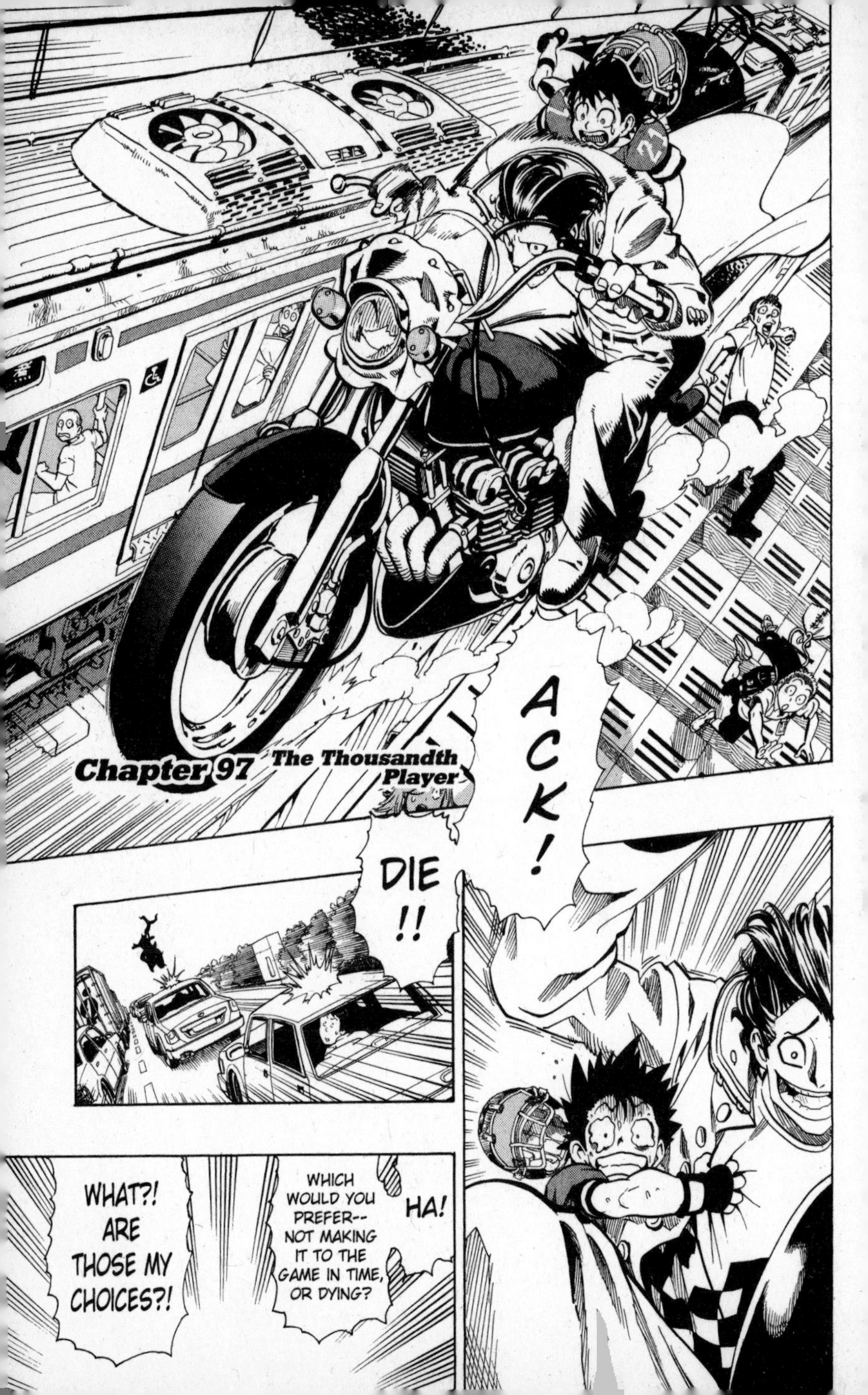
Chapter 97 The Thousandth Player
ACK!
DIE!!
HA!
WHICH WOULD YOU PREFER-- NOT MAKING IT TO THE GAME IN TIME, OR DYING?
WHAT?! ARE THOSE MY CHOICES?!

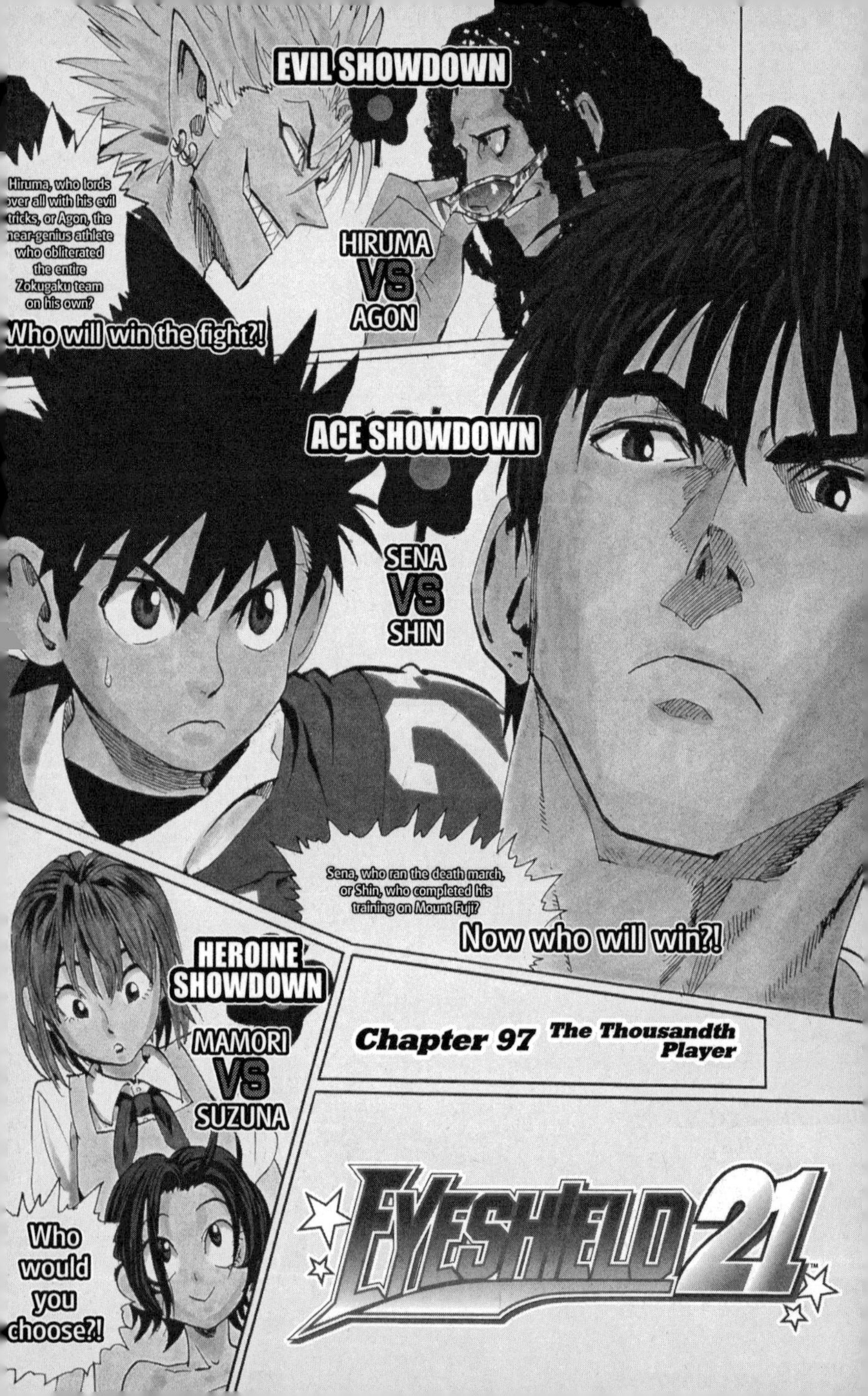
EVIL SHOWDOWN
HIRUMA VS AGON
Hiruma, who lords over all with his evil tricks, or Agon, the near-genius athlete who obliterated the entire Zokugaku team on his own?
Who will win the fight?!
ACE SHOWDOWN
SENA VS SHIN
Sena, who ran the death march, or Shin, who completed his training on Mount Fuji?
Now who will win?!
HEROINE SHOWDOWN
MAMORI VS SUZUNA
Who would you choose?!
Chapter 97 The Thousandth Player
EYESHIELD 21

Special 2nd Serialization Anniversary Your Vote Will Decide Who Wins!

Eyeshield 21 Ten Match-ups!!

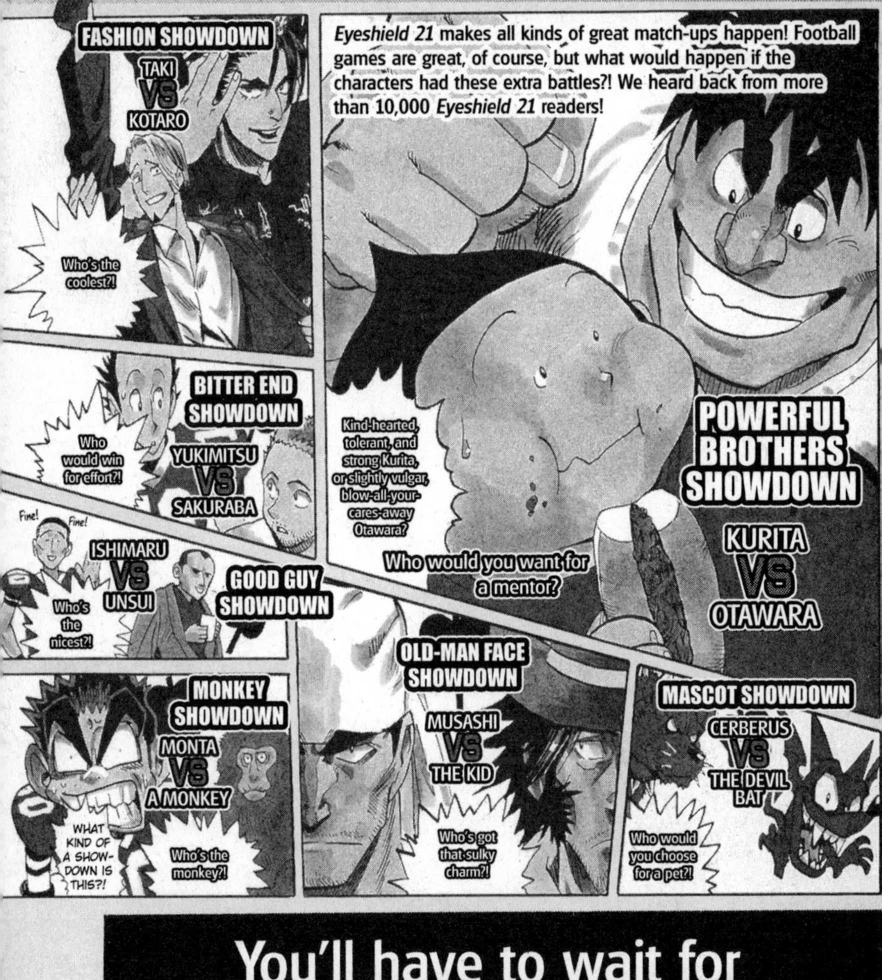
Eyeshield 21 makes all kinds of great match-ups happen! Football games are great, of course, but what would happen if the characters had these extra battles?! We heard back from more than 10,000 *Eyeshield 21* readers!
POWERFUL BROTHERS SHOWDOWN
KURITA VS OTAWARA
Kind-hearted, tolerant, and strong Kurita, or slightly vulgar, blow-all-your-cares-away Otawara?
Who would you want for a mentor?
FASHION SHOWDOWN
TAKI VS KOTARO
Who's the coolest?!
BITTER END SHOWDOWN
YUKIMITSU VS SAKURABA
Who would win for effort?!
GOOD GUY SHOWDOWN
ISHIMARU VS UNSUI
Fine!
Fine!
Who's the nicest?!
MASCOT SHOWDOWN
CERBERUS VS THE DEVIL BAT
Who would you choose for a pet?!
OLD-MAN FACE SHOWDOWN
MUSASHI VS THE KID
Who's got that sulky charm?!
MONKEY SHOWDOWN
MONTA VS A MONKEY
Who's the monkey?!
WHAT KIND OF A SHOW-DOWN IS THIS?!

You'll have to wait for Volume 12 for the exciting results!!

THIS POLL WAS TAKEN IN JAPAN.

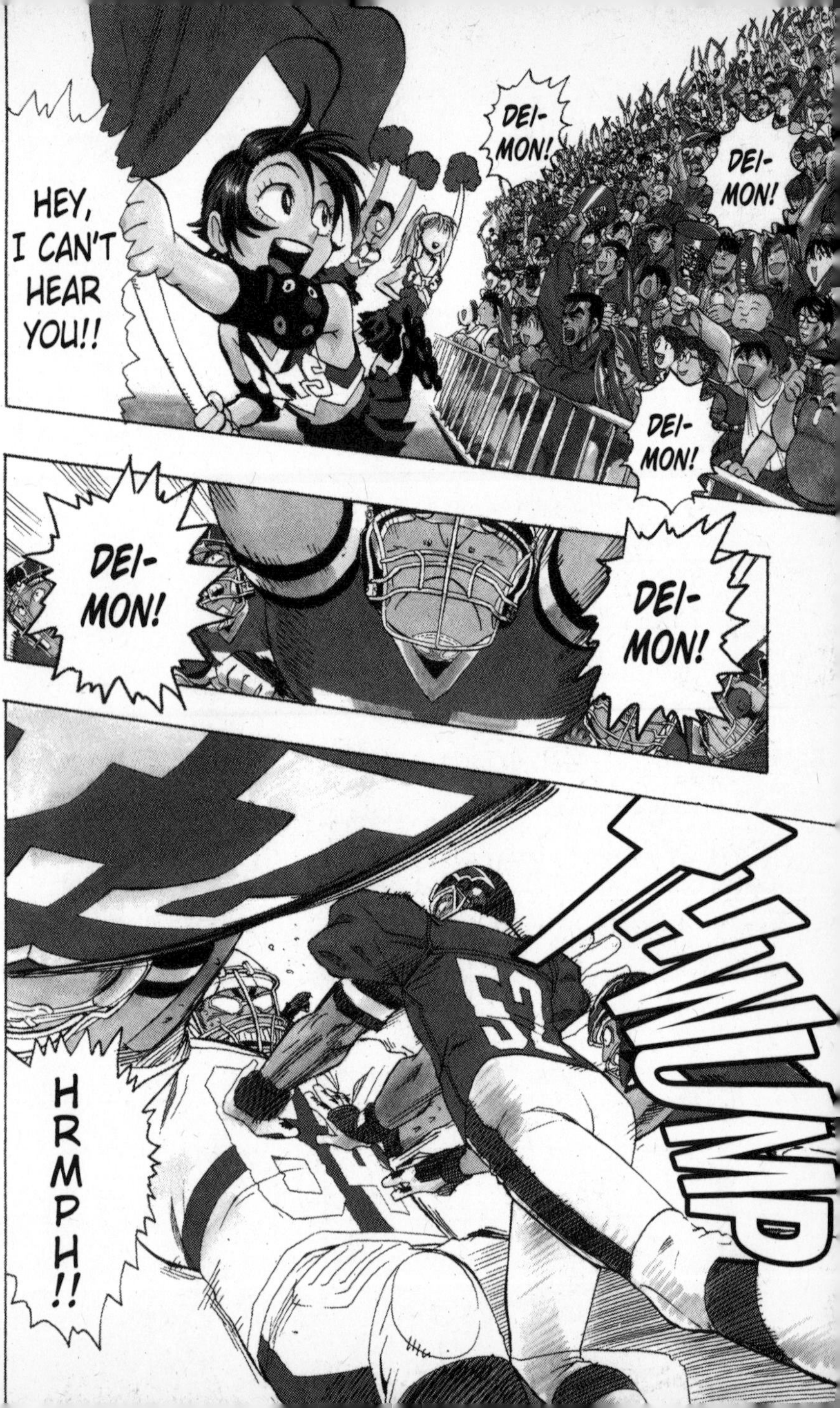
DEI-MON!
DEI-MON!
DEI-MON!
HEY, I CAN'T HEAR YOU!!
DEI-MON!
DEI-MON!
THUMP
HRMPH!!

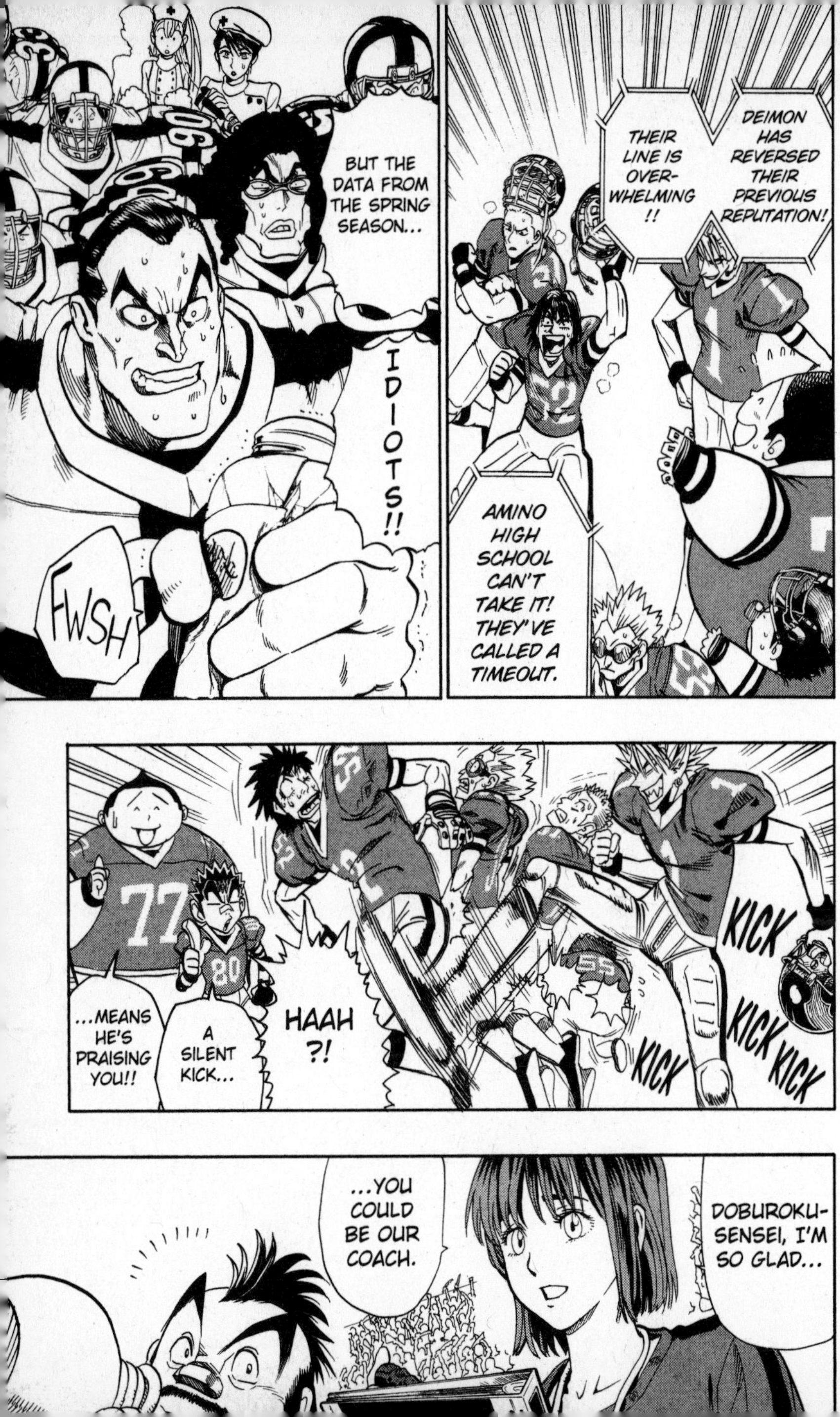
DEIMON HAS REVERSED THEIR PREVIOUS REPUTATION!
THEIR LINE IS OVER-WHELMING!!
AMINO HIGH SCHOOL CAN'T TAKE IT! THEY'VE CALLED A TIMEOUT.
BUT THE DATA FROM THE SPRING SEASON...
IDIOTS!!
FWSH
KICK
KICK
KICK
KICK
HAAH?!
A SILENT KICK...
...MEANS HE'S PRAISING YOU!!
DOBUROKU-SENSEI, I'M SO GLAD...
...YOU COULD BE OUR COACH.

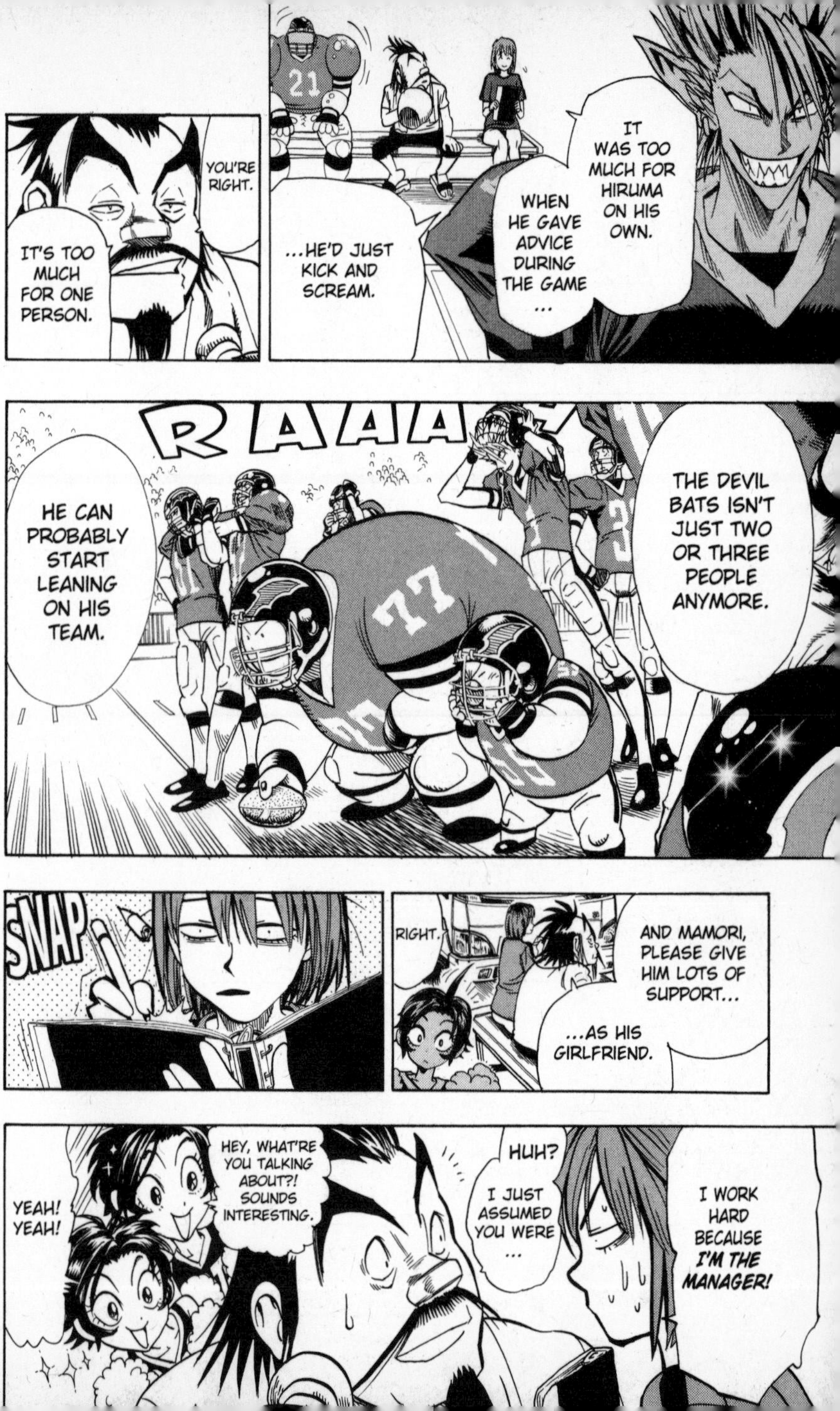
IT WAS TOO MUCH FOR HIRUMA ON HIS OWN.
WHEN HE GAVE ADVICE DURING THE GAME ...
...HE'D JUST KICK AND SCREAM.
YOU'RE RIGHT.
IT'S TOO MUCH FOR ONE PERSON.
RAAA
THE DEVIL BATS ISN'T JUST TWO OR THREE PEOPLE ANYMORE.
HE CAN PROBABLY START LEANING ON HIS TEAM.
AND MAMORI, PLEASE GIVE HIM LOTS OF SUPPORT...
...AS HIS GIRLFRIEND.
RIGHT.
SNAP
I WORK HARD BECAUSE *I'M THE MANAGER!*
HUH?
I JUST ASSUMED YOU WERE ...
HEY, WHAT'RE YOU TALKING ABOUT?! SOUNDS INTERESTING.
YEAH! YEAH!

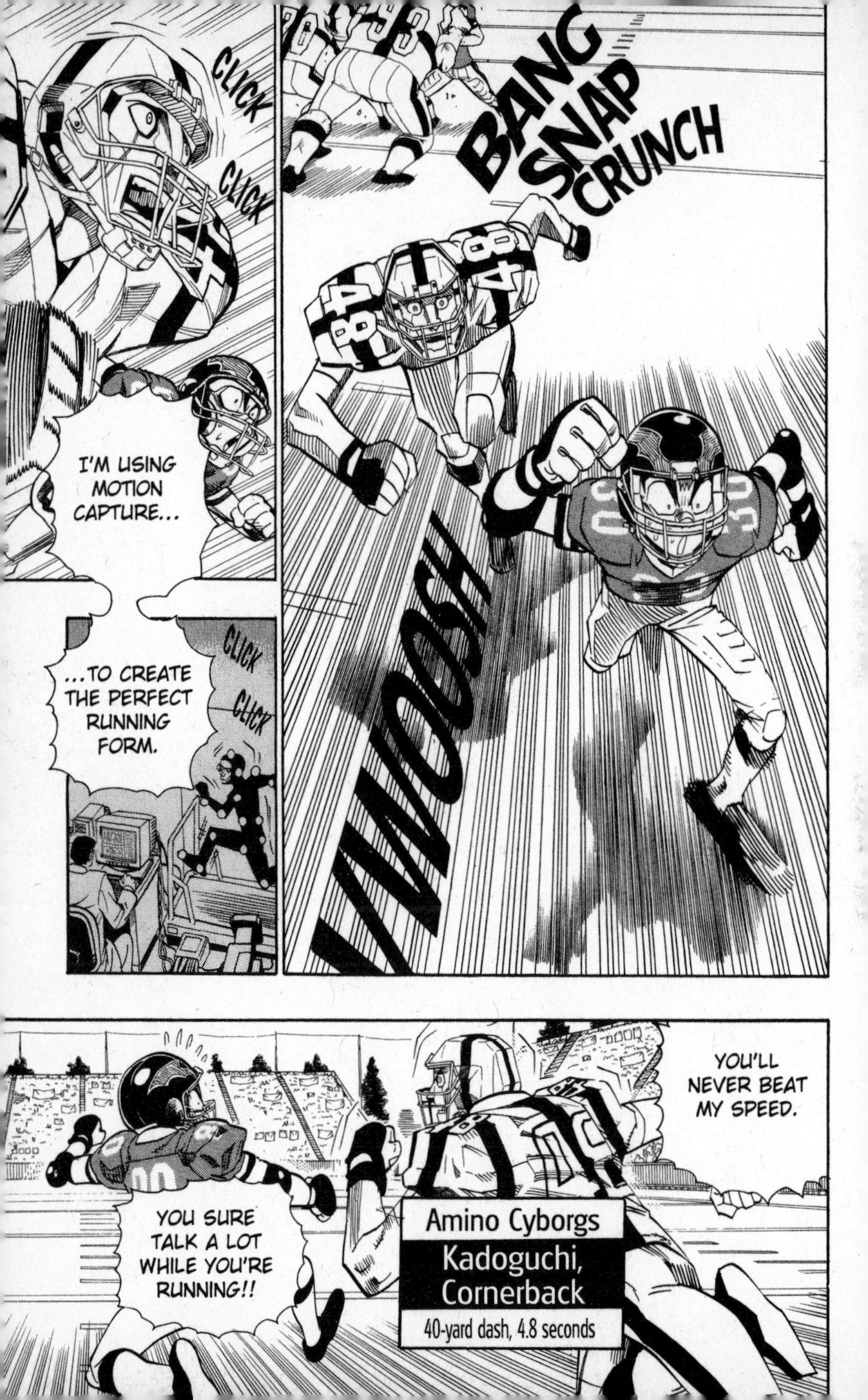
BANG
SNAP
CRUNCH
WHOOSH
CLICK
CLICK
I'M USING MOTION CAPTURE...
CLICK
CLICK
...TO CREATE THE PERFECT RUNNING FORM.
YOU'LL NEVER BEAT MY SPEED.
Amino Cyborgs
Kadoguchi, Cornerback
40-yard dash, 4.8 seconds
YOU SURE TALK A LOT WHILE YOU'RE RUNNING!!

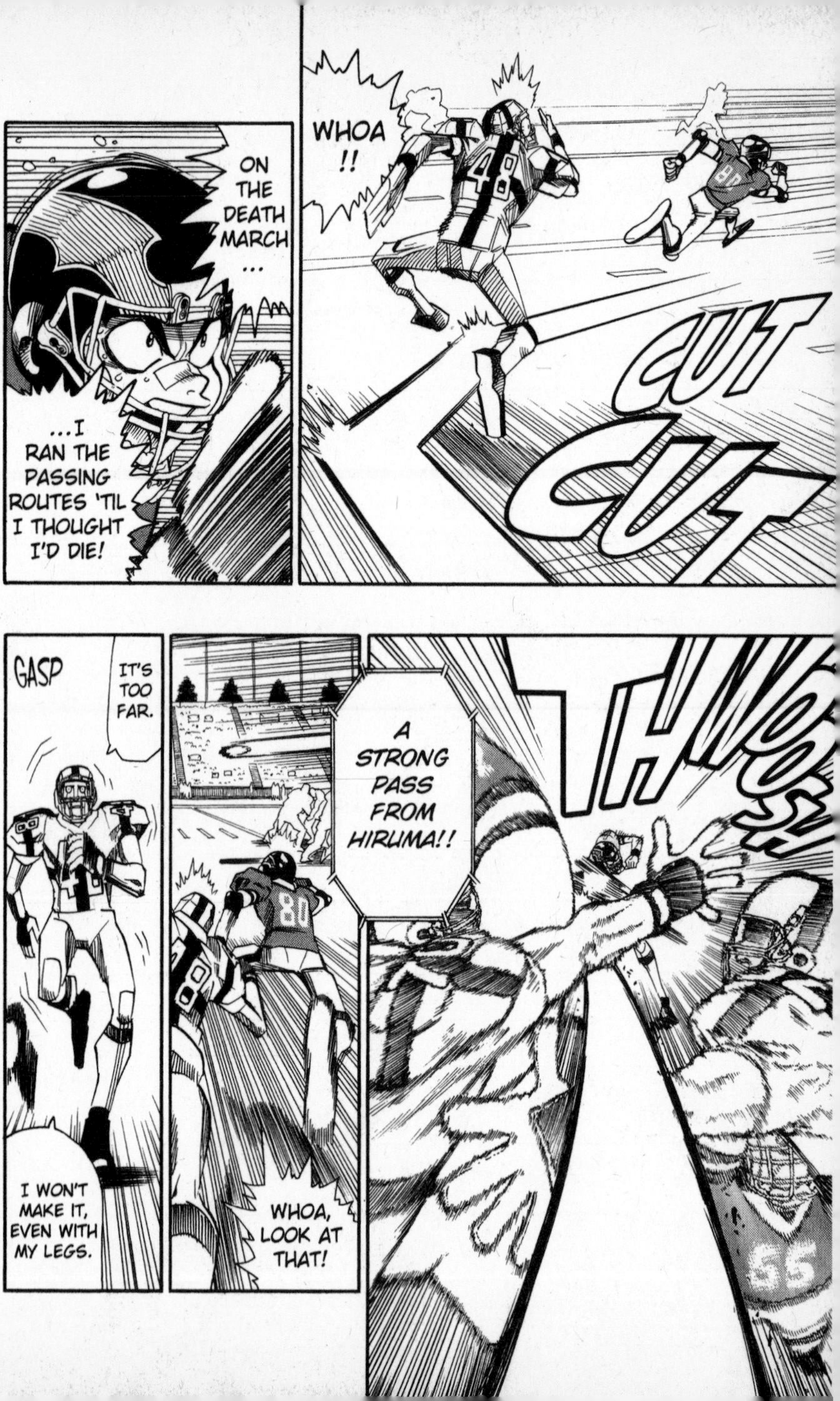
WHOA !!
CUT
CUT
ON THE DEATH MARCH ...
...I RAN THE PASSING ROUTES 'TIL I THOUGHT I'D DIE!
THWOOSH
A STRONG PASS FROM HIRUMA!!
WHOA, LOOK AT THAT!
GASP
IT'S TOO FAR.
I WON'T MAKE IT, EVEN WITH MY LEGS.

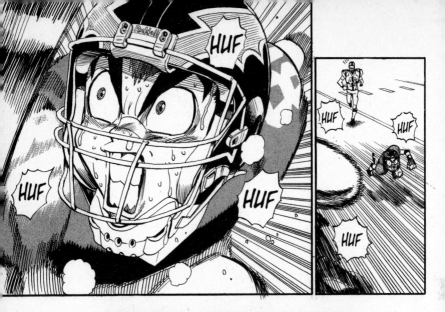

HUF

HUF

HUF

HUF

HUF

HUF

I DON'T BELIEVE IT!

NO WAY! HE CAN'T ...

NNGH-YAH!

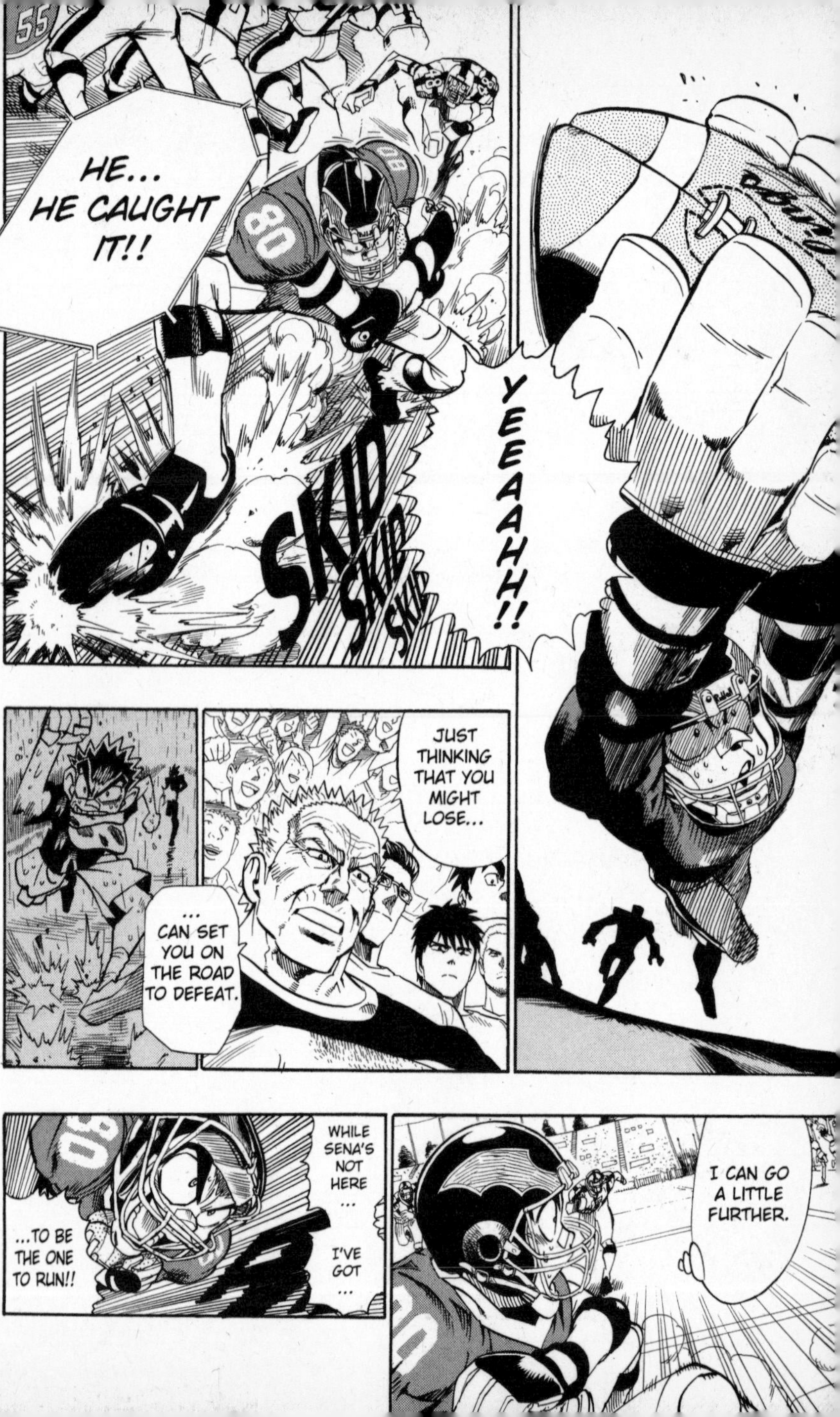
YEEAAHH!!
HE... HE CAUGHT IT!!
SKID SKID SKID
JUST THINKING THAT YOU MIGHT LOSE...
... CAN SET YOU ON THE ROAD TO DEFEAT.
I CAN GO A LITTLE FURTHER.
WHILE SENA'S NOT HERE...
I'VE GOT...
...TO BE THE ONE TO RUN!!

DA DUM

!!

MONTA VS Munakata

SWSH...

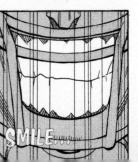

SMILE

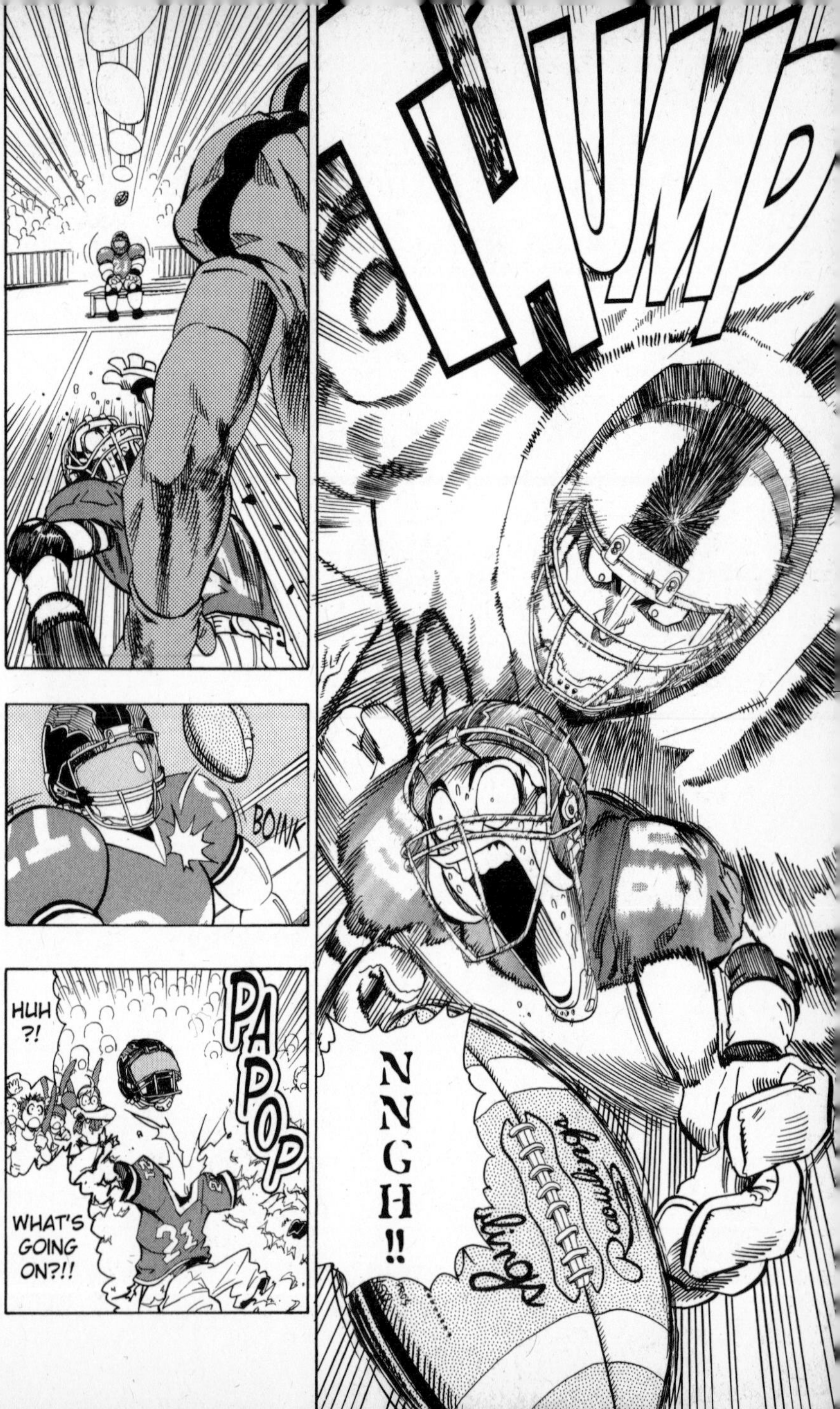
THUMP
NNGH!!
BOINK
HUH ?!
PAPOP
WHAT'S GOING ON?!!

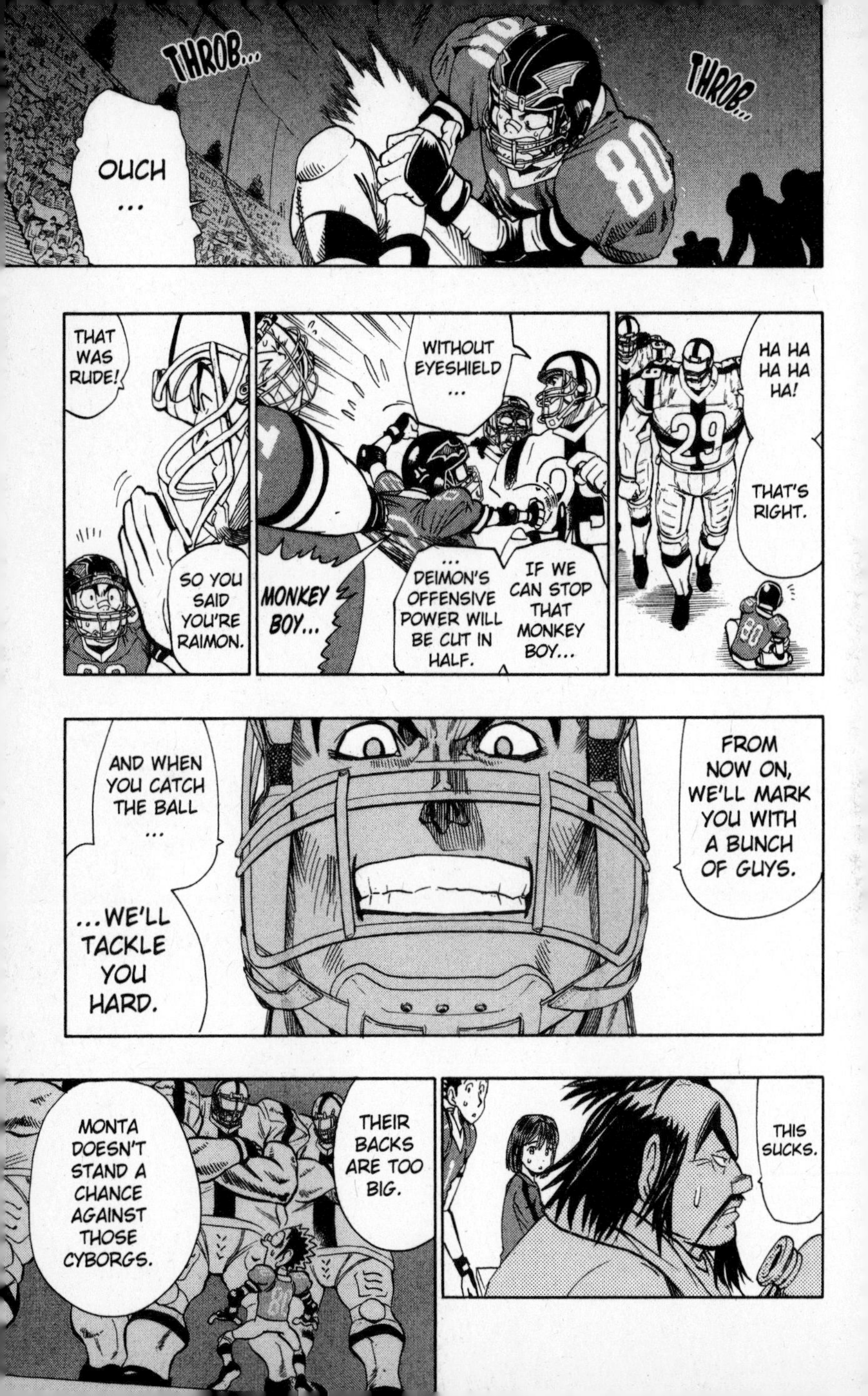
THROB...
THROB...
OUCH ...
HA HA HA HA HA!
THAT'S RIGHT.
WITHOUT EYESHIELD ...
IF WE CAN STOP THAT MONKEY BOY...
... DEIMON'S OFFENSIVE POWER WILL BE CUT IN HALF.
MONKEY BOY...
THAT WAS RUDE!
SO YOU SAID YOU'RE RAIMON.
FROM NOW ON, WE'LL MARK YOU WITH A BUNCH OF GUYS.
AND WHEN YOU CATCH THE BALL ...
...WE'LL TACKLE YOU HARD.
THIS SUCKS.
THEIR BACKS ARE TOO BIG.
MONTA DOESN'T STAND A CHANCE AGAINST THOSE CYBORGS.

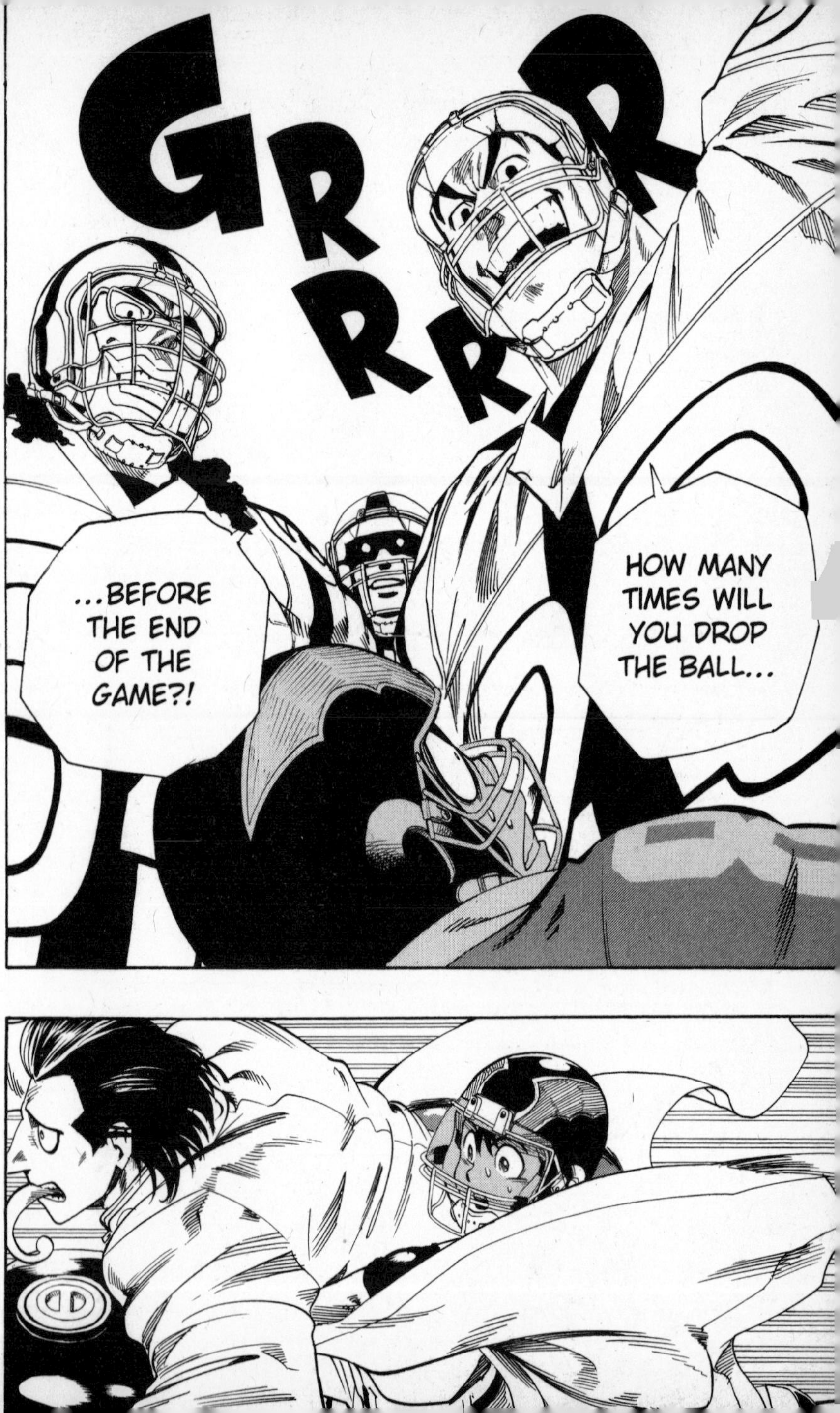
GRRRR
HOW MANY TIMES WILL YOU DROP THE BALL...
...BEFORE THE END OF THE GAME?!

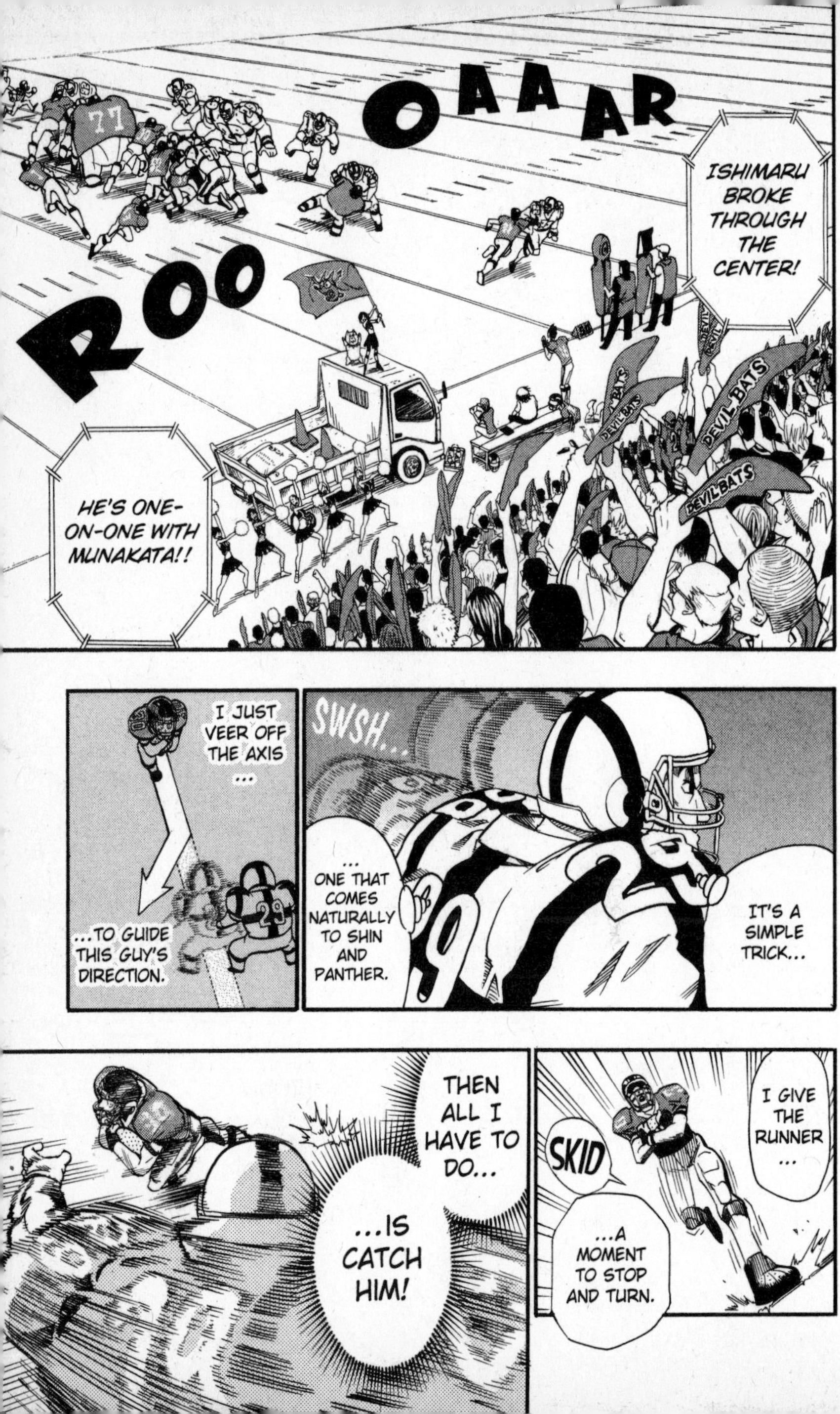
ROOOAAAR
ISHIMARU BROKE THROUGH THE CENTER!
DEVIL BATS
DEVIL BATS
DEVIL BATS
HE'S ONE-ON-ONE WITH MUNAKATA!!
SWSH...
IT'S A SIMPLE TRICK...
...ONE THAT COMES NATURALLY TO SHIN AND PANTHER.
I JUST VEER OFF THE AXIS ...
...TO GUIDE THIS GUY'S DIRECTION.
I GIVE THE RUNNER ...
SKID
...A MOMENT TO STOP AND TURN.
THEN ALL I HAVE TO DO...
...IS CATCH HIM!

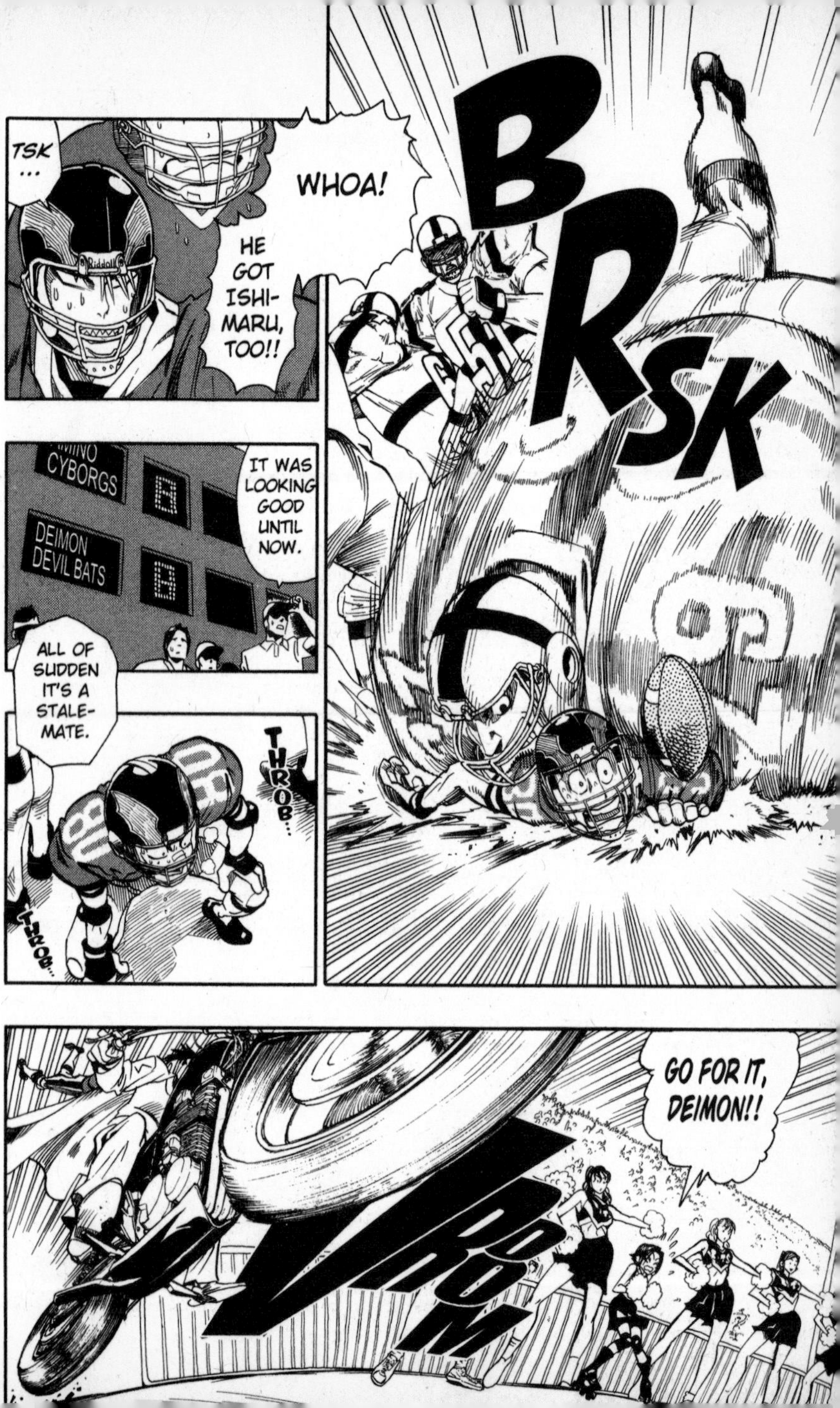
BRSK
WHOA!
HE GOT ISHI-MARU, TOO!!
TSK ...
CYBORGS
DEIMON DEVIL BATS
IT WAS LOOKING GOOD UNTIL NOW.
ALL OF SUDDEN IT'S A STALE-MATE.
THROB...
THROB...
GO FOR IT, DEIMON!!
VROOM

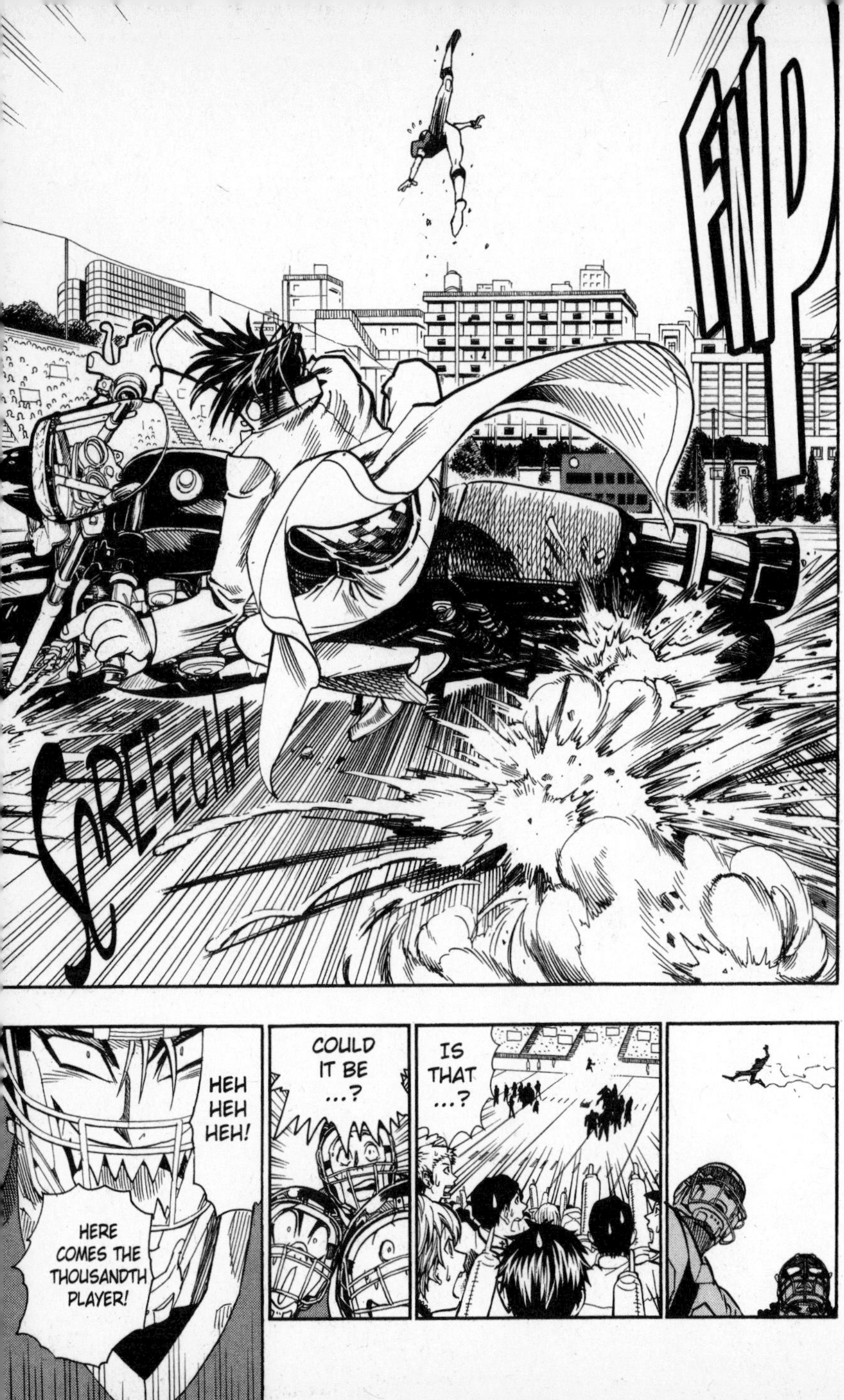
SCREECH!!
IS THAT ...?
COULD IT BE ...?
HEH HEH HEH!
HERE COMES THE THOUSANDTH PLAYER!

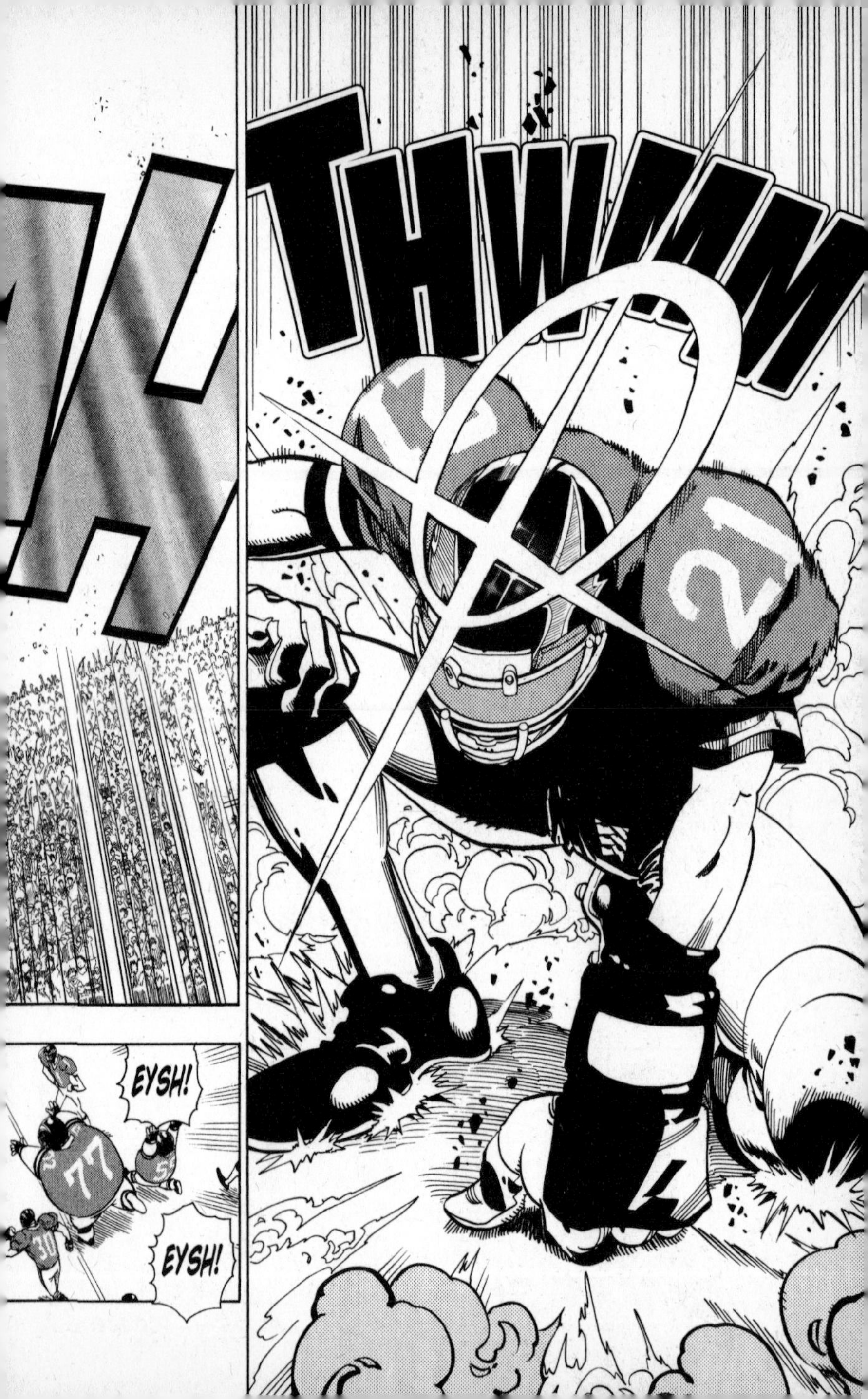
THWAMM
!!
EYSH!
EYSH!

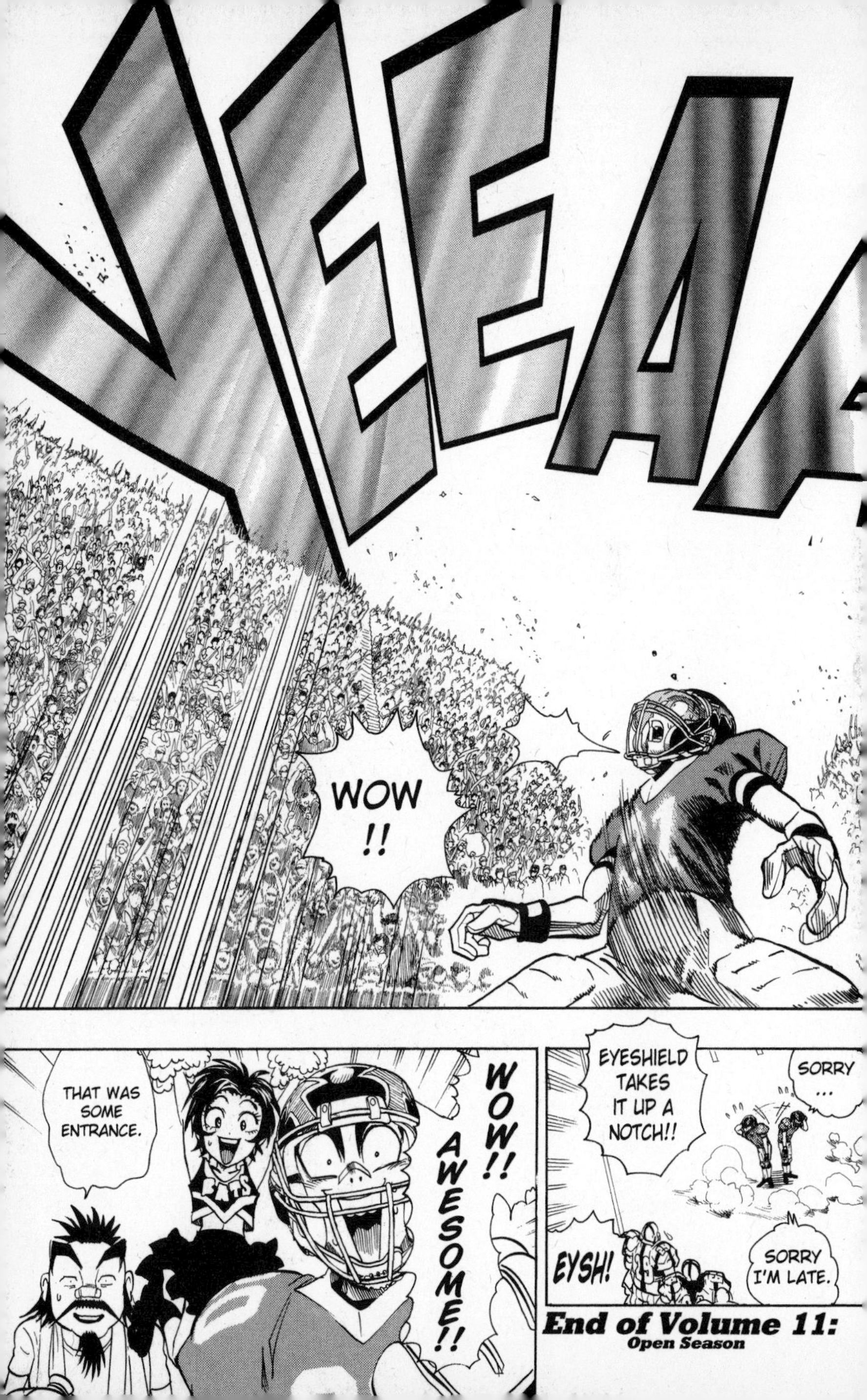
YEEAA
WOW !!
SORRY ...
EYESHIELD TAKES IT UP A NOTCH!!
SORRY I'M LATE.
EYSH!
WOW!!
AWESOME!!
THAT WAS SOME ENTRANCE.

End of Volume 11:
Open Season

Eyeshield 21 Survey Corner **Devil Bat 021**

Investigation File #029

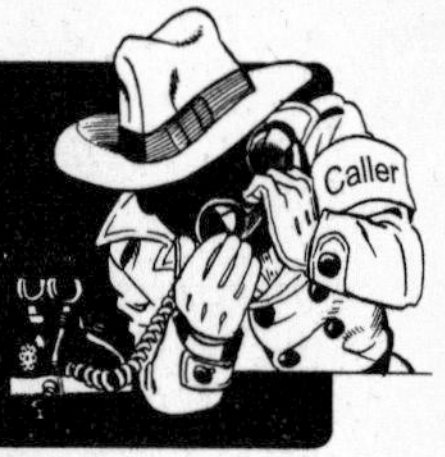
Caller

Find out the names of each team's mascot!

S.K., Chiba Prefecture

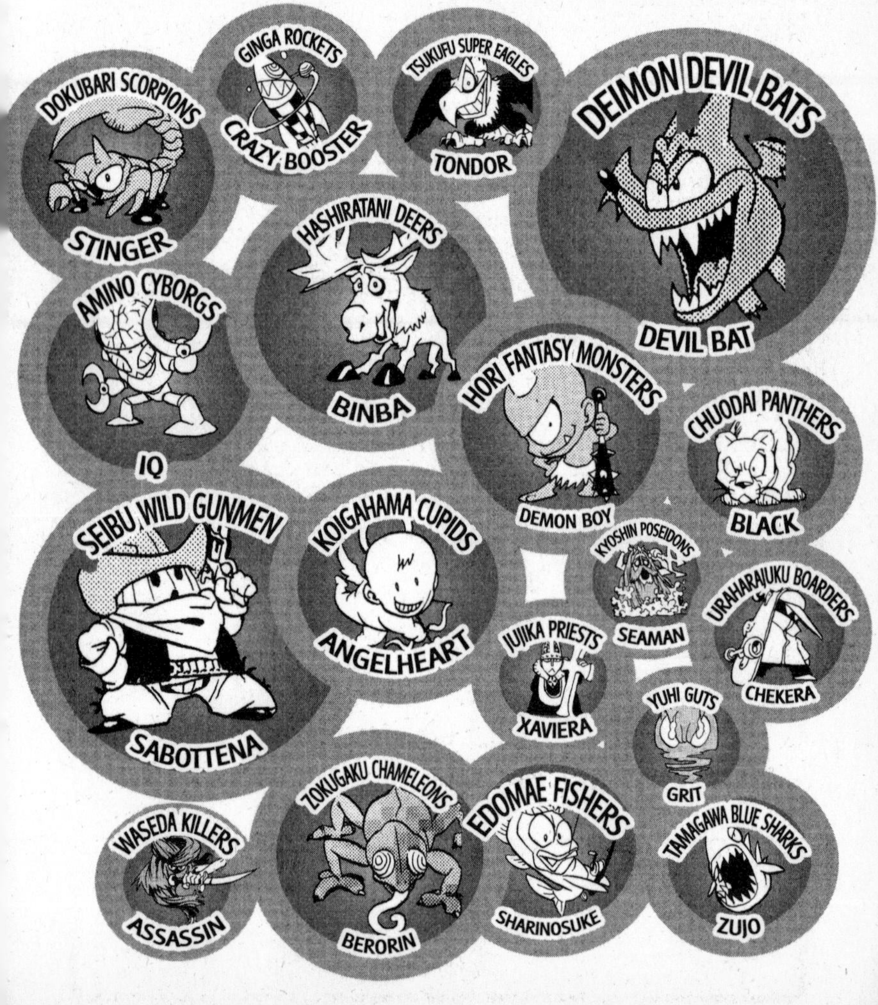
DOKUBARI SCORPIONS
STINGER
GINGA ROCKETS
CRAZY BOOSTER
TSUKUFU SUPER EAGLES
TONDOR
DEIMON DEVIL BATS
DEVIL BAT
HASHIRATANI DEERS
BINBA
AMINO CYBORGS
IQ
HORI FANTASY MONSTERS
DEMON BOY
CHUODAI PANTHERS
BLACK
SEIBU WILD GUNMEN
SABOTTENA
KOIGAHAMA CUPIDS
ANGELHEART
KYOSHIN POSEIDONS
SEAMAN
IUJIKA PRIESTS
XAVIERA
URAHARAJUKU BOARDERS
CHEKERA
YUHI GUTS
GRIT
WASEDA KILLERS
ASSASSIN
ZOKUGAKU CHAMELEONS
BERORIN
EDOMAE FISHERS
SHARINOSUKE
TAMAGAWA BLUE SHARKS
ZUJO

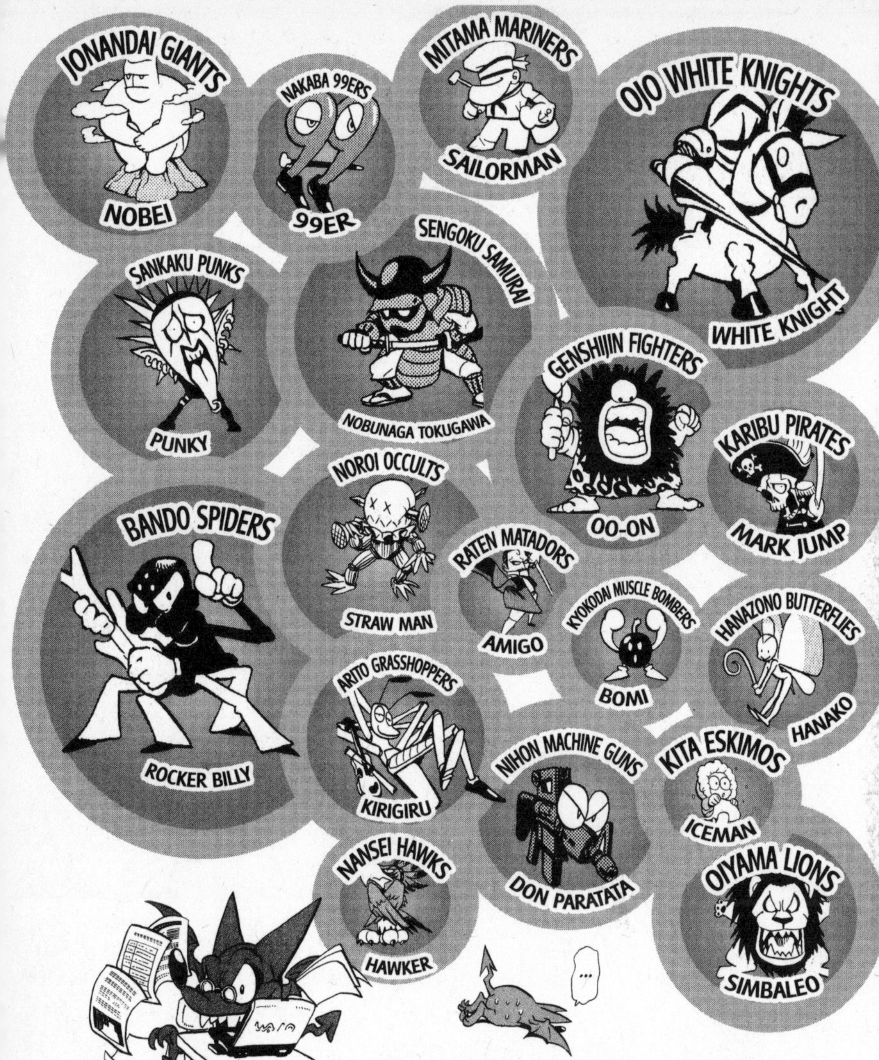
JONANDAI GIANTS
NOBEI
NAKABA 99ERS
99ER
MITAMA MARINERS
SAILORMAN
OJO WHITE KNIGHTS
WHITE KNIGHT
SANKAKU PUNKS
PUNKY
SENGOKU SAMURAI
NOBUNAGA TOKUGAWA
GENSHIJIN FIGHTERS
OO-ON
KARIBU PIRATES
MARK JUMP
BANDO SPIDERS
ROCKER BILLY
NOROI OCCULTS
STRAW MAN
RATEN MATADORS
AMIGO
KYOKODAI MUSCLE BOMBERS
BOMI
HANAZONO BUTTERFLIES
HANAKO
ARITO GRASSHOPPERS
KIRIGIRU
NIHON MACHINE GUNS
DON PARATATA
KITA ESKIMOS
ICEMAN
NANSEI HAWKS
HAWKER
OIYAMA LIONS
SIMBALEO
...

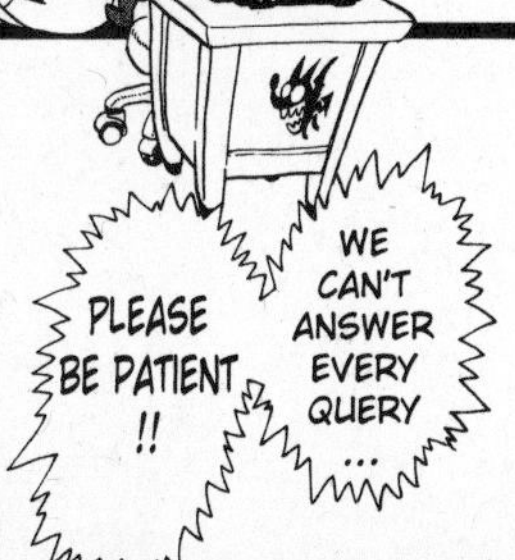
WE CAN'T ANSWER EVERY QUERY...
PLEASE BE PATIENT!!

Send your queries for Devil Bat 021 here!!

Devil Bat 021
Shonen Jump Advanced/Eyeshield 21
c/o VIZ Media, LLC
P.O. Box 77010
San Francisco, CA 94107

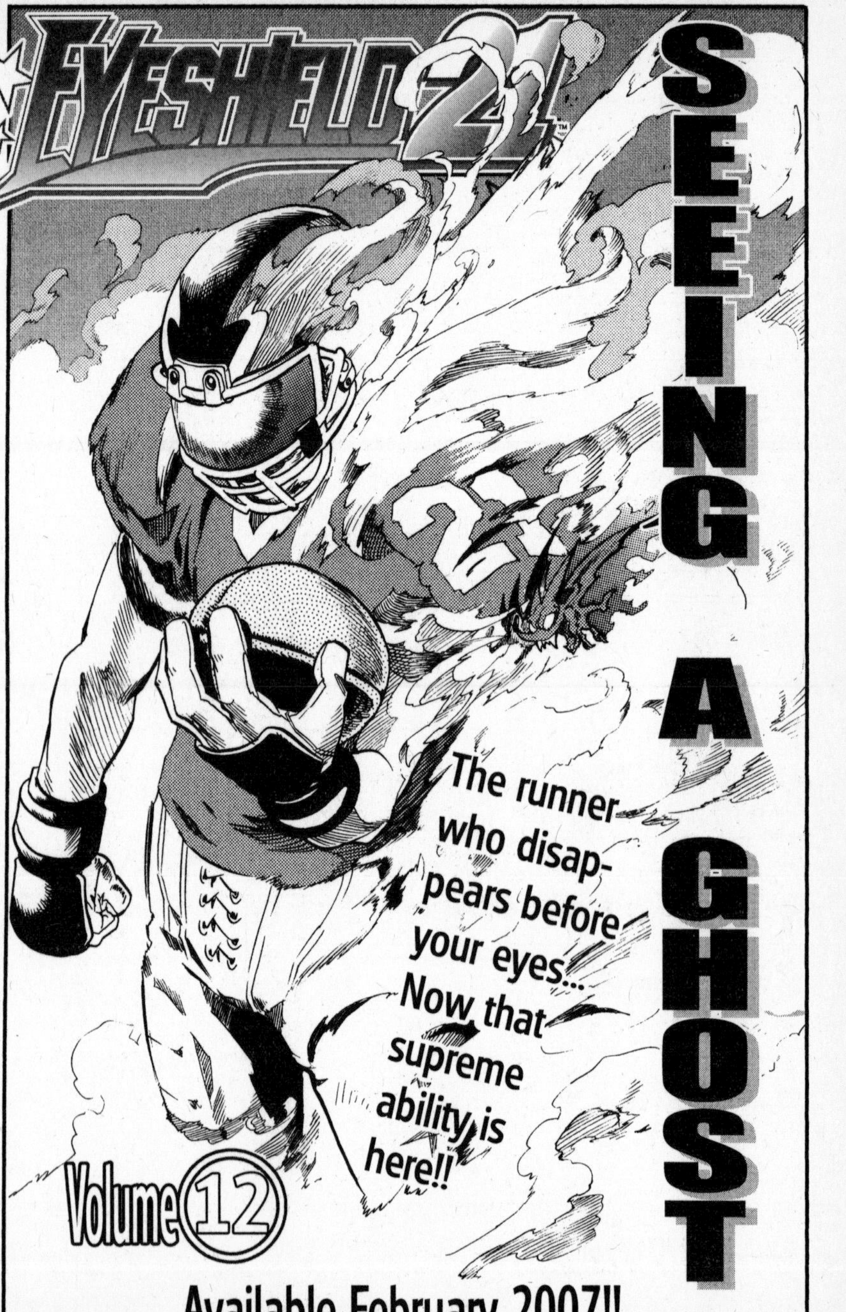

EYESHIELD 21™
SEEING A GHOST
The runner who disappears before your eyes... Now that supreme ability is here!!
Volume 12
Available February 2007!!

Story:
Riichiro
Inagaki

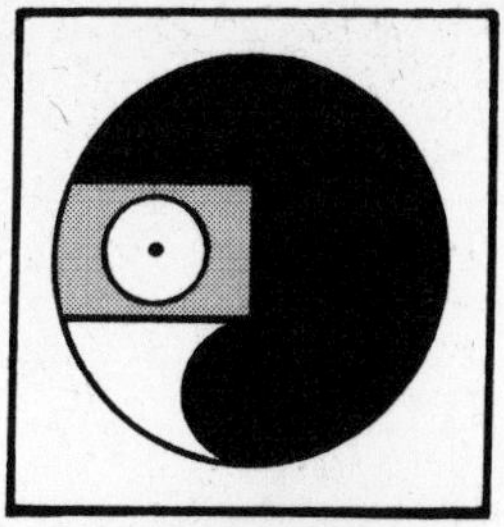

Art:
Yusuke
Murata

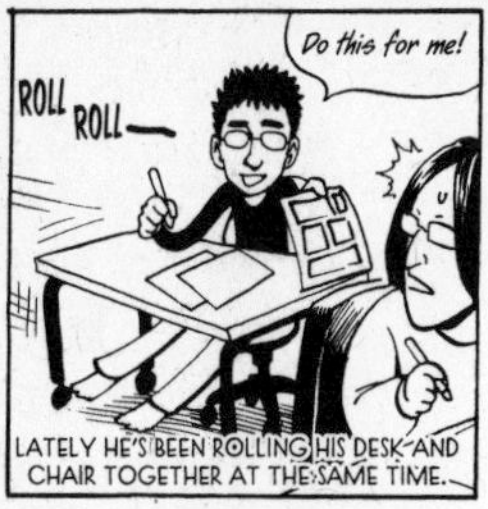
Do this for me!
ROLL ROLL—
LATELY HE'S BEEN ROLLING HIS DESK AND CHAIR TOGETHER AT THE SAME TIME.

Chief:
Akira
Tanaka

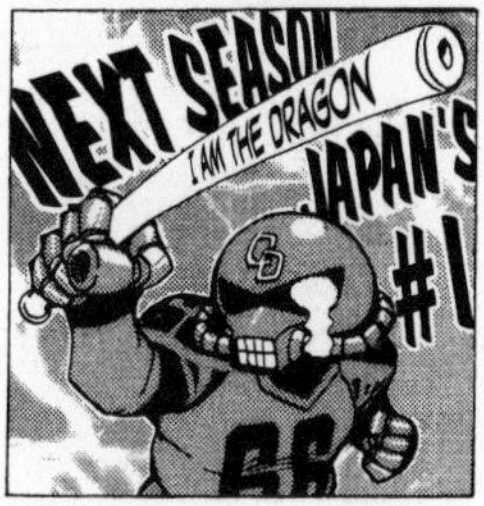
NEXT SEASON
I AM THE DRAGON
JAPAN'S

Takahiro
Hiraishi

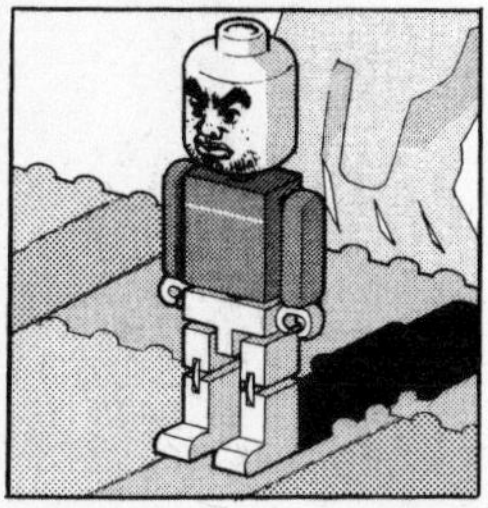

Kentaro
Kurimoto

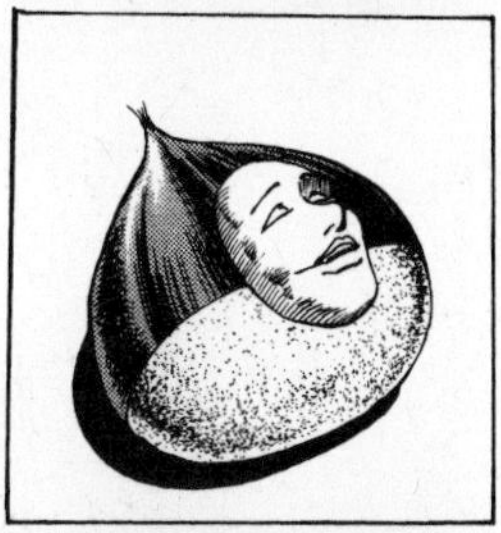

Akira
Nishikawa

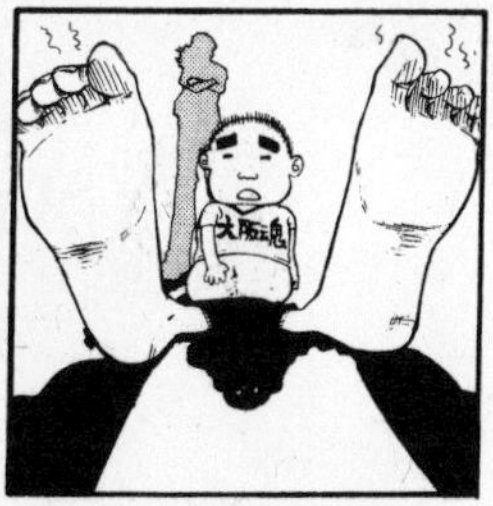

Yūji
Furuyama

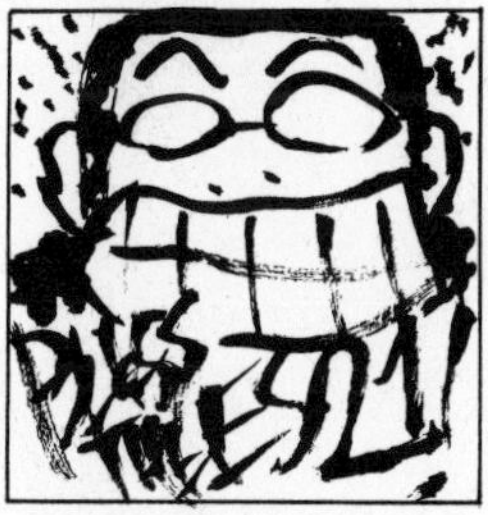

Masayuki
Shiomura

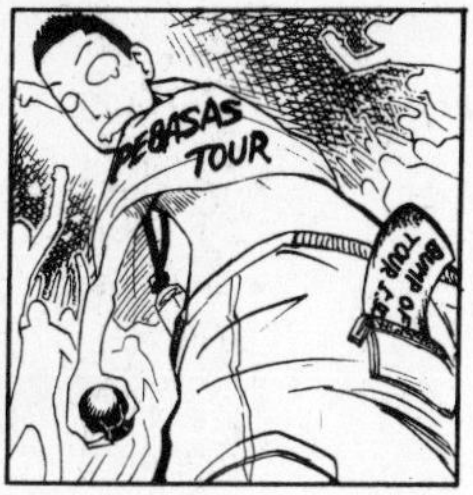
PEGASAS TOUR

Sanmi
Yi

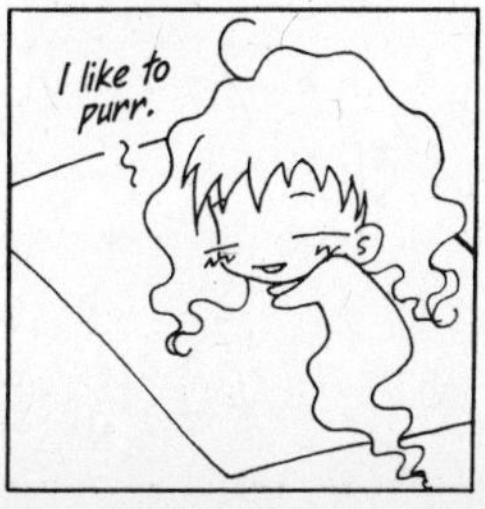
I like to purr.

STAFF

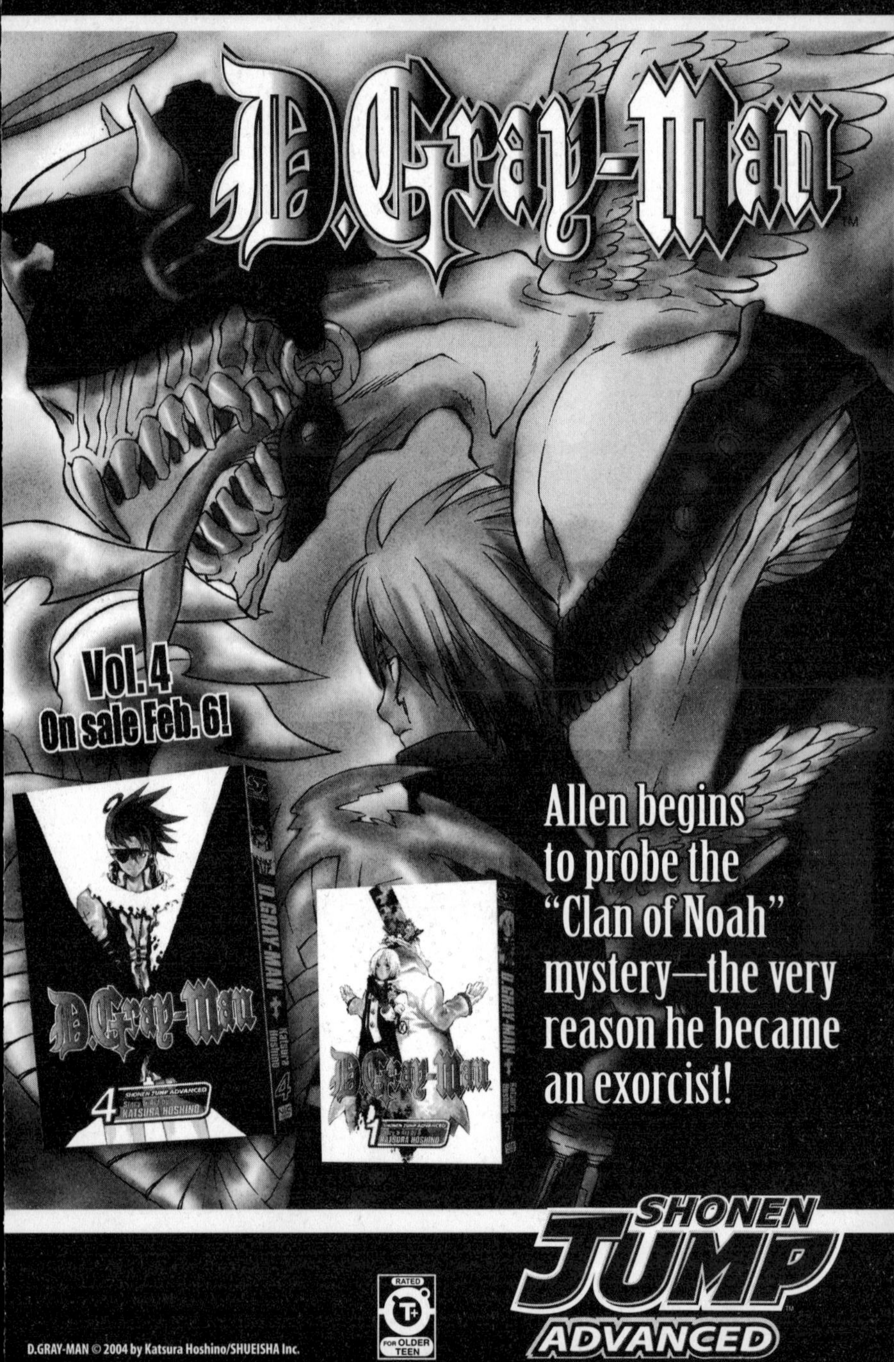
D.Gray-Man™
Vol. 4
On sale Feb. 6!
D.GRAY-MAN
KATSURA HOSHINO
Allen begins to probe the "Clan of Noah" mystery—the very reason he became an exorcist!
SHONEN JUMP ADVANCED
RATED T+ FOR OLDER TEEN
D.GRAY-MAN © 2004 by Katsura Hoshino/SHUEISHA Inc.

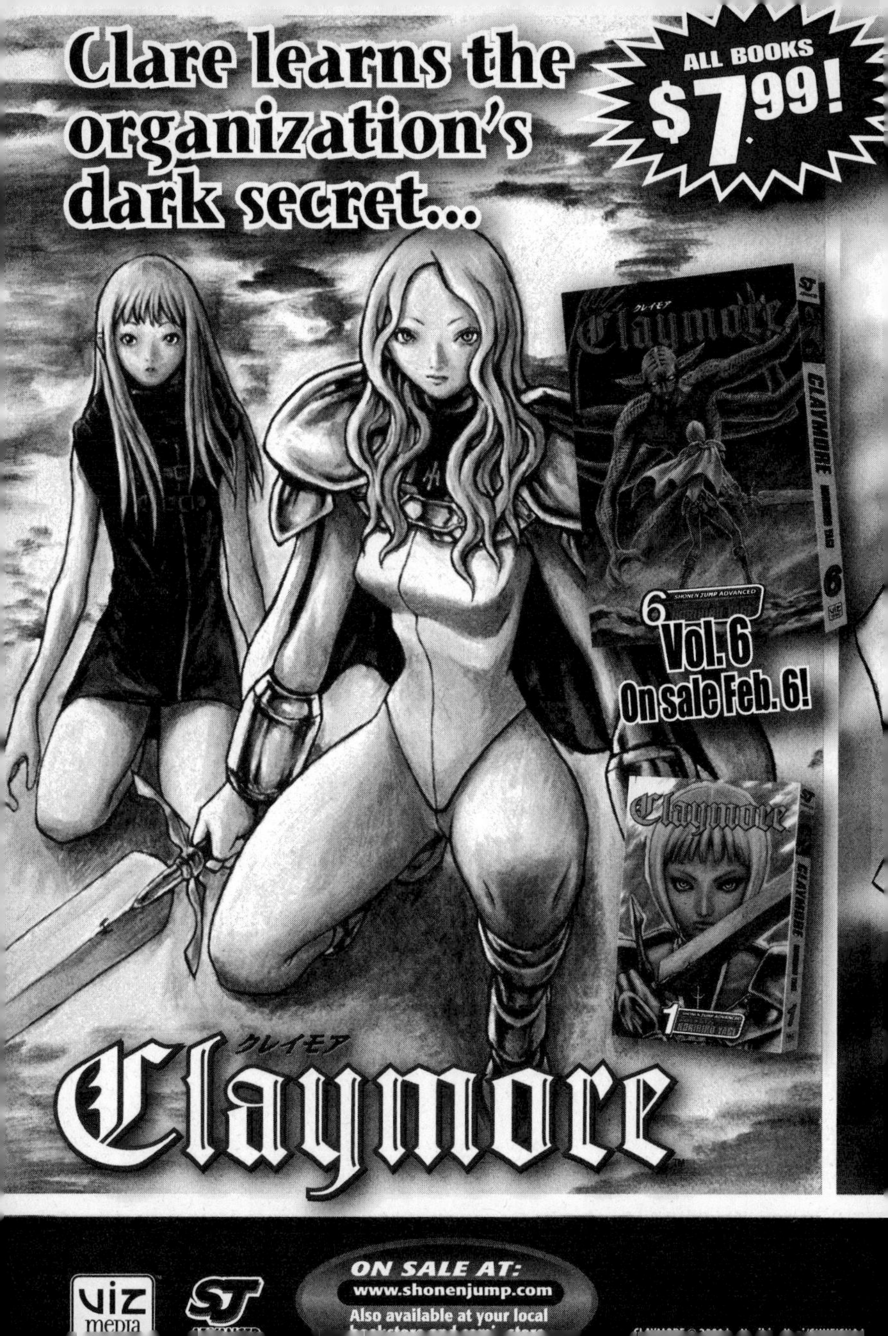

Clare learns the organization's dark secret...
ALL BOOKS $7.99!
Vol. 6
On sale Feb. 6!
クレイモア
Claymore
ON SALE AT:
www.shonenjump.com
Also available at your local

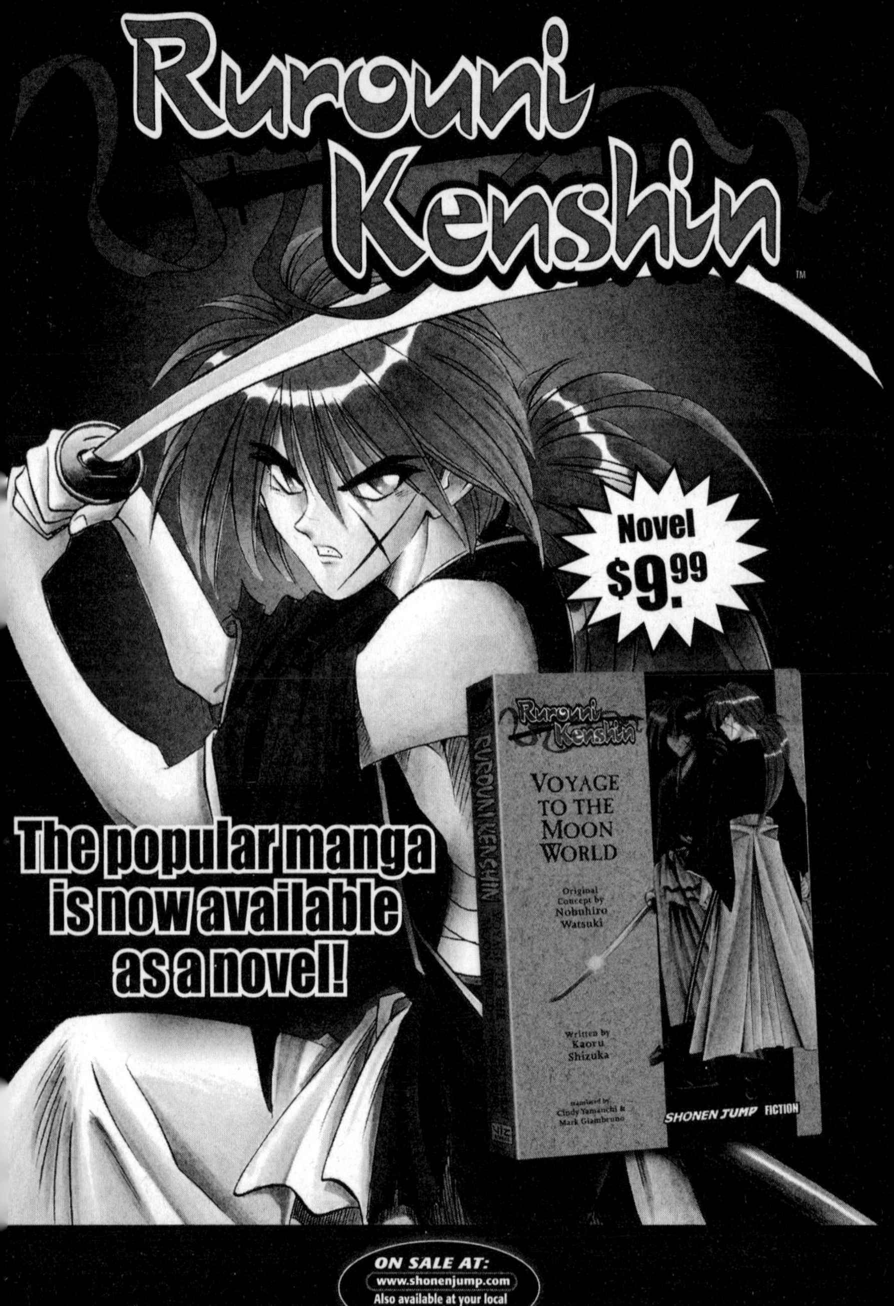
Rurouni Kenshin™
Novel $9.99
Rurouni Kenshin
RUROUNI KENSHIN
VOYAGE TO THE MOON WORLD
Original Concept by Nobuhiro Watsuki
Written by Kaoru Shizuka
translated by Cindy Yamauchi & Mark Giambruno
SHONEN JUMP FICTION
The popular manga is now available as a novel!
ON SALE AT:
www.shonenjump.com
Also available at your local bookstore and comic store.

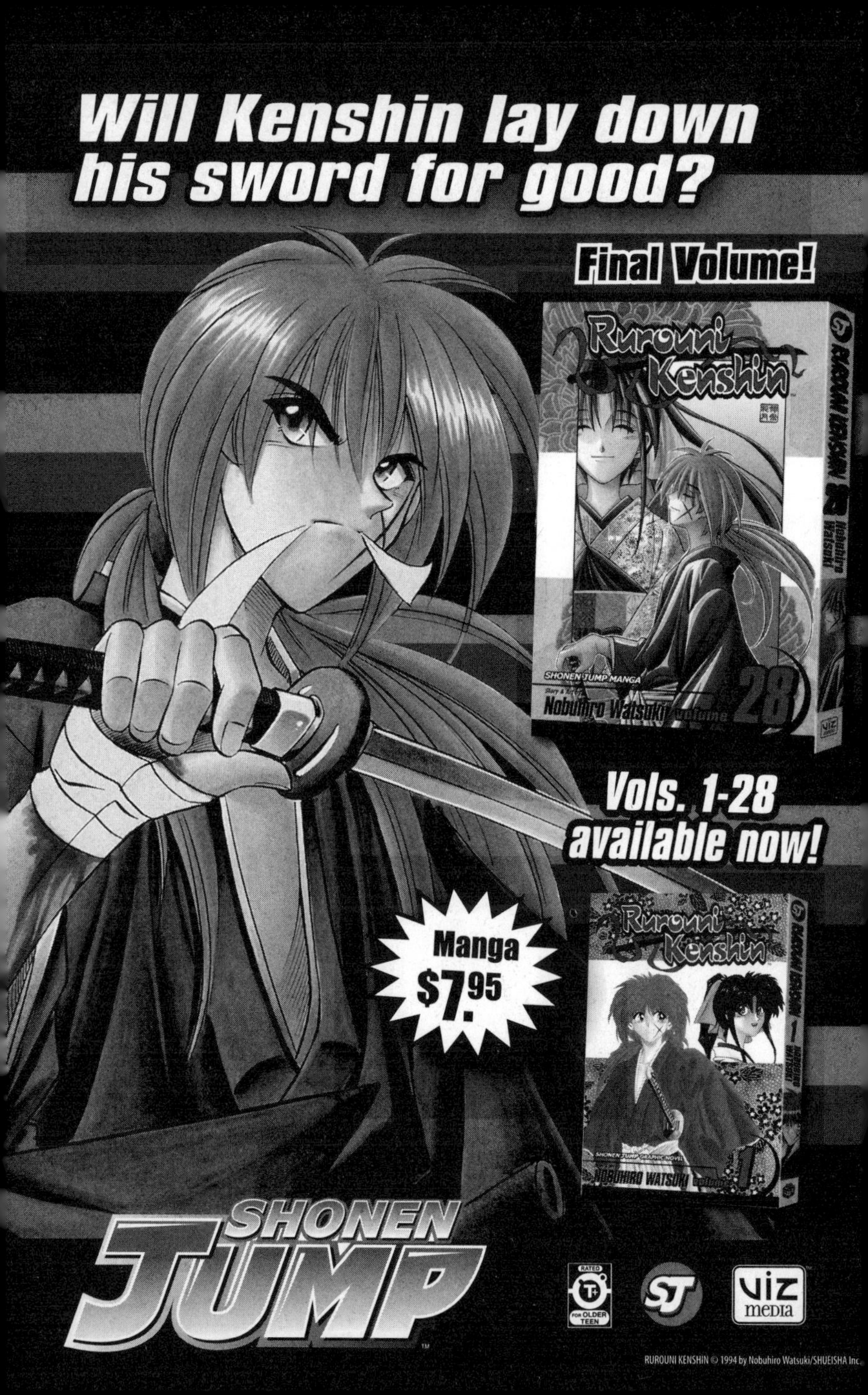

Will Kenshin lay down his sword for good?
Final Volume!
Rurouni Kenshin
SHONEN JUMP MANGA
Nobuhiro Watsuki volume 28
Vols. 1-28 available now!
Manga $7.95
Rurouni Kenshin
NOBUHIRO WATSUKI volume 1
SHONEN JUMP
RATED T+ FOR OLDER TEEN
SJ
VIZ media
RUROUNI KENSHIN © 1994 by Nobuhiro Watsuki/SHUEISHA Inc.

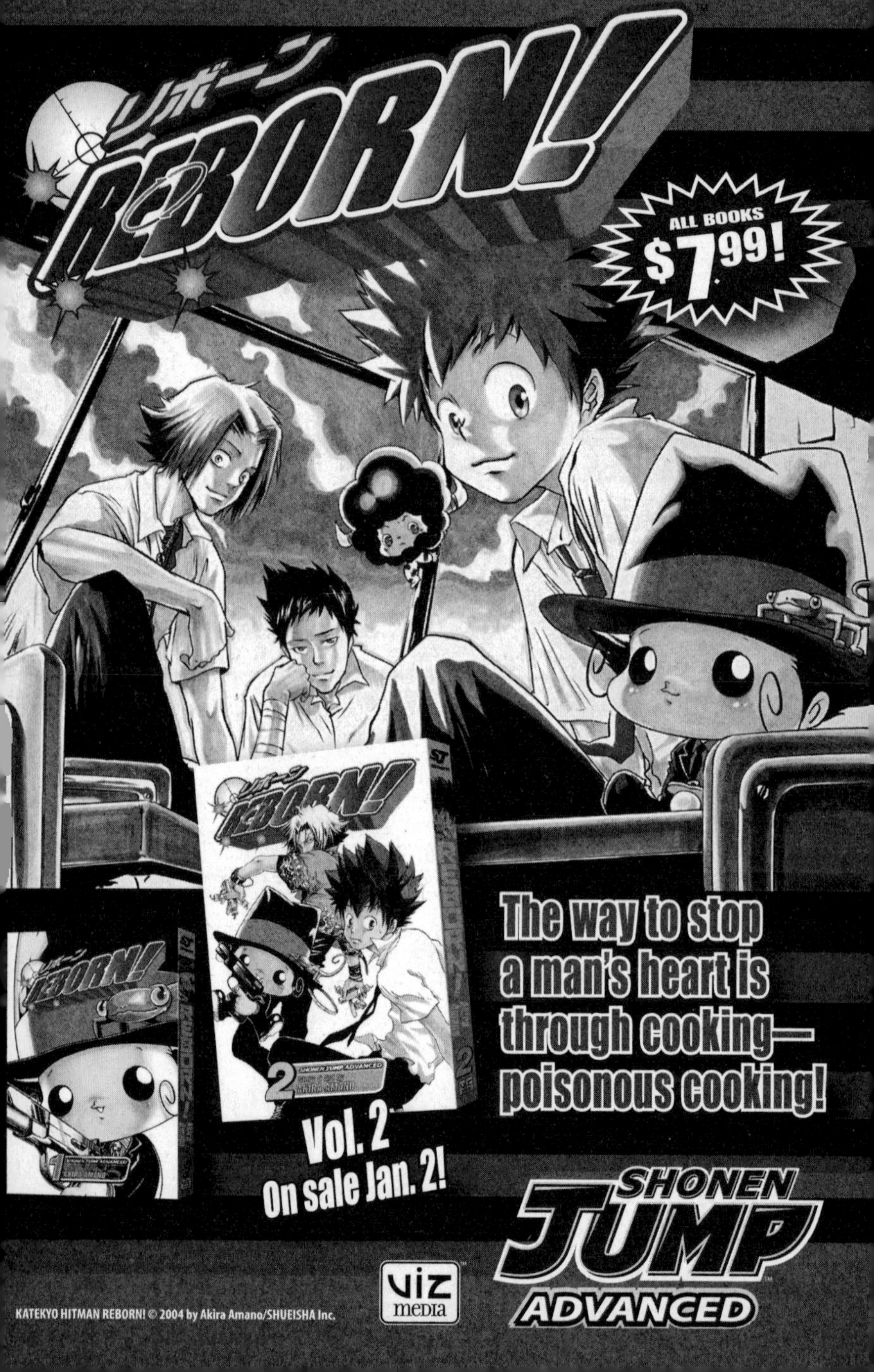

REBORN!
ALL BOOKS $7.99!
The way to stop a man's heart is through cooking—poisonous cooking!
Vol. 2 On sale Jan. 2!
SHONEN JUMP ADVANCED
viz media
KATEKYO HITMAN REBORN! © 2004 by Akira Amano/SHUEISHA Inc.

Tell us what you think about SHONEN JUMP manga!

Our survey is now available online.
Go to: www.*SHONENJUMP*.com/mangasurvey

Help us make our product offering better!

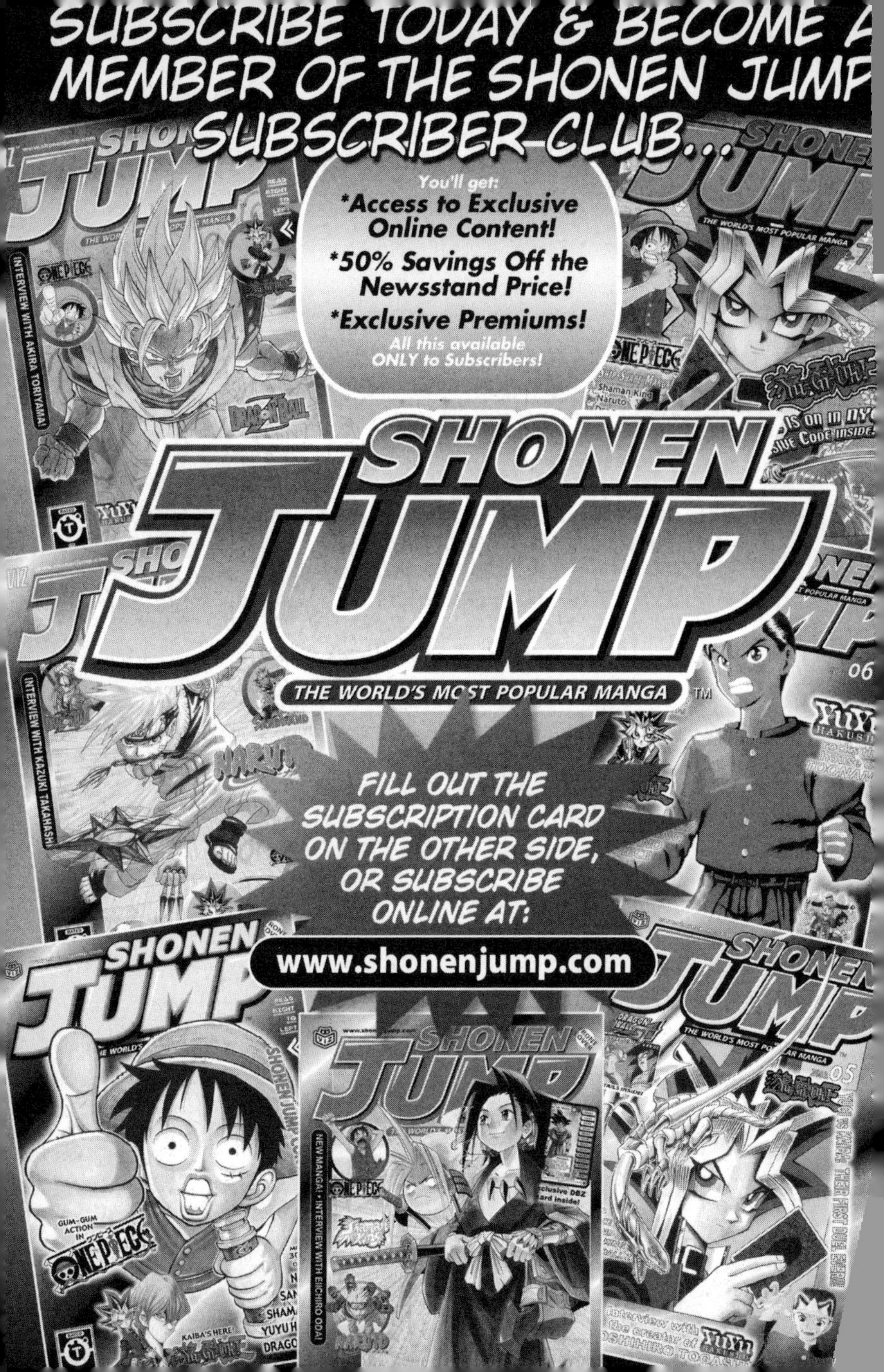
SUBSCRIBE TODAY & BECOME A MEMBER OF THE SHONEN JUMP SUBSCRIBER CLUB...
You'll get:
*Access to Exclusive Online Content!
*50% Savings Off the Newsstand Price!
*Exclusive Premiums!
All this available ONLY to Subscribers!
SHONEN JUMP
THE WORLD'S MOST POPULAR MANGA
FILL OUT THE SUBSCRIPTION CARD ON THE OTHER SIDE, OR SUBSCRIBE ONLINE AT:
www.shonenjump.com

SHONEN JUMP

THE WORLD'S MOST POPULAR MANGA

**SUBSCRIBE TODAY and SAVE
50% OFF the cover price PLUS enjoy
all the benefits of the SHONEN JUMP
SUBSCRIBER CLUB...**

YE
(12 issu
LOW S
up for

only
2995!

NAME

ADDRESS

CITY   STATE   ZIP

E-MAIL ADDRESS

☐ MY CHECK IS ENCLOSED   ☐ BILL ME LATER

CREDIT CARD: ☐ VISA   ☐ MASTERCARD

ACCOUNT #   EXP. DATE

SIGNATURE

CLIP AND MAIL TO ➤   SHONEN JUMP
Subscriptions Service Dept.
P.O. Box 515
L 61054-0515

Ma
Ca   w 6-8 weeks for delivery.
PE   A Inc.